the Bible for a change

Foreword by Rev Dr Ash Barker
Edited by David Painting

MONARCH
B O O K S

Published by **Monarch Books**
www.lionhudson.com
Part of the SPCK Group
SPCK, 36 Causton Street, London, SW1P 4ST
and by the **International Bible Reading Association**
5–6 Imperial Court, 12 Sovereign Road, Birmingham, B30 3FH
Tel: 0121 458 3313; Fax: 0121 285 1816
www.ibraglobal.org
Charity number 1086990

ISBN 978 1 80030 030 9
e-ISBN 978 1 80030 031 6
ISSN 2050-6791

First edition 2021

A catalogue record for this book is available from the British Library

Printed and bound in the UK, July 2021, LH29

Fresh From The Word aims to build understanding and respect for different Christian perspectives through the provision of a range of biblical interpretations. Views expressed by contributors should not, therefore, be taken to reflect the views or policies of the Editor or the International Bible Reading Association.

The International Bible Reading Association's scheme of readings is listed monthly on the IBRA website at www.ibraglobal.org and the full scheme for 2021 may be downloaded in English, Spanish and French.

Contents

Foreword

Welcome to the latest edition of *Fresh From The Word*.

The same Holy Spirit that inspired the Scriptures can captivate and call us into action today through these Scriptures. If ever there was a time when we needed to be sustained and empowered by the Spirit in this way, it is now.

I am a person who needs to rise at 5 a.m. to prepare for my day. For over 30 years I've lived and served on the front line of urban poverty on three continents and lead people who intentionally put themselves in harm's way. I've learned that if I don't prepare for my day well, then I will be washed away by the unsaid compulsions of others, and often of my own heart. In this sacred time of morning stillness, I can sit with the Scriptures and re-connect with Who and what is most essential, ready for all that will be thrown my way.

Fresh From The Word is a proven resource designed for those dissatisfied with the world today and ready for thoughtful and committed change. Whether you are just starting out reading the Bible or have spent your life immersed in its stories, there are always new insights here to inspire and inform our actions, lives and engagement with the planet. *Fresh From The Word* brings together in one volume inspiring daily and weekly reading Bible themes with some of the world's most insightful theologians, biblical scholars and creative writers, as well as innovative church leaders and peace activists. We can all engage with the Scriptures in more meaningful ways as a result. This book is a gift to us and our world.

At a time when religious fundamentalism is on the rise, misusing sacred texts to radicalise for hate, people of Christian faith need to be especially diligent. The Bible misread can oppress and inflict pain, but the vital discipleship of Jesus engages us with the Bible as a liberating force for deep compassion and justice in our lives and the broader world. If we can consistently and relentlessly be animated by the Bible's big hope for God, people and the earth living in harmony together, then we can resist hate and become the revolution of love we want to see in the world.

This volume can help make sacred the daily habit of engaging the Scriptures for change. This is what the world needs from us now.

Rev Dr Ash Barker (www.seedbeds.org)

How to use *Fresh From The Word*

How do you approach the idea of regular Bible reading? It may help to see daily Bible reading as spiritual exploration. Here is a suggestion of a pattern to follow that may help you develop the discipline but free up your mind and heart to respond.

- Before you read, take a few moments – the time it takes to say the Lord's Prayer – to imagine God looking at you with love. Feel yourself enfolded in that gaze. Come to scripture with your feet firmly planted.
- Read the passage slowly before you turn to the notes. Be curious. The Bible was written over a period of nearly 1,000 years, over 2,000 years ago. There is always something to learn. Read and reread.
- If you have access to a study Bible, pay attention to any echoes of the passage you are reading in other parts of the biblical book. A word might be used in different ways by different biblical authors. Where in the story of the book are you reading? What will happen next?
- 'Read' yourself as you read the story. Be attentive to your reactions – even trivial ones. What is drawing you into the story? What is repelling you? Observe yourself 'sidelong' as you read as if you were watching a wild animal in the forest; be still, observant and expectant.
- What in the scripture or in the notes is drawing you forward in hope? What is closing you down? Notice where the Spirit of Life is present and where negative spirits are, too. Follow where life is leading. God always leads into life, even if the way feels risky.
- Lift up the world and aspects of your life to God. What would you like to share with God? What is God seeking to share with you?
- Thank God for being present and offer your energy in the day ahead, or in the day coming after a night's rest.
- Finally, the † symbol is an invitation to pray a prayer that has been written for the day's reading. You are invited to say these words aloud or in silence with thousands of other readers around the world who will be reading these notes on the same day in dozens of languages.

Introduction from the Editor

Welcome to the 2022 edition of *Fresh From The Word*! This is my first year as editor and I'd like to thank Nathan Eddy for his faithful editorship, leaving me with a wonderful team of writers and advisers. We each take on our roles aware of the rich heritage and the lives we've touched in previous years, while seeking to bring new vision for the lives yet to be reached.

As a reader of *Fresh From The Word*, I've always enjoyed getting to know the writers a little through their brief biographies. This year, I've had the privilege of discovering something more of the personal journeys that underpin their writing.

From insightful readings on grief and loss – written not as an academic study of Scripture, but through the tears of personal tragedy – to those about facing hostile powers written between blackouts and coordinating relief efforts for those devasted by flooding: real people in real situations.

From seasoned writers to those writing for the first time. Female, male, single, married, confident, doubting – all bringing their personal experience of God to bear on the passages, demonstrating how Scripture has shaped who they are as well as what they believe.

I'd like to honour them, not just for a willingness to exercise their gifts on our behalf, but for the godly way in which they have done so: showing humility and grace in their responses, accepting additional commissions when, because of the pandemic, others were unable to do so. And for their generosity of spirit in writing for us at a time when their own challenging circumstances demanded attention.

And they've written, as ever, to a creative and inspirational reading plan. We journey through Luke, walk (and swim) with Jonah. We have our minds expanded through Revelation and our hearts touched as God uses kisses to express his love for us. We find encouragement in 'facing the darkness' and we enjoy looking at 'a colourful Bible'. From Corinthians through Kings, we are drawn together as we read the same passages each day.

From around the world geographically and from around the church theologically, the IBRA community of writers and readers is a wonderful foretaste of heaven: where those from every tribe and every tongue will be present with the one who unites us all – Jesus.

I commend this edition to you,

David Painting

Acknowledgements and abbreviations

The use of the letters a or b in a text reference, such as Luke 9:37–43a, indicates that the day's text starts or finishes midway through a verse, usually at a break such as the end of a sentence. Not all Bible versions will indicate such divisions.

We are grateful to the copyright holders for permission to use scriptural quotations from the following Bible versions:

GNT   Scriptures quotations marked GNT are taken from the Good News Bible © 1994 published by the Bible Societies/HarperCollins Publishers Ltd UK, Good News Bible© American Bible Society 1966, 1971, 1976, 1992. Used with permission.

MSG   Scripture quotations marked MSG are taken from The Message. Copyright © by Eugene H. Peterson 1993, 1994, 1995, 1996, 2000, 2001, 2002. Used by permission of NavPress Publishing Group.

NEB   Scripture quotations marked NEB are taken from the New English Bible © Oxford University Press and Cambridge University Press 1961, 1970. Revised English Bible © Oxford University Press and Cambridge University Press 1989.

NIV   Scripture quotations marked NIV are taken from the Holy Bible, New International Version. Copyright © 1973, 1978, 1984, 2011 Biblica, formerly International Bible Society. Used by permission of Hodder & Stoughton Ltd, an Hachette UK company. All rights reserved. "NIV" is a registered trademark of Biblica. UK trademark number 1448790.

NIVUK Scripture quotations marked NIVUK are taken from the Holy Bible, New International Version Anglicised. Copyright © 1979, 1984, 2011 Biblica, formerly International Bible Society. Used by permission of Hodder & Stoughton Ltd, an Hachette UK company. All rights reserved. 'NIV' is a registered trademark of Biblica. UK trademark number 1448790.

Walking in the light

1 Light in the darkness

Notes by **Stephen Willey**

Stephen has a city centre ministry in Coventry, England and has recently been involved in the City of Culture celebrations there. For many years he was engaged in industrial chaplaincy and work against human trafficking. He is committed to transformation in areas of multiple deprivation, especially encouraging those who are young or vulnerable, inside and beyond the church, to discover their value and meet their potential. Stephen is married and has two grown up children. Stephen has used the NRSVA for these notes.

Saturday 1 January
Light for the new year

Read Genesis 1:1–5, 14–19

Darkness covered the face of the deep, while a wind from God swept over the face of the waters. Then God said, 'Let there be light'; and there was light. And God saw that the light was good; and God separated the light from the darkness.

(verses 2b–4)

Sometimes, in the snow and icy wind of January, a glow appeared on the slag heaps in the town of Consett. Red hot slag was a by-product of the transformation that was going on in the Iron Works. Within furnaces, cold stones of iron ore, limestone and coal were being converted into steel. Memories of those days, when the town could be seen far off by its red glow, belong to an older generation now, but that glow was a sign of a living, creative town.

As we start this new year together, how does the heat of God's creativity draw us into a new time? Whatever that first Genesis light was like, at the beginning of all things, it presaged a wonderful transformation. Out of chaos came light, life and goodness. At this time of the year, as we simultaneously look back and forward, can the fire of God's love change things, especially if they are hard and cold? God says, 'Let there be light', and perhaps we don't think of a process as violent, hot, or bright as the inside of a blast furnace, but that intense fire echoes creation, as God invites us to new beginnings.

† Fire of God's loving, burn in our hearts as the new year begins. So may our lives shine with your creation's transformation.

Sunday 2 January
Not overcome by darkness

Read John 1:1–9

[John the Baptist] came as a witness to testify to the light, so that all might believe through him. He himself was not the light, but he came to testify to the light. The true light, which enlightens everyone, was coming into the world.

(verses 7–9)

I was feeling anxious and somewhat out of control as I approached the dual carriageway with no headlights. First one headlight had gone and then, shortly afterwards, the other one died. I had only dim sidelights. I saw that this road was unlit, unlike the well-lit streets I had been on. Then I was on it, struggling to see my way. As I drove, I realised that not only was I struggling but I had become dangerous – even potentially deadly. If someone were to be walking on the road ahead I may not see them until it was too late. I slowed down to a crawl and sighed with relief when I returned to the well-lit streets near home.

Without light it is possible to become dangerous and even to despair of finding a way, but with light, there is hope. John the Baptist points to the light which will help us find our way. That light will help us recognise the truth about things and people, a light that helps us to be seen by others and can prevent us missing their presence among us, thus causing damage. John the Baptist witnessed to a light which had an entirely different quality from the shadows. The light of Jesus, the Word, came into the world to show that there is a way (John 14:6). Christ offers the hope of an unquenchable light for all who are in darkness: the true light that enlightens everyone.

† Jesus, light of our lives, shine into this new year and accompany us through whatever lies ahead. We ask this in and through your glorious light. Amen

For further thought

Can I make a resolution to live in Christ's light, so my steps do not damage others but lead where God would have me go?

Monday 3 January
God will give light

Read Luke 1:68–79

By the tender mercy of our God, the dawn from on high will break upon us, to give light to those who sit in darkness and in the shadow of death, to guide our feet into the way of peace.

(verses 78–79)

I was a youth worker, working with unchurched young people who spent much of their lives on the streets, and I was confronted by their need each day. All around me I saw the hurt and damage that those young people were suffering, and saw how their suffering often led to the suffering of others. My work was deeply challenging and almost overwhelming. It felt like a flood of need was swamping me and I had nowhere to turn. Then I discovered, for the first time in my working life, that I could turn to someone – an older, wiser person whose experience of life enabled him to reflect on the lives I was encountering. Through his care I rediscovered the God who touches lepers and heals the sick, or those considered unclean.

I think it was the look in my supervisor's eyes, a look of compassion and care, for suddenly the tender compassion of our God broke like a new dawn, releasing something within, as tears filled my eyes. Since that first meeting I have (many times) found my work demanding even to the point of being overwhelming, but even now I can remember that look of compassion, and for a moment, at least, the dawn from on high breaks in on me.

This poetry in Luke speaks to the heart. If the shadows around should seem impenetrable, hear the words of Zechariah, allow the light of compassion to rise in your heart and then, even in the midst of shadows, let the light guide your feet in the way of peace.

† Holy God, by your tender compassion, may your light rise in me. By your gracious dawning light, may my life be a source of comfort to those who share my road this year.

For further thought

Is there poetry, music or art that lights up your heart? How could it be integrated into your prayers this year?

Tuesday 4 January
Seeing a great light

Read Isaiah 9:2–7

The people who walked in darkness have seen a great light; those who lived in a land of deep darkness – on them light has shined. You have multiplied the nation, you have increased its joy; they rejoice before you.

(verses 2–3a)

'Why is light good?' (Gen 1:4), I wondered, while cycling up a hill on a country lane. It wasn't a question I'd asked before – I'd always known that light was good. But why? As I contemplated this, I arrived at the top of the hill where a gate led into a field with cabbages and trees, and birds on telegraph wires. I paused. Without light … Without light, not only would I not see this scene because my eyes would not be able to see, but the scene would be unseeable, impossible. Those trees, cabbages and plants, and hence the birds, and all animals need light for food, growth and life for survival itself.

Without light what would this world be? Impenetrable darkness, from which no life could ever emerge. There would be no eyes to perceive beauty's absence. Without light we would not be able to do or be anything. Light brings forth life. And so, in Isaiah, God's light gives life to the people who walked in deep darkness. It brings hope, life and joy to the people

Isaiah tells of the birth of a child who is given to those in darkness. That light, born among us, makes life possible in all its contrasting colours and forms. That light offers abundant life.

† Light of God's loving, joy of colour and contrast, we adore you! Speak into our shadows with creative words, through your light free us to display our beauty more fully.

For further thought

How will I and my community celebrate light in the beauty of colour, contrast and form this year?

Wednesday 5 January
Wake up, arise and shine!

> **Read Isaiah 60:1–6**
>
> *Lift up your eyes and look around; they all gather together, they come to you; your sons shall come from far away, and your daughters shall be carried on their nurses' arms. Then you shall see and be radiant; your heart shall thrill and rejoice.*
>
> (verses 4–5a)

I walked from one village to another most days, to go to work. There was one far off field which always seemed to glow with a translucent green. I used to love to see that field and I would look for it as I went on my way, even when the mist hid it. That radiant field drew my eye and lifted my spirits on days that felt challenging or lightless.

The Magi (Matthew 2:1–12) followed a star which had caught their attention. Starlight and wisdom drew them to a brightness beyond any starlight or wisdom they had previously known. As they knelt at the side of the Christ child, there was the light that they had come to see, shining with a brightness never before known on this earth. Radiant child! Christlight! And their faces were surely radiant too, as they contemplated the gift and gave their gifts of gold, frankincense and myrrh. And later, when they reflected on that day, would not their hearts thrill and rejoice?

I am still, at times, drawn to that luminous green field, though I haven't seen it for years. I value the gift of having seen it when I felt lost or uncertain. The Magi's vision of the Christ child echoes through Isaiah. Christ, born of Mary, brighter than the brightest star, is a sign of hope for the people.

† Christ, announced by angels, let our eyes be drawn to you. By your radiance lift up our hearts and grant that we may reflect your radiance in the world around us.

For further thought

There are many things which might distract, but what draws my eyes and lifts my heart?

Thursday 6 January (Epiphany)
Light dawns

Read Psalm 97:1–12

[The Lord] guards the lives of his faithful; he rescues them from the hand of the wicked. Light dawns for the righteous, and joy for the upright in heart. Rejoice in the Lord, O you righteous, and give thanks to his holy name!

(verses 10b–12)

We had a long journey from the north of England to eastern France. The town I left was dark and I slept on the coach after walking around on the ferry in the cold, grey, pre-dawn light.

When I woke from my sleep, I lifted up the blind on the coach window. Fields of sunflowers in full bloom shone gold in bright summer's sun against a blue cloudless sky. Colours I had never seen before. Me, a boy from the north of England. Such light, such golden joy, was unexpected, even undeserved. I had lived all my life, until then, unaware that this vibrant, golden light existed.

For the Magi, upright in heart, as they studied the stars for God's revelations, their quest, faithfully following the star, led not to sunflowers, blue skies and sunshine, but to the very glory of God. The promise of Isaiah was fulfilled. Their eyes saw the sight of the holy infant, cradled in his young mother's arms. Such a light dawning, such joy! They had hoped for a king, but they were unprepared for what they had discovered: the One who came to rescue them and the people of the world. As the Magi brought forth their gold, it was surely dull in comparison with the gift they had received. God's love, undeserved, born to us.

† Glorious God, keep us faithful and true. Open our eyes to your holiness and by your grace show us joy of your presence in our midst.

For further thought

What precious gifts could I resolve to give to God this year?

Friday 7 January
Light shines out of darkness

Read 2 Corinthians 4:1–6

For it is the God who said, 'Let light shine out of darkness', who has shone in our hearts to give the light of the knowledge of the glory of God in the face of Jesus Christ.

(verse 6)

One summer, my father had been invited to bring us, his family, to Ohio, in America. Ohio seemed strange. So many new things to see. But, to me, more spectacular than the tourist attractions, was something new to me during the warm nights – fireflies – hundreds of them, floating in the air and glowing intermittently with their yellow-green light. We tried to catch them in jam jars – we wanted to get a 'jar of light' – but though we caught some, they stopped glowing for us once they were in the jar. To a 12-year-old, their light made the night seem enchanted. I discovered very quickly that you could not capture the quality of those nights in a jam jar!

The radiance of Jesus' face – his light in our darkness – is not something we can capture like fireflies in a jar. The glory of God is there for us to see – and for those who see him, he re-creates the world, making it beautiful and strange and new. Jesus' divinity, acknowledged by the Magi's gift of frankincense, is the very holiness of God. Such holiness, the light of God's glory, seems beyond us. Yet, as the writer of 2 Corinthians says, that light, the glory of God, through Christ's face, shines in our hearts.

† God of glow-worms and fireflies, God of the stars in space and the sparkling light on the water, radiant and beautiful Saviour, shine in our hearts we pray.

For further thought

Are there places where I try to trap Christ's light in a jar rather than seeing it transforming the darkness?

Saturday 8 January
Come to the light

Read John 3:17–21

The light has come into the world, and people loved darkness rather than light ... all who do evil hate the light and do not come to the light, so that their deeds may not be exposed. But those who do what is true come to the light.

(verses 19b–21a)

I suppose we have all placed things in the shadows. My sister moved the sofa to cover a stain from a spilled drink. The burglar, who I heard but never saw, came at night. A person has long hair to hide their God-given ears that stick out at right angles. And me? I confess, I have sometimes left unspoken that which needed to be revealed in the full light of day.

Why not keep things in the dark? The burglar got hold of some money. I can leave the truth untold and avoid the conflict it might cause. If our body has something that shames us, why not hide it from others? Why not remain hidden – hiding the truth of who we really are, especially if it might shock or hurt those we want to love us?

Fearing exposure, it is possible to fly to the shadows. But what do we give up if we choose darkness?

We give up the myriad, contrasting colours of creation and the beauty of diversity; trust, honesty and fireflies; stars and the light on the water. Turning from the light of the resurrection, it is possible to choose a kind of death, or a kind of half-life in the shadows. The Magi brought myrrh as their third gift presaging Jesus' death, but the Creator of light overcomes the shadows of death, inviting all into the light of loving, the joy of colours, the fires of creation, the words of life. All this for each of us, because the light has come into the world.

† Jesus, your light is never overwhelmed, speak the word of transformation into our lives. By your merciful grace, dispel the shadows I have cast and enter my darkness to make me beautiful in your sight.

For further thought

What does Christ's light reveal in the places of shadow in my life, or my community? Is there some transformative action I can take?

Walking in the light

2 A light to my path

Notes by **Kate Hughes**

Kate worked for the Anglican Church in Southern Africa for 14 years, including as an editor at the Theological Education by Extension College in Johannesburg. Since her return to the UK, she has worked as a freelance book editor specialising in theology. She lives in a small council estate in Coventry with her Cavalier King Charles Spaniel, she is involved in her local Anglican church where she preaches regularly, and also volunteers with the Pets as Therapy charity. Kate has used the NRSVA for these notes.

Sunday 9 January
A lamp to my feet

Read Psalm 119:105–112

Your word is a lamp to my feet and a light to my path.

(verse 105)

The Christmas before I started writing these notes, I became very focused on the words from the first chapter of John's Gospel: 'The light shines in the darkness, and the darkness did not overcome it' (John 1:5). The darkness did its best to overcome and destroy the man who was the light of the world, the light of God's love burning steadily and indestructibly in the world he had made.

A month after Christmas 2019, Covid-19 arrived – and, for many people, life became very dark indeed. And yet there is always a light through the dark, if we trust God's promise and look out for it. It will guide my feet so that I don't stumble and it will show me the way I need to go. As we try to live in God's way, as citizens of his kingdom and followers of Jesus, we shall discover that the light is there for us too. This week, we shall be finding out more about it: how we need to behave in order to receive God's light and to live in that light.

† Show me your way, O Lord, and lead me by your light, now and always.

Monday 10 January
Live justly and in the light

Read Isaiah 58:6–11

If you offer your food to the hungry and satisfy the needs of the afflicted, then your light shall rise in the darkness and your gloom be like the noonday.

(verse 10)

When you look at the world with its wars and injustice, its massacres and cruelty, the terrible things that human beings do to each other both nationally and one to one, it is tempting to wonder where the light of God is in all of this. There are times when God's light shines like a beacon in the world, but more often God works through his faithful people.

Whenever we allow God's love to shine through us, there is also God's light. Whenever we act justly, set people free from literal bondage or the bondage of sin, feed the hungry, give a home to the homeless, refuse to speak evil of others, that is when God's light shines in the darkness. Each act of obedience shines like a star, a pinpoint of God's light that the darkness can never overcome. Multiply this by the billions of God's people in the world, and there is quite a lot of God's light penetrating the darkness. Or, to change the metaphor, a spring of water is poured out onto parched land, a spring that never runs dry.

† Help me today, Lord, to bear my part in bringing your light to a world of darkness.

For further thought

How have you enabled God's light to shine today, even by actions that seem tiny but contribute to the worldwide effect?

Tuesday 11 January
Walk in the light

Read John 12:35–36

While you have the light, believe in the light, so that you may become children of light.

(verse 36)

In this passage, Jesus, the light of the world, is speaking to his disciples while he is still with them. While they can look at him and see what being light is like, it should not be difficult to believe that the light of God exists and that they can follow it. The problem comes when God's light seems to have been swallowed up by the darkness of a sinful world. That must have been how the disciples felt during and after the crucifixion: how could they believe in the light? Yet, as John says at the very start of his Gospel, God's light can never be overcome by darkness.

We may not have the man Jesus physically still with us, but we can believe that God's light is still with us, still leading us, still confronting the darkness of sin. If we believe in the light, we shall discover many examples in our own lives and in the life of the world of God's light confronting darkness and not being overcome. The love of God, which unwaveringly responds to all that sin can throw at it, lights up our world and our lives. We can show that we are part of God's family and citizens of his kingdom by passing on his light to others when, like Jesus, we do not allow evil to stop us loving them.

† Lord, help me to share the light of your love with others, and never let the darkness of sin and evil overcome me.

For further thought

What, in practical terms, does it mean to be 'children of light'?

Wednesday 12 January
The armour of light

Read Romans 13:11–14

Put on the armour of light ... put on the Lord Jesus Christ.

(part of verses 12 and 14)

Under cover of darkness, evil can flourish. But we have emerged from the darkness of sin and walked – perhaps blinking and bleary-eyed – into the light of the new day of salvation. However, the darkness never ceases trying to overcome us, and we need help in our new walk in the light. We need the sort of protection provided by a suit of armour, and for us that is God's light. But not just any light but *the* light – the light of the world, the Lord Jesus Christ. It is by his Spirit that we can fight on the side of the light, take God's light into the territory of darkness, and remain safe.

When the prodigal son came home, his father wrapped the best robe around him (Luke 15:22) so that he was clothed in his father's love and welcome. When we say that we trust God, we are clothed in the Holy Spirit, the Spirit of Jesus, who enables us to belong to the light and to share it with others. That is our armour. In the early days of Christianity, at baptism new believers were immersed in water and, coming out, were then clothed in a white robe. By the light of candles, this new robe must itself have shone like light; they were clothed in the light of the Lord Jesus Christ. We may not have been baptised in that way, but all of us can receive that shining robe and let its light shine out on others.

† Clothe me with your light, Lord Jesus, with your armour against the darkness.

For further thought

Think of one person who is in the darkness of sorrow, sin, depression or sickness and let God's light flow through you to them.

Thursday 13 January
From darkness into light

Read Colossians 1:9–14

Joyfully giving thanks to the Father, who has enabled you to share in the inheritance of the saints in light. He has rescued us from the power of darkness and transferred us into the kingdom of his beloved Son.

(part of verses 11–13)

The power of darkness: left to themselves, human beings find it so easy to do what is wrong, to side with the darkness of the world, not to have the courage or the power to resist temptation, to take the easy way out by attacking, bullying and mistreating others to get what they want. Without the knowledge of God, human beings are trapped in the darkness of sin. But Good Friday and Easter Day changed all that. Jesus on the cross, steadfastly and unchangingly showed God's love and forgiveness; he showed that human beings do not need to be chained and imprisoned by sin, they do not need to be dragged down into darkness. They have a choice. They can choose darkness, or they can choose to join the others who have chosen God, who have chosen to belong to that great company of the faithful, the saints. Those who choose the light are citizens of God's kingdom, the foretaste of what God's rule will be like when that kingdom finally comes in all its glory.

The writer of Colossians describes what it is like to be one of the faithful: it is about knowing God and his will, about spiritual wisdom, about pleasing God, bearing fruit, being made strong, experiencing God's glorious power, about endurance and patience, redemption and forgiveness. Walking in the light.

† I choose light, I choose the kingdom, I choose God.

For further thought

Can you remember an occasion in the past week when you deliberately chose God, chose the light? For example, stopping yourself making a hurtful remark?

Friday 14 January
Blinded by the light

Read Acts 26:12–18

To open their eyes so that they may turn from darkness to light and from the power of Satan to God, so that they may receive forgiveness of sins and a place among those who are sanctified by faith in me.

(verse 18)

This is Paul's definitive confrontation with the light. He was in the darkness of misunderstanding what God wants of his people. Saul, as he was then, thought that the new movement of the followers of Jesus was so wrong that the only way of dealing with it was to kill or imprison the people involved. As a Pharisee, Saul prided himself on keeping God's law, clinging to the covenant that God had made with his people in the time of Moses. God's faithfulness demanded obedience from his chosen people. But so focused were the Pharisees on aligning themselves with the God of the covenant that they could not recognise that God could do something new, could do things differently. They saw Jesus and his followers and saw only the darkness of disobedience, heresy, and a threat to the Jewish nation. Something unusual had to happen to Saul to shake him out of this outlook, this blindness, and make him able to see in the light, to see the light in Jesus.

Somewhere along the line, the Jews had become so focused on their current problem of living under the Roman occupation that they had forgotten that they were meant to be sharing their special relationship with God with all the nations of the world. Living in the light for Paul meant not just living as a devout Jew, it meant taking the Jewish experience of God, transformed in the life, death and resurrection of Jesus, into the darkness of the Gentile world. God's amazing love gives forgiveness and new life to Jew and Gentile alike.

† Loving Father, thank you that all of us, Jew and Gentile alike, can be given a place with your saints in the light.

For further thought

The Jewish experience of God as his chosen, covenant people, is clearly important. But how does Jesus shed light on it and extend it by his life, death and resurrection?

Saturday 15 January
Children of light

Read Ephesians 5:8–14

For once you were darkness, but now in the Lord you are light. Live as children of light.

(verse 8)

In the Bible, being 'a child' of someone meant that you replicated them. There was a clear family resemblance. There was a strong possibility that you would grow up to practise the same trade as your father. Your name probably reflected your relationship to him: Simon bar Jonah = Simon son of Jonah. The Bar Mitzvah ceremony in modern Judaism makes a Jewish boy the Son of the Commandment or Law, a member of the family of the chosen people, the keepers of God's law.

So, what does it mean to live 'as children of light'? If we are children we are expected to reflect the personality of our Father, to have a family resemblance to God and to all the other children of light. So, we reflect 'all that is good and right and true' (verse 9), as shown us in the life and work of the Son of God, Jesus of Nazareth. In order to do this, we need to 'find out what is pleasing to the Lord' (verse 10) and not simply avoid the unfruitful works of darkness but expose them to the light, show them up for what they really are and help others to avoid them. We can only do this if we allow the Holy Spirit, the spirit of Jesus, to guide us and empower us. Living in the darkness makes it impossible for us to be the people that God has created us to be; we stumble through life, losing our way. Like so much of God's creation, we need light in order to flourish. So, we need to wake up and turn our back on the darkness that so much resembles death. And then 'Christ will shine' on us (verse 14).

† O Lord, help us to turn away from darkness and walk with you in the light.

For further thought
What kind of darkness particularly concerns you? Pray for those who are trapped in it.

The Gospel of Luke (1)

1 Healer and teacher

Notes by **Alesana Fosi Pala'amo**

Alesana is Head of Department for Practical Theology at Malua Theological College, Samoa. An ordained minister of the Congregational Christian Church Samoa, his research interests include social ministries, Pacific research methodologies, theology and pastoral counselling. Alesana has a PhD from Massey University New Zealand through his research on Samoan pastoral counselling. Alesana and his wife, Lemau, co-founded a pastoral counselling agency called Soul Talk Samoa Trust, and their sons Norman, Alex and Jayden attend college and primary school in Samoa. Alesana has used the NRSV for these notes.

Sunday 16 January
Deep water teaching

Read Luke 5:1–11

When he had finished speaking, he said to Simon, 'Put out into the deep water and let down your nets for a catch.'

(verse 4)

This week we shall read and learn about Jesus being a healer and a teacher. For today's reading, Jesus is a teacher. There is a common practice in Samoa that when an issue appears unresolved while discussed by *matai* (title holders) at their village council meetings, or parents with their family members, wisdom known as *t'f'* is sought. To do this, a metaphorical reference to deep-water fishing – *tu'utu'uileloloto* – is often heard by these community and family leaders. The idea is that out in the deep waters there are larger fish to be caught compared to the size of the fish found closer to shore; further out in deeper waters, profound learning and thus wisdom are found.

Jesus taught his first disciples in a similar way, instructing them to cast their nets out in the deep. Today's reading involves Jesus calling Simon Peter and his fellow fishers, James and John, sons of Zebedee. Through his deep-water fishing lesson, Jesus taught his first disciples to repent, follow him and catch people. We too are summoned for this purpose, to repent, follow Jesus and lead others to share in the glory and abundance of life in and through our Lord Jesus Christ.

† Our Saviour, help us to cast our nets into deeper waters and to serve you and catch more people to share in your love. Amene

Monday 17 January
Healing through cleansing

Read Luke 5:12–26

Then Jesus stretched out his hand, touched him, and said, 'I do choose. Be made clean.' Immediately the leprosy left him.

(verse 13)

When awaiting anxiously the results of an exam, or an outcome that is life-changing, cleaning keeps us busy, distracting us from our nerves of anticipation! The Monday following White Sunday in October is the day that candidates receive the results of the entrance exams for Malua Theological College in Samoa. On such a day, 20 years ago, I found such a distraction in mowing our lawn and trimming our hedges while awaiting the results of the exam. As it turned out, the life-changing outcome from that exam to train and serve God as a minister continues to this day, with my family and me being stationed at Malua Theological College. While being 'cleansed' of anxiety in this way is helpful, the cleansing Jesus brings is more profound!

Considered unclean and untouchable by those around him, Jesus broke down such a mindset by reaching out, touching and cleansing the sick man of his leprosy. This cleaning wasn't just a distraction from the problem, this was God reaching out and touching the problem, dealing with it at the source. Likewise, with the paralysed man. The root of all our paralysis, directly or indirectly, is sin. As a result of his friend's faithful and costly actions, Jesus is able to cleanse the man of his sins, enabling him once again to walk. Of course, the authorities objected to Jesus forgiving sins, but as John puts it 'If we confess our sins, he who is faithful and just will forgive our sins and cleanse us from all unrighteousness' (1 John 1:9).

If we will come to him, Jesus cleanses us too.

† Lord God, thank you that you heal us and cleanse us. May we always seek in you pathways for healing our pain and cleansing us from our sins. Amene

For further thought

Is there someone who needs your help by bringing them to Jesus? Don't let the uncleanness of others stop you from bringing them to Jesus.

Tuesday 18 January
Lord of the Sabbath teaches with food and drink

Read Luke 5:27–6:5

Then he said to them, 'The Son of Man is lord of the sabbath.'

(verse 5)

Previously working as food and beverage cost controller for one of Sydney's iconic city hotels, the Sydney Boulevard, my role involved costing recipes, and monitoring the effective movement and storage of all food and beverage items in the hotel. Occasionally I needed to run stocktakes for the bars and restaurants on Sundays, especially when month-end fell on this day. I always felt uneasy working on a Sunday, especially when my work obligations clashed with my church commitments or prevented my attendance at Sunday worship.

The Scribes and Pharisees were more than uneasy about Jesus doing what they considered to be work on the Sabbath, they were horrified. Their legalistic worldview had blinded them to the truth about God. In today's passage, Jesus gives a context for the Sabbath law – that the Sabbath is made for all humankind to enjoy rest, that the Sabbath is for humankind, not humankind for the Sabbath, and above all, that the Son of Man is lord of the sabbath. He alone has the right to define what is appropriate and what isn't.

This teaching was so helpful to me in understanding that if a task must be done on the Sabbath such as food preparation, then such a task is not in breach of the Sabbath law, because the law is rooted in the character of God, who does good every day of the week. So, if an activity on the Sabbath is absolutely necessary for one's survival and livelihood, then such activity should be done. Yet, if life can still function without attending to that activity on the Sabbath, then maybe wait for another day to carry out the task – and enjoy resting with God!

† Help us God to know when to carry out a task on Sundays, or not, so that we can enjoy the blessings of rest and keeping your Sabbath holy. Amene

For further thought

How can we approach God's law without being trapped in legalism?

Wednesday 19 January
Called to teach and heal

Read Luke 6:6–19

On another sabbath he entered the synagogue and taught, and there was a man there whose right hand was withered … They had come to hear him and to be healed of their diseases.

(verses 6 and 18a)

For the Congregational Christian Church Samoa that I belong to, Sunday is the Sabbath and the primary day of worship. Yet for parishes of my church outside of Samoa, Sunday is also when other events are held following the usual Sunday worship. Events such as parish meetings, youth groups, and choir practice are done when parishioners congregate for Sunday worship, due to the vast distances some members have to travel to attend church.

It was the same for the crowds in this passage. The multitudes had gathered from great distances to witness Jesus' ministry and to listen to his teachings about God's blessings, human relationships and ethical and moral living. These followers yearned to be healed from their diseases, as word spread across the Judean countryside of Jesus' miraculous healings.

Should Jesus send them home unhealed, simply because it is a particular day of the week? Is that what God is like, more interested in a rule than a person? 'Stretch out your hand' he commands, restoring the man (verse 10).

Once we commit ourselves to God as a Christian, we are called as both teacher and healer. We become teachers to share about Jesus' teachings including doing good and saving life, every day. We also become healers, in sharing the good news that through Christ all things are possible.

† Our Loving God, use us as vessels to teach others about your grace and eternal love, and the healing and comfort you provide where all things are possible through you our Lord. Amene

For further thought

Remind ourselves that God calls us all to share on to others the good news of Christ as teacher and healer for all life's challenges.

Thursday 20 January
Healing truth

Read Luke 6:20–36

Blessed are you who are poor, for yours is the kingdom of God. Blessed are you who are hungry now, for you will be filled. Blessed are you who weep now, for you will laugh.

(verses 20–21)

As a child in Samoa, we played with slingshots made from tree branches. Those that formed a perfect 'Y' were the best. I remember making a very good one using rubber tubing from bicycle tyres. Mysteriously, after a short time of enjoying it, I found my slingshot split into two, as if cut by a sharp object. A jealous cousin eventually confessed about 30 years later!

Jesus shone light onto darkness revealing the truth: that blessing comes from discovering that you have nothing, that real nourishment comes when you are starved of the world, that joy comes when we are honest about our grief. But people living in darkness responded like a jealous cousin, seeking to destroy, to throw him out, to discredit him.

And when we seek to be light, we should expect a similar response. This hurts because the emotional pain scars deep into one's non-touchable existence, tempting us to respond in the same way. But Jesus, as teacher and healer, shows us that those who seek to hurt us are truly to be pitied; they may have what the world counts as blessing: riches, status, approval, but this is all they will ever have. It is what they desired and God, in his grace has given it to them. Tragically, the gold will tarnish, the food and fine clothes rot, the hoarded goods will be stolen, their status will pass to the next generation leaving only emptiness. Understanding this stirs compassion, making forgiveness easier.

† Lord God help us to forgive others who have done wrong against us, just as we seek your forgiveness for our sins. Grant us healing by forgetting as well. Amene

For further thought

When darkness seeks to engulf, how do we help one another to keep shining?

Friday 21 January
What goes around comes around

Read Luke 6:37–49

Do not judge, and you will not be judged; do not condemn, and you will not be condemned. Forgive, and you will be forgiven.

(verse 37)

I suppose the one thing that everyone knows about a boomerang is that it is supposed to return to you when you throw it! The first time I ever threw a boomerang as a youngster, it didn't return to me. Knowing what it *should* do isn't enough, there is a technique that is needed in order for it to work. Eventually, an Aboriginal friend at Matraville in Sydney taught me the skills I needed. To my surprise I quickly learned how to throw a boomerang the correct way, and watched it circle back in a loop to where I caught it.

Today's passage catches this idea of what you do to others coming back to you, like a boomerang that returns to the thrower when done correctly. 'In everything do to others as you would have them do to you' (Matthew 7:12a). The teaching is that whatever deeds you do for someone, either good or bad, these are what you wish others to return to you someday. The skill that we need to develop as Christians is to pursue doing good deeds for others, demonstrating our correct use of this moral and ethical guide given by Christ. Only then can we 'catch the returning boomerang' and reap in the benefits of God's love, when kindness and love are reciprocated to us by others.

† Lord, help us to do good deeds to others by sharing the love you have for us, so that others can also rejoice in your abundance and blessings. Amene

For further thought

Do we often expect people to show kindness to us – yet we avoid doing the same? Let us do good to others as Jesus has taught.

Saturday 22 January
A healing word

Read Luke 7:1–17

But only speak the word, and let my servant be healed.

(verse 7b)

A measles outbreak in Samoa led to eighty-three fatalities, most of whom were children under five years old. As well as the natural grief, several locals blamed the government and health officials for neglecting the vaccination against measles, an illness that rarely leads to fatalities in this modern era. We had no solutions to the problem – we couldn't bring back their loved ones, we couldn't bring justice. But we could bring the presence of God into the situation.

Sitting with the grieving, sharing their tears. Praying with them, standing together in the pain, my wife and I offered emotional and spiritual support to the bereaved families. We witnessed first-hand how this simple presence or singing a hymn brought peace in the midst of the pain for many of the bereaved families.

And we saw this time and again, as we mobilised teams of ministers, theological students, and medical professionals to visit the bereaved families; the presence of God in our presence gave space for their anger and softened bitter hearts.

Jesus is the healing word, as today's reading demonstrates. For the centurion who had faith in Jesus to heal his slave, he sought and found the healing wonders of Jesus' word. For the widow who lost her son, Jesus resurrected the young man from death with his word to 'rise'. Our Lord is the healing that his faithful seek, to bring about peace and comfort for the broken and troubled world that we live in.

† Our healing and gracious God, please continue to bless as the healing word that we seek in our times of need. Grant us peace and comfort always. Amene

For further thought

Do we sometimes seek healing for our troubles away from Christ? Nothing is impossible to our Lord; all we need is to believe.

The Gospel of Luke (1)

2 Good News for the poor

Notes by **Alex Cameron**

Alex is a humanitarian aid worker with Medair, a non-governmental emergency response organisation (NGO). She wrote these notes while in Lebanon responding to the Syrian refugee crisis, two months after the Beirut explosion and in the middle of the Covid-19 outbreak. She was born and bred in London but has had the amazing opportunity to work across the world with inspirational people trying to make their bit of it better. Alex has used the NIV.

Sunday 23 January
Who are the poor?

Read Luke 7:18–35

Go back and report to John what you have seen and heard: The blind receive sight, the lame walk, those who have leprosy are cleansed, the deaf hear, the dead are raised, and good news is proclaimed to the poor.

(verse 22)

In my work, we ask questions and carry out endless assessments to establish what and where the needs are. Sometimes they are simple, like providing food in a drought. Sometimes they are complex, such as attempting to improve land and property rights when rebuilding after an explosion. I have met many people whom most would consider poor, but never have any of them answered that what they needed was for good news to be proclaimed!

It makes sense to me that Jesus restored sight to the blind and life to the dead, but surely it would be more of a miracle to lift the poor out of their poverty... unless Jesus was not talking about those who are materially poor? Sight is provided to those who need to see, cleansing is given to those in need of being cured from a horrendous, contagious disease, and good news is given to those in need of hope.

The poor Jesus is speaking about are those who are spiritually, not materially, poor. When I read this passage, I see all of us as being poor; we all need hope and the good news to be proclaimed to us. While it's not the first thing we think about, who in this world doesn't need to hear good news?

† Father we come before you knowing that we are poor and in need of your good news. Help us this week to open our hearts to hearing it.

Monday 24 January
What is the Good News?

Read Luke 7:36–50

Therefore, I tell you, her many sins have been forgiven – as her great love has shown.

(part of verse 47)

This passage gives me so much hope! This woman breaks every social norm of the time to come and wash Jesus' feet, and the Pharisees are shocked by the events. It's commonly thought that this woman was probably a prostitute, she came to the Pharisee's house uninvited, interrupted their meal and proceeded to wash Jesus' feet with her tears, dry them with her hair and anoint them with oil. I think if I were one of the Pharisees, I'd be a little shocked too! They see it as highly inappropriate for a man claiming to be a prophet to allow the woman to do this. They probably expected Jesus to throw her off and demand she go and make herself clean. Instead, Jesus starts talking to them about forgiveness and how this woman is demonstrating love!

Jesus sees it all differently, he already knows why she's there. He sees a woman bursting with love, kneeling before her Saviour, and demonstrating that love in the best way she can think of. He doesn't tell her to go and perform a certain ritual, or even dictate how she should now live her life. He just tells her that her sins are forgiven.

The Good News is that we can all be forgiven and restored in our relationship with God. This woman, although her sins were many and who didn't do anything in the 'right' way, was forgiven. God forgives us and accepts our love in all the ways we choose to show it.

† Father forgive us; for all the things we know we have done wrong and for all the things we have failed to do.

For further thought

How can you demonstrate your love for Jesus today?

Tuesday 25 January
What should we do with the Good News?

Read Luke 8:1–18

But the seed on good soil stands for those with a noble and good heart, who hear the word, retain it, and by persevering produce a crop.

(part of verse 15)

How is that New Year's resolution going for you? Three weeks into January and I've normally hit a stumbling block with mine. Week 1 is normally good, I've got that drive of a 'new year, new me' attitude; I'm eating more healthily, exercising more, and starting to learn that new language/read more books/better myself in some way. By week 2, the regular commitments of life have started to interrupt the good schedule of the first week; working long hours has led to microwave meals, Netflix to unwind and sleeping longer. By week 3, I'm normally feeling quite unimpressed with myself and my ability to keep any of my resolutions; sometimes this gives me renewed energy to try again, but normally it leads to me giving it up.

If the seed in this parable was my New Year's resolution, then for many years it has fallen on paths, rocky ground and among thorns. Just as fields and gardens need to be maintained in order for there to be good and fertile soil, I know I have to continuously cultivate my heart in order for the Good News to find good soil to grow in. Hearing the Good News is not enough, we need to continue to work to ensure it produces fruit in our life.

I first heard the Good News long ago, but there are still moments when I realise that the thorns are beginning to grow. The worries of this world can crowd out faith, but even small things, like remembering to pray each day, help me to start cutting back those thorns and returning to the fertile soil.

† Lord, help us to cultivate our hearts. Give us the power to chase off the birds, dig up the weeds and cut down the thorns. May your Good News be what is growing there.

For further thought

What seeds is God trying to sow in your life? What sort of ground are they falling on?

Wednesday 26 January
Have a little faith

Read Luke 8:19–39

'Where is your faith?' he asked his disciples.

(verse 25a)

'What have I got myself into this time?' Before I went to Ghana, I was warned about the 14-hour bus ride from Accra to Bimbilla, but no one mentioned the ferry! It had already been a rough day; I'd had to run after the bus and I'd started to feel really sick following the goat curry I'd eaten for lunch. Now I was faced with this ferry and then finding the right bus on the other side of the river.

'God, why am I here?' I asked again. God has led me into some difficult situations where, at the time, it has been a struggle to understand why I am there. This was one of them! As I got off the bus, I was struggling to hold back tears when suddenly a woman appeared at my elbow, grabbed my arm and started ushering me toward the boat. We got to the front of the queue before she realised that I still had money, not a ticket, in my hand. She didn't speak English, so she grabbed my money and disappeared into the crowd. I started to panic slightly, but she quickly returned with a ticket. She got me safely on board, avoiding the manoeuvring vehicles and goats joining us. She stood to the side when we reached the other bank and I had to run off and throw up. Then she made sure I got on the right bus. To me she felt like my guardian angel.

Every time I've been in those situations, I've encountered wonderful people who have helped me out of them. I truly believe this is God nudging me to have a little faith!

† Lord, help each of us to have a little more faith today.

For further thought
Who can you be a guardian angel to today?

Thursday 27 January
Faith and healing

Read Luke 8:40–56
Daughter, your faith has healed you.

(verse 48)

So far this week we have begun to explore who the poor are and why they are in need of Good News. We've looked at what that Good News is, how we can cultivate it, and asked God to grow it in us. Today, we start to think about how that impacts how we live our lives.

In this passage we witness the faith of two different people: Jairus, the synagogue leader desperate to save his daughter, and the bleeding woman grabbing the edge of Jesus' cloak. Jairus seemingly was not bothered who saw him approach Jesus for help, whereas the woman tried everything to not have to identify herself. But Jesus calls her to the front of the crowd, out of the shadows and into his light. Her faith has already healed her physically, but Jesus wants to heal her from shame and even calls her 'Daughter'!

Having seen the woman healed, it must have felt crushing for Jairus to be met by the news that his daughter had died, but Jesus asks Jairus to continue to have faith, even in the face of people laughing at the idea that anything could now be done. In healing Jairus' daughter, Jesus brings her back from the darkness of death – and with her, the whole family.

Faith and healing go hand in hand. It's not always the miraculous healing of disease and death, but it is also the healing from shame, grief and darkness. Jesus pulled the woman out of the darkness of shame and Jairus' daughter out of the darkness of death. I believe God asks us to spread the Good News, going to people in dark places, and walking with them into the light.

† Father, we pray today that you will help us come alongside people in darkness. Help us to share with them your Good News and begin the walk into the light.

For further thought
Who do you know who needs healing, leading from darkness to light?

Friday 28 January
Living by faith

Read Luke 9:1–17

Take nothing for the journey – no staff, no bag, no bread, no money, no extra shirt.

(verse 3)

When deploying into an emergency response situation, you can't always predict what conditions you might be walking into, or how long you will be there, so you prepare by taking a little of everything, cramming it all into one or two suitcases. Clothes, laptops, ropes, water filters, mosquito nets, tents, sleeping bags, medicines and emergency food are just some of the things I have lugged through various airports around the world.

Once on the ground, aid agencies have huge logistics teams to procure and distribute the emergency aid provisions. In the aftermath of the Beirut explosion, it took at least forty staff and volunteers in my organisation to distribute 2,000 emergency shelter kits for 10,000 people in the following weeks. Similarly, other NGOs had huge operations providing food for all the people whose kitchens were no longer operational.

I can completely understand the Twelve when they come to Jesus telling him to send the crowds away – the need can feel overwhelming! And if I had been one of them being sent out, I'd have asked Jesus if it was OK to at least take a snack for the journey! But Jesus asks them to give it all up and live by faith. He provides when they need it. Sometimes God does it through a little boy's lunch box, and sometimes he does it through the generosity of donors to teams of NGOs; but he does provide!

† Father, there are moments when we doubt your provision and try to provide for ourselves. Increase our faith to know that you will provide when we are in need.

For further thought

Who can we be God's provision for?

Saturday 29 January
Taking up our cross

Read Luke 9:18–36

Whoever wants to be my disciple must deny themselves and take up their cross daily and follow me.

(verse 23)

We started this week with John sending his disciples to ask Jesus whether he was the one they were waiting for and we end it with Jesus asking his disciples who they think he is. Peter answers, 'God's Messiah'. Jesus then tells them what they should do to follow him, and it's not an easy ask; deny yourselves and take up your cross and follow me.

It can seem a really scary prospect! When I look at the examples of the disciples, these instructions led many of them to their deaths. Am I ready to sign up to that?

For me, the key word in this verse is 'daily'. Jesus doesn't reveal everything to his disciples at once. It takes them months of travelling with him till he asks, 'Who do you say I am?' (verse 20) and only after this conversation does the Transfiguration happen where the voice from the cloud declares, 'This is my Son' (verse 35). God knows when we are ready to follow him on the next stage of the journey, he knows whether the seeds of Good News are sitting on rocky or fertile ground in our hearts and prepares us, so we are ready for what comes next. In Matthew 6:34, Jesus says, 'do not worry about tomorrow'. We are not asked to see into the future and worry about tomorrow, but we are asked to daily seek God over ourselves and follow him.

† Father, help each of us to put ourselves aside today and pick up our cross. May you prepare us for what is coming next and give us peace to know it is in your hands.

For further thought

Who do we have in our life who inspires us to follow Jesus in this way?

Weather warnings

1 And it rained!

Notes by **Mark Mitchell**

Mark has largely been engaged in the aid and development sector over the last twenty-five years. As such, Mark tends to read the Bible through a social justice or emergency management lens. He is constantly inspired by or seeking to inspire others with God's heart for the poor or those impacted by disasters. Based in New Zealand, he lives with his wife, Julia, who is a a health adviser, and two daughters at high school. Mark has used the NIV for these notes.

Sunday 30 January
A part of creation

Read Jeremiah 10:11–13

But God made the earth by his power; he founded the world by his wisdom and stretched out the heavens by his understanding.

(verse 12)

We should need no reminding that God created all things by his power, wisdom and understanding. We read in the original creation account in Genesis that when God looked at all he had created, he saw that it was good. In Psalm 19:1, the heavens declare the glory of God and if you have ever looked across the horizon watching a lightning storm, it is easy to see the majesty in his creation. Storms are majestic, inspiring and awesome but they can also be destructive, and it can be easy to be terrified by 'signs in the heavens' (verse 2).

How we see storms depends on where we are living. If our homes are built in accordance with building regulations and on a solid foundation, we can perhaps relax and enjoy the majesty and power in a storm. If, however, our homes are less well constructed, we have reason to fear the storm. How we build a house does not prevent the storm from coming but it does change our perspective.

By living by God's ways, when storms come, what we see is the glory of God's creation not the chaos. Sometimes it takes the force of the storm to be reminded of his power, wisdom and understanding.

† Lord, help me to build my life in accordance with your ways so when the storms come, I see you, your glory, your majesty.

Monday 31 January
God's blessing

Read Deuteronomy 11:10–15

… then I will send rain on your land in its season, both autumn and spring rains, so that you may gather in your grain, new wine and olive oil.

(verse 14)

The Egyptians referred to the Nile as the 'river of life'. The river provided water to the crops through irrigation channels, which meant that the further from the river you lived, the less access you had to this life-giving water. (Even now access to the water is by negotiation with those whose land is closer to the source.) Moreover, in Egypt, there is very little rain to feed the Nile or to provide comfort and sustenance for those living at distance from it (around 29 mm of rain per year in Cairo!)

By contrast, when the Israelites crossed the Jordan to the promised land, they arrived in a place of mountains and valleys that drinks rain from heaven. In this new land, it predictably rained during two seasons: at the end of autumn (seedtime) and in spring (before harvest) – termed the former and latter rain (Jeremiah 5:24). And this rain came in equal measure to everyone – a sign of God's love and care for all.

Similarly, Matthew 5:45 tells us that the rain, God's blessing, is available to all, righteous or unrighteous, and is irrespective of what we might do to deserve it. It is clearly, God's will to bless all people, the gospel is good news to all, but as today's reading reminds us, this blessing is dependent upon how we respond to the gospel.

Even in a mountainous land, rainwater can run off and be lost. To prevent this, it is important to identify ways of capturing the water and directing it to where it is needed. The blessing is there, but our obedience allows the blessing to be harvested and bear fruit.

† Lord, help me love you and to be faithful to your commands that I may receive, and help me to share your blessings.

For further thought

How are you actively collecting God's blessing? Is it being channelled to where it is needed most?

Tuesday 1 February
Do not forget

Read Jeremiah 5:20–25

I made the sand a boundary for the sea, an everlasting barrier it cannot cross. The waves may roll, but they cannot prevail; they may roar, but they cannot cross it.

(part of verse 22)

Throughout the Bible, waters are pictured as a place where evil can reside. From God holding back the waters in Genesis to create a safe place for humankind, to the storm on the lake in the Gospels, waters and evil are synonymous.

In a similar vein, in this conversation with Jeremiah, God points out that that it is He who holds back the threatening waters. The roaring seas are constant with disaster ever present, yet God stands in the gap between the storms of life and his people, just like the beach between the land and the sea. Without the beach we see the destructive force of the waves breaking against hard rock and causing cliffs to crumble. And yet waves lose all their power and energy in the sand. On the cross, Jesus acts as the beach – the relentless waves of evil, doing their worst against his broken body. But because he stands between us and the waves, by the time they reach us they have lost their power.

And yet, God's people have become ambivalent about the God who protects and provides. They forget that God not only holds back the waves but, out of his love for them, provides for all their needs and ensures the regularity of the rains required to produce a good harvest.

In spite of this God is merciful. At personal cost, he gently holds back the disaster and continues to provide for our every need whether we remember him or not. Yet how much better is it to praise him with all our being and not forget all his benefits (Psalm 103:2)? To include praise to him at the time of harvest and to remember him and all his blessings?.

† Lord, help me to remember all your benefits.

For further thought
We often ask why there is so much suffering in the world. Perhaps we could reflect on how much more there would be if God were not even now, holding back the flood.

Wednesday 2 February
And it rained

Read Genesis 7:11–24

In the six hundredth year of Noah's life, on the seventeenth day of the second month – on that day all the springs of the great deep burst forth, and the floodgates of the heavens were opened. And rain fell on the earth forty days and forty nights.

(verses 11–12)

When I compared this reading to that of yesterday, I am reminded that God doesn't always hold back the waves. In fact, this was the time that God allowed the floodgates to be opened. The thing that strikes me about this, however, is how precisely the date of the flood was recorded. This was clearly an important date to God. He, like us, remembers specific anniversaries and commemorates them. I can almost imagine him relating the story as Moses writes Genesis. The sadness and the pain it still caused him is important to note; God is not indifferent to grief.

While through the flood God was bringing to an end a period of corruption, he also wanted to save people through Noah. In 2 Peter 2:5, Noah is called a 'preacher of righteousness'. If building a big boat wasn't clear enough, Noah was clearly sharing God's plan with those around him. Ultimately, God's plan was to restore humanity to himself.

In a fallen world, disasters will continue to occur, and God's plan is still that we should be prepared for them, whether by building a boat or in other practical ways. God continues to grieve for humanity and has compassion on all, particularly the most vulnerable. As Christians who hear from God, we should have compassion for those in need and determine how to respond. Likewise, we know that God can bring about good from bad situations in order to bring people back to himself.

Just as Noah was faithful, so God is faithful in providing his protection. What is our part?

† Lord, in the midst of disaster help me to see how I can be a preacher of righteousness and help those in need.

For further thought

How can we have the same mind as Christ – putting ourselves between evil and the vulnerable?

Thursday 3 February
Our response

> **Read Leviticus 26:3–5**
> *If you follow my decrees and are careful to obey my commands.*
>
> (verse 3)

Wading through the law of Leviticus can be a challenge. I think you can justifiably pat yourself on the back if you manage to get through the full book! Even so, as you read through the book of laws for priestly duties and the liturgical calendar, it is easy to wonder how much is still relevant.

And yet, it is clear that the idea of the law continues through into the New Testament. After all, Jesus said he didn't come to abolish the Law but to fulfil it (Matthew 5:17). So, what is its relevance to today?

Our reading told the Israelites that if they followed his decrees and laws that God would send rain (a metaphor for blessing, Isaiah 44:3–4). But if not, he would withhold that blessing to get their attention. In short, the end of this book of Law presented a conditional covenant: If you do this, I'll do that; if you obey the law, I will bless you. Easy to see this as a mechanical exercise – you press these buttons and I do this. Yet when pushed further, Jesus, indicated that the whole Law could be summed up as loving God and loving people (Matthew 22:37–39), relational not transactional.

Paul then speaks of a 'new covenant' and John records the 'new' commandment given by Jesus: 'Love one another' (John 15). And while this is true for each of us, I am reminded that the original covenant was addressed to the whole of Israel not to individuals. It is a collective covenant. We know that God's desire is to bless us collectively, that he is faithful to his promises. Our response must be a collective faithfulness to our side of the covenant.

† Lord, thank you for your faithfulness despite our unfaithfulness. Give us the grace to respond with soft hearts.

For further thought

In what ways can we be faithful collectively – as church, and as nations, in responding to God's love?

The power of a storm

Read Exodus 9:22–33

Then the Lord said to Moses, 'Stretch out your hand toward the sky so that hail will fall all over Egypt – on people and animals and on everything growing in the fields of Egypt.'

(verse 22)

In today's reading, we read of the seventh plague: the plague of hail. As with the previous plagues, God tells Moses to warn Pharaoh of what is about to happen. What makes this plague different, however, is that God tells the Egyptians what to do to protect themselves: 'Give an order now to bring your livestock and everything you have in the field to a place of shelter, because the hail will fall on every person and animal that has not been brought in and is still out in the field, and they will die' (verse 19). Even in the middle of God's judgement, in his mercy he was showing them a way out, a way to redemption.

The plagues are a reminder that God judges harshly those who oppress. As we see at the start of the book of Exodus, God was responding to the cry of his people in response to the oppression by the Egyptians (Exodus 3:9–10). God's approach in addressing oppression was to challenge the systems and beliefs of the day (Exodus 12:12). Each of the plagues are thought to directly oppose the gods of Egypt. The hail came from the sky which was represented by the god 'Nut'. Aside from demonstrating his power over the natural elements, here God was diminishing the power of the Egyptian belief systems and dismantling the very structures holding the Israelites captive.

† Lord we pray for those that are held in slavery and oppression and declare your freedom for them.

For further thought

What are the gods today that hold us captive?

Saturday 5 February
The sun brings forth

Read Deuteronomy 33:13–16

May the Lord bless his land with the precious dew from heaven above and with the deep waters that lie below.

(verse 13)

Contrast today's reading with that of yesterday. Moses who had previously called the plagues on Egypt is now announcing blessing on the tribes of Israel. Specifically, in the passage we read, he was prophesying blessing over Joseph from the full range of all that God had created: the dew from heaven would water his crops, waters from the deep would water his animals, the sun would help to ripen the fruit and the moon would guide the agricultural calendar through to harvest.

In spite of many challenges through his life, Joseph remained faithful to God and the dreams that God had for him. As a result, he was ultimately used by God to save his family and all of Egypt. As we have been seeing, faithfulness to God results in blessing – a blessing that went beyond Joseph's life to the generations that followed (Deuteronomy 7:9).

This contrast – plague and blessing – reminds us of the sun following a storm: the warmth dries up the rain, new life appears, and hope is restored. So often it is at these moments that we see God's permanent sign of promise – a rainbow.

As we learn in the Abrahamic covenant (Genesis 12:2–3), we are blessed to be a blessing. In God's circular economy, as we bless others God provides everything required for all of our needs. As Paul said in response to the generosity of the Philippian church: 'And my God will meet all your needs according to the riches of his glory in Christ Jesus' (Philippians 4:19).

† Lord, help us to be light and warmth to those in the storm.

For further thought

Where in the cycle are we? In the storm with darkness all around? The sun is coming because the Son has come.

Weather warnings

2 Watering the earth

Notes by **Jane Gonzalez**

Jane is a Roman Catholic laywoman. Retirement has offered her opportunities to spend more time in Spain, where she and her husband have a home, and to indulge her creative side. She is currently writing haikus (17-syllable poems) and illustrating them with her own photos. Projects for the future include weaving and collage. In between all this, she remains an active member of her local parish, particularly in the Justice and Peace Group. Jane has used the NRSVA for these notes.

Sunday 6 February
The desert shall bloom

Read Job 29:21–23

After I spoke they did not speak again, and my word dropped upon them like dew. They waited for me as for the rain; they opened their mouths as for the spring rain.

(verses 22–23)

I am not at my best first thing in the morning and I don't like early starts! Sometimes, of course, life dictates arising early: trains to catch, jobs to go to, appointments to be kept. And although it's not my preferred time of day, the early morning has its charms. There is an untouched feeling, especially on a bright day; the sense that the world is pregnant with possibilities if we can only find time to look and listen.

A vivid memory of this is being in the garden at home, looking over my notes before an important exam, and being aware of the softness of the day: the early sun, and the grass beaded and sparkling by the dew that had fallen. I drank in the promise of the day, as Job's listeners drink in his words. Dew, in arid and desert places of the earth, promises and produces a miraculous springing forth as the parched ground responds by flowering and flourishing. Thus, too, is the word of God that speaks to us. It is often as gentle as dewfall; as quiet as the first hours of dawn. But if we pay attention it will bloom within us.

† Father, refresh my mind and heart with your life-giving words. Give me the patience and courage to take time to listen.

Monday 7 February
Water, water, everywhere ...

Read Isaiah 19:5–10

There will be bare places by the Nile, on the brink of the Nile; and all that is sown by the Nile will dry up, be driven away, and be no more. Those who fish will mourn; all who cast hooks in the Nile will lament.

(verses 7–8a)

I live in the south of England, not far from London. It's a gentle area with an undulating landscape criss-crossed by an abundance of chalk streams, virtually unique in the world. Our local one, the Gade, has recently been restored to maintain its traditional meandering route and its margins have become places where children paddle and families gather. The unobtrusive animal and aquatic residents of this quiet habitat have a chance to flourish.

The Nile may seem far removed from a small chalk stream. It is a mighty river. It sustains major eco-systems and is the lifeblood of many nations and communities. Without it, Egypt would be a barren waste. But the demands of the modern world threaten both the Nile and the Gade. Over-extraction, disturbance of the flow by damming, disputes over entitlement to water – and the often selfish demands of modern life.

Isaiah's dire warnings are addressed to the enemies of Israel – a judgement on them if they do not change their ways. It can be tempting to think that this is all just ancient history but there is a warning here for us. Whether we live in the Nile valleys or near a chalk stream, we prejudice God's creation at our peril. If we do not maintain a proper balance between human activity and the natural world, if there is not appropriate respect for other creatures, the drought, famine and loss of life and livelihood foretold by the prophet will happen in our day. We will be authors of our own destruction and, in the words of Pope Francis, our own judgement.

† Father, creator of all things, all creation is my neighbour. Give me the grace to love and care for it.

For further thought

Do I take easy access to water for granted? If appropriate, contact your water supplier and find out how you can save on your consumption.

Tuesday 8 February
A good deed every day

Read Acts 11:27–30

The disciples determined that according to their ability, each would send relief to the believers living in Judea.

(verse 29)

As I write these words, the UK has moved into a third period of lockdown, as we try to stem the tide of infection caused by the coronavirus and its more virulent mutations. The new year is barely a few days old and the hopes raised by the development of vaccines and their roll-out have yet to be fulfilled. For many people January can be a long, dreary month and this year things seem greyer and less hopeful than usual.

It can be facile (and harmful) to trot out encouraging phrases and platitudes when the future for many seems bleak and uncertain. Yet there are reasons to be cheerful. For me, these lie in the small acts of kindness, love and generosity of so many. Before Christmas, for instance, our goddaughter raised £200 for a homeless charity. She was sponsored for the hours she spent sleeping outside in the garden in a large cardboard box. She raised both money and awareness of the plight of rough sleepers. Our postman not only delivers our mail but does shopping and collects prescriptions for an elderly neighbour. So many people do so much – each 'according to their ability' as the writer of Acts puts it.

As Christians we are called to change the world, to be salt and light, to feed, clothe, support and nurture those in need. These are the demands of discipleship and they can feel daunting; sometimes impossible to achieve. But God demands only that we do something – the best we can, even if it seems insignificant. He will do the rest.

† Father, I thank you for the kindnesses shown to me. Help me to do my best to bring the Good News to others.

For further thought

A quote often attributed to Mother Teresa says 'Not all of us can do great things. But we can do small things with great love.' Where can you make a difference?

Wednesday 9 February
Signs of the times

Read Jeremiah 18:14–15

Does the snow of Lebanon leave the crags of Sirion? Do the mountain waters run dry, the cold flowing streams? But my people have forgotten me, they burn offerings to a delusion.

(verses 14–15a)

For me, walking has always been a pleasurable experience. It is more than a hobby. I now possess the requisite hiking boots, waterproofs and an app for finding footpaths – but I'm just as happy setting off from my front door for a walk. I grew up in the 1950s when few people had cars and my parents remained resolutely carless all their lives. We walked everywhere. 'Nature rambles' with my father were the greatest fun: there was always something to remark upon or observe and we learned about trees and flowers and the seasonal changes around us.

Walking allows me to fall into step with the rhythm of the seasons. Passing along an area of common ground, I see a line of horse chestnut trees. For me, these symbolise the inexorable cycles of birth, death and regeneration: the bare branches of winter, the 'sticky buds' of spring; white candle-shaped flowers in summer and the shiny hard fruit of conkers in autumn before bareness returns. All as planned by the Creator and so often forgotten by us in our busy lives as we flash past in our cars.

Jeremiah points out the steadfast fidelity of God to his people referencing the rhythms of the natural world. When we stop seeing God at work around us, we can so easily be seduced to believing in our own ways and works – and into worshipping the idols of success, glamour or comfort. We cease to walk in the paths of righteousness when we cease to walk with God.

† Father, I try to walk in your ways but often stumble from the path. May I never lose sight of you as my goal and compass.

For further thought

St Teresa of Avila said that God was in 'the pots and pans'. Can I too find God's presence in the ordinary and everyday things of life?

Thursday 10 February
I give you my word

> **Read Isaiah 55:8–12**
>
> *So shall my word be that goes out from my mouth; it shall not return to me empty, but it shall accomplish that which I purpose, and succeed in the thing for which I sent it.*
>
> (verse 11)

At the time of writing we are looking forward to celebrating our daughter's wedding. The current restrictions imposed in the UK by the Covid-19 crisis limits the wedding to fifteen persons. We are in a peculiar situation, therefore, in planning for the happy day. Hopefully, by July, things will have improved and we will be able to host a celebration as well as a marriage. In the meantime, we plan for a variety of scenarios and numbers! My husband is preparing his speech even though it may have to be issued via social media rather than in person!

Of course, the most important part of the day will go ahead. Come what may – they will marry. They will, in time-honoured fashion, exchange vows and make promises. They will give each other their word – to be faithful. 'For better, for worse, for richer, for poorer …' In days gone by the vows included the phrase, 'I plight thee my troth' which means 'I pledge you my truth'. The words stand for commitment, loyalty and a wholehearted acceptance from both parties of the covenant into which they are entering.

Words matter. We live in a world where words are often twisted and debased; where some people reduce the truth to mere personal opinion or 'alternative' versions of reality. It can be hard to sift the truth from the lies. As Christians we know where the truth is to be found – in the word of God, incarnate in Jesus and present in scripture. God has given us his word. It is for us to be faithful to it and bring it to fruition.

† Father, give me faith to know that your promises come true. Help me to be patient because I know that you hear and answer me.

For further action

Take some time to reflect on the Beatitudes in Matthew (5:3–12). How can you make these words come true in your own life or in others'?

Friday 11 February
Blessed assurance

Read Isaiah 43:1–7

When you pass through the waters, I will be with you; and through the rivers, they shall not overwhelm you; when you walk through fire you shall not be burned, and the flame shall not consume you.

(verse 2)

In early January, we celebrated the feast of the Epiphany and in accordance with tradition we took down our Christmas decorations and packed them away for another year. This year, however, I left the wreath on the door and the nativity set will remain on the mantelpiece, with its lights, until the feast of Candlemas. I'm not alone – according to my newspaper, a significant number of people, both church and non-churchgoing, have decided to keep their festive lights and trees for the time being. These have become tangible signs of the hope that Christmas brings and of the need we have of reassurance that there is light at the end of the very dark tunnel in which the whole world finds itself at present.

I am blessed in having someone to share my experience of that darkness, but the global pandemic has highlighted loneliness and alienation within our societies at a time when we cannot easily reach out to others in comfort or friendship. When interaction is reduced to shouting at each other from two metres' distance. For the lonely, isolated, bereaved and anxious, hope can seem non-existent or very far away and many people, of all faiths and none, ask, 'Where is God?' in all this (see Psalm 42).

As Christians we can find hope and consolation in God's promise to be with us, in the here and now, whatever befalls. The coming of Emmanuel celebrated each Christmas fulfils the proclamation of Isaiah centuries before. God is with us – through 'dungeon, fire and sword', as the old hymn by Frederick Faber says. Therein lies our assurance.

† Father, I believe that you are with us, in good times and in bad. I believe – help me to grow even more steadfast in faith.

For further thought

What signs are there in your life that mark you out as a person of hope? Consider how you can bring the light of hope to others.

Saturday 12 February
Are you sitting comfortably?

Read James 5:13–18

The prayer of the righteous is powerful and effective. Elijah was a human being like us, and he prayed fervently that it might not rain, and for three years and six months it did not rain on the earth.

(verses 16b–17)

When I was very small – and before we owned a television set at home – my mother and I tuned in to *Listen with Mother* on the radio. This 15-minute programme was broadcast every day for pre-school children. There were songs, nursery rhymes and a story. Before the story started the presenter would ask, 'Are you sitting comfortably?' Then she would pause, before adding, 'Then I'll begin …'. It was recognised that, in order to fully enjoy the story, you needed to be in the right frame of mind to listen. To be seated, comfortably, with the temptation to fidget reduced!

In my own prayer life, I am trying to spend more time sitting comfortably in the presence of the Lord. I am conscious of the need to listen more intently to him rather than bombarding him with words. Especially when he knows better than I do what I need. James, in our passage, exhorts us to turn to God in every situation. It is reminiscent of Paul's call to 'unceasing prayer'. And heartfelt prayer, like Elijah's, certainly brings results. But does unceasing or fervent prayer always mean unleashing a torrent of words?

Sometimes our words might even get in the way of real communication with God. The mind chatters unceasingly, intruding and distracting us. There is a still, small voice of God that wants to talk with us, sit companionably with us, but it needs calm and space and stillness in order to be heard. When we are sitting comfortably, then the Lord will begin.

† Father, give me the grace to be silent in your presence. Help me to accept that you know better than I do what is necessary for me to flourish.

For further thought

Daniel O'Leary talks of 'exploring the shy secrets of God' (*The Tablet*, 17 May 2008). Try to find some quiet prayer time. Where does God want to take you?

It started with a kiss

Notes by **Helen Van Koevering**

After living in Southern Africa for most of her adult life, Helen, raised in England, moved to the USA in 2015. Helen is a rector of St Raphael's Episcopal Church in Lexington, Kentucky, where her husband serves as bishop. She has previously served as a parish priest and as Director of Ministry for the rapidly growing Anglican Diocese of Niassa in northern Mozambique during a decade of extensive and transformative church growth. Now, with the lens of missionary spirituality gathered in those formative years in Africa, she is discovering new perspectives for life-giving faithfulness in her new context. Helen has used the NRSVA for these notes.

Sunday 13 February
Jacob steals Esau's birthright

Read Genesis 27:1–27

'Are you really my son Esau?' He answered, 'I am.' Then [Isaac] said, 'Bring it to me, that I may eat of my son's game and bless you.' So he brought it to him, and he ate ... Then his father Isaac said to him, 'Come near and kiss me, my son.'

(part of verses 24–26)

Many say they study the Bible to learn how to live good, loving, moral lives. Yet there are many stories that scandalise. Isaac and Rebekah, with their sons, Esau and Jacob, show us a family as real then as now. A system that every family might recognise with rivalries, parental favouritism, anger, covetousness, deceit and conspiracy. Yet we judge the actions of these ancient families from our own point of view. As we read of Esau and Jacob, we might regard Esau as the wronged party, the underdog, the one who loses his birthright and blessing through no fault of his own. Rebekah and Jacob conspired against him to cheat him, and that kiss of a son to his dying father was not loving and obedient, but deceitful and dishonest. We might think that, by any moral standard, Jacob should be disqualified as the proper bearer of the promise of God. Certainly, God's choice of Jacob makes no sense by any human standard seeking to express morality.

God's choice of a scoundrel scandalises us. This won't be the only time that God chooses a less-than-righteous, scandalous person in the unfolding story of redemption and restoration. I wonder in what ways God scandalises you?

† Loving God, you see in us who we are becoming. Thank you that you choose to include all, even me, in your kingdom come.

Monday 14 February
Kisses of his mouth

> **Read Song of Solomon 1:1–5**
>
> *Let him kiss me with the kisses of his mouth! For … your anointing oils are fragrant, your name is perfume poured out … Draw me after you.*
>
> (part of verses 2–4)

The Song of Solomon weaves a startling celebration of faithful lovers and the mutuality of their love as strong as death (Song of Solomon 8:6) into a love reflected in the renewed life of the earth itself (Song of Solomon 2:10–13) and sealed by the love of the resurrected Christ and the church. Being a song which is predominantly written in a woman's voice, with many images relating to the natural world, we hear voices not traditionally heard as authoritative.

The woman's voice calls us to the centre of the poem, the natural world to see anew, take note of the details and receive the invitation to learn of love and life from the lush and fertile landscape of grace. These are ethical calls to learn from God's world so that we might enjoy and care for one another and the world. The Song points us toward restored relationships, the earth rejoicing with the lovers as healing and renewal are seen rooted in unquenchable love as fierce as the grave (Song of Solomon 8:6–7).

Here, in the Song's evocative poetry, we glimpse God's restorative love lived out. The sensual metaphors for infused, intoxicating, compelling, relational love in the Song reflect the love that first called the world into being, sustains it season by season, reveals beauty, and draws us into new life beyond death itself. And God's extravagant love, responding to the desires and needs of the world, is met in faithful relationships and glimpsed in a kiss of mutual love.

In short, the Song models an ethical stance: to see the lover in others and in our landscapes.

† Beloved One, open our eyes so that in your love we see love as our guide in all our relationships, known and new, and in the world in which we live.

For further thought

Pause for a moment with a view of nature and note what you can hear, smell, touch as God's loving presence with you.

Tuesday 15 February
Naomi, Ruth and Orpah

Read Ruth 1:6–18

[Naomi said], 'The Lord grant that you may find security, each of you in the house of your husband.' Then she kissed them, and they wept aloud … Ruth clung to her … 'your people shall be my people, and your God, my God.'

(parts of verses 9, 14 and 16)

The book of Ruth, set in Israel's early, pre-kingdom years, begins with tragic loss and grief for one Israelite family. Naomi loses her husband and her two sons. Rather than continue in the land not her own, Naomi decides to return to Judah. Much is left unsaid about the causes of these deaths and the barrenness of the daughters-in-law after 10 years' marriage. And in a book that barely mentions God, we are left to discern God's presence in the women's mutual kindness, words, tears and kisses. All we know for sure is Orpah turns back and Ruth prefers becoming a foreigner herself to leaving Naomi. Ruth's clinging to her mother-in-law is a gift of grace that Naomi cannot at first see in her bitterness.

The narrator sees things differently, attributing none of Naomi's tragedies to God, and near the end of the book, it is the Bethlehemite women who articulate to Naomi what has been evident all along, that Ruth's love is worth more than seven sons. Grace is walking right beside Naomi, unseen, yet refusing to leave her. Ruth communicates presence. She will worship the God that Naomi believes abandoned her, and she will do what even Naomi's closest kin couldn't do: remain.

The end of the story transforms the beginning as divine kindness and compassion is seen as having written the narrative that began with a kiss.

† Loving God, may I always remember that your presence and compassion accompany me and those I love always. Amen

For further thought

Take some time today to remember the ups and downs of your own life story, and what you learned of God through it all.

Wednesday 16 February
Jonathan and David's bond

Read 1 Samuel 20:34–42

David ... bowed three times, and they kissed each other, and wept with each other ... Then Jonathan said to David, 'Go in peace, since both of us have sworn in the name of the Lord, saying, "The Lord shall be between me and you, and between my descendants and your descendants, for ever."'

(part of verses 41–42)

David was a Bethlehem shepherd of the tribe of Judah, the youngest son of eight with a harp and a slingshot and anointed to be the next king; Jonathan was the oldest son of King Saul, trained in the art of war, and of the tribe of Benjamin. From David and Jonathan, despite their differences, we learn of the spirituality of friendship.

Key to their relationship was seeing what God saw in each other: men after God's own heart (1 Samuel 13:14). Each saw the other as a warrior and a man of faith who served the living God. And their friendship, sealed in a covenant, provided each of them with God-given courage, strength and faithful love that Jonathan showed toward David at Horesh (1 Samuel 23:16), and David declared in a lament after Jonathan's death (2 Samuel 1:23–26), and continued in his care for Jonathan's orphaned, lame son as one of his own (2 Samuel 9:11).

In the kiss of faithful friendship of today's passage, we catch a glimpse of God's friendship. Though their lives were threatened by their loyalty to each other, they loved the other as they loved their own selves. This is a friendship embodied in God's Son, Jesus, who tells us to love our neighbours as ourselves (Matthew 22:39), lay down our lives for one's friends (John 15:13), and live as friends of God (John 15:15). This friendship is the gift of God offered to us all.

† Lord Jesus Christ, what a privilege that you call us your friends!

For further thought

Consider close friendships you have known. Consider the hurts, the beauty, joy and love you have shared. What of God have you learned through these?

Thursday 17 February
Amassa kissed and killed

Read 2 Samuel 20:1–13

Joab said to Amasa, 'Is it well with you, my brother?' And Joab took Amasa by the beard with his right hand to kiss him. But Amasa did not notice the sword in Joab's hand; Joab struck him in the belly.

(verses 9–10a)

Today's kiss between the cousins, Joab and Amasa, is in complete contrast to yesterday's kiss between the friends, David and Jonathan. Amasa was a nephew of David, and cousin of Joab, David's military commander, as well as a cousin of Absalom, David's son. Family jealousy and hatred in action, not dissimilar to that of Cain and Abel was the issue for them – and so many families ever since. After crushing a revolt and restoring David as king, David appoints Amasa, 'my bone and my flesh' (2 Samuel 19:13), as his military commander, replacing the fiercely loyal and suspicious Joab who had killed Abner and Absalom for standing in his way. He didn't trust Amasa, so, feigning family affection, he murdered him.

The sixth commandment listed in Deuteronomy 5:17 is 'you shall not murder'. It is clear that when we do not love our neighbours as ourselves, when we disconnect through our own fault, word and deed, when we do not recognise family as our closest neighbours, we hurt relationships not just with one another but with God. Our harsh words and actions, though they may not kill, can damage, hurt and destroy others, intentionally or not. Those others may be as far away as our global neighbours, or as close as our next of kin.

† Lord, show me where I need to be reconciled with my neighbour, and teach me the path of reconciliation. Forgive me when I have not loved my neighbours as myself. Amen

For further thought

What blocks me from living and loving my neighbours with authenticity? What do I need to learn about them, myself and the world today?

Friday 18 February
Judas kisses Jesus

Read Matthew 26:47–56

Now the betrayer had given them a sign, saying, 'The one I will kiss is the man; arrest him.' At once he came up to Jesus and said, 'Greetings, Rabbi!' and kissed him. Jesus said to him, 'Friend, do what you are here to do.'

(verses 48–50a)

It is in Judas' kiss in the shadow of the cross that we know there is a thin line between faithful friendship and painful betrayal. Just before this kiss, Jesus shared the last supper with his closest followers. But at this table of belonging and wholeness, we also see death finding its way through betrayal. One of you, Jesus says, will be my betrayer.

We might wonder with the Gospel writers why and how Judas did such a thing, but the truth is that Judas is not excluded from the table – he shares in the bread and the wine that represent Jesus' body and blood, the life that would deliver us from sin and death. Jesus' faithful friendship is in striking contrast to the faithless kiss of Judas, but also, as we read, in all the disciples that Jesus had hand-picked to walk this road.

It is in the kiss of Judas' betrayal that we are reminded that our righteousness leans entirely on Jesus' gift of body and blood, and that the gift of grace and Jesus' faithfulness remains. The meal Jesus shared with all his disciples carried a promise: 'I tell you, I will never again drink of this fruit of the vine until the day when I drink it new with you in my Father's kingdom' (verse 29). That meal was the first of many meals in a kingdom that will know no end, where all will be nourished and made whole, where relationships with God and one another are mended, where resurrected life is real.

† Lord Jesus, we have all fallen short of the glory of God. May we recognise our need and your loving embrace of us as we follow you on your way today. Amen

For further thought

Have you known betrayal of a friend? How did it feel? How did it change you?

49

Saturday 19 February
The Holy Kiss

Read 2 Corinthians 13:11–13

Greet one another with the kiss of peace … The grace of our Lord Jesus Christ, the love of God, and the fellowship of the Holy Spirit be with you all.

(verses 12–13, GNT)

This week, we have heard of the kisses of deceit, passion, commitment, promise, death, and betrayal. Kisses that reveal the whole range of human emotions and the wide range of human relationships. We have witnessed God's love in friendships given to us in biblical characters. Now, we are to learn about the meaning of Paul's call to the people of Corinth to live as friends of God with one another: 'mend your ways; take our appeal to heart; agree with one another; live in peace; and the God of love and peace will be with you' (verse 11, NEB). Let love and peace be verbs. Let the way we interact with one another bring us together like a kiss of peace.

Don Richardson, in his book, *The Peace Child* (2005), tells the story of two villages who ended their conflict by offering the other one of their children. Brought up and loved by the other tribe, Richardson sees in this 'peace child' a redemptive analogy for Jesus, which calls us to forgiveness and to transformed relationships. That kiss of the triune God's peace has been reflected in treaties between enemies through time and around the world, and the path of history has been changed. That kiss of peace has been evidenced when great minds have come together over new scientific breakthroughs with the potential to move the world forward. That kiss of peace is like that kiss of a couple's farewell, a parent's greeting, or a friend's embrace. This kiss agrees with the presence of the God of love and peace with us.

† God, you call us to new life that begins in the way we live in your world. May we be the change you call us to be, for the sake of your glory. Amen

For further thought

Where does our world and our community need a 'kiss of peace'?

Jonah

Notes by **Emma Wagner**

Emma spent 13 years in missions, leading and pioneering teams and initiatives to reach out and share God's love. Now in her mid-thirties, Emma lives in Scotland with her husband, three children, and her sourdough starter, Doris. Under her pen name Emma Browne, she writes contemporary Christian romance novels featuring ordinary women setting out to change the world, finding love and exploring their faith along the way. Emma has used the NIVUK for these notes.

Sunday 20 February
God calls – Jonah flees

Read Jonah 1:1–6

But Jonah ran away from the Lord and headed for Tarshish.

(verse 3a)

Jonah knew two things: the people of Nineveh were horrible people who had done awful things and deserved to die, and God is a merciful God who longs for all people to turn from wickedness and find his love. So, when God tells Jonah to go to Nineveh, Jonah runs in the opposite direction. Because Jonah was not going to be the one to tell the people of Nineveh about the loving God who cared about them. If God wanted to speak to those people so badly, he could find somebody else to go.

When I think of people that have inflicted hurt and fear on me and on those around me, I think that God might have to love them – because that is what he's like – but he's going to have to find somebody else to let them know. The idea that God would want *me* to urge *those people* to turn toward God and receive his mercy and love doesn't always fill me with joy.

Yet even when I can't find anything about those people to love, God still loves them and he invites me to join with him in reaching out to them.

† Father, thank you for your mercy. Help me to share in your love toward those who have hurt me.

Monday 21 February
Disobedience hurts others

Read Jonah 1:7–17

I know that it is my fault that this great storm has come upon you.

(verse 12b)

The storm wasn't God's punishment for poor Jonah – that's not what God is like. However, by Jonah choosing to go his own way; evil was stirred up and the storm was given free rein. And that storm raged not only on Jonah – he wasn't alone on the boat going to Tarshish – so when the storm grew on the sea, the crew and passengers were terrified. Evil unleashed impacts us all whether we were the ones to unleash it or not.

The natural consequence of us acting out of hurt, unforgiveness, or pride is that hell – with its earthquakes, pandemics and discord – is unleashed. However, when we are willing and able to lay aside our hurt, unforgiveness or pride, the kingdom of heaven with its love, harmony, and well-being is unleashed. *We* have the power to unleash the kingdom of heaven, or to allow evil a foothold in this world. And whichever we unleash – heaven or hell – will have an impact on the people around us. It's like Jesus said in Matthew 16:19: 'I will give you the keys of the kingdom of heaven; whatever you bind on earth will be bound in heaven, and whatever you loose on earth will be loosed in heaven.' Our choices matter.

What are the areas of my life in which I am choosing to hold on to hurt? In what ways are my choices stirring up a storm? And what do I need to let go of in order to partner with God to unleash the kingdom of heaven?

† Father, show me the impact of my choices. Help me to leave hurt and unforgiveness behind and to choose to unleash the kingdom of heaven.

For further thought
Evil unleashed looks like war, pandemics and terror, but what does the kingdom of heaven look like in your context today?

Tuesday 22 February
Jonah's prayer in the whale

Read Jonah 2:1–10

In my distress I called to the Lord, and he answered me. From deep in the realm of the dead I called for help, and you listened to my cry.

(verse 2)

When God created the world, he parted the land from the sea. As time went on, people came to understand the sea as being evil – held back from the good dry land – and throughout the Old Testament, the sea is often alluded to as being dangerous, or evil. When Jonah chooses to leave God's good plan and the dry land, he goes to sea; and here he faces the consequences of his choices. Here, in the depths of the sea, in the face of evil, he has an 'aha' moment. Jonah cries out to God, and finds that even there, God will hear his cries. Even in 'the realm of the dead', God is not far away. God is close by and willing to listen, even when Jonah has chosen to do the exact opposite of what God has asked him to do. And God doesn't say, 'Well Jonah, why should I listen when you've been so stupid?', but the merciful God wades into the sea and saves him. God takes him from the depths of despair, and Jonah is given a new chance to do life differently.

God could easily have given up on Jonah and picked somebody else to go to Nineveh. He could have shrugged his shoulders and left Jonah in the realm of the dead. But he doesn't do that. Instead, God chooses to show Jonah that he is merciful and kind. Patient and loving. And he will be merciful, kind, patient and loving toward Jonah just like he wants to be merciful, kind, patient and loving toward the people of Nineveh.

† Father, thank you for not giving up on me, even when I choose to go my own way. Thank you for saving me again and again.

For further thought

Are you experiencing the depths of the sea? God is near enough to hear you when you cry out to him.

Wednesday 23 February
Jonah preaches – eight words

Read Jonah 3:1–4

Forty more days and Nineveh will be overthrown.

(verse 4b)

Jonah got his second chance, and this time he went with a willing heart and did his utmost to persuade the people of Nineveh to turn toward God, right? Nope, that's not exactly what happened. Sure, Jonah went to Nineveh and he preached, but he didn't have much to say. His sermon consisted of eight words and it really wasn't the most inspiring of sermons. Still, somehow, it worked.

Maybe Jonah's sermon worked not because of what he was saying with his words, but because of what he was communicating by coming to see them. Perhaps the people of Nineveh were able to listen to Jonah's sermon and be convicted by it only because they saw Jonah's act of obedience to God in going to preach to his enemies. Jonah's obedience to God preached a sermon so inspiring that the people of Nineveh listened and changed their ways.

Maybe you would rather get on a ship and go the opposite direction of where God is calling you to go. Maybe you're terrified at what he is asking you to do. That's okay – feel the fear, but don't let it stop you from being obedient to God. It is through our obedience to God that God's purposes come about here on earth. We get to partner with him in bringing his kingdom to this earth – and all we have to do is follow God where he leads us. Yes, sometimes it's costly, but what a privilege!

† Father, help me to be obedient to you today, even when it is costly.

For further thought

How is God calling you to follow him today?

Thursday 24 February
Nineveh repents

Read Jonah 3:5–10

Let everyone call urgently on God. Let them give up their evil ways and their violence.

(verse 8b)

Humankind was always called to follow God's way and to enjoy living in relationship with him, and whenever we leave that relationship and choose to go our own way, things tend not to go well. Jonah found this out on the sea to Tarshish, and now it's the people of Nineveh's turn to find out that choosing evil ways and violence leads to destruction. But, as he likes to do, God extended his hand one last time to the people of Nineveh and offered them life again.

Shaken to their very core by Jonah and his sermon, the people of Nineveh realised their violence and wicked ways were leading them towards destruction. They didn't deny their sin – instead they owned up and took responsibility for their actions. They agreed with God that the ways they had been living were not good, they took some time out to pray and to change their ways, and they called out to God again, hoping he might save them.

God saved the people of Nineveh from their destruction because he is merciful and kind, patient and loving. But, in order to save them, God required that they take responsibility for their actions and decide that they wanted him and his ways instead. God couldn't have saved them from their wickedness if they kept inviting the storm into their lives by continuing to choose wickedness.

God wants to save us from evil too. But he requires that we take responsibility for our actions, turn away from wickedness, and that we choose to walk in his life-giving ways instead.

† Father, show me where my actions invite evil to take hold. Help me take responsibility for my sin and thank you for giving me second chances as I trust in you and leave wickedness behind.

For further thought
Are there areas of your life where you need to agree with God, take responsibility and change your ways?

Friday 25 February
Jonah's anger at God's mercy

Read Jonah 4:1–4

I knew that you are a gracious and compassionate God, slow to anger and abounding in love, a God who relents from sending calamity.

(part of verse 2)

Though Jonah is an adult, here we see him throwing a full-blown tantrum, complete with his dramatic 'Take my life, for it is better for me to die than live' (verse 3). Being a mother of three, I've witnessed my share of tantrums, and they aren't pretty; there's shouting and crying and anger, and blame thrown around like confetti. When my children have a tantrum, I'll get to hear things like 'You're the worst mum in the world!' But Jonah isn't angry because God is the *worst* God ever – Jonah is angry because God is the *best* God ever. God is gracious and compassionate, patient and loving – and it's really frustrating Jonah! Why can't God be mean, vengeful and hateful when it comes to Jonah's enemies?

I think this is one of the most beautiful scenes the Bible has to offer. It tells us everything we need to know about what God is like. God isn't in the least threatened by Jonah's anger. God is not contemplating sending a bolt of lightning to kill Jonah off. No, because God knows that tantrums are clever in that they function as a shield which allows the person to hide that they are hurting on the inside. So, God doesn't get angry at Jonah, he doesn't tell him off, or strike him down. Instead, he responds to the hurt inside Jonah. God sees his pain and tries gently to reason with him.

† Father, thank you for being big enough to handle all my emotions, and for responding in kindness.

For further thought

Have you ever felt angry at God? Have you told him? It's okay to have a tantrum at God – he can handle it.

Saturday 26 February
Jonah's lesson from God

Read Jonah 4:5–11

And should I not have concern for the great city of Nineveh, in which there are more than a hundred and twenty thousand people who cannot tell their right hand from their left – and also many animals?

(verse 11)

God responds to Jonah's tantrum by acknowledging Jonah's sense of justice but appealing to his compassionate side. God argues that the people of Nineveh really need help and, now that they can see that, then why shouldn't he help them? Would Jonah really want God to be the kind of god that would wipe them out? Surely not. If Jonah wanted God to be that kind of god, he too would be dead. It was only by God's grace that Jonah had survived to this point.

The book of Jonah doesn't tell us what happens next. We don't get to find out how Jonah responds. Will Jonah agree with God and follow him, or will he choose an alternative route? But the question is bigger than Jonah: it echoes to us today. Will we choose to join with God in loving our enemies and do our best to share God's heart with them? Or will we choose to stay in our hurt, selfishness and pride, and go our own way instead? Having read the book of Jonah, we know that following God and going his way isn't always easy – it will likely confront our pain – but it is a way that brings life, whereas the consequences of choosing our own way leads to destruction. It gives evil a foothold and stirs up a storm.

We get to choose.

† Father, help me to see past my hurt, and to partner with you in loving *all* peoples. Even my enemies.

For further thought

Walking with God sometimes will confront our pain. If you were to tell God about your pain today, what would you say?

The Gospel of Luke (2)

1 Preparing for ministry

Notes by **Jan Sutch Pickard**

Jan is a former Warden of the Abbey in Iona. Earlier, she edited publications (Now, Connect, the Prayer Handbook) for the Methodist Connexion, and is a 'Local' (lay) preacher. Having served twice on the WCC Ecumenical Accompaniment Programme in Palestine and Israel, Jan continues to support monitoring and non-violent action there, praying for justice and peace. With the Iona Community she shares this commitment and works on liturgy that reflects ordinary life as well as God's goodness. Jan has used the NRSVA for these notes.

Sunday 27 February
My Father's house

Read Luke 2:41–52

After three days they found (Jesus) in the temple, sitting among the teachers, listening to them and asking them questions. And all … were amazed at his understanding and his answers. He said … 'Why were you searching for me? Did you not know that I must be in my Father's house?'

(verses 46–47 and 49)

A lively-minded child I know was told off by her teacher for shouting out interesting information in class. It was probably disruptive. And she risked being called 'teacher's pet' – always first with the answers. What would she make of the story of the boy Jesus in the temple? In some Sunday school pictures, the teachers of the law look impressed; Jesus looks smug!

His parents were relieved and surprised to find him there, but while the temple was an impressive setting for theological dialogue, it wasn't the only place where the boy Jesus had a chance to listen, learn and prepare for leadership in his community. In the synagogue in Nazareth, boys of his age would have been schooled like Jewish boys today, learning about their faith, memorising key scripture passages.

But also, in family religious observances; in the workshop helping his father; at the bake-oven watching his mother: like any child he will have questioned and commented and learned about life. The world (not just the temple) was his Father's house – the place of learning through living. That's true for the small child who asked and answered too many questions in class, true for the child in each of us.

† The whole world's your home, God. May we learn from, and care for, all who share it, aware that we'll never know all the answers. Amen

Monday 28 February
The realities of repentance

John's urgent message echoed the prophecy in Isaiah. 'Prepare the way of the Lord ... the crooked shall be made straight, and the rough ways made smooth' (verses 4–5). Would John's hearers have felt their hearts uplifted? Or did he put the fear of God into them, and then put their feet on the ground? And what's the message for us, in our time?

Instead of setting Isaiah's words to the music of Handel's *Messiah*, how about the sound of sirens, feet crunching on broken glass, surrounded by boarded-up houses and the graffiti of gangs? We may imagine an austere, beautiful desert landscape but to John's hearers the wilderness was a waste place, full of challenges, as an inner-city scene might be for us. A place where desolation and discord don't just threaten but penetrate human lives; people becoming a danger to each other and themselves – self-destructive. So, the soaring hymn of promise, in John's preaching, comes in the context of harsh condemnation. Repentance means turning around, choosing a new way. Transformation isn't possible unless individuals and institutions change.

That's true for us too: if our values are distorted, are we up to the task of 'draining the swamp', transforming the wilderness?

The people cried out, 'What then should we do?' (verse 10). And John's answers are wonderfully down-to-earth, about sharing resources, feeding the hungry, not cheating, acting fairly, not misusing power. These are the realities of repentance, a practical preparation for ministry. Then we might have some chance of changing the world.

† Turn us around God, turn our world upside down. Set us facing the other way, show us new priorities, and stay at our side – as we find a different way into your future. Amen

For further thought

Look in your newspaper, in the broadcast news, or on social media, for situations where repentance is urgently needed. How can you respond?

Tuesday 1 March
Son of Adam, Son of God

Read Luke 3:15–38

When all the people were baptised, and when Jesus also had been baptised and was praying, the heaven was opened, and the Holy Spirit descended upon him in bodily form like a dove. And a voice came from heaven, 'You are my Son, the Beloved; with you I am well pleased.'

(verses 21–22)

Volunteering with a local historical centre, I enjoy responding to enquiries about genealogy. Research can be complicated: in this part of the world, most folk seem to be called MacLean, with many called Donald or John: hard to know who's who!

Luke's Gospel offers a family tree with a wider array of given names. But what's the point? We read 'Jesus was the son (as was thought) of Joseph' (verse 23). This list – going back to Adam – only gives one version of the story. For instance, no women are mentioned here, not even Mary his mother. And his Father?

Yet, as I've learned in the historical centre, genealogy is a serious pursuit for some, a question of identity, a way of answering, 'Who do you think you are?' That's a question that was asked again and again by an oppressed people yearning for a saviour. They asked whether John was the Messiah. John said he was just the messenger. And Jesus? Who was he? What ministry could he offer to a wounded society?

What questions were in his mind, walking with the crowds to the Jordan, as he went down into its muddy waters, part of a mass baptism? What did it mean for him, to ask to be baptised? Was this a turning point for him? And was he the only one to see the dove, a sign of the Spirit, settle on him, to hear the affirmation, 'You are my Son, the Beloved'? What did these words mean? What possibilities? What encouragement? What weight of responsibility?

Who do you think you are, Jesus?

† Picture that scene: the flowing river in which each person is immersed – dying to their old life; crowds on each bank – wondering witnesses; dazzling infinity above – a dove descending; words of blessing – 'Beloved'.

For further thought

Think of an occasion when it's meant much to hear your name spoken. Make time to talk with someone lonely today, greeting them by name.

Wednesday 2 March (Ash Wednesday)
Yearning for bread, testing vocation

Read Luke 4:1–13

Jesus … was led by the Spirit in the wilderness … he was famished. The devil said to him, 'If you are the Son of God, command this stone to become a loaf of bread.' Jesus answered him, 'It is written, "One does not live by bread alone."'

(part of verses 1–4)

The flat stones of the desert, baking hot, are a reminder of daily bread, of the basic nourishment that all need. God in human form knew the gnawing hunger which is felt today by a mother in a refugee camp who's given the last food to her children, by a prisoner of conscience on a hunger strike, by a farming family whose crops have failed because of drought, by a child who has come to school without breakfast yet again. While we share distress and anger that people suffer like this, we know that the causes lie deep and the world needs God's word of compassion and justice to bring about change.

Being part of that change can be a ministry to which we are called. In exploring his call, Jesus needed to be aware of the pull of God's Spirit and the push of the devil – the conflicting powers at work around us, and often in us. These are given graphic form in a dialogue between the devil and Jesus. The accounts of Jesus' temptations in the synoptic gospels remind us of how complex that calling may be. We're reminded of how overwhelming economic issues (the need for daily bread) can be. There's also the lure of power for anyone in leadership, and the struggle to hold on to faith – testing God.

While Jesus responds with the words of scripture, it's clear that this isn't a reflective retreat, or an exercise in proof texts, but a picture of a person wrestling to bring into reality that which he knows in his heart and mind.

† (With pauses for reflection). Just and merciful God … deliver us from temptation … do not test us beyond our enduring … save us in the time of trial. Amen

For further thought

Learn about different kinds of bread, worldwide, including the flatbread of the Middle East. If time, make bread – and share it!

Thursday 3 March
Today it is coming true

Read Luke 4:14–21

When he came to Nazareth, where he had been brought up, he went to the synagogue on the Sabbath day, as was his custom. He stood up to read, and the scroll of the prophet Isaiah was given to him. He unrolled the scroll.

(verses 16–17)

The day that we came to Nazareth, a visiting church dignitary was being welcomed with a service in the Church of the Annunciation. I was accompanying a group of young people, on a first visit to Jerusalem and the West Bank, to meet and listen to some of their Israeli and Palestinian peers. In Nazareth, we met a student group brought together by Sabeel, 'the Way', a liberation theology organisation based in Jerusalem.

Not invited to the service, and being a bit scruffy, we went instead up the street to the old synagogue, which dates back to the time of Jesus. It's now disused, so we felt free to step into the cool of this high-ceilinged space, and simply to be quiet for a while, reflecting. Then I handed my battered little Bible (on my desk as I write now) to one of our group, opening it at this passage. James read aloud, into the silence of the centuries. Then we prayed.

I thought afterwards how very close these young people were to the start of their Christian journey. For them ministry would take many forms; only some would offer for ordination or to serve the church (James, I think, was studying physics). All of them, though, after this visit to the Land that we call Holy, would have a deeper awareness of different lives, of people protesting against injustice and asking, 'Where is God?' and others showing steadfast faith. Then back home, with all eyes on them, they would be committed to share what they had seen and heard, of holy places and welcoming people; of human wrong, but also God at work.

† Good news for the poor, freedom from prejudice and fear, clear seeing, healing – may these become true of the way we live together, today. Amen

For further thought

Reflect on the word 'today' – the reality of our world now. Read aloud, slowly and mindfully, 'the Galilean manifesto' (Luke 4:18–19).

Friday 4 March
Controversy and authority

March

The Gospel of Luke (2) – 1 Preparing for ministry

> **Read Luke 4:22–37**
> *All spoke well of him … amazed at the gracious words that came from his mouth. They said, 'Is not this Joseph's son?' … And he said, 'Truly I tell you, no prophet is accepted in the prophet's home town …'. When they heard this, all in the synagogue were filled with rage.*
>
> (verses 22, 24 and 28)

When my son was about 10 years old, an elderly relative asked, 'Do you think you'll grow up to be a minister like your father and your grandfather?' Startled, the boy asked, 'Wouldn't I have to be a Christian first?' Maybe she thought he was making light of a ministry she valued. But it's not (usually) a family business!

The people of Nazareth were proud of 'one of their own' young people, reading so well in the synagogue. In Jack Rosenthal's award-winning play *Bar Mitzvah Boy*, the young man at the heart of a celebration runs away from it. Outside, his sister asks whether he was afraid, forgot the words? No, he was questioning the context: relatives, neighbours, wanting him to conform to their idea of a nice Jewish boy. Then and there, he recites the verses he learned. The words of scripture aren't the problem, or their message – it's the narrow social expectations.

It was so hard for the congregation in Nazareth to hear a message that questioned the safe and familiar – that they wanted to destroy the speaker. It took a distressed man in Capernaum to recognise 'the Holy One of God'. It took an act of healing to convince the onlookers of Jesus' authority.

How does this complex story relate to our faith community? Whom do our familiar rituals alienate? What words and actions have real authority? Can we enlarge our sense of belonging to be more inclusive? Can we live with the risk of the gospel as well as its reassurance? How do we rediscover the liberating message of the Word?

† Spirit of God, help me find the words to tell your truth; may I be part of your work of healing and hope; bless me to see and say and be good news. Amen

For further thought
Reflect on the questions in the last paragraph, spend time with the one that speaks most urgently to you.

Saturday 5 March
The mutuality of ministry

Read Luke 4:38–44

After leaving the synagogue he entered Simon's house. Now Simon's mother-in-law was suffering from a high fever, and they asked him about her. Then he stood over her and rebuked the fever, and it left her. Immediately she got up and began to serve them.

(verses 38–39)

This nameless woman has something she wants to give. It's not just a square meal for her son-in-law and friends, as soon as she's feeling better. It's a much deeper service than simply providing a meal. Hospitality and welcome, providing a place of safety where restoration is possible. Ministry is mutual.

At the start of Jesus' ministry, he's moving on restlessly, from the Jordan into the wilderness, from Nazareth to Capernaum, synagogue to a home then besieged by crowds, from one busy place to another, from Galilee to Judea. It's the kind of ministry which today quickly leads to 'burn out'. Jesus is driven by his mission: 'I must proclaim the good news of the kingdom of God to the other cities also; for I was sent for this purpose' (verse 43). Times of solitude sustain – but the crowds keep gathering, hoping for healing, and teaching that will encourage them.

But what can help, heal and encourage Jesus? Simon's mother-in-law offers hospitality. In the Gospels, we're aware of other places where Jesus is welcomed – like Bethany, home of Martha and Mary and Lazarus. It's not just four walls and food. It's the hospitality of the heart: Mary's listening, Martha's plain speaking, then, when Lazarus dies, Mary's tears and Martha's outburst of anger, followed by an affirmation of faith, 'I believe that you are the Messiah, the Son of God, the one coming into the world' (John 11:27). Mary and Martha enable Jesus himself to weep, and to feel their faith.

Like the women who stand at the foot of the cross, come to the empty tomb and run to tell the world, they minister to Jesus and also share the Good News.

Blessing: Go out with joy, walk in God's Way, grow in God's Love, and live the Good News, today and every day. Amen (from a sermon by Bill Pollock, Minister in Mull)

For further thought

Think about what mutuality of ministry means to you. Write your own blessing for someone whose ministry has inspired you.

The Gospel of Luke (2)

2 Down from the mountain

Notes by **David Painting**

David's passion is to equip people to encounter God more profoundly. A science graduate, he held senior roles in industry and commerce alongside a pastoral ministry in Baptist churches in the UK. Having spent time in YWAM (Youth With A Mission), he currently divides his time between software development, co-leading a house church, teaching and writing. Most recently he was a theological adviser and data contributor to the Infographic Bible project. David enjoys being a grandfather and all things related to space. He is excited to be Editor of *Fresh From The Word*. David has used the NRSVA in these readings.

Sunday 6 March
A God who comes down

Read Luke 9:37–50

But Jesus rebuked the unclean spirit, healed the boy, and gave him back to his father.

(verse 42)

Confused, Moses asks God to define himself (Exodus 3:13). 'I am who I am', God responds; 'get to know me', the invitation. But Moses doesn't want the trouble of getting to know, he just wants to be told. Extraordinarily, God doesn't insist, but comes down to Moses' level, describing his character in the Law – an accommodation revealing even more about himself than the words now written on stone. Having received, Moses comes down the mountain to share what he has discovered.

This week, like Moses, we see Jesus come down a mountain to reveal who God is: a God who comes down and meets us where we are, experiencing our circumstances, our hopes, our pain.

'How long must I bear this?' Jesus asks, distraught as he witnesses the effects of sin in the lives of the father and son in this passage. How much less painful it would have been to have remained in heaven, untouched by this reality. Yet in this encounter, we see the whole story of the Bible: a Father, heartbroken at the devastation caused by sin, a people unable to heal themselves, and Jesus who comes down, shares our pain, pushes back evil and restores us lovingly to the Father.

† Thank you, Lord, that you didn't insist that I reach your heights, but came down to find me.

Monday 7 March
Getting rid of idols

Read Luke 9:51–62
Follow me.

(part of verse 59)

We all have the need to be loved, to know who we are, to have a sense of worth. When we seek to satisfy these from a fallen world, it's like fuelling a gas-powered car with diesel – it causes problems! Displacing God is idolatry, and it breaks God's heart – because it always leads to pain and suffering.

Moses came down the mountain eager to share what he had discovered about God, only to be confronted with an image of God that the people had made up – the idolatry of a golden calf. Jesus came down from the mountain and faced the same: people satisfying their needs from the world – their need for *value:* 'Who is the greatest in our group?' (verse 46), for *belonging:* 'Tell them to stop, they're not part of us' (verse 49), 'Those Samaritans won't work with us, shall we call down fire?' (verse 54), for *identity:* 'Let me first say goodbye to family' (verse 59).

Our deepest needs can only be met in relationship with Jesus, but relationship requires us to be real about where we are. So often we are scared to do that, frightened of not being liked, not being approved. The good news is that we can stop pretending, maybe we're not the mature leader we'd like to be, maybe we're more like the child that Jesus pointed to, maybe our life is not the together version we'd like to present, maybe we're actually a bit of a mess – like the Samaritan woman Jesus would visit one day.

It's okay, it is *you* he has come down to meet, not an idolised version of you.

† Thank you for loving the real me, help me to trust in your love.

For further thought

Are there needs that you are fulfilling from a fallen world rather than a loving Jesus?

Tuesday 8 March
Sheep among wolves

Read Luke 10:1–16

Go on your way. See, I am sending you out like lambs into the midst of wolves.

(verse 3)

If the first challenge is to understand what God is like – that he really wants relationship with you, that he has really come down to where you are to meet you – the next challenge is harder! 'Follow me' is an invitation to emulate him, to become like him.

Of course, following the Shepherd has its wonderful moments: mountain top views, green pastures, still waters – wonderful, yes please! But sometimes following leads down from the mountain into the shadowy valleys that reek of death. As he prepares these new followers, he warns them that they are going as sheep among wolves, that birds might have nests, but the Son of Man has nowhere to stay (9:58). But still, he invites them: 'Follow me' (9:59).

Within 30 years of that invitation, all but one of the Twelve and countless other believers would have died as a result of following Jesus. Some of you reading these notes may face the same, all of us who follow will face challenges. There were some then and many now who heard the invitation, counted the cost, shook their heads and turned away. Yet those who followed went out and saw the kingdom break into people's lives. Being like Jesus makes God visible! Being like Jesus makes space for the Holy Spirit to act: evil was cast out, wholeness restored, death defeated, light shone, darkness was dispelled – individuals, families, communities and nations were transformed.

The imperative 'follow me' is rarely accompanied with a guarantee of safety but it always carries an assurance of his presence. 'Be strong and of courage … For the Lord your God is with you' (Joshua 1:9).

Take Jesus into the world.

† Lord, help me to be like you, to carry you into the world so that you can bring light and life.

For further thought

Counting the cost and choosing to follow is at the heart of our faith. When the cost seems too high, remember his presence. He understands, he stands with you.

Wednesday 9 March
Go and do the same

Read Luke 10:17–37

You shall love the Lord your God with all your heart, and with all your soul, and with all your strength, and with all your mind; and your neighbour as yourself.

(verse 27)

Moses was always impressed with power. He grew up in the palace surrounded by splendour and saw how powerful leaders acted. He presumed that God, being all-powerful, would act like a bigger version of Pharaoh: insisting on his own way, lashing out when crossed, moving people around like pawns to do his bidding. When God called him to lead the people out of Egypt, he acted on this belief, killing the Egyptian, then later, having power encounters with Pharaoh's magicians.

And like Moses, the disciples quickly focused on power. Having been sent out, they come back rejoicing at the signs of the kingdom: 'even the demons obeyed us' (verse 17). Jesus acknowledges God's power and sovereignty, 'I saw Satan fall like a bolt of lightning' (verse 18), but then he realigns their focus, encouraging them instead to take joy from the fact that they are known by heaven. Known by name, for who they really are – and loved for that, just as we are called to love God for who he is, not for who we have believed him to be: a God who comes down the mountain to care for us. Unlike the self-important priest who ignores the man in need (verse 31), or the religious zealot more interested in selling his fixed view of God than showing God's love (verse 32). But like the Samaritan who lays aside his differences, counts the cost to reputation and wallet and out of compassion, goes to where the man is and cares for him (verse 35).

† Lord, help me to love like you love, like I am loved.

For further thought

Reflect on how God exercises his omnipotence: not for self-gain but in self-control; withholding his righteous anger, even when his Son is nailed to a cross.

Thursday 10 March
Friends with God

> **Read Luke 10:38–11:13**
>
> *For everyone who asks receives, and everyone who searches finds, and for everyone who knocks, the door will be opened.*
>
> (verse 10)

We're blessed to have close friends who know us for who we are, with whom we can be ourselves. We can truly relax when we're with them, we don't have to put on a show – they know us too well to be impressed by the outward! Spending time with them is always a highlight; a 'green pastures' moment, a mountain top time to survey the bigger picture, regain perspective and re-energise.

Bethany was such a place for Jesus – and Mary, Martha and Lazarus, such friends. In providing a banquet, maybe Martha was trying to impress Jesus with her cookery skills, more likely, she simply wanted to make him feel welcome and honoured. When Mary didn't help, it felt to Martha as if Mary was disrespecting their honoured guest. But Jesus doesn't want to be the honoured guest, he wants to be friends and gently disarms Martha's distress.

Isn't it hard to receive this truth? That God doesn't want us to waste time trying to earn his love, seeking to perform, to impress, to be worthy. We already are. Before we did anything, even before we breathed, he already loved us. What he longs for is not our service, but our presence. Mary understood and Jesus gently resets Martha's mind: 'You're busy with lots of dishes – one would do, then, like Mary, we could spend time being together' (verses 41–42 paraphrased).

And in that relationship, our Father longs to serve us: providing for our needs, forgiving our sin, directing our paths (11:2–13).

Relax. You can be you. You are loved by the King of kings, your closest friend.

† Pray through the 'Lord's Prayer' (Matthew 6:9–13).

For further thought

Make some space today to notice Jesus beside you. Feel his arm on your shoulder, look at the gleam in his eyes, the warmth of his smile. Watch how eagerly he makes space for you, listens to you, laughs with you.

Friday 11 March
Restoration

Read Luke 11:14–32

But he said, 'Blessed rather are those who hear the word of God and obey it!'

(verse 28)

The kingdom of God is radically different from the kingdom of this world and those who rely on the world will be shaken and discomforted when its foundations begin to crumble. As Jesus and his followers began to bring that kingdom into realty, as God's will began to be done 'on earth as it is in heaven', those whose power and wealth depended on the status quo realised that the religious system that they had so carefully constructed was about to fall down: what need of religious lawyers and teachers, priests and temple if what was required was nothing more than to love God and your neighbour? For them, there was only one solution – to discredit or destroy Jesus.

They began by trying to trip him up debating the law, only to have him put the law into context. Now they try to discredit him by claiming that his power comes from evil. Jesus points out that a divided kingdom must fall, that the foundation of the kingdom is love, not power. Power might free you from a demon, might heal you miraculously, might feed you dramatically – wonderful signs for sure! But if you don't receive the love of God and respond to it by loving, in the end, you've received nothing of lasting value – and you might even end up worse off (verse 26).

But here's how it all ends, says Jesus: with the one who is truly evil defeated by the one whose strength is measured in love, not power alone. And having bound the enemy, the Lion of Judah plunders his domain, taking back all that was stolen.

† Lord, help us bring the kingdom, to see the transforming power of love.

For further thought

What has the enemy stolen from you? Jesus has bound the enemy and taken back *everything* you lost. The Father is lovingly waiting to restore it, in this life and the next.

Saturday 12 March
Seeing the light

> **Read Luke 11:33–54**
>
> *Woe to you lawyers! For you have taken away the key of knowledge; you did not enter yourselves, and you hindered those who were entering.*
>
> (verse 52)

Jesus has great mercy and compassion on those with no choice: those who cannot choose because they have no resources – the poor. Those who cannot choose because of life's circumstances – the sick. Those who cannot choose because they do not know another way – those who have been misled or mistaught. Those who cannot choose because others impose their will on them – the oppressed and enslaved.

Throughout the Gospels, Jesus stands with such people, advocates on their behalf and defends them. On the cross he pleads with his Father that they might be forgiven because 'They do not know what they are doing' (Luke 23:34).

But to those who have the light, who have the ability to choose, he judges according to that light. To the rich he looks for generous choices, to the powerful that they use their power compassionately, to the learned that they use their knowledge to make wise choices. 'From everyone to whom much has been given, much will be required' (Luke 12:48).

To the blind, he gladly brings sight, but to those who see the light but choose to stay in darkness, his message is clear. You will reap what you sow, you will not ultimately escape the consequences of your choices. God is not mocked.

This week, we saw Jesus come down from the heights to where the people were, unambiguously shining light on who God really is. A God of compassion, of justice, a God of kindness and truth. Above all, a God of love.

We too have seen that light. Now, we are without excuse.

† Lord, I once was blind to who you are, but now I see. Thank you, Jesus.

For further thought

Following Jesus will require everything we have. Being light in dark places will cause problems. What will sustain you?

Facing the darkness

1 Despair

Notes by **Dr Delroy Hall**

Delroy has over 30 years' experience in vocational ministry as well as being a trained counsellor. He is committed to dealing with human pain while developing trust, so people can recover and thrive. He has lectured nationally and internationally. In 2017, he was appointed as the chaplain for Sheffield United Football Club. Outside of his ministerial responsibilities, Delroy keeps fit by swimming, cycling and running. He is married to Paulette and has twin daughters, Saffron and Jordan. Delroy has used the NKJV for these notes.

Sunday 13 March
Grief over sin

Read Exodus 32:19–35

Then he took the calf which they had made, burned it in the fire, and ground it to powder; and he scattered it on the water and made the children of Israel drink it.

(verse 20)

It is clear from this section of scripture that Moses is far from happy. He grieves over the sin of the people, but there is something many overlook as the scriptures are read. One aspect of grief is anger. 'How could this thing happen?' we may ask ourselves – and a whole range of other questions when our lives have been devastated. We are heartbroken when we have lost someone or something that is precious. We grieve if we have trusted someone or something and we have been disappointed. In such a case, we have lost trust. Let us be clear. Grief is universal, but it is personal. Deeply so.

We see Moses' angry response. Can you imagine? He took the calf that the Israelites had made, ground it into powder, sprinkled on the water and made them drink it. He was angry, but the Israelites feared the anger of God even more.

In the biblical narrative, people experienced loss often through disobedience. The main reason why grief is so painful is that an important attachment has been broken whether by death or another form of loss. With further reading there is an unspoken driver in Moses' life. He loves God and he loves his people too. Deep pain is always experienced when we have loved and are severed from what we have loved.

† Father, Moses reminds us of how much you are grieved when we live our lives in ways which dishonour you. Please forgive us.

Monday 14 March
Death of David's son

Read 2 Samuel 12:15–23

But now he is dead; why should I fast? Can I bring him back again? I shall go to him, but he shall not return to me.

(verse 23)

This is every parent's nightmare. Your young child is sick, almost to death, rendering you and your family feeling powerless. Whether you are a believer or not, like David you will do everything possible to bring your child back.

Maybe that is darkness you face right now. Fearing the loss of a child and it your only child. How can life be so cruel you may be thinking, and dare I say it, Lord, how could you put us in this position? How could you?

I have heard it said more than once that when we pray for healing for a loved one it often is not so much about them but our fear of losing them.

David shows us a way in which we can handle someone dying. It is more to do with his mindset and how he views God coupled with a pragmatic approach to life.

David acknowledges his son is now dead and there absolutely nothing he can do about it other than find solace in God. No doubt he is grieving, but to pine after something that will never return is futile. Look what he does though. In his time of grieving and lived darkness, he spends time comforting his wife. We learn from this that when are having our struggles in life it helps us if we help others.

† Lord, in our time of darkness, despair and needing your comfort and love, help us to take our mind off ourselves and remind us to extend love, compassion and mercy to others.

For further thought

Are you going through a difficult time, your own darkness? If so, is there anyone you can help right now during their difficulties?

Tuesday 15 March
Elijah's despair

Read 1 Kings 19:1–18

It is enough! Now, Lord, take my life.

(part of verse 4)

When we think of Elijah, we major on his exploits, his battle and victory over the pagan worshippers and the miracle of rain. Then we read this strange portion of scripture where he is fleeing due to a contract on his life. From conquering the enemy to now running for his life, have we ever considered the emotional and psychological stress he would have experienced and the range of stress hormones flowing through his veins? The prophet was human, exhausted, and possibly experiencing a depressive moment – the accumulative effect of what he had experienced.

Some may find it ironic how, after such an experience, one could feel as Elijah did. Well, it happens. How many people, after a great time, have felt low? How many believers would admit that in their lifetime they have secretly uttered, 'It is enough! Now, Lord, take my life'?

One of the features of exhaustion or burnout is how a person can feel as though they are the only one suffering in such a manner. If the statistics are true, in the UK one in four people have mental health concerns. It is far more common than we realise.

What then is the remedy for exhaustion or burnout? Certainly not another church service or prayer meeting. Rest and refreshment are what is needed, including stillness so one can hear and listen. Listen, not only to God but to what your body is trying to tell you. Believe it or not, while we do not worship our bodies, listening to them is just as important as listening to God.

† Saviour and friend, you have called us to listen to you, but through your word you have taught us the importance of physical rest. Help us to listen and be obedient to what we hear.

For further thought

Are you going through a low time in your life? What are you doing to help yourself other than attending church or having another prayer meeting?

Health of Job

Read Job 2:1–13

And when they raised their eyes from afar, and did not recognise him, they lifted their voices and wept.

(verse 12a)

The book of Job is problematic. It talks of human suffering while silently asking: is there any purpose in suffering? Even if as a reader you do not know Job's specific illness, you can make a safe conclusion. It was grim.

He has boils, he is scraping his skin and his wife challenges him. 'Do you still hold fast to your integrity?' (verse 9). She tells him to curse God and die, perhaps through embarrassment, seeing the dreadful physical condition of her husband. His friends appear later and due to his condition, fail to recognise him from a distance. When they meet him, they weep while tearing their clothes, symbolising grief, and mourning. Aghast, they sit with him for a week, without uttering a word.

When our health deteriorates significantly it is a dreadful experience. Two years ago, due to a combination of situations, I developed a severe case of eczema – the worst I have experienced. From my chin to my ankles, I was covered with eczema. It was not painful. It just itched profusely and I felt incredibly unwell. This led to being hospitalised for three days and having two severe episodes of shedding huge amounts of skin. Not pleasant.

How does Job respond? He recognised life was full of good and the not-so-good, but he refused to blame God. Often, God uses our crises as a way of getting us to stop when we have ignored the early warning signs. While God does not cause tragedies in our lives, he can use them for us to be still in preparation for something else.

† Loving Lord, when life crises happen we do not believe you have caused them, but you often allow things to happen so we can hear you. Lord, heal our situation, hearts, and our ears.

For further thought

Are there warning signs in your life you know you are ignoring? Don't! Your life is in God's hands. Do not wait for a crisis.

Thursday 17 March
Overwhelming guilt

Read Psalm 38:1–22

I am troubled, I am bowed down greatly; I go mourning all the day long. For my loins are full of inflammation, and there is no soundness in my flesh. I am feeble and severely broken; I groan because of the turmoil of my heart.

(verses 6–8)

One simply cannot ignore the beauty of Old Testament poetry. It is said that if you ignore such poetry you ignore over one third of the Bible. Today's reading is richly littered with poetic imagery letting us know the plight of the psalmist.

The above abstract is showing how the writer conveys the depth of his guilt. Even if you do not love poetry, the language used paints a vivid picture. There are forty-five words and within this nugget of biblical text, twelve of those words are expressing the writer's guilt.

Have there been times you have been overwhelmed with guilt and are unable to articulate your feelings? Perhaps writing poetry or reading the Psalms captures the depth of your emotions. He expresses eloquently emotions that are often ragged, raw and uncontrollable. Reading such literature can help us in gaining clarity, describing a way through the swampy dilemma of feeling immense guilt, while offering hope.

Poetry is so powerful that in the UK there is poetry on prescription where doctors will prescribe certain poems for their anxious, nervous and depressive patients to read, to help them in their moments of stress and anguish.

Overwhelming feelings of guilt render us feeling powerless, condemned, destitute and alone, wanting to escape the feeling immediately but reading many of the Psalms gives us hope.

'Do not forsake me, O Lord; O my God, be not far from me! Make haste to help me, O Lord, my salvation!' (verses 21–22).

Feelings of guilt over what we have done do not need to stay with us forever.

† Jesus, lover of my soul, do not let me become so guilt-ridden that all joy flows out from my life. Remind me that you are the physician and forgiver of my soul. Amen

For further thought

If you are feeling overridden with guilt and need a place that echoes your feelings, pray this psalm knowing that God is our light at the end of a dark tunnel and he will hear you.

Man of sorrows

Read Isaiah 53:1–12

A Man of sorrows and acquainted with grief.

(part of verse 3)

'A Man of sorrow and acquainted with grief.' With a name like that one might want to get rid of it as quickly as possible.

We live in a world, in the West more so, where we prize luxury and the easy life. Hardship, effort, struggle and suffering are not things we associate with a successful or helpful life. Yet regardless of who we are while we are in our flesh, we will experience dark moments of life.

I recall a church where I was the pastor for a few years. I was the new kid on the block. I went to visit an aged member who spent most of her adult life being unwell. Imagine my surprise after introducing myself, she introduced herself by saying that she believed she was 'born to suffer'. How sad is that? I do not remember my response, but as I read this scripture that pastoral moment revisited me. Jesus, our 'Man of sorrows and acquainted with grief' is someone for all of us.

When we go through dark periods in our lives, at some point, it is good to remember that Jesus is one acquainted with our despair. Again, following on from our previous reading, the beauty of Old Testament poetry portrays the essence of the pain and anguish of life – all of which Jesus willingly went through for us. The songwriter, Philip Bliss, captures it well in 1875 when he penned,

> *'Man of sorrows,' what a name*
> *For the Son of God who came;*
> *Ruined sinners to reclaim!*
> *Halleluiah! what a saviour!*

What a saviour indeed. Astonishing!

† Divine Lord, Man of sorrows, what a name! Father help me to learn to retreat in you in times of need as you understand me when many others will not.

For further thought

Often, we carry burdens for too long. Why struggle needlessly when we know someone who is waiting to help us carry the load? Turn to the one with the incredible name.

Saturday 19 March
Weeping prophet

Read Jeremiah 20:1–18

Why did I come forth from the womb to see labour and sorrow, that my days should be consumed with shame?

(verse 18)

God says to Jeremiah, what do you want to hear first, the good news or the bad news? Jeremiah responds, I will hear the good news first. Well, the good news is that I have called you from the womb. You cannot beat that thought, Jeremiah. The bad news, says God, is that you are going to suffer, greatly.

Reflecting on this passage, I am reminded of the many clients who have attended counselling sessions and who have this belief, not uttered like Jeremiah, but with similar sentiments, 'Why was I born?'

Earlier, Jeremiah decides not to talk about God – but, ultimately, he cannot help himself as the words refuse to remain within the confines of his body. They spill out of him like they have a mind of their own. The consequences of this uncontainable utterance are pain, being mocked and derided, and tears.

Standing for the truth, and in Jeremiah's case, acting as a divine 'whistle blower,' that is, an employee who reports the wrongdoing of people or organisations to authorities, means life is going to be tough. The life and times of a whistle blower is tough but what makes it worse is that normally the whistle blower leaves their job and seeks alternative employment because the working conditions and relationships have changed, but not Jeremiah. No. He must remain within the same environment, confessing and prophesying against God's people.

Maybe you are someone who would love to move from where you are because life has become so difficult as you want to live authentically, but God wants you to remain as a voice and mouthpiece of conscience of the organisation. He has not served your release papers yet.

† Lord, cannot you see what is happening to me. Can't you see? I have spoken the truth. I dislike where I am, but I will trust you want me here. Grant me grace to be obedient.

For further thought

Are you in a place where life has become tough? What support do you have while you fulfil what the Lord has called you to do?

Facing the darkness

2 Worry and anxiety

Notes by **Simei Monteiro**

Simei is a Brazilian poet and composer. She has worked as Worship Consultant at the World Council of Churches in Geneva, Switzerland. She is interested in worship and the arts, and her book, *The Song of Life* (ASTE/IEPG, 1991), explores the relationship between hymns and theology. As a retired missionary from the United Methodist Church, USA, she lives in Curitiba, Brazil, with her husband Rev Jairo Monteiro. They have two daughters and three grandchildren. Simei has used the NRSVA and NIVUK for these notes.

Sunday 20 March
Anxiety and the heart

Read Proverbs 12:25

Anxiety weighs down the human heart, but a good word cheers it up.

(verse 25, NRSVA)

Our world is experiencing a time full of insecurity. Most of us do not know what normal life is anymore!

Anxiety is to suffer by anticipation; it is a misinterpretation of time when your life timing is excluding the 'here and now'! It is the opposite of mindfulness.

One of the techniques therapists use to help people in an anxiety crisis is to talk quietly and positively to the person. If we want to help someone to overcome this crisis, we need to put ourselves in the place of the other. We must act with empathy!

Listening to the person is better than talk. Sometimes the 'good word' is simply 'I'm here for you'. By contrast, reciting phrases coming from self-help books is not helpful since the person will think you are not considering his or her real suffering.

As we try to keep ourselves mindful, we can remember this biblical verse: 'But I have calmed and quieted my soul, like a weaned child with its mother' (Psalm 131:2a).

As God's children, in the middle of our uneasiness, we can feel comforted and wrapped in God's holy arms. That is all we need and want right now.

† Eternal Healer, help me not be anxious. Take me in your mothering arms and make me hear your whispering: 'I am here for you!'

Monday 21 March
Do not worry

Read Matthew 6:25–34

Is not life more than food and the body more than clothes? Therefore do not worry about tomorrow, for tomorrow will worry about itself. Each day has enough trouble of its own.

(verses 25b and 34, NIVUK)

I read somewhere that, for people in some parts of the world, everyday life is like death and resurrection. We are alive all day long and die in the night. The next day is a new life to be lived, and you need to spend it wisely! The past does not exist anymore, and the future is uncertain so let's take this day as a unique gift from God!

During the time of the current pandemic, soon after lockdown began, we saw people rushing to supermarkets, banks and pharmacies to get all kinds of goods and emergency supplies and store them all at home. There was some alarming news about a general bankruptcy of the economy around the world; fear of starvation started to grow among individuals and families.

Is life more than food?

It seemed not, and people were more and more worried about what to do in such a situation when you must stay home and discover ways to make your life possible.

After six months locked down, we discovered we had so many things we were not eating or dressing in, and many people started to share goods and clothes. Less is more!

Home life was very simple: pyjamas and real food to eat; all the family participating. The world became small. Soon we discovered that the most important thing was to enjoy this new life with its daily routine in family and create new activities. Time to study and play with the children, to make music with the whole family: watch worship and prayer time online and Holy Communion.

More content and fewer accessories!

† Dear Giver of Life! Help us to be content with what we have for each day, trusting you will provide food and clothes as you did for the Hebrews during their journey in the desert.

For further thought

'Is not life more than food and the body more than clothes?' How could this be applied to our lives?

Tuesday 22 March
All who are weary

> **Read Matthew 11:28–30**
>
> *Come to me, all you who are weary and burdened, and I will give you rest. Take my yoke upon you and learn from me, for I am gentle and humble in heart … For my yoke is easy and my burden is light.*
>
> (part of verses 28–30, NIVUK)

How can a burden be lighter? I am now old, and now I start to feel the weight of years and surprisingly, of small things! So, I decided to get rid of some household items and clothes.

As Brazilians, we eat rice and beans every day, and we used to cook beans for the whole week using the largest pressure cookers we can find. Recently, I discovered mine is now too heavy to handle. It is a time to remember what the Bible says: that a day will come when even a grasshopper will be weighed down (Ecclesiastes 12:5)!

What does it mean to carry a light burden? What kind of lightness is this? I do not want to carry any burden, but I know that, in this world, burdens are part of our human condition. So, what makes a burden light?

There is an old story about a little Scottish girl who was trudging along, carrying as best she could a boy who was younger but seemed almost as big as her. Seeing her struggling, someone asked if she was tired. With surprise, she replied: 'No, he's not heavy; he's my brother.' The love she had for her brother gave her enough strength for such a feat!

The yoke Jesus offers is easy and the only reason is that such easiness is love! Love is what makes the burden light. Then we can cope with all burdens we have to carry because God is with us and his love gives us strength and resilience, and our faith will become a very effective fuel in our daily life.

† Dear God, help me to take life easily and smoothly and make others' burdens lighter too. Give me a desirous vision of eternity where all the heavy loads will exist no more.

For further thought

Can you remember a moment in your life when, by God's grace, your heavy burden seemed lighter?

Wednesday 23 March
Who shall separate?

Read Romans 8:35–39

Who shall separate us from the love of Christ? Shall trouble or hardship or persecution or famine or nakedness or danger or sword? No, in all these things we are more than conquerors through him who loved us.

(verses 35 and 37, NIVUK)

Reading these scriptural verses, I was struck by the thought that through the love of Christ and with the help of God, we can overcome anything! I was surprised how deep and wide that possibility is. We can see that it involves our whole experience in life – even when we are in danger of death! I gave thanks to God because I believe in it and have experienced it.

But what does it mean to be 'more than conquerors'?

After meditating on Christ's own victory and his love for human beings, it came to my heart that we are more than conquerors if we, after winning a battle against something, do not stop our course but continue our journey keeping hope.

Once, in one country of Latin America, there was a severe flood in remote areas, and the rescue of survivors was almost impossible. The weather was so bad, and the rescuers tried to save people as best they could. Some survivors were on the roofs. After a long wait, a pregnant woman, who was already in labour, was finally lifted up to the helicopter and, immediately after, gave birth to a baby girl. All the rescuers were happy and when all arrived safely to the shelter one of the rescuers asked her if she had a name for the baby, and she said: 'She will be called Victoria Esperanza. (Victory Hope) That is all I've got right now!'

Yes, we can be 'more than conquerors'! Our God's victory in Christ is our victory and opens the gate to our final conquest, heaven!

† Dear Giver of Life; help us to keep our hope in every situation we face; if we win a battle or lose it. Help us live and enjoy the depth of your love.

For further thought

Have you ever won a battle against something? How was the taste of being victorious? What are your hopes now?

Thursday 24 March
Don't lose heart

Read 2 Corinthians 4:16–18

Therefore we do not lose heart. Though outwardly we are wasting away, yet inwardly we are being renewed day by day. For our light and momentary troubles are achieving for us an eternal glory that far outweighs them all.

(verses 16–17, NIVUK)

At the time of writing, hearing questions about when we are going to get out of the pandemic, we feel we are really losing heart. There is still no guarantee that we will get the vaccine soon and we remain locked down since we are in the 'risk' group. We really do not know when this trial will end and, each day, each month, and now for almost one year, we are at risk of losing hope that we can overcome this situation and get back to our everyday life: the new normal!

As Christians, based on the wonderful promises we find in the Bible, we are led to believe we will have a healthy, wealthy and happy life. Also, in our world today, it is so common to hear preachers saying that if you follow Jesus you will have happiness, success and comfort!

Maybe this is true – but it is not forever! The day of trial comes suddenly, and you may be disappointed because you did not think it could happen to you. But it can happen even to the best of us!

At Christmas 2019, we had a wonderful time. We met as a large family in my niece's house; we sang Christmas songs and enjoyed the communion around a table. My brother seemed very happy, celebrating with my sister-in-law their second Christmas as a married couple. Now both are dead. During the months of mourning, we have experienced different feelings; sometimes being angry against this crazy situation and sometimes smoothly accepting the finite nature of life and longing to be renewed day by day.

† Pray for all those who are on the verge of losing heart – because they are emotionally, mentally or physically exhausted. Pray that they can find hope and trust in God's grace.

For further thought

What have you done when you felt like you were losing heart? From whom or from where did you get help?

Friday 25 March
Don't be anxious

> **Read Philippians 4:6–7**
>
> *Do not be anxious about anything, but in every situation, by prayer and petition, with thanksgiving, present your requests to God. And the peace of God, which transcends all understanding, will guard your hearts and your minds in Christ Jesus.*
>
> (verses 6–7, NIVUK)

When we think of peace, we often think it means the absence of conflict. We see many attempts to bring this about: peace conferences, peace rallies, treaties between nations. But these verses tell us that peace ('*shalom*') means so much more than this understanding. The search for peace is also present in our personal lives – when we reach the bottom of the well, the natural cry is to ask God for help, for peace.

The peace of God: what kind of peace is this?

If we think about Jesus in the garden of Gethsemane, in deep anguish, distressed at what he will endure this following day – being torn apart, physically, emotionally, spiritually – he wasn't scared to lament to God his loneliness, his desire to find a different way or even, on the cross, his sense that God had abandoned him. He cast all his anxieties on God. And, in being honest in this way, while trusting in God's love, the miracle happened. Peace came.

Learning from Jesus' experience, we can perceive how confident he was in the love of his Father. The one thing we can do when we are facing suffering is to trust that – however unlikely it might seem – still, God loves us. That no matter how broken we may be, God, in his sovereignty, can and will restore and make us whole. We can be confident that God is there for us! Peace will come. This confidence comes from God's amazing grace and is unfathomable for human minds!

† God of peace, allow us to be completely overflowed by your mercy. Let us accept your gift of peace which goes beyond our own understanding; guard our hearts and minds through Christ Jesus. Amen

For further thought

Have you experienced something like being inundated by God's peace without even having asked for it? Were you surprised?

Saturday 26 March
Cast our anxieties

Read 1 Peter 5:7–10

Cast all your anxiety on him because he cares for you. And the God of all grace, who called you to his eternal glory in Christ, after you have suffered a little while, will himself restore you and make you strong, firm and steadfast.

(verses 7 and 10, NIVUK)

We are blessed to have professionals to help us with our health issues – it is so good to have others walk with us through times of trouble. Sometimes though, it can be a long process, stressful for the patients and the healthcare professionals, and both need somewhere to bring their anxieties. God offers himself to be the perfect receptacle; the care of God – his love, mercy and grace – are where we can cast all our anxieties. That is wonderful!

When I lost my brother and my sister-in-law as a result of Covid-19, the whole family was devastated. We could not understand how death came in such a short time. We had been looking forward to seeing and embracing our dear ones, now we were not allowed to be present or even give a proper burial to them.

I was surprised to feel comforted by little expressions, sometimes just an emoji posted on my Facebook page or a short message through WhatsApp. It was a peace that made no sense, it was beyond understanding – all these small comments and signs had no right to comfort me, I was in despair, longing for care and peace. And yet they did, God was there for me even in these little things. They represented and reminded me of God's love, and I was able to cast on God all my anxieties without any shame or fear; I felt free to do it trusting in his love and care.

I learned so much by humbling myself under God's hands, by trusting God's love, even when I couldn't see it directly.

† Dear God, thank you for being the repository of my fears and anxieties. Help me to be confident in your love and purposes, wholeheartedly and without restrictions! Your grace is better than life!

For further thought

Have you ever been comforted or lifted by emojis and signs sent by friends through your social media? Who can you bless today?

Facing the darkness

3 Doubt and fear

Notes by **Jane Gonzalez**

For Jane's biography, see p. 37. Jane has used the NRSVA for these notes.

Sunday 27 March
No laughing matter

Read Genesis 18:1–15

The Lord said to Abraham, 'Why did Sarah laugh, and say, "Shall I indeed bear a child, now that I am old?" Is anything too wonderful for the Lord? At the set time I will return to you, in due season, and Sarah shall have a son.'

(verses 13–14)

Lent is the liturgical season which challenges us to confront the areas of our lives that hinder the working of God's grace within us. Often it is not a question of 'big sins' but rather that the fears and anxieties of daily life connive to suppress hope and to smother trust in God's loving providence.

I write these reflections against a national and international background of fear and anxiety. The global pandemic – Covid-19 – remains a threat to everyone's health and well-being. The future seems far less certain than we considered it to be a year ago. Nobody is immune from a malignant and capricious virus with its unknown and frightening repercussions. The normal (false?) securities have been upended. Yet the year winds inexorably onward.

In the UK, autumn is here with a magnificent harvest of fruits and berries. It has followed on from a good summer and a beautiful spring and announces, as always, the prospect of winter and the promise of a better year to come. Everything arrives – in due season. The challenge for us, as for Sarah, is to keep the hope and trust in that God's time is not our time, but he always keeps his word.

† Father, help me to live each day well. Calm the fears and anxieties that lead me into doubt and mistrust.

Monday 28 March
You've got a friend

Read Matthew 11:1–6

When John heard in prison what the Messiah was doing, he sent word by his disciples and said to him, 'Are you the one who is to come, or are we to wait for another?'

(verses 2–3)

One of the most rewarding periods of my life was the ten years I spent as a visitor in my local prison. My role, as part of a small group of volunteers, was to act as a friend to those inmates who had nobody to visit them. Some had no family to speak of; some were ashamed to let their family or friends know where they were. Most of the men I visited were doubly disadvantaged – they were from overseas and struggled to express themselves in English. I'm a linguist and speak fluent Spanish.

Prisons are places of isolation, doubt and dependency. Life is uncertain. You are at the mercy of a routine that may change overnight. The loss of control over the basics of existence can be the hardest thing to adapt to. Visits help those incarcerated to experience some kind of normality, dignity and humanity and to face fear and darkness with a companion who does not judge.

John, in common with most prisoners, is reliant on news from outside. It's no wonder that even a strong-minded and focused individual like him has a 'wobble'. It is not surprising that doubts creep in. What was crystal clear on the outside starts to seem shaky and unfounded. John faces the inevitability of death and he questions previous certainties and convictions. Was his path the true one? What if he has been mistaken in pointing out Jesus as the one to follow? He seeks – and fortunately – gets the reassurance he needs to still his fears and doubts. He is blessed in his friends.

† Father, sometimes I feel imprisoned by doubt and fear. Thank you for the people in my life who bring me hope and comfort. Help me to reach out to the lonely and unloved.

For further thought

Consider how you might help prisoners and their families. The Bible Society (www.biblesociety.org.uk) works to make Bibles available for every prisoner who wants one.

Tuesday 29 March
Body of proof

Read John 20:24–29

Then he said to Thomas, 'Put your finger here and see my hands. Reach out your hand and put it in my side. Do not doubt but believe.' Thomas answered him, 'My Lord and my God!'

(verses 27–28)

Friends visited us recently for a socially-distanced cup of tea and a catch-up, in person. Both have shielded themselves in accordance with government guidelines and therefore our communication has been via social media platforms. Social media sites have been a godsend but it was refreshing to meet physically rather than virtually! One of our friends has replaced his old mobile with a new smart phone as he has (finally!) realised that modern communication methods have their place and their benefits. For many people, the ability to go online for worship, shopping and maintaining relationships has been a lifeline.

Of course, social media and the internet have their drawbacks. We are all too aware of how fake news and misinformation can be spread and how social media outlets can be manipulated with malicious or criminal intent. Sometimes, lies are spread in good faith or with honourable intentions. We seek confirmation and proof before we trust what others claim – such as turning to websites such as Trustpilot to check if our purchases are all that they are made out to be.

We can sympathise with Thomas then, forever known as a doubter. On the heels of a week of rollercoaster emotions, betrayals, disappointment and the seeming death of hope comes the announcement of something unbelievable, incredible: Jesus is alive. It is very human to ask for a tangible sign rather than take that leap of faith. Yet that is precisely what we are asked to do on a daily basis – believe, even though what we see might seem to discredit what faith tells us.

† Father, help me to remember the words of Thomas when I am tempted away from you. May I say and believe that you are, 'My Lord and My God'.

For further thought

Reflect on James 3:5–10. Do I contribute to disbelief or misinformation by gossip or by passing on opinions and viewpoints without checking their veracity?

Wednesday 30 March
The eye of the beholder

Read James 1:5–8

If any of you is lacking in wisdom, ask God, who gives to all generously and ungrudgingly, and it will be given you. But ask in faith, never doubting.

(verses 5–6a)

I love going to the seaside. Some of the fondest memories of childhood are of coach trips to the coast as a family. It didn't matter to us whether the beach was shingly, stony, sandy or muddy – there was always something to do or find: castles, rockpools, seaweed … We would return home with souvenirs not just from the gift shop or funfair but also with shells and pebbles and little bits of glass worn smooth by the sea's relentless ebb and flow. In the UK, we call it beachcombing – finding small treasures in unexpected objects stranded on the shore.

The acquisition of wisdom might well be described as a kind of spiritual beachcombing. How is wisdom acquired? The sages of old saw it as a distillation of life's experiences. It was not a question of learning or intellectual achievement but more about knowledge and understanding gained from pondering life and its ups and downs. From seemingly unpromising objects and detritus, we can discern beauty and usefulness. In the same way, in the Christian life, we may sift through and reflect on the many experiences that shape us and through which we start to become wise. Everything washed up on the shore may have beauty and purpose. Everything – even the darkest of days or harshest of griefs – can help us become more faithful and loving followers of Christ. James asks us to pray without doubt – to pray, then, with hope. Hope is the bag into which we may put the bits and pieces from the shore that will turn into beautiful things for God.

† Father, help me to welcome whatever life throws at me. May I seek the truth in all and discern your will for me.

For further thought

It can be painful to reflect on past hurts or sorrows. But can you see times when dealing with darkness has helped you grow? How did you regain hope?

Thursday 31 March
Gazing into the sanctuary

Read Psalm 34:1–7

I sought the Lord, and he answered me, and delivered me from all my fears. Look to him, and be radiant; so your faces shall never be ashamed. This poor soul cried, and was heard by the Lord, and was saved from every trouble.

(verses 4–6)

The months of restrictions and curbs on normal activity due to Covid-19 have affected everyone – not least faith communities. In the UK, worshipping communities responded in a variety of ways during lockdown with live streaming of services and imaginative ways of praying together via social media. Our churches accepted the sacrifice of abandoning gathering together as a necessary contribution to the health and well-being of the nation. It was sad to be unable to celebrate the major feasts and festivals together. Lent, Easter, Pentecost passed us by.

Or so it seemed … Here at home, the enforced inactivity of lockdown was surprisingly productive spiritually – walking in a wooded glade after a spring shower brought to mind the psalmist gazing on God in the sanctuary; after watching Maundy Thursday mass, my husband and I washed each other's feet; we kindled a new fire on Holy Saturday and watched the service from our shed: there were many ways in which God was present to us, without the need to be in a church or designated 'holy place'. The space in our home, our garden and in the natural world was our sacred space.

Of course, it has been a joy to return to church and to gather as a parish – albeit at a distance and wearing masks. But God is not confined in church and maybe this is the lesson to be (re)learned from this year. In the midst of great fear and trembling and an uncertain future, there is one sure thing: God is with us – in the unexpected and the unfamiliar 'new' normal as much as in the old.

† Father, help me to resist the allure of what is safe and cosy. Give me the grace to embrace change and the courage to follow you along new paths.

For further thought

The world is God's sacred space. Are we doing enough to protect it? Look at some environmental projects local to you and consider what you and your church can do to support them.

Deliver us from evil

Read Psalm 55:1–7

My heart is in anguish within me, the terrors of death have fallen upon me. Fear and trembling come upon me, and horror overwhelms me. And I say, 'O that I had wings like a dove! I would fly away and be at rest.'

(verses 4–6)

Researching my family tree has become an important interest over the last few years. I am now the 'matriarch' of our small family and, along with my sister, feel that it is important that the younger members of the family partake of our memories and know the roots that we share. So far, we haven't discovered any celebrities or a fabulously wealthy relative living abroad – we are relentlessly ordinary. The most shocking disclosure so far is not even the suicide of our grandfather – this was an open secret within the family – but rather the history of the mental illness that he suffered. This was hidden from our father and from his brothers. It remained unacknowledged and unspoken. To all intents and purposes my grandfather was expunged from the family history – there are no photos or mementos of him.

Nowadays, we understand that the stresses and worries of living can often result in mental health issues. Similarly, as Christians, we know that faith, even great faith, is no guarantee against doubt or crippling anxiety or the sensation that God has abandoned us. But there should be no shame or stigma attached to such doubt and darkness. The great saints experienced it – the dark nights of the soul, the inability to pray, the dread that God is not there. We will all question at times, especially when things go wrong or we are suffering. There are no easy answers, but the psalmists did not hide it – they voiced it, screamed it, got it out into the open. God is strong enough to bear our pain.

† Father, sometimes the pain of this world is too much. Help me to feel your loving arms around me whenever I want to run away and hide. Give me strength to carry on.

For further thought

Mental health issues are more talked about today but there is still shame and stigma for many. If you can, consider joining or supporting an organisation that provides support for those who are suffering or suicidal.

April

Facing the darkness – 3 Doubt and fear

Saturday 2 April
On the threshold

> **Read Joshua 1:1–9**
>
> *As I was with Moses, so I will be with you; I will not fail you or forsake you. Be strong and courageous; for you shall put this people in possession of the land that I swore to their ancestors to give them.*
>
> (verses 5b–6)

I have a friend who is a Catholic priest in Canada. He is not the greatest of correspondents and I often learn that he has moved parishes by tracking him across the very big diocese where he resides. He seems to move every couple of years – unlike our own clergy, in the UK, who tend to stay for eight to ten years. Any change brings apprehension, though, on both sides. Parishioners may fear a new broom intent on sweeping clean. The incoming priest may be anxious and doubtful about how to fill the shoes of a well-loved predecessor.

Joshua certainly had some very big shoes to fill. How daunting to be chosen to complete Moses' task and to lead the Hebrew people on the next stage of their journey! But how comforting to have God's reassurance and encouragement as he takes up the role of leader: 'Be strong and courageous'!

These words are particularly relevant for faith communities today – as we adjust to life in a world where old certainties have fled. Nobody knows what the post-Covid church will look like. There seems to be a great desire in both spiritual and secular realms for a new normal – not a return to the old – a sense that this is a *kairos* moment (right, critical, opportune). Like Joshua we stand on a threshold. It may not be a new broom but maybe we need to trust in the promise of God that he will be there. Can we forsake the sameness and safety of the past and create a church that can really accompany the lost into light? To a promised land?

† Father, I want to do your will but often I am afraid to take the risk of following you in faith. With your grace I will be strong and courageous in seeking to do better.

For further thought

Read Luke 5:5. What dreams or aspirations do you have for the future? Is it time to fulfil these and risk venturing out into the unknown? What is God asking of you at this moment?

The Gospel of Luke (3)

1 Journey to Jerusalem

Notes by **Terry Lester**

Terry has served the Diocese of Cape Town as an Anglican priest for over 35 years. He is a father and grandfather and works in Constantia where he serves a diverse community, a veritable microcosm of South Africa. He is passionate about community building and reconciliation, and chairs an NGO called 'Constantia Heritage and Education Project' which records the stories of those displaced from here to other parts of the Cape Flats ensuring that these stories of overcoming adversity are honoured and celebrated. Terry has used the NRSVA for these readings.

Sunday 3 April
The walk of life

Read Luke 18:31–19:10

See, we are going up to Jerusalem, and everything that is written about the Son of Man by the prophets will be accomplished. For he will be handed over to the Gentiles; and he will be mocked and insulted and spat upon. After they have flogged him, they will kill him.

(part of verses 31–33)

Pilgrims who made the journey to Jerusalem would recite the 'Song of the Ascents' from the Hebrew psalter which lists the dangers on the way, from the sun by day to the moon by night. Also, those dangers posed by 'enemies' who direct evil toward the pilgrim. Alongside are the added dangers of the sheer physical toll and the hazards posed by wild animals. But distractions can also divert the pilgrim. Those regarded as perpetually unclean who saunter along the way represent a threat to ritual purity too. Then there are the opportunists, like tax collectors, who regard pilgrims as easy prey for a shakedown and charge their 'add-on' tax. All these hazards the pilgrim sought to avoid – no wonder they soaked themselves with: 'The Lord is your keeper', 'If the Lord had not been on our side' and 'those who trust in the Lord are like Mount Zion'!

As Jesus journeys to Jerusalem, he too encounters others but instead of regarding them as hazards and avoiding them, he engages them, knowing that their help too comes from the Lord! It is only in engaging the world around us with its many challenges that we too can say, 'The Lord has done great things for us' (Psalm 126:3)!

† Lord, help me to not regard anyone as a distraction but as a fellow pilgrim seeking to walk the way that leads to life. Amen

Monday 4 April
Yet more miles to go

Read Luke 19:11–28

As they were listening to this, he went on to tell them a parable, because he was near Jerusalem, and because they supposed that the kingdom of God was to appear immediately.

(verse 11)

Jericho is a significant town on the road to Jerusalem. It provides the ideal stop for the travel-weary pilgrim who has made it through the first part of the harsh mountainous terrain from the Jordan basin below. Arriving in this lush oasis town after the arduous mountain paths is a considerable achievement. By now the pilgrim has walked more than halfway and might feel justifiably self-satisfied with their achievement. But the journey isn't over, the work not yet complete.

Just as in the story, those entrusted with the master's resources might picture the reward and commendation promised at the master's arrival, thinking that their work is complete. But we are told that the master's return is delayed and, as with the pilgrim, the journey is far from over. Jerusalem is the destination and there remains much that still needs to be endured, not to mention work that still needs to be done. The master has equipped the servants with all that is needed according to each's ability. In this delayed time, they are to work tirelessly till the very moment he appears and takes the throne.

In South Africa, we would not have overcome what we did were it not for the herculean efforts of many. Yet daily, nearly 30 years on, we are reminded that we have not yet arrived at that place where dignity and justice are a daily reality for all. We can't rest yet and fully enjoy the lush setting as there are still miles to go for justice and dignity to reach all.

† Lord Jesus, you invite us to follow you. Help us to follow to the end for even though the cross awaits, so too does the resurrection. Amen

For further thought

Building God's kingdom on earth as in heaven is not a short sprint but a marathon, more a cross country than a stadium track race!

Tuesday 5 April
Shouting stones!

Read Luke 19:29–48

As he came near and saw the city, he wept over it, saying, 'If you, even you, had only recognised on this day the things that make for peace.'

(verses 41–42a)

For many years during the dark apartheid decades there was a law prohibiting gatherings of more than two people – the Riotous Assemblies Act. Gathering and making common purpose to march or protest by more than two people alongside each other was punishable by law. The Black Sash – an organisation of mostly white women who opposed the repressive laws and their effects, especially on black people and their families – organised protests. They wore a black sash, held up placards and stood a few metres apart, making it difficult for law enforcement officers to arrest them, since no law was being broken – technically! It proved most effective and frustrated the racist rulers no end!

This story of Jesus and his disciples descending the Mount of Olives is a turning point in the narrative. Jesus – prophetically riding on a donkey as his ancestor David had – might have been ignored by the authorities. But the people hailing him as king, could not. It wasn't just the words, which would be sure to alarm the Romans, it was that these people felt empowered to express themselves that was the real problem. The people had long wanted an end to the excesses of organised religion and the injustices they had suffered at the hands of the authorities. And in Jesus they had found one who empowered their voice, and it shook those in power. 'Tell your followers to be quiet', they demand. But there are things that truly make for peace and these cannot be silenced!

† Dear Lord Jesus help us not only to pray for peace but to work so that it is established in all the corners of the world you love. Amen

For further thought

If you become fatigued working for a more just order, don't stop – instead, form alliances, work together and support others in this struggle.

The Gospel of Luke (3) – 1 Journey to Jerusalem

Wednesday 6 April
Telling the Good News

Read Luke 20:1–19

What then does this text mean: 'The stone that the builders rejected has become the cornerstone'?

(verse 17)

The reading tells, with chilling casualness, the seeming ease with which violence is unleashed and the frightening way in which it escalates! Two examples from my part of the world come to mind:

In 1994, as South Africa was celebrating its emergence from decades of violent repression and the dashed hopes and aspirations of millions of its people under apartheid, just a few hours away Rwanda was entering its own nightmare. The violence which neighbour unleashed on neighbour, built up over years of repression of Rwanda's people along tribal and racial lines, culminated in the horror that played out on its streets and villages.

A few years earlier, I had visited Juba in South Sudan to pay my respects and honour John Garang, their first president. There had been so much hope and goodwill emerging after 25 years of war with Khartoum. His untimely death, and the subsequent strain of holding a fractured nation together, soon took its toll and yet again, they took to the bush and have been embroiled in ongoing conflict since.

And of course, it isn't just this region which has seen conflicts, violence remains the go-to for many.

As Jesus makes his way to the city of peace, where God's name dwells, he challenges them. Knowing that their violence would soon spill over against himself, he challenges them to consider the meaning of the scripture, that the rejected stone has become the cornerstone.

† Lord Jesus, it is enough that you died for all! Help us to choose life no matter how hard. Amen

For further thought

What are the ways in which we can reduce intolerance, anger and conflict so that it doesn't boil over into greater chaos?

Thursday 7 April
The bare necessities

Read Luke 20:20–40

Then give to the emperor the things that are the emperor's, and to God the things that are God's.

(verse 25)

It is very refreshing to hear someone break something down to its simplest form, or a complex and delicate argument distilled to its absolute essentials. It lands most refreshingly on the ear especially in a world so often filled with verbose bluster. 'Jesus loves me this I know', a much-loved song, asserts a profound truth wrapped in a catchy tune. It is a truth about Jesus which grown-ups would do well to return to often! Or Paul to the Roman Christians, after long and convoluted reasoning involving deep theological concepts, breaking it all down to a few simple words: 'Let love be genuine'.

In today's reading the passage cautions against those who love to bamboozle and tie people up in knots with their cunning arguments designed to catch someone out. The Scribes and Pharisees had tried this with Jesus and had failed – he simply tells them to, 'give to the emperor the things that are the emperor's, and to God that which is his'. And his actions match the simplicity of his words. Striding resolutely toward Jerusalem with the profoundly simple purpose of redeeming that which was God's. The simplicity of a shepherd: the sheep is lost; I will find it and bring it home. The simplicity of a father: my child is lost; I will seek them and welcome them back. The simplicity of love: my loved ones are dying; I will die instead.

But the simplicity of the words and actions demand an equally simple answer. In the light of God's ultimate demonstration of love, whose are you?

† Lord Jesus Christ, help me not to lose sight of the basics: your love, your embrace and you reaching out to all, and help me to follow you in these. Amen

For further thought
It is said that 'less is more'! In an age of wordiness, in an age of rampant consumerism, how can I adapt to less?

Friday 8 April
With the end in sight

Read Luke 20:41–21:11

He said, 'Truly I tell you, this poor widow has put in more than all of them.'

(verse 3)

Living with someone who has a terminal illness can be both a huge learning and a blessing. It was that for me. My wife died a few years ago aged 52, after living with cancer for 20 years. As we entered the last stages of the disease and her movements became more difficult and her pain a bigger challenge to manage, we chose to focus on what was important and necessary for both of us and for our adult children as we journeyed together. We cared for and supported each other and created an environment which gave confidence to her to tackle chores albeit from the comfort of her bed. In this way she remained active and engaged in life in the home. Focusing always on the possible rather than the losses, we adjusted and became a team and celebrated small things giving huge pleasure rather than being disheartened by what was too difficult or exacted too high a toll. Through small but meaningful acts we expressed mutual love and support overshadowing regret and sadness.

She died next to me in our bed, in the early hours of the morning, me, holding her hand as she exhaled for the last time. Accompanying someone to death can thus be a wonderfully life-giving experience, notwithstanding the pain and sadness overshadowing the journey. We can choose to walk it together or run ahead of each other and miss those opportunities for connecting even in life's most dire moments.

Those who encounter Jesus as he nears his end appear so busy in their own worlds that they miss the One offering life!

† Dear Lord Jesus, help me to find in each and every moment of my journey the things which make for life. Amen

For further thought

There are some wonderful podcasts on grief and loss, on death and dying which are really all about living. Find a few to listen to.

Saturday 9 April
Standing tall

Read Luke 21:12–28

Now when these things begin to take place, stand up and raise your heads, because your redemption is drawing near.

(verse 28)

One of the first things which impress visitors to Cape Town is the imposing mountain which sits in the middle of the metropolis. As kids growing up here, we have criss-crossed the many paths which take you up and over the mountain. It was therefore going to be very special taking my children on their first walk to the top! We set off early from below the cableway making our way up Platteklip Gorge. The children seemed buoyed by their excitement and ran ahead with friends, who were visiting from abroad, being equally excited. The path consists of steps set out at quite a steep gradient and snakes up the mountain. With each step, your unfit legs feel heavier and heavier as your initially brisk pace slackens to a saunter and your bouncy demeanour is reduced to a crawl! My youngest's legs gave in under her and I had to carry her, as my chest hurt with each deep breath. What was such an exciting prospect when we set off became drudgery wishing it to end. 'A few more steps', I kept coaxing, but as you turned a bend, the steep incline sat there like a menacing goader.

And then, suddenly, there it was: the last few steps and the table! The view is breathtaking, the feeling indescribable. The assaults of doubt evaporate replaced by joy and exhilaration, and the world is again a wonderful place!

Raising drooping hands and looking up is the posture of discipleship, says Jesus.

† Lord Jesus, we turn to you in the hurly-burly and in life's assault on our hope and faith. Help us Lord. Amen

For further thought

Don't be overwhelmed when you are on the journey to seeing that better vista, that more glorious view, for it is there within your reach.

The Gospel of Luke (3)

2 Your king comes to you

Notes by **Bola Iduoze**

Bola is an entrepreneur, author, conference speaker and mentor. She specialises in helping people grow through practical application of spiritual principles. Bola began her career as an accountant over 20 years ago and her entrepreneurial journey in 2000. Since then she has trained, coached and mentored over 700 home business owners around the world. In addition, Bola co-pastors Gateway Chapel alongside her husband Eddie. They have two children, Asher and Bethel. Bola has used the NIV in these notes.

Sunday 10 April (Palm Sunday)
His word will come to pass

Read Luke 21:29 – 22:6

Heaven and earth will pass away, but my words will never pass away.

(verse 33)

I grew up in a small town in Nigeria called Ibadan and went to a little Baptist church where Sunday school was an essential part of the development of every child within the area. Our Sunday school teacher taught us how God does not fail in ensuring the night shows up on time and daylight equally appearing without fail. He would say, 'Just as God will never mix up day nor night, he will never miss ensuring his words come to pass without fail. Though the governments may change very frequently,' – which was then a common experience with one government being in power and giving loads of promises, and the other coming in and ignoring previous promises – 'God does not change.'

I was taught that God is stable and, irrespective of the changes around, we can depend on his promises. That knowledge created a strong sense of dependency on God and his word in my mind and a remembrance that our God is not man.

I would therefore like to encourage you with the same words today – that irrespective of what life seems to throw at you, the word of the Lord spoken to you will be established in your life.

† Father, thank you for being a dependable God whose words do not fail. Help me to stay focused on your word and promises today.

Monday 11 April
The greater is called to serve

Read Luke 22:7–30

But you are not to be like that. Instead, the greatest among you should be like the youngest, and the one who rules like the one who serves.

(verse 26)

One of the most remarkable parts of growing up in a home with five siblings is the constant struggle to be served by others. I grew up within a culture where the younger ones do more chores than the older and the younger serves the older, of course within reason! This whole being the greater and the one to be served continues to the school setting where the school seniors expect to be served by the junior students. The whole concept of service being expected by the greater is not something strange for a typical Nigerian child – which I was. Growing up and finding yourself in the position where you are being served seems to be the biggest incentive to studying and moving up the years in secondary schools!

The lesser serving the greater is not a strange concept but Jesus changed that by stating that Christianity sees things differently. Jesus encouraged his disciples to serve even if in a greater position and he showed this to them through his actions, feet washing and teachings.

Serving others, even those you deem yourself greater than, is a key part of Christianity and a great reflection of the Spirit of God in us. A true reflection of humility, therefore, is to be quick to serve and not to be served.

† Father, grant me grace to be humble and open enough to serve others, even when I think I am greater than them, in Jesus name. Help me stay humble today, Lord.

For further thought

Serving others is a great sign of Christ in us. If Jesus at this crucial time in his life took time to teach his disciples about this, then we should live by this principle.

The Gospel of Luke (3) – 2 Your king comes to you

Tuesday 12 April
Prayer for strength in the time of stress

Read Luke 22:31–53

An angel from heaven appeared to him and strengthened him. And being in anguish, he prayed more earnestly, and his sweat was like drops of blood falling to the ground.

(verses 43–44)

As Jesus progressed toward the final days of his life and understanding the pain and persecution that would come his way within the next few days, he was in a state of anguish and went to God to pass the burden of the upcoming challenge to his Father. He went to ask for help from his Father and the Bible makes us understand that an angel came from heaven and strengthened him. What an amazing lesson this is.

My husband Eddie and I have been to Israel quite a few times and one of the places we do not fail to visit is the garden of Gethsemane in Jerusalem. On most occasions, I will stand there and look toward the old city of Jerusalem, on which Jesus would have cast his eyes, knowing fully well that he was going to be crucified when he got there. He was walking toward a place where he would suffer for a sin he did not commit. That is difficult – but he still went ahead and did it. But not before he requested help from his Father in the place of prayer.

Prayer is a useful tool every believer can use to handle any challenge of life. Every time we cry to the Lord, he sends his angels and strengthens us.

Do you need help or strength today? Then take the issues to God because he still answers prayers and still sends his angels to minster to us as well as provide us with strength on a daily basis.

† Father, when my heart is overwhelmed, remind me to cry to you and trust you for strength from above to be able to overcome any challenge of life.

For further thought

Jesus in preparing for the difficult task of the crucifixion ahead of him had to set time aside to pray. After that, the angels came to minister to him and strengthen him.

Strength for the time we are weak

> **Read Luke 22:54–71**
>
> *The Lord turned and looked straight at Peter. Then Peter remembered the word the Lord had spoken to him: 'Before the rooster crows today, you will disown me three times.' And he went outside and wept bitterly.*
>
> (verses 61–62)

As young children in a large family setting, playing games was a general practice. One such game is 'I promise'. This was a game we played to show that we will keep certain secrets. Although sometimes, circumstances do not allow us to keep such promises, at other times it's just sheer indiscipline that stops the keeping of them. As I read through today's story, I felt sorry for Peter and could equally identify with him as I look at the weakness of our flesh.

Peter was a disciple of Jesus who had in mind to follow Jesus through the time of his persecution and he felt that he would be there for Jesus no matter what happened. Jesus had talked about what was going to come, but Peter was so confident in his own ability to stand by Jesus through the tough times.

As Jesus proceeded in his period of trial, Peter, being certain he was never going to betray Jesus did not expect the occurrence of the denial. After he betrayed Jesus – just as Jesus had predicted – Peter saw him and went out to cry bitterly. He repented and regretted this situation. But a great lesson has been learned and that is: we cannot depend on our flesh. We can have a desire but lack the ability to follow through on it because our flesh is weak. We need therefore to continue to pray for strength and understand that we should not put our confidence in our flesh.

† Father help me to fix my eyes upon you and strengthen me through every phase of life. Let me not rely on my flesh but upon your ability to sustain me always.

For further thought

Peter desired to support Jesus, but his flesh failed him. This shows that our flesh is inadequate in fulfilling promises but there is strength from above.

April

The Gospel of Luke (3) – 2 Your king comes to you

Thursday 14 April (Maundy Thursday)
What will you do with the opportunity?

Read Luke 23:1–17

When Herod saw Jesus, he was greatly pleased, because for a long time he had been wanting to see him. From what he had heard about him, he hoped to see him perform a sign of some sort.

(verse 8)

The scripture says that Herod had wanted to meet Jesus for a long time, based on what he heard about Jesus. The opportunity was presented to him, but he never took advantage of it.

I remember a time in my life when I had the opportunity to sit with my mentor. I thought I was prepared; only to realise that I was not! I was in so much awe that I left wishing I had used the time more effectively. So I totally understand that it is possible to wish to meet someone and then, when you meet them, to realise that you were not as prepared as you thought you should be.

What happens when what we have always wanted is presented to us? It does not matter what opportunity we have if we are unprepared to take advantage of it and achieve anything of value with the chance that we are given. There were a few people that met Christ briefly whose lives changed after that, but sadly we could not say that about Herod because Christ coming into his life never made any difference.

A big lesson to learn from this story is that we should always ensure we take advantage of the opportunity God has presented to us. And to always ask ourselves the question – what if the door is opened for us to meet the person we always wanted to meet, how will we react, and what impact will that make in our lives?

† Lord, prepare me not to miss any opportunity you present me so I can live a life of more impact and purpose every day in Jesus name.

For further thought

Herod desired to meet Jesus, but when Christ came, nothing changed. Jesus coming into our lives should make a difference. How have we changed?

Friday 15 April (Good Friday)
Forgiveness is a decision, not a feeling

Read Luke 23:18–38

Jesus said, 'Father, forgive them, for they do not know what they are doing.' And they divided up his clothes by casting lots.

(verse 34)

Forgiveness is a decision and not a feeling. I once felt wrongly accused and wanted to lash out and correct the unjust situation. I felt I needed to tell anyone that cared to listen that the story was untrue. At the same time, I felt the person at the heart of this story deserved to be punished and exposed for their wrong thoughts and words. I realised that these feelings were overcoming my long-learned thought of 'forgiveness being a decision'.

After a good cry, I read the above scripture and realised what Jesus went through: where a lot of the parties present in his day and at the time of his crucifixion had their own agendas and strongly pushed those forward. The people were not concerned about the impact of their words and actions on Jesus. Jesus, in the midst of that unfair and unjust situation, however, made a decision to forgive and showed that decision with his action and words, asking his Father to forgive.

Of course, when someone wrongs us, they should acknowledge that and do what they can to put things right. But when they don't, looking at that scripture helped me to put in perspective my hurt and pain as well as helping me to go back to my original understanding of forgiveness. We do not always feel the emotions of forgiveness, but we can make that decision, act on it and then the feeling will follow (sometimes slowly!).

Like Jesus, we can make a choice to forgive no matter how hard we find the actions of others.

† Father, thank you for showing me, with the example of Jesus, how to forgive and help me remember that I can make the decision to forgive, starting from praying for the person who offends me.

For further thought

Forgiveness is a decision. Jesus chose to forgive and that was enabled through the strength given to him after he prayed.

The Gospel of Luke (3) – 2 Your king comes to you

It's never too late for anyone

April

The Gospel of Luke (3) – 2 Your king comes to you

Read Luke 23:39–56

Then he said, 'Jesus, remember me when you come into your kingdom.'
Jesus answered him, 'Truly I tell you, today you will be with me in
paradise.'

(verses 42–43)

The Bible does not give us the names of the thieves on the cross, yet one attained the most exciting result after meeting with Jesus – even that late in life. He was in his dying moments and he prayed a prayer asking Jesus for help to get into the kingdom of God.

That prayer showed that the man believed that Jesus was going into a kingdom that was potentially better than where he was likely to go, and he requested Jesus' help to get into this better kingdom. Jesus showed that that prayer did not come too late in life but promised him paradise just because of the request he made.

I once heard the story of a gentleman who was on his sickbed and had a friend come to share Christ with him. After Jesus was introduced to him, this man insisted that his past was just too messed up for Jesus to forgive him. He refused to accept Jesus just because he felt it was too late for him.

The thief on the cross who asked for help from Jesus had a different eternity awaiting him and I want to focus on the fact that God's grace is always available to us no matter how far gone in sin or disobedience we have been. All we need to do is to ask him and he will make his grace available for us.

† Jesus, thank you for showing us that it is never too late to call on you for help at the time of our need.

For further thought

One of the two thieves on the cross made a last-minute decision that determined his eternal destination. It is never too late.

The Gospel of Luke (3)

3 Your king reigns

Notes by **David Painting**

For David's biography, see p. 65. David has used the NIVUK and NRSVA for these notes.

Sunday 17 April (Easter Sunday)
Not by power

> **Read Romans 6:1–14**
>
> *We were therefore buried with him through baptism into death in order that, just as Christ was raised from the dead through the glory of the Father, we too may live a new life.*
>
> (verse 4, NIVUK)

When Einstein conceived his famous equation, $E=mc^2$, he knew that it could be used to build a weapon of catastrophic power. Just a few years later, it was. If we discover how to do something, at some point, someone does it. We haven't learned the lesson of Eden: just because it is there doesn't mean you should eat it, just because you can, doesn't mean that you should.

Perhaps our thinking is influenced by the enemy, it never crosses his mind that a God who is infinitely more than he is might choose not to exercise those attributes: that omnipresent God might allow himself to be constrained to a woman's womb. That omniscient God might become an unknowing baby. That omnipotent God might allow himself to be nailed to a cross.

And so, we start with this verse, to remind us that the reign of this king is achieved through love, not power, that his plans are accomplished through genuine relationship, not by controlling every detail and that victory is sometimes disguised as death.

And if we are to be true subjects of this king, we must share the same values, the same nature. Not by might, nor by power, but by his Spirit.

† Father, open my eyes to just how big you are, and yet how personal – how you lift me up, how you step down, how you love.

He is not here

Read Luke 24:1–12

Why do you look for the living among the dead?

(part of verse 5, NIVUK)

When the women went to the tomb, they wanted to grieve, to lament, to gain some closure by properly saying goodbye. And to do that, they needed a body, the body of Jesus. Yet when they arrive, the tomb is empty and the angel's words meaningless. 'He is not here' wasn't good news for them, it was catastrophic. They had all this pain, all this disappointment, all this anger, all this grief – and now they were left holding it. They had the myrrh in their hands, the bandages – everything they needed, and now instead of anointing and wrapping, instead of leaving it with Jesus, all they could do was turn around and carry the pain back into their lives.

Of course, for them, 'He is not here' quickly became 'He is risen' – and mourning turned to garlands of praise!

But how many people are stuck in that in-between time before daybreak on Easter Sunday? People who continue carrying the symbols of death: the pain of loss, the fracturing of trauma, the debt that others have imposed. People for whom there have been no first rays of dawn, no whispered 'Mary', no joy-filled hug, no 'He is risen' moment. People who are just holding on, with nowhere to take the pain. The king reigns, but the kingdom is not yet here.

Perhaps you are in that place – like the women, in the gloom, surrounded by death, with nowhere to go with your pain. He knows, he feels it too. May you find him in the place of the living.

† Lord, help me to cry out to you. Lead me from the place of death to the place of life.

For further thought

Who needs you to be a place where they can grieve and lament? Who can you help see the risen Lord?

Tuesday 19 April
Hope renewed

Read Luke 24:13–27

But we had hoped that he was the one who was going to redeem Israel.

(verse 21a, NIVUK)

'We had hoped.' Perhaps the saddest words we can utter. We had hoped, but now, by implication, hope is gone. The loss of a loved one whose dying took with them our hopes. The loss of health that deprived us of carefree days. The loss of career, the loss of a friendship, the loss of innocence. And with those losses, the loss of hope.

Along with the crowds, these two men had pinned their hopes on Jesus: of religious freedom, of the Romans being kicked out, of a better future, a more just society, a kingdom where good reigns. They had been disappointed before, so many false messiahs had come and gone, but this time, this time they had really believed. Jesus' words and works had resonated, had burned within them, hope had been ablaze in their hearts.

Hopes that had been cruelly extinguished along with the sun; spreadeagled before them and nailed to a cross. Desolate, they left Jerusalem, walking wearily away from the city of peace into the approaching night.

And when we lose hope, we so often do the same. For whatever reason, hope dies, and we find ourselves walking away from the peace of Christ into an increasingly dark place. Weariness descends on us and all we want to do is go somewhere familiar, shut out the night and curl up.

Have you experienced that? Is it where you are right now? You may not see him yet, may not believe it to be possible. But day is coming, the sun is about to rise, Jesus, the King, is with you.

† Lord, help me to walk with those who are hopeless today.

For further thought

Are there areas of your life where, perhaps because of disappointment, you are walking away from peace?

Wednesday 20 April
Bread and wine

Read Luke 24:28–43

They got up and returned at once to Jerusalem. There they found the Eleven … Jesus himself stood among them and said to them, 'Peace be with you.'

(parts of verses 33 and 36, NIVUK)

Have you ever seen someone you know and not recognised them? The dentist or doctor greeting you across the street. Your mind struggles to place them. You recognise the face, the voice – you know that you know them, and yet you don't! Your knowledge of them is tied to a setting, the doctor's surgery, the dentist's chair. And without the setting, you don't recognise them.

Why didn't these two recognise Jesus as he walked with them? Because they knew Jesus was dead, that his body was in a cold dark tomb outside Jerusalem. The physical setting was wrong, along with the theological one: God was all powerful, not one who could be held by nails. Yet there was something familiar in this man's voice, the way he spoke of God that resonated and encouraged them to invite him into the house. Something about his demeanour that made it natural for him to take the lead when the meal was ready.

And here it was, bread and wine; their minds must have been taken back to what they had seen or heard of that last supper. Bread and wine, brokenness and shed blood and now they recognise him. This is what God is like, one who steps down, one who draws near, one who reigns by giving everything.

And that which was impossible – to take another step in the hopeless dark – becomes more than possible in this new light. Quickly, they return to the place of peace, to Jerusalem, to the encouragement of others who have also seen. Jesus is alive, this is our God, peace be with you.

† Lord, open my eyes to the extent of your love for me – that you would do this.

For further thought

Why not take some bread and wine and hear again the voice of Jesus, affirming, encouraging and bringing peace?

Thursday 21 April
Witnesses

Read Luke 24:44–52

You are witnesses of these things. And see, I am sending upon you what my Father promised; so stay here in the city until you have been clothed with power from on high.

(verses 48–49, NRSVA)

When those first visitors arrived at the tomb, they discovered two things. First, Jesus wasn't there and, second, the graveclothes were neatly folded. A dramatic statement about the things of death: they were no longer needed. Jesus, having risen from the dead, chooses this as a prophetic outworking of his words on the cross: 'It is finished!' (John 19:30). The law, the prophets, the psalms have all, like those graveclothes, been wrapped up, their purpose of describing what God was like completed by the full revelation of Jesus.

As Paul put it in 1 Corinthians 13:12, previously they had seen God 'through a mirror, dimly'. 'Now', Jesus says, 'you can see clearly that the Messiah needed to suffer and rise on the third day so that a new message might ring out across the world. Sins forgiven, a new life made possible. You are the first to see it, the first to witness it' (paraphrased).

He was talking about you. 'First to witness' implies others will witness later. You are implicit in Luke 24, part of the unfolding story. You are a witness to God's love and mercy; you too can wait in the place of peace to receive power to testify.

Witnessing isn't about lecturing others, it isn't about reciting a formula, it isn't about handing out leaflets of other people's testimony. It's about you sharing the kingdom life that Jesus has won for you: the victories over temptation, the forgiveness when you gave in, the joy when prayer was answered, the lament when it wasn't, the sense of peace in the storm and above all, the presence of the king.

† Thank you for life in all its fulness, for the victory of resurrection, for the empowering of the Spirit.

For further thought

What does witnessing mean to you? Does this reading challenge you to re-evaluate that perhaps?

The Gospel of Luke (3) – 3 Your king reigns

April

Friday 22 April
Restoration

Read Isaiah 52:1–10

The Lord will lay bare his holy arm in the sight of all the nations, and all the ends of the earth will see the salvation of our God.

(verse 10, NIVUK)

We came home one day to a waterfall cascading through the kitchen ceiling. Where there had been smooth plaster, now a gaping, jagged hole. Everywhere we looked the damage was more than we had thought. It felt hopeless.

When those first exiles returned to Jerusalem, they were overwhelmed and devastated. The beauty of the Temple utterly gone – and with it, any sense of God being with them. It was hard even to see that this had been a city, not one stone was left on another and the walls that had so often defended, behind which they had felt so secure, were razed to the ground, the doors and gates completely burned.

We had a very kind insurance person. She came and looked and assessed, she sympathised and, step by step, walked us through a process of restoration. Gradually, we began to see a bigger picture, a more hopeful outcome. Ezra and Nehemiah did the same for those first returnees. Slowly, they began to clear the space, to rebuild, to restore. When there was opposition, they handled it and ensured the work prospered.

How lovely are the feet of them that bring good news (verse 7). How the world needs people like these, people who don't deny the pain, who don't pretend that the devastation isn't real, but who walk with us, holding our heads up to see beyond the immediate to what lies beyond.

The new kitchen was far better than the old. In the end a new Temple was built, new walls complete. And even the ends of the earth saw that God saves.

† Lord, thank you that you save, that you act, that nothing can prevent your purposes.

For further thought

All these stories of restoration took time and involved people. Of course, God could fix it instantly. But he doesn't, he works lovingly with us, giving us significance.

Saturday 23 April
Your kingdom come

Read Psalm 150

Let everything that has breath praise the Lord. Praise the Lord.

(verse 6, NIVUK)

I remember vividly the night that our first grandchild was born. The culmination of a difficult nine months followed by a long labour. Hour after hour, waiting for news, praying, hoping, fearing. The longer it went on, the higher the anxiety, the brief messages only serving to raise more unanswerable questions. Finally, the call: 'Come and see your new grandson.'

When that longed for hope becomes real – a baby in your arms – real joy and praise flood out and nothing can quite do it justice! Not all the musical instruments, not all the fine words, not all the dance, not all these combined can express what leaps from our heart.

The good news that Jesus proclaimed was simple: 'The kingdom of God is at hand'. Whether it was seen in the justice of the kingdom, or the compassion of the king, it was there. It was there in Simeon holding the newborn and declaring, 'I have seen with my own eyes, the salvation of God'. It was there as Jairus' daughter was raised; it was there as Legion was freed; it was there as Mary wept with joy, hugging the risen Jesus.

Wherever Jesus is made visible, wherever hope is renewed, wherever salvation comes, the king and the kingdom are there. This is how our God reigns. Not often in the showy, outward exertion of power, but in the quiet, unseen, subversive choices of his people.

The evidence may not yet be visible, all the signs may point to death. Yet, our God reigns; victory, like the dawn, is coming. Praise the Lord!

† Lord, your reign doesn't always mean that your will is being done right now. Help me look beyond that to the coming king.

For further thought

Reflect on key events in Luke, from the annunciation to the ascension – God's will being exercised through the free choices of his people.

All creatures great and small

1 Great

Notes by **Paul Nicholson SJ**

Paul is a Roman Catholic priest belonging to the Society of Jesus, a religious order popularly known as the Jesuits. He currently works in London as Socius (assistant) to the Jesuit Provincial. He edits *The Way*, a journal of Christian spirituality, and is author of *An Advent Pilgrimage* (Kevin Mayhew, 2013) and *Pathways to God* (Catholic Truth Society, 2017). Since being ordained in 1988, he has worked principally in ministries of spirituality and of social justice and was novice-master between 2008 and 2014. Paul has used the NRSVA for these notes.

Sunday 24 April
All God's creatures

Read Genesis 1:20–25

*And God said, 'Let the earth bring forth living creatures of every kind'
… And it was so. God made the wild animals of the earth of every kind, and the cattle of every kind, and everything that creeps upon the ground of every kind. And God saw that it was good.*

(part of verses 24–25)

Zoology was my first passion. Toward the end of my schooling, I decided either to dedicate my life to zoological research or become a priest. At university, I studied 'living creatures of every kind'. Ultimately, the call to ordained ministry prevailed. But I've never lost my concern for all God's creatures.

Today's reading sets the scene for two weeks' prayer when we'll consider the rich variety of animal life that is one of God's greatest gifts to us. Some are directly useful, providing our food and clothing. Some are beautiful, leading us to praise. Some don't seem to serve us at all – were you ever drawn to thank God for mosquitoes? – but have their own place in our planet's great web of life. All are known to God, who called them into being, and pronounced them good.

Since *Fresh From The Word* is read worldwide, you will have the particular animals of your own locality to thank God for. Even in big cities, there will be some to catch your attention. In central London, where I live and work, there are pigeons and spiders, cats and dogs. And God still looks on them each day, and still judges them good.

† Look out for the animals that are nearest to you today, and take time to thank God for their presence in your life.

Monday 25 April
How big is your God?

Read Job 41:1–15

Can you draw out Leviathan with a fish-hook, or press down its tongue with a cord? Can you put a rope in its nose, or pierce its jaw with a hook?

(verses 1–2)

The blue whale is the largest creature ever to live upon this planet. It can reach a length of 30 metres, and weigh up to 200 tons. The writer of the book of Job must at least have heard of whales, and uses them as the basis for his idea of Leviathan the great sea monster. Even with modern technology, whale-hunting is a dangerous business (and is, thankfully, becoming less common). With the boats and equipment of biblical times, it must have seemed like the height of folly to attempt it.

So, when God wants to contrast his own power with Job's weakness, Leviathan is one of the examples he offers. God doesn't want to crush Job, or mockingly put him in his place. But it is important to show that Job cannot expect to understand fully everything that God does, everything that happens to him, and that at times he will have no option but to trust. If Job cannot imagine taming even a single whale, how can he hope to fully comprehend the God who creates the galaxies?

One of the things that people of faith have to be on their guard against at times is a tendency to want to domesticate God, to create a small, cosy idol of God who is able to affirm me but never challenge me. The greatest theologians have recognised that when they have drawn all their ideas together, 'God is always greater'. It is a useful reminder, now and then, in our own prayer to make sure that the God we are worshipping isn't too small!

† Creator God, the natural world speaks in so many ways of your greatness. As I contemplate the great wonder of creation, I praise you for all your gifts.

For further thought

Why is the hunting of whales controversial among many people today? What is your own opinion of the matter?

Tuesday 26 April
You may not withhold your help

Read Deuteronomy 22:1–4

You shall not watch your neighbour's ox or sheep straying away and ignore them; you shall take them back to their owner. You shall not see your neighbour's donkey or ox fallen on the road and ignore it; you shall help to lift it up.

(verses 1 and 4)

In any society that relies heavily on small-scale farming, the kind of society where the book of Deuteronomy was first produced, domestic animals are one of the main sources of wealth. The loss of such animals, therefore, by theft or straying, represents a huge threat to a person's livelihood. It is understandable, then, that in God's guidance about how to live a blessed and fully human life, these precepts encouraging care, not just for your own livestock, but for those of your neighbour, find a place.

Impulses to ignore this guidance are two-fold. First, it must have been tempting to simply absorb a stray animal into your own flock or herd – 'finders, keepers', as the saying goes. Second, what is being commended here may put the finder to some inconvenience or expense. Lifting up a fallen ox cannot be easy, and housing, feeding and watering a donkey until its owner claims it may be a costly business. But the benefits come, not simply in terms of animal welfare, but in enjoying the kind of society in which people look to the interests of their neighbours as well as their own.

Few of us have to deal on a day-to-day basis with straying sheep or fallen oxen. But the principles behind this passage are as relevant today as they ever were. Am I prepared to give the needs of those around me something of the same care and concern that I give to my own? Even if this is somewhat costly at first, it benefits all of us in the long run.

† Lord Jesus, who said that love of God and neighbour sums up all God asks, help me to attend to the needs of those around me with the same concern I show to my own.

For further thought

How ready do you find yourself to accept others showing you their care and concern when you yourself are in need?

Wednesday 27 April
Confidence in time of peril

Read 1 Samuel 17:32–47

David said, 'The Lord, who saved me from the paw of the lion and from the paw of the bear, will save me from the hand of this Philistine.' So Saul said to David, 'Go, and may the Lord be with you!'

(verse 37)

I had never noticed before how many references to animals this story contains. There are the lambs and sheep the shepherd David protected; the lions and the bears preying upon them; the dogs that Goliath resisted being compared to; and the carrion birds and scavenging beasts who will feed off the corpses of the Philistine army. Of all these, the lions and the bears first catch the attention.

The fact is that lions (wholly) and bears (partially) are meat-eaters. It is their nature to feed on other animals, as they attempt to feed on David's flock, and even on David himself, given the chance. The nineteenth-century scientists who propounded the theory of evolution were shocked by the extent of what the poet Tennyson called 'nature red in tooth and claw'. Isaiah dreams of a time when 'the leopard shall lie down with the kid' (Isaiah 11:6), but without a radical change to the leopard's digestive system, that will never happen. This system of predator and prey is part of the nature of our world, something we have no choice but to acknowledge and accept.

The lions and bears in this passage are not being invoked as evil monsters who should know better, but as natural forces that God has offered David protection from. And if God has offered protection from these, it gives David grounds for confidence that God will not withdraw his protection when the boy comes up against the strong warrior, Goliath. We know the end of the story. David's confidence is not misplaced, and the carrion birds and scavenging beasts do not go hungry!

† Lord, you know the dangers and difficulties I face – not lions and bears, but everything in my life that threatens me. Protect me, as you protected the shepherd David.

For further thought

Many argue today that reducing meat consumption is part of our Christian duty to care for creation. What is your view on this?

All creatures great and small – 1 Great

117

Thursday 28 April
Following in God's paths

Read 1 Samuel 6:7–16

The cows went straight in the direction of Beth-shemesh along one highway, lowing as they went; they turned neither to the right nor to the left, and the lords of the Philistines went after them as far as the border of Beth-shemesh.

(verse 12)

There is a story told of Ignatius of Loyola, founder of the Jesuit order to which I belong. Once while travelling, he fell into the company of a Muslim. They spoke of their respective faiths, finding much in common. But before they parted, the Muslim said something the headstrong Ignatius later took as an insult. He couldn't decide whether to pursue and attack the Muslim. Coming to a fork in the road, he let the mule he was riding decide which road to take. The mule chose the path the Muslim had not taken, so Ignatius was saved from a brawl or worse.

In this passage, it is cows that are allowed, by their choice of paths, to indicate God's will. The Philistines, in defeating Israel, had captured the ark of the Covenant, the symbol of God's presence with his people. Soon afterwards, a plague broke out among the Philistines. Their priests suggested they return the ark to Israel. If the cows took it straight back, the Philistines would recognise that the God of Israel sent the plague. If they wandered aimlessly, the plague would be regarded as a random sickness. Sure enough, the cows went straight back to the Jews, the Lord showing his power through them.

It may take us a certain suspension of disbelief to think that God shows his will by influencing an animal's choice of path. Yet as Christians, we need to believe that God has plans for us; and if he has plans, he has given us ways to recognise what those are, and how we can follow them.

† Lord God, you choose many different ways to indicate to us the paths we should take. Give us the power to recognise your leading, and the desire to follow the paths you map out.

For further thought

Many speak and write nowadays about discernment, the art of recognising how God prompts us to action. You might read or think about this today.

Friday 29 April
The power of the tongue and its speech

Read James 3:3–5

If we put bits into the mouths of horses to make them obey us, we guide their whole bodies .... So also the tongue is a small member, yet it boasts of great exploits.

(verses 3 and 5)

There was a time when warhorses represented the height of military technology for the Jews, the equivalent of an armoured tank or supersonic fighter jet today. The use of horses in battle had transformed warfare, and whoever had mastery of cavalry would prevail over his enemies. When the psalmist contrasts those who trust in horses with those who trust in the Lord (Psalm 20:7), it is precisely because the horse's power and strength is so impressive.

Yet, astonishingly, it only takes a small thing like the bit in a horse's mouth to enable the rider to control all that power. James's train of thought leads him from that to the power of the tongue – itself a small thing in the mouth – to do good or ill, and thus guiding and shaping whole human lives. All the more reason, then, to ensure that it is used for good, and curbed when it would tend to harm, as a rider curbs his mount.

This reading offers an invitation to recognise the truth of that in our own lives. There are likely to be words that you have said, times when you have spoken, that have done great good to others, guiding and consoling them. There are also, perhaps, times when a word of gossip or slander has done damage that is difficult to repair. Seeing more clearly, with God's help, the ways in which your own tongue has acted for good or evil here can be a powerful spur to speaking more carefully and lovingly in the future.

† I ask you, Lord, to help me to speak only for good, never for harm, always to build up, and never to tear down; to speak always in love, and never in hate. Amen

For further thought

Spend some time today recalling a time when something you said was of real help to another person, and thank God for that time.

All creatures great and small – 1 Great

Saturday 30 April
The scapegoat bearing the sins of the people

Read Leviticus 16:15–22

Then Aaron shall lay both his hands on the head of the live goat, and confess over it all the iniquities of the people of Israel, and all their transgressions, all their sins, putting them on the head of the goat, and sending it away into the wilderness.

(part of verse 21)

I belong to a Christian tradition that is rich in signs and symbols: bread and wine, oil and incense, crucifixes and statues. Other parts of the Christian church rely less on these, and at times have even by and large rejected them. Yet we as humans are embodied creatures, and it is not easy for us to approach the God who is spirit wholly without the help of more earthly things.

The word 'scapegoat' has passed into popular culture now, and would be widely understood as one who takes the blame for something not his or her fault. Here, though, in the Jewish law, we find its origin, and a more restricted meaning. The goat here is part of a ritual in which a people acknowledging their departure from God's ways are led to an experience of God's forgiveness. The goat (which we may hope will thrive in the wilderness, even as we may fear that its fate will be less happy) is a symbol of the people's sins being removed from them, leaving them free to serve God more wholeheartedly in the future.

Later, John the Baptist, himself a dweller in the wilderness, will recognise Jesus as the Lamb of God who will carry away the sins of the people. All of us, perhaps, experience our faults and failings as too hard to bear at times, and yet impossible to escape from by our own power alone. We need to know that these will not burden us eternally, that there is One who can and will free us from them.

† Jesus, Lamb of God, you take our sins upon yourself as the goat took on the sins of the people of Israel. Accept my thanks for your merciful and forgiving love.

For further thought

Scapegoating and blaming the innocent seem to be a common pattern of human behaviour. Do you ever find yourself blaming others for your own shortcomings?

All creatures great and small

2 Small

Notes by **Pete Wheeler**

 Pete leads St Peter's, a revitalised Anglican church in a deprived 1960s estate in Aylesbury, UK. Having spent 20 years working as a musician – composing, producing and licensing music for film and TV – he trained at St Mellitus Theological College, London. He is married to and leads church with Ali, a graphic designer. They have two children. As well as music, Pete's creative downtime involves not enough golf and lapsang souchong tea. Pete has used the NIV and MSG for these readings.

Sunday 1 May
Bees

Read Judges 14:8–14

When he rejoined his parents, he gave them some, and they too ate it. But he did not tell them that he had taken the honey from the lion's carcass.

(verse 9b, NIV)

My friend Phil is a beekeeper. I watch with fascination at the comings and goings of the hives in his garden. Over 50,000 flights a day per colony take off and land. Bees are industrious. Their strength is in the fact that they don't operate alone. Together they are a hive of activity and their purpose is clear – to selflessly put the queen first for the good of the whole hive.

In this curious story in Judges 14, we meet Samson, a man who is physically strong, but is really very weak. He is selfishly determined to go his own way, defying his parents' wishes to marry a Philistine girl, and defying them again by feeding them honey gathered from an 'unclean' place – the carcass of a lion he had killed. In fact, we eventually see that Samson only truly becomes strong when he is at his weakest – fully reliant on the Holy Spirit to fulfil his calling, giving everything for the good of his people in the very last five minutes of his life.

Journey with me through this week, encountering 'all things wise and wonderful' to remind us how creation itself reflects God's qualities (Romans 1:20).

† God of all things, remind me today that your strength is found in my weakness. Lead me to fulfil your will in and through me. Amen

Monday 2 May
Consider the ant

Read Proverbs 6:6–11

You lazy fool, look at an ant. Watch it closely; let it teach you a thing or two. Nobody has to tell it what to do.

(verse 6, MSG)

In the UK I might be described as having 'ants in my pants' – a saying for those who, like me, find it hard to sit still.

Ants may rival bees for busyness! Solomon recognises the lesson they can teach us about working hard. Ants are designed to be proactive. 'Nobody has to tell it what to do', says Solomon. They just get on with the task at hand. Cooperation, communication, teamwork and relationship – ants are a great example of how creation reflects these godly qualities (Romans 1:20). When we are not sure what we should be doing, this may be the prompt we need to simply get on with building God's kingdom – proactively loving our neighbour, resolutely acting justly, tirelessly pursuing his presence.

Solomon might argue that things that are worth achieving usually involve hard work. His wisdom is aimed at those who would think otherwise. Much of Solomon's own life's work was spent constructing the Temple (1 Kings 6). An incredible feat of construction, resourcefulness and beauty. And yet... for all Solomon's wisdom and the Temple's splendour, reflecting God's glory, it wasn't quite what God desired. For God had already shown his people, Israel, that he was no longer to be restricted to a mountain, a tent or even a temple.

Be sure then to listen well. Locating yourself in your 'colony' (church family) will help you listen and discern where best to focus your kingdom-building activity, through hard work, selflessness and good communication.

Surely, of all God's creatures the ant would testify, 'teamwork makes the dream work'!

† God of my busyness, above the noise of my life, cause me to quieten, that I might hear your voice, wherever I am reading this right now. Send your Holy Spirit and fill me today.

For further thought

Every colony of ants has pioneers, creating new paths, leaving signs for others to follow when they find new habitats and sources of nutrition. Is that you?

Tuesday 3 May
An army of locusts

Read Joel 1:1–7

Has anything like this ever happened in your days or in the days of your ancestors?... it has the teeth of a lion, the fangs of a lioness. It has laid waste my vines and ruined my figtrees.

(parts of verses 2, 6, and 7, NIV)

The people of Israel had become stubborn and arrogant – unwilling to change, to follow God's lead, or to turn away from their sin back toward him. It is the prophet Joel who sees the warning signs – his prophecies being fuelled by a voracious army of locusts. Joel recognised the signs – that this flying cloud of teeth and death was a forewarning for the nation of Israel.

If ants and bees form colonies, the locust is an army – a munching militia, stripping fields of crops in minutes. A swarm can contain in excess of 500 million locusts, eating up to 80 kilotons of food in a day, meaning nothing is left unscathed. Even the tree bark is stripped and eaten in minutes (verse 7). Truly incredible.

My wife, Ali, and I recently recognised a work pattern developing that, if left untouched, would grow into a deeper, unhealthy problem. We made ourselves address it openly. We call that process 'keeping the drains clear'. It's easy to leave stuff sitting in the drain. But, inevitably, ignoring it will result in drains 'overflowing', causing surrounding damage and requiring deeper, more extensive repairs.

The locusts were a sign. What's your gauge for, and how accountable are you, to addressing what's wrong? Perhaps you rely on a trusted, truth-speaking friend, or a regular retreat for listening to what God is saying through the rhythms of your life. What areas might need change or repentance? Today, ask the Holy Spirit to convict you of any drains that need a clear out, and any areas where transformation must come. Don't be afraid.

† Gentle Spirit of God, help me to recognise the signs of things that need to change. Be gentle with me today as I let you down into the drains to see what needs clearing. Amen

For further thought
If you need a gauge, why not ask a friend to become your accountability partner? Or, as suggested, perhaps a retreat or quiet day to really listen well.

Wednesday 4 May
Fishing

Read Matthew 4:18–22

'Come, follow me,' Jesus said, 'and I will send you out to fish for people.' At once they left their nets and followed him.

(verses 19–20, NIV)

Have you ever gone back to where it all started? Back to where you began, or where you heard Jesus' voice for the first time, rising above the wind and storms, transcending everything else that sought to drown it out?

Do you need reminding of the moment of your calling?

For Peter, Andrew, James and John, this is the moment that changed everything forever. They know about fish and how to catch them. Fishing requires tenacity, endurance, adaptability and learned wisdom. Jesus affirms these existing gifts and skills by asking the fishermen to use them to become fishers of people. But in doing so, Jesus is going to show them that he is the master fisherman.

There have been many times that I have had to remember my calling – allowing myself to return to that moment when I finally listened and let Jesus speak clearly to me. I remember how things got worse before they got better, and life is still sometimes difficult. But that's the point. Our callings are rarely without trouble, inconvenience or sacrifice (Matthew 16:24)!

In my fishing kit, I have a 'spinner'. It's a hook designed to look like a tiny, limping fish as it drags through the water. As the little flash of silver glides past, bigger fish are tempted to follow and take the bait.

So, now consider… is there something shiny and attractive in your life that is drawing you toward it? Is this your reminder that Jesus' voice is the *only* one to follow? Today, stop and listen for his voice. Let it transcend all others.

† Jesus, take me back to where it all began. Re-ignite and affirm in me the calling you have placed on my life. Show me more. Take me further. Amen

For further thought

Today, remember and reflect on your calling. This may revolve around *who* you are called to be, rather than a place or a thing you do.

Thursday 5 May
Birds

Read Genesis 8:1–12

After forty days Noah opened a window he had made in the ark and sent out a raven, and it kept flying back and forth until the water had dried up from the earth.

(verses 6–7, NIV)

In the UK, if you attempt to eat chips by the seaside, you will most likely get a visit from above. Seagulls are adept at stealing your freshly fried food by dive-bombing you from the skies before heading out oceanwards with the prize in their beak, so that you have no hope of retrieving it. If you're really unlucky, they'll leave you a gift of their own making on your shoulder, or worse.

A raven contrasted against a dove are the central characters for the conclusion of the flood. It's a little unclear why Noah used a raven first, but it seems likely that it had something to do with 'carrion' – dead mammals that the raven could feed on. Historically, the raven has long been associated with death, a reputation that was likely augmented by this flood story. The raven's flight 'back and forth' may indicate that there was plenty of food for it. In sending the dove, Noah sets his search upon new life.

The dove, however, finds no habitable land on its first journey. In the second, a good news message is returned in its beak! However, the dove's third outing signals that death no longer prevails and that new life has begun!

Similarly, on the third day, Easter morning, Jesus asks Mary why she is out looking for the dead (John 20:11–18). Realising what God has done, she is re-tasked to bring the good news of new life to the disciples.

The deep waters of death have receded and hope abounds. Today, let's fix our gaze upon the good news of new life in Jesus.

† Mighty God, help us to trust you, even when things appear to be 'dead in the water' – when all hope seems lost. Even then, you are working for our good. Amen

For further thought

Have you ever considered that something as simple as feeding the birds is a worshipful act of loving God's creation? Perhaps not with chips, though.

Friday 6 May
A venomous snake

> **Read Acts 28:1–6**
>
> *When the islanders saw the snake hanging from his hand, they said to each other, 'This man must be a murderer…' But Paul shook the snake off into the fire and suffered no ill effects.*
>
> (part of verses 4–5, NIV)

The bright green boomslang, the black mamba which is able to stand up to 6 feet like a pole, the spitting cobra, the rainbow boa, the highly venomous but rather ordinary looking common brown, sea snakes, the monstrous anaconda – the list goes on. Snakes come in a fascinating array of species and variety, adapted to an incredible range of habitats across the world.

Our fear of snakes is understandable. They carry a very real threat of pain – even death. It is a primordial fear. We are warned early on in our ancient creation story, that temptation comes via the serpent. Be alert to this.

As Paul reaches down to collect firewood, he must have recoiled in surprise and pain at the bite of a venomous snake. Having survived a shipwreck, this dangling serpent affirmed the locals' suspicions of evil intent.

Now, it would be pretty easy here for me to start drawing metaphors concerning 'shaking off the snakes'. But I wonder if Luke (the author of Acts) includes this in his narrative simply to show us that God is faithfully working and protecting Paul amid shipwrecks and snakebites. The minds of the Maltese are settled, and Paul goes on to heal many through the laying on of the same hands that were bitten.

I have an irrational fear of spiders. An irrational fear helps no one. But maintaining a healthy respect for those things that can harm us, drag us off course and disrupt us, is wisdom. Nevertheless, we submit that God, through Jesus as redeemer, is able to work through these things when we let him and trust him.

† God of creation, as you faithfully protected Paul, would you protect us as we go about our lives? Keep us from harm, that your will might be done in all things. Amen

For further thought

John 16:33 says: 'In this world you will have trouble. But take heart! I have overcome the world!'

Care for all living things

> **Read Exodus 23:10–12**
>
> *But during the seventh year let the land lie unplowed and unused. Then the poor among your people may get food from it, and the wild animals may eat what is left. Do the same with your vineyard and your olive grove.*
>
> (verse 11, NIV)

Our church runs a community garden in its grounds. It's used for building relationships and growing seasonal food that is distributed throughout the community. Local organisations and schools use it to teach horticulture and how to grow (and cook) healthy, seasonal vegetables.

Community gardens are a great place for ministry and mission. They have a positive effect on people's physical and mental health, promoting community cohesion. Our local GP surgery 'socially prescribes' people to the garden, in tandem with any medication they need.

A key to our relationship with all creation is to remember that it all belongs to Yahweh. The people of Israel experience the reality of God's covenant through Yahweh's provision of the land and its creatures. When they are out of kilter with it there are very real consequences (Numbers 16:31–35).

The covenantal 'rhythm' includes a year of 'jubilee' – a sabbath for the land, when it can rest and lie fallow. A time to celebrate its fruitfulness, but also to encourage others to make use of it too! Verse 11 implies that this practice was to be extended to all assets.

How we relate to creation is now defined by our new covenant in and through Jesus Christ. I hope that this week has been a helpful and fun reminder of how the care of all living things, and our relationship with the world, is entirely Christian. As we pray 'your kingdom come' we remember that this is where God's kingdom is coming, 'on earth as in heaven'. Join me in leaving it in a better shape than we found it!

† Lord of the land, sky and sea, you have given us your creation to tend and care for. Transform our relationship with your world, that we would use it to care for all living things. Amen

For further thought

Have you ever considered where you might transform a space near you for the good of creation and your community?

Readings from Revelation

1 An open door into heaven

Notes by **Eve Parker**

Eve is a Postdoctoral Research Associate at Durham University, focusing on inclusion and diversity in Theological Education. She holds a PhD from St Andrews University, Scotland, that explored a Christian theology with sacred sex workers in South India. She has previously worked for the Council for World Mission and the United Reformed Church, and is passionate about intercultural ministries and liberationist theologies. She is married to James, and they have two children, Minerva and Iris. Eve has used the NRSVA and NIVUK for these notes.

Sunday 8 May
Witnessing as solidarity

Read Revelation 1:1–3

Blessed is the one who reads aloud the words of the prophecy, and blessed are those who hear and who keep what is written in it; for the time is near.

(verse 3, NRSVA)

The book of Revelation is challenging; it presents us with an apocalyptic vision from John of Patmos – a prophet in exile who speaks out against the oppressive earthly empire under which he exists. At the time of John's revelation in Asia Minor, the Roman state ruled, the emperor himself was given divine status, and the political, military, religious and economic power of Rome meant that anyone who disobeyed the state's authority was in danger. Despite this, John calls on all who hear and read his prophecy to be true witnesses to the Word that opposes the rule of Rome.

To be a witness means to live in the light of Jesus Christ, the ultimate witness, whose testimony of faith led to his death on the cross. Witnessing means listening to the voices that have been marginalised by earthly empires, the poor, the oppressed, those excluded and silenced by the dominant system. Today, this means listening to the cries of the refugees escaping war and persecution. It means hearing the struggles of the poor and challenging the consciences of those within the system to acknowledge the atrocities of systemic greed and state violence. Witnessing demands solidarity in the struggle for liberation.

† God, let us bear witness to the prophets who have been silenced by earthly empires, and speak out in solidarity with the downtrodden.

Monday 9 May
God's chosen at the throne

Read Revelation 4:1–11

And whenever the living creatures give glory and honour and thanks to the one who is seated on the throne, who lives for ever and ever, the twenty-four elders fall before the one who is seated on the throne … they cast their crowns before the throne, singing.

(part of verses 9–10, NRSVA)

When I teach my students about the book of Revelation, I begin by playing the spirituals, songs sung by African American slaves that offer profound theological insights into the scriptures and speak from the experiences of those who have been downtrodden by the evils of racism and slavery, yet live in hope of the promised land. 'Deep River', is one such spiritual that speaks to Revelation 4:

> *That promised land, where all is peace?*
> *Walk into heaven, and take my seat*
> *And cast my crown at Jesus' feet*

In Revelation 4:1–11, John envisions the divine throne and heavenly realm, where the living creatures and the twenty-four elders, those who are God's chosen people, belong to God's throne and will go on to commission and deliver God's judgement. The song of the slaves envisions a heavenly throne, where they are the elders who cast their crowns at the feet of Christ, and it is they who go on to impose God's judgement on those who have sinned so gravely in the human world. Unlike those who have ruled on earth, the one who is seated on the throne is worthy 'to receive glory and honour and power' (Revelation 4:11). The spirituals uncover the prophetic hope of John's revelation that speaks to the struggles and suffering of the people on earth who exist at the underside of earthly empires, including those who have experienced the atrocities of racism, and envisions a world that can be realised today – where white supremacy is conquered through resistance and solidarity.

† May we resist tyranny in all of its forms. May we glorify the worthy one and call out the oppressor. May we sing in hope and give thanks to the one seated on the throne.

For further thought

What role do the tyrants of history and today play in how we understand scripture?

A kin-dom of every tribe

Readings from Revelation – 1 An open door into heaven

Read Revelation 5:1–14

You are worthy to take the scroll and to open its seals, for you were slaughtered and by your blood you ransomed for God saints from every tribe and language and people and nation; you have made them to be a kingdom and priests serving our God.

(part of verses 9–10, NRSVA)

Earthly empires often profess exclusivist nationalist ideologies that create cultures of belonging and *un-belonging*, where 'tribes' of people are segregated, marginalised and oppressed, for their identity, ethnicity, language, class and sexuality. At the heart of such social and political systems is the desire to have and maintain power – power that operates in the interest of the elites. Today such power rests in the hands of the wealthy nations and the free-market economy, where there exists a great divide between the rich and the poor. Such powers control access to basic resources such as healthcare, housing, food and clean water – restricted to certain 'tribes' and 'people'.

In contrast to such earthly kingdoms, John witnesses a kingdom to come that is made up of 'saints from every tribe and language and people and nation'. Instead of a kingdom of inequality, John's vision portrays an intercultural *kin-dom*, of diverse tribes, languages and people. Together with the heavenly creatures, they worship the slaughtered Lamb who is worthy to take the scroll and, as we read on in Revelation, the content of the scroll exposes God's plan unfolding. It is revealed that it is the Lamb – not the unjust rulers on earth – who holds ultimate power and who 'will reign on earth' (5:10). The Lamb is Jesus, who was slaughtered by the Romans, and it is Jesus who holds the plan of God, the plan that exposes the myth of Rome's unlimited power and ultimately the downfall of Rome. The power rests with God on the heavenly throne and the Lamb who reveals the eternal intercultural kin-dom.

† Lamb of God, may we find comfort and strength in the promise of your kingdom to come.

For further thought

How can we work toward creating inclusive kin-doms in the here and now?

The four horsemen

Read Revelation 6:1–11

I heard the voice of the fourth living creature call out, 'Come!' I looked and there was a pale green horse! Its rider's name was Death, and Hades followed with him; they were given authority over a fourth of the earth, to kill with sword, famine, and pestilence.

(part of verses 7–8, NRSVA)

The opening of the seals leads to the unfolding of God's judgement and, in the apocalyptic scenes that follow, John reveals that there will be four horsemen unleashed upon the world – said to symbolise religion, war, famine and death. Such imagery is shocking and terrifying to the reader, especially when a world of famine, war, religious persecution and death are realities experienced by *others* in distant lands. Yet when such texts are read in the context of a refugee camp where families have escaped brutal sectarian conflict, been displaced from their homes and met with violence, famine and ultimately the constant fear of death, then the four horsemen have already been unleashed, only they have not been sent by God but by humanity. The powerful nations, though, often turn a blind eye to such struggles; like Rome, they seek to portray an illusion of peace, stability and prosperity, while masking the injustices of a system of inequality. So, they turn away the boats of refugees that arrive on the beaches and incite hatred through propaganda and policy.

In contrast, God hears the cries of the oppressed, saying, 'how long will it be before you judge and avenge our blood on the inhabitants of the earth?' (verse 10). Unlike the leaders on earth, God 'robes' (verse 11) and comforts those who have suffered, and in response to the suffering comes the promise that justice will be delivered.

† Lord, approximately 700 million people are going hungry, wars are being fought in the name of religion, pandemics of inequality are running rampage, help us to robe and comfort the suffering.

For further thought

What can we do to better educate ourselves about those who suffer from religious violence, war and famine?

May

Readings from Revelation – 1 An open door into heaven

Thursday 12 May
Quenching thirst with the water of life

Read Revelation 7:1–17

*They will hunger no more, and thirst no more; the sun will not strike
them … for the Lamb at the centre of the throne will be their shepherd,
and he will guide them to springs of the water of life, and God will wipe
away every tear from their eyes.*

(part of verses 16–17, NRSVA)

Food poverty and lack of access to clean water is a reality faced by
hundreds of millions of people worldwide today. As a consequence
of climate change, water is scarce for many of the most vulnerable
communities, due to rising temperatures, droughts and less
predictable weather conditions much of the world's population is
suffering from thirst and lack of sanitation. Water is also being used
as a weapon of war, with more powerful nation states restricting
access to water supplies, forcing people to die of thirst or resulting
in the displacement of entire communities.

In Revelation 7, John's vision offers hope for those who have
suffered from such realities. There is the promise of something
better to come, where those who have been oppressed will hunger
and thirst no more. John envisages a heaven in which the thirst
of those who have 'come out of the great ordeal' (verse 14) will
be quenched, they will be guided to the 'water of life', water that
flows from 'the throne of God and of the Lamb' (Revelation 22:1),
that offers 'eternal life' (John 4:14). The number of people who are
seen rejoicing before the throne of God is great, though they have
suffered immensely through times of persecution, their faith was
strong, and from the wrath of God they have been delivered to a
place of comfort, where their tears will be wiped away. Those who
had no water will thirst no more, the Lamb that was slaughtered
will be their Shepherd, their cries that were silenced have been
heard by the One who will wipe away their tears.

† Lamb of God, may we journey with you through earthly tribulations to receive the
water from the spring of eternal life.

For further thought
Think of those who are forced to travel great distances for access
to water that should be a basic human right.

The burning of the earth

> **Read Revelation 8:1–13**
>
> *The first angel blew his trumpet, and there came hail and fire, mixed with blood, and they were hurled to the earth; and a third of the earth was burned up, and a third of the trees were burned up, and all green grass was burned up.*
>
> (verse 7, NRSVA)

Before the great tribulation is silence 'for about half an hour' (verse 1), followed by incense offered with the prayers of the saints (verse 4) and suddenly a scene of intercession becomes one of God's judgement being delivered, as the angel throws the censer of fire from the altar to the earth and the world is hit with raging storms and terrifying scenes of destruction, blood, fire and violence. But the violence that unfolds from the trumpets is unleashed against the environment, as the earth, trees and grass are burned up. The imagery in the vision brings to mind the extent to which the earth's resources are currently being destroyed as a result of the climate crisis.

Humankind's overconsumption has cost the earth greatly, as our consumerist lifestyles are unsustainable and have wreaked havoc on the ecosystem. Consequently, the world is warming at an alarming rate, we are experiencing more heat waves and wildfires, and the World Health Organisation has declared climate change as the greatest threat to health in the twenty-first century.

The Roman Empire, as with the powerful nations of today, was also guilty of abusing the natural resources of the world. Revelation critiques Rome's belief that it rules the cosmos and can freely exploit earthly resources, by exposing the ways in which God, humanity and the environment are all connected. Further revealing that it is not humanity that has power over the universe but God, who created all things, and humanity must recognise that we are inseparable from nature. Our survival depends on how we treat the planet which we have already damaged extensively.

† God of the universe, who created all things, may we do better at caring for the world around us.

For further thought

Reducing household waste and energy is one way to live a more sustainable lifestyle and help protect the planet.

May

Readings from Revelation – 1 An open door into heaven

Saturday 14 May
Eternal life

Read Revelation 12:1–17

She gave birth to a son, a male child, who 'will rule all the nations with an iron sceptre'. And her child was snatched up to God and to his throne. The woman fled into the wilderness to a place prepared for her by God...

(verse 5–6a, NIVUK)

The imagery of the nameless woman of Revelation 12 who is depicted as heavenly, appearing beneath the moon and clothed in the sun, is closely related to the mythology of the goddess Roma, of the Roman imperial regime who was depicted in a similar light. Yet, in contrast to the false myths of Rome, John's vision is said to be of the mother of Christ, clothed in heavenly sun, who gives birth to the one who will rule. The image stands in stark contrast with another woman described in Revelation 17, as the 'mother of prostitutes' who is clothed in earthly extravagance, said to drink the blood of martyrs and is referred to as 'Babylon'. Her fate is one of eternal suffering in contrast to that of the woman of Revelation 12, who after giving birth, is exiled to the wilderness, where a dragon comes for her and sends a great flood from his mouth to destroy her, yet the earth saves her and swallows up the flood.

The woman is said to be symbolic of the faithful on earth whom God will ultimately save. However, what is made apparent is how difficult faith can be: the woman gives birth in pain, she has her son taken from her to be kept at the throne of God, and is sent to the desert in exile where she is further tormented. She endures significant suffering, and yet throughout her struggles remains faithful. John wants his readers to know that though there may be great suffering on earth, God will reward the faithful with eternal life.

† God in heaven, let me be truthful in my endeavours and faithfully serve you no matter what trials await.

For further thought

How can we help comfort those who are struggling and support those who are afraid in the 'wilderness'?

Readings from Revelation

2 A new heaven and a new earth

Notes by **Alesana Fosi Pala'amo**

For Alesana's biography, see p. 16. Alesana has used the NRSV for these notes.

Sunday 15 May
Unmarked by the beast

Read Revelation 13:1–18

Also it causes all, both small and great, both rich and poor, both free and slave, to be marked on the right hand or the forehead, so that no one can buy or sell who does not have the mark.

(verses 16–17a)

Today's reading reveals a vision of two beasts as witnessed by John the Apostle. The first beast, described as a seven-headed creature, symbolises for us today mighty and great secular powers – including greed, wealth, power – all things that people worship and follow that are not Christ-centred. The second beast represents all false teachings that manipulate God's faithful away from him. In the vision, the mark of the beast is found on the right hand or the forehead with the name of the beast or the number of its name – 666. I propose that the mark of the beast for us today has been digitalised, where most of humankind are connected to each other in the virtual and online world.

This week, I will present blueprint markers for a new heaven and a new earth, proposed by our readings. Beginning with today's passage, the first blueprint marker is to be unmarked by the beast. Although we are more likely to be connected in the virtual world through different technologies, it is still possible to be unmarked by the beast. Christ has marked us with his blood as the sacrificial Lamb, so that we can overpower all beasts that we encounter.

† Lord God, thank you for marking us with the blood of Christ who has saved us from our sins through his death and resurrection. Amene

Monday 16 May
Babylon the great is grounded

Read Revelation 17:1–18

They will make war on the Lamb, and the Lamb will conquer them, for he is Lord of lords and King of kings, and those with him are called and chosen and faithful.

(verse 14)

The second blueprint marker for a new heaven and a new earth is where the great and small nations of the world are considered alike. Although there are differences in land masses and populations for such nations, all nations are aligned to the same fate. Such a time was the Covid-19 coronavirus pandemic that impacted the world throughout 2020 and 2021. It became a time when all nations great and small were grounded on many levels due to the pandemic. International travel was grounded for all nations, where even domestic borders were closed. Large global companies and industries were grounded as the workforce became infected and lockdowns restricted employment. Babylon the great was grounded – no more great nations, no amount of wealth could buy a way out of the pandemic. All nations great and small were subjected to the same pandemic. It became a time when all nations needed to unify, having the great nations lead the way with access to resources and data, to develop a vaccine and re-start the world toward recovery and regeneration.

Today's reading describes how the great secular nation identified as Babylon that symbolised the Roman Empire of its time, was grounded. With all its worldly desires and raging war against Christ as the sin-city, such a place is compared to being a great harlot of immoral living and unethical lifestyles. A new heaven and new earth is where there is no more sin, where Christ has conquered all evil and the faithful chosen are without blemish and exalted by the blood of the sacrificial Lamb.

† Our powerful and supreme God, help the fallen world rise above sin and unnecessary overconsumption to be satisfied with lesser, in your mercy and through your providence. Amene

For further thought

Live to work or work to live? Is our living all about working, or do we work just enough to live? The latter allows rest.

Tuesday 17 May
Hallelujah! An eternal union!

Read Revelation 19:1–16

And the angel said to me, 'Write this: Blessed are those who are invited to the marriage supper of the Lamb.' And he said to me, 'These are true words of God.'

(verse 9)

The third blueprint marker for a new heaven and a new earth is an invitation to fellowship with the Lord for eternity. The first part of today's reading is where John the Apostle hears the content of his vision. One of the expressions he hears loudly as voiced by a great multitude is 'Hallelujah', the Hebrew term for 'Praise the Lord', used four times here in the book of Revelation and no other place in the New Testament. As a word translated into all languages such as 'Alleluia' in Greek and 'Aleluia' in Samoan, praising the Lord here is for salvation and giving glory and power to God, for he has passed judgement upon Babylon. Symbolic of the ruling Roman Empire of the time, Babylon had fallen, a valid reason for exalting God.

'Hallelujah' is heard again at the proclamation of the marriage between Christ the Lamb and the church, his bride, also understood as the new Jerusalem. The invitation disclosed is a blessing that only the faithful will receive. Being invited to any event is great, for it shows that one's inclusion and participation in the event is valued. To be invited to the divine marriage between Christ and the church is an incomparable blessing, since one who accepts the invitation shares in the eternal nature of this union.

The second part of today's reading is where John sees the content of his vision. This again is reason to praise the Lord, for Christ the rider on the white horse as the King of kings and Lord of lords has reigned victoriously over evil.

† Christ our Redeemer, thank you for being the rider on the white horse and overcoming all the evil beasts in our lives. Amene

For further thought

Hallelujah reminds us – like many songs that share the same title – to praise our Lord, for all that he continues to do for us.

Readings from Revelation – 2 A new heaven and a new earth

Wednesday 18 May
A new heaven-earth

Read Revelation 21:1–14

See, the home of God is among mortals. He will dwell with them; they will be his peoples, and God himself will be with them … Death will be no more; mourning and crying and pain will be no more, for the first things have passed away.

(part of verses 3–4)

John the Apostle continues to see and hear the contents of his visions. Today's reading describes a vision about a new heaven and a new earth, specifically, the new holy city, the new Jerusalem. As the centre-point of readings for this week, the fourth blueprint marker for a new heaven and a new earth is what I propose to be called a new heaven-earth.

This new heaven-earth has properties from both realms – heaven and earth. As a new heaven, the holy city, the new Jerusalem comes down out of heaven and becomes the new dwelling place for God. As a new earth, the worldly Jerusalem of old is now a new holy city measured with its city gates from east, north, south and west, and its city wall of twelve foundations of the twelve apostles.

There is hope for the faithful Christian: beyond the world we live on earth, there are blessings awaiting us in a new heaven-earth. For us to realise such beauty and joy, we have to live through this life and realise that there is much more that awaits us. The struggles, pain, and hurt will be no more, as God dwells with his people in a new heaven-earth and suffering on all levels will be of the past. There will be no more crying, no more feeling sad or overwhelmed, and no more death; we will enjoy living with God dwelling among us in a new heaven-earth.

† O God, thank you for a new heaven-earth that supersedes the current world we live. Continue to teach us to conduct our lives today to demonstrate that our hearts have accepted you as Lord. Amene

For further thought

Do we live only for the now forgetting a new heaven-earth that God has prepared for us all to inherit through faith in Christ?

Thursday 19 May
Open borders

Read Revelation 21:15–27

Its gates will never be shut by day – and there will be no night there.

(verse 25)

The fifth blueprint marker for a new heaven-earth from today's reading is open borders. Due to the Covid-19 pandemic, 'open borders' was a status many nations required for economic recovery, yet the health and safety of the nation took priority. Samoa closed its international borders early into the pandemic, a government strategy that may have contributed to Samoa's status of no positive Covid-19 cases for the most part of 2020. Many Samoan nationals remained abroad due to international border lockdowns, with several lobbying groups demanding open borders for repatriation flights of returning Samoan citizens. Once the Samoan borders were relaxed and repatriation flights began, Samoa realised its first two positive Covid-19 cases late into the year.

Open borders to a new heaven-earth means that the opportunity is open for all regardless of nationality, age, gender and economic, political and social standings in society, to the new holy city, the new Jerusalem. The glamour and splendour of the new holy city is presented with all its precious stones, jewels, city gates and wall. There are some underlying blessings of this new holy city that set it apart from any other city: the gates are open continuously, there is no darkness as continuous light emanates from the glory of God, there is nothing false or evil, and the only temple in the city is God and the Lamb. Although there are open borders, the only valid entry into the new holy city is to be written in the Lamb's book of life – through accepting Jesus Christ into one's life as Lord and Saviour.

† Lord God, thank you for the opportunity to dwell in your glory for eternity. May our hearts be open in accepting Christ as our Saviour. Amene

For further thought
The chance to rejoice in God's grace eternally is there for our taking; we just need to reach out and accept Jesus Christ as Lord.

Friday 20 May
River of life and healing

Read Revelation 22:1–7

On either side of the river is the tree of life with its twelve kinds of fruit, producing its fruit each month; and the leaves of the tree are for the healing of the nations.

(verse 2b)

The sixth blueprint marker for a new heaven-earth is the river of life and healing. Rivers, streams and creeks are all bodies of water that flow, with rivers being the largest, creeks the smallest and streams in between. All three provide life to their surroundings and flow downwards from elevated positions. Rivers eventually become outlets to the various seas around the world. When my family and I lived at the Protestant Theological University in Kampen, The Netherlands, I recall the Ijssel River that flowed through the city as a source of life along its river banks. I often noticed fishers cast their rods along the river, and the abundant vegetation near the water. Families enjoyed picnics and swimming during the summer months, and in winter of that year, the surface of the Ijssel River froze and some local youth ice-skated across the river.

The river from the vision of today's reading is like no other, with its source originating from the throne of God and Christ the Lamb. The river runs in the middle of a new heaven-earth, and flows toward and into eternal life. The new holy city has built itself around the river that gives life and heals the broken world, affected by disease, discrimination, poverty, political unrest, natural disasters and abuse in its physical, mental and emotional forms. The tree of life found on either side of the river of life and healing becomes a beacon of hope, with leaves that heal the broken world from all its pain. The new heaven-earth never sees night or evil, and God as light shines forever.

† O God, thank you for being our source of life and healing from all the pains of this world, like a river that flows from your glory to everlasting life. Amene

For further thought

Do we build our lives around worldly things that come to pass, or the river of life and healing that begins from and continues to God?

Saturday 21 May
Alpha and Omega

Read Revelation 22:8–21

I am the Alpha and the Omega, the first and the last, the beginning and the end.

(verse 13)

Alpha and Omega remind us today that all things begin from and return to God. As the first and last alphabet letters respectively of the original Greek language in which the New Testament was written, Alpha and Omega represent the beginning and the end. From today's reading, the seventh and final blueprint marker for this week of a new heaven-earth is our Lord Jesus as the Alpha and Omega, the beginning and end of all things. The number seven is important in this final book of the Bible – used 52 times and understood as a godly number symbolic of completeness. In the Genesis creation story, God created all things within six days and on the seventh day, God rested as creation was complete.

Jesus Christ as the beginning means that once the person has accepted Jesus as Lord, one becomes a new creation of righteous living worthy to honour God. Jesus Christ as the end means that when one's life journey comes to its end through death, the faithful Christian is completed and returns to God. The time in-between – from the beginning and the end for the faithful believer – is where the devoted Christian prepares for Jesus' return. We do so by enjoying and appreciating the life that God has gifted us, acknowledging God and all his abundant blessings. When our life journey becomes complete at its end and we return to God, he allows us rest from this world into the new heaven-earth that he has prepared for us. Lord Jesus as Alpha and Omega, is our beginning and our end, and inspires our lifetime in-between.

† Our loving God, thank you for creating us in your likeness. May our lives reflect your love as we prepare to join you in your everlasting kingdom, a new heaven-earth that awaits us. Amene

For further thought
Let us live in the world today by sharing the love of God that embraces us and know that God awaits us with love in eternity.

May

Readings from Revelation – 2 A new heaven and a new earth

The Bible's divine body imagery

1 Breath

Notes by **Erice Fairbrother**

 Erice is an Anglican priest and Associate of the Order of the Holy Cross in Aotearoa, New Zealand. She writes and leads meditations drawing on New Zealand voices and imagery, encouraging a spirituality that enables God to be heard in the culture, language, and accents of her own country. She is a publisher and a poet who is passionate about supporting emerging voices in her community and through creative writing. Erice has used the NRSVA in these notes.

Sunday 22 May
Renewing the earth

Read Psalm 104:24–30

The earth is full of your creatures ... living things both small and great ... When you send forth your spirit, they are created; and you renew the face of the ground.

(part of verses 24–25 and 30)

From time to time, on the shores of New Zealand, whale strandings occur. Beautiful, strong creatures suddenly vulnerable and in need of rescue. People spend hours with them until they can be guided back out to sea and survive. Each time strandings happen, we see anew an outpouring of respect for life and for the part they play in creation.

To be part of 'renewing' God's earth and all the creatures in it has become an imperative that nations everywhere are having to respond to – a work that for us as Christians is about participating in the work of saving this planet which God has made and in which we are called to ensure it survives human abuse and neglect. The Hebrew scriptures this week portray the earth as embodying images of God – in tangible forms of breath, of creating life, of discernible presence and divine vulnerability. As we meditate on them, may we find the same dedication as those who care for the whales – being alongside God's creation until the face of God's earth is renewed and rebirthed.

† Lord, help us to see the earth as an expression of who you are. Let it awaken in us a more urgent care for our vulnerable and fragile creation.

Life of God's life, breath of God's breath

Read Genesis 2:4b–9, 18–22

Then the Lord God formed the man from the dust of the ground, and breathed into his nostrils the breath of life; and the man became a living being ... And the rib that the Lord God had taken from the man he made into a woman ...Then the man said, 'This is at last bone of my bones and flesh of my flesh'.

(parts of verses 7 and 22–23)

Local poets gather every month to read their work and encourage each other to develop their talent. Recently a poet suggested that when poems are presented in written form, they are just words 'dead' on a page. He likened poems in books as 'trapped' and unable to communicate deeper meaning. He, like many in our group, 'reads' his poems without paper or book in his hands, and for him only performance poetry is authentic. What he was overlooking was the power of words to transform and be transformed, when a reader takes them, and in reading breathes new life into them.

I remember sitting with my mother who was dying. Although I had been told that she was unable to hear or respond, during my visits I would read aloud her favourite psalms. It was a real joy when I heard her begin to complete a verse whenever I stopped for a moment. The psalms were inaccessible to her in her prayer book, but as I breathed them into speech, they became living words calling a deep responsiveness from her.

Did God experience a similar joy when he breathed his breath into the earth creature he had made, creating 'a living being'? There is a sense of joy in the response of the man to the woman God makes, when he recognises her as being of his own form and flesh. We too can know that joy as we give form and breath to God's presence in our world, when we seek, through word and action, to make God's justice and peace recognisable on earth.

† Begin your prayer times this week with a few moments of simply breathing. Breathe in and out, feeling the gift of breath. Notice how it settles your body and brings peace in your soul.

For further thought

Think of a time when you have been to a performance you knew well and experienced anew. What brought it alive differently for you?

The God who knits and weaves

Read Psalm 139:13–18

For it was you who formed my inward parts: you knit me together in my mother's womb. I praise you, for I am fearfully and wonderfully made ... My frame was not hidden from you, when I was being made in secret, intricately woven in the depths of the earth.

(part of verses 13–15)

On entering our Anglican Cathedral in Napier, visitors pass a table displaying beautifully knitted garments and shawls. Closer inspection shows that they are there to be blessed during a morning liturgy once a month. The garments include tiny baby clothes and soft warm beanies, each one knitted by women caring for the needs of vulnerable newborns in our hospitals and community. There are larger coloured shawls which are also given out to older worshippers to add extra warmth when they come to pray during our colder months. In other churches in New Zealand, a visitor may find small woven baskets – tiny portable cots for new babies to be kept close to their parents; including being crafted to be safe enough for mother and child to lie close together in the night. Lovingly woven in Maori communities, these too are blessed for the holy work of caring for the littlest among us.

These works of human hands present us with a beautiful metaphor for the intimate, caring and creative love of God. Feminine imagery of God in the Hebrew scriptures, as captured in today's psalm, reminds us that this too is part of God's nature. Like the women who meet to knit for vulnerable babies, God knits us together in our mother's womb and safely weaves us into being. This is a God who looks – watching as a mother watches, as we are formed and given life. Such holy touch and craft reveal God as one who is intimate and active in our lives. The psalmist is astounded as he contemplates God in this way.

† Give thanks for someone who has nurtured and cared for you. Give thanks that they were able to be like God for you in those times.

For further thought

The psalmist is astounded by God's work. What do you find most astounding about God?

May

The Bible's divine body imagery – 1 Breath

Wednesday 25 May
A God with ears

Read Exodus 2:23–25

Out of the slavery their cry for help rose up to God. God heard their groaning, and ... took notice of them.

(parts of verses 23–25)

As a teacher some years ago now, I would often find myself surrounded by a group of excited children, all bursting to respond to something that I might have just asked. How often I would find myself saying, 'I can only listen to one of you at a time!' As I write this reflection today, I am aware that there is a similar clamour for my attention – and indeed calling for all of us to pay attention. This time, however, the clamour of voices is not bursting with excitement but, in contrast, are voices of concern and despair; voices of creation 'crying for help', voices of asylum seekers, of those without food or shelter, and voices from refugee camps. So many other voices from people and places of suffering. The luxury of being able to hear the cry of just one at a time is not possible.

Today we read of God hearing the groaning of the Israelites – a whole nation under oppression crying out in agony. God not only hears their cries but notices, that is, he is also responsive to the needs that reach his 'ears'. Our part in responding to great need is, at heart, a work of faith; faith that God still hears, still notices. Faith reminds us that even though issues threaten to overwhelm our world, it is still God's world and God still holds it in his hands. It is this faith that allows us to believe that even the smallest of responses we make, is to share with God in his work of renewing creation and making people whole.

† Pray that every prayer be an action and every action a prayer.

For further thought

Kindness is usually related to human relationships. How would being kind to the earth show we hear and are responsive to the groaning of God's creation?

Thursday 26 May (Ascension)
What are our eyes focused on?

> **Read Acts 1:1–11**
>
> *While he was going and they were gazing up toward heaven, suddenly two men in white robes stood by them. They said, 'Men of Galilee, why do you stand looking up toward heaven?'*
>
> (verses 10–11b)

It's a good question. This account of Jesus ascending to God is one that calls us to reflect. What might this ancient narrative be saying to us right now? In our own context? A context that has been hugely changed in the face of a deadly pandemic, alongside continuing global oppression, poverty, and inequality.

When someone we love or who has had an important role in our lives leaves for work, or travel or to live somewhere else, it is not always easy to let them go. Yet somehow the possibility they will be back or will be able to be contactable is a comforting thought. When New Zealand went into lockdown in 2020, our borders were closed. For me, with close family and young grandchildren living overseas, the impact slowly took effect. I realised I no longer had the certainty that we would meet again. National lockdown eased but our border closures didn't. Gradually, I realised I had to learn to relate differently, to find a different way of continuing my close, intimate relationships – one that didn't depend on physical togetherness whether in joy or in sadness.

What do we look for at such times? Do we focus on what was, or do we have faith enough to shift our focus to where God is with us in present reality? This is the faith the men in white called the disciples to. A faith-relationship embodied, able to be seen and lived as Christ had lived it physically with them; a call to a new kind of holy relationship focused in this earthly life whatever complexities emerge.

† Our Father in heaven – your will be done on earth as it is in heaven.

For further thought

Take this week to reflect on where and at what times you have had to adjust the lens of your faith to find new ways of being with God, with others.

God sits

Read Psalm 47

God is king over the nations; God sits on his holy throne.

(verse 8)

Some of my fondest memories from my time as a theological student are around the evening lectures with our New Testament teacher. A Catholic priest and revered scholar, he would arrive – often without notes – and, sitting down in front of us, begin to teach. His formal instruction on the New Testament narratives were often illustrated from his own experiences of travelling around the Middle East as a young seminarian. Yet the remaining impression I have of him is the peace that surrounded him. He never stood to teach, he sat in front of us and yet was totally connected to us. From the way he came into the room to his unhurried way of seating himself, he communicated a deep sense of peace. It drew a response of great respect from us, his students.

There is something about being seated. It can invite a sense of drawing near, closeness. The psalmist describes God seated before his people, letting them into his holy space and making his presence accessible, a presence evoking thanksgiving and praise. Sitting is an act that is stilling, calming, often communicating a sense of peaceful confidence. In a world where peace is not the norm, our quiet stillness can communicate much about the peace that God alone can give. I have a friend who sits with the very ill in a local hospice where she offers, in a silent wordless presence, the peace and reassurance of God's love to the dying. There are many ways to be present. Psalm 47 suggests that to sit with others can be as powerful as words.

† Pray for wisdom to know when to speak and when to be still.

For further thought

Does the gospel depend on our words or our presence? Or is it about a balance we need to pursue more intentionally?

May

The Bible's divine body imagery – 1 Breath

Saturday 28 May
Awesome God

Read Psalm 115:1–11

You who fear the Lord, trust in the Lord! He is their help and their shield.

(verse 11)

In this, our last reading for the week, we meet God as one in whom we can stand in awe. Where we have explored images of God that we can relate to; a God who knits, who sits, who weaves, who breathes, who listens and lives, present and active with us and for us, we now read of God who is also beyond the limits of our own lives. God is life itself. God does not put 'fear' into us – rather our God evokes awe as we experience his work and creative action in our lives. We truly are the work of God's hands and because of that he commits to being the source of our protection and our shield.

In contrast, in verses 4 to 8, the psalmist describes the folly of putting faith in things. Contemporary desires for accumulating wealth in all its forms or spending excessively on things are wonderfully imaged in the description of the gods that are the work of human hands. In this twenty-first century, however, idols can be more subtle. It can be hard to identify where they might be and the part they might play in our lives. After all, some possessions are necessary, others give genuine pleasure, and still other possessions like money can enable us to address injustice and other pressing issues that threaten our lives and our world.

Trust is a great way of measuring modern idolatry. The psalm helps us as, in verse 11, we read: 'trust in the Lord' – a trust in which we encounter the living God. Eternally trustworthy. Truly awesome!

† Pray that our trust may be strengthened, our sense of awe and holy fear never diminished.

For further thought

What do I trust the most when I am happy? Where do I invest my trust when I am not in a good space?

The Bible's divine body imagery

2 Tears

Notes by Kristina **Andréasson**

 Kristina was ordained priest in the Church of Sweden in 2007. She worked in south Sweden before she moved to work for the Swedish Church in London in 2014. In 2019, she started serving in the Church of England as Associate Vicar of St John's Wood Church in London. To her, the many images of God in the Bible tell us how God is always more, but images can also help us feel closer to God, maybe especially in hurt and pain. Kristina has used the NRSVA for these notes.

Sunday 29 May
God's robe fills the earth

Read Isaiah 6:1–5

In the year that King Uzziah died, I saw the Lord sitting on a throne, high and lofty; and the hem of his robe filled the temple. Seraphs were in attendance above him.

(verses 1–2a)

On a Sunday in late May in London, the parks will normally be crowded with people, especially if the sun is shining. Some of the parks are also filled with all kinds of flowers at this time of year making a vibrant, colourful scene, everywhere you look.

In Isaiah's vision, the hem of God's robe filled the temple, as if to say that not a spot or corner of the temple floor was missed by God's robe. What if God's robe looked like the flowers filling the park on a sunshiny day in London?

Isaiah saw God on a throne. Yet he doesn't describe what God looked like. Maybe no words could do God justice. Maybe it is for you and me to imagine the vision of God on the throne. But we get to hear about the robe, God's glory filling the earth.

There are so many people in the London parks in summer, and like the hem of a robe, the smallest flower touches each differently depending on how they feel. I imagine a robe of summer flowers growing and spreading, making its way all over earth, not missing a single spot or corner, reaching all people, whoever they are, whatever they feel of joy or sadness.

† God of life, let us sense your presence in joy and in sadness, even if just the hem of your robe. Amen

God weeps, with us and for us

Read Jeremiah 8:22–9:11

*O that my head were a spring of water, and my eyes a fountain of tears,
so that I might weep day and night for the slain of my poor people!*

(verse 1)

He was very tall, and in his old age he still had wide shoulders and a strong posture. I remember him well, just outside the chapel. He took his hand and stroked my cheek. His hand felt so big and strong, as if to speak of many years of hard work and labour.

One could say that I had just taken a funeral for a very old person who had passed away peacefully. But one could also say that we just had a funeral for that man's little brother. The old man said nothing but stroked my cheek as tears were running down his face. The memory has remained with me, as an image of how much love there is in tears.

Like his, tears can speak of the love we carry for someone else. Other times tears can also say something about self-love, when we ourselves have been hurt.

The old man looked as if his life story could speak of strength in many ways. But when he was saying goodbye to his little brother and allowed his tears to fall, maybe he wasn't filled with strength, but filled with love. We might not feel like our strongest self when tears are falling, but it is human to weep, and it is human to be weak sometimes.

When weeping, some strength might be gone, but love is not gone. Almighty God weeps with us, and weeps for us when we can't, or won't. A God who weeps might not be an image that speaks of strength, but it does certainly speak of a love that is still alive.

† God of life, be close when I am hurting, until the very last tear. Be my fountain of tears when I can't cry myself. Fill me with love when I am weak. Amen

For further thought

God weeps. Does that clash with an image of God as almighty, or is it rather the opposite?

Tuesday 31 May
God looks with love

Read Psalm 33:6–22

The Lord looks down from heaven; he sees all humankind. From where he sits enthroned he watches all the inhabitants of the earth.

(verses 13–14)

There is a restaurant in London where you dine in complete darkness. You will have to feel your way on the table, and guess what it is you're eating. The waitresses and waiters have visual impairments.

Is it an intimidating thought that God sees *everything*, watches *all* humankind? Maybe, in one way, it could be – especially if seeing was all that God did.

When I return to my memories of the restaurant visit in complete darkness, I realise how those are different from other restaurant memories. I still remember the shape of the glass, the name of our waiter, which part of the plate that tasted the best. I also remember very clearly how I felt that day. I guess the waiter would be able speak about how you notice other things more when you can't see very well.

I believe that tells us something about in what way God watches us. God understands how our lives shape us. God remembers each and every one of us by name. God keeps in mind how different parts of the world, how different contexts play a part in who we are and what we do. God knows our feelings and counts them as important.

God sees every one of us, but not in an intimidating way, as God also notices those things that might get lost when we only look. God sees us all, but not in a supervising way that would create fear or shame. God watches us through loving eyes that take in consideration what might not be clear to our eyes.

† God of life, thank you for seeing the good that others might not see, and for seeing also hurt and pain that is covered up and hidden from the rest of the world. Amen

For further thought
If God watches us and sees every one of us, is there really anything that we can't talk to God about in our prayers?

Where is God's face?

> **Read Psalm 80:1–7**
>
> *Restore us, O God; let your face shine, that we may be saved.*
>
> (verse 3)

Do we ever feel God's face shine upon us? I think so – in those moments when it is like a ray of light reaches us, giving us some strength, and brightens us up within. I think it can sometimes be something so small as when you wake up one morning, heavy minded and not your happiest self, but then you pull away the curtain and the morning sun fills the room. It reaches your heart, and suddenly you hear the birds singing, despite everything. Another time it might be the opposite though, the bright warm morning sun clashes with the feelings you have within, it is simply too bright. Maybe then, God's shining face is more captured in the little cat, still curled up in bed, raising his head, squinting with his eyes, as if to say, 'No, it is not time to get up yet!'

Other days we might have to go outside and seek God's face. But there are rooms with no windows, homes without company, and it is not possible for all of us to open the door and go outside. Where is God's face then? Maybe God's face then is more to be found wounded on the cross, crying, 'Why have you forsaken me'? A wounded face letting us know that we are never alone.

But when we meet God's shining face, whether it is in the morning sun, a grumpy cat, or something else – let us treasure it, as I think it has the power to reflect on others, and someone else might also feel saved, even if only for a day.

† God of life, let your face shine, that me might be saved, if only to find the strength for one more step. Help us recognise your face in others. Amen

For further thought

When did you last see God's face? Could it be that we sometimes miss it?

God understands everybody

Read Isaiah 42:14–17

For a long time I have held my peace, I have kept still and restrained myself; now I will cry out like a woman in labour, I will gasp and pant.

(verse 14)

If you are a priest serving the Church of Sweden, you will most likely have many confirmation classes and be a part of your church's youth group. They are so many – the teenagers and young adults I've met throughout the years.

I have often told them about the image of God crying out like a woman in labour. It is an unexpected image of God and therefore so important. Not all of us will experience labour but imagine what the image can do when it is given to a group of teenage girls, or young female adults. God knows the physical pain of labour. That must mean that God knows what it is to have a female body.

Whatever you feel about yourself, body and soul, as a young female, you can talk to God about it. God also understands that. God cries out in labour. It is so important as it reminds us that if God can do that, then God can also see and understand the wounds behind every single #MeToo.

And of course, telling youth groups about this image, I believe it can be something for the teenage boys and young men to hear as well. Let us return to Isaiah's vision and think of what image of God we put on that throne. If that image somehow feels far away from our own body and soul, then God crying out in labour reminds us that God is more than just one image. Whatever scars or worries our souls and bodies might carry, God will understand. We can share it with God.

† God of life, you have created me and embrace me wholly. Let me know that there is no worry and no scar that you wouldn't understand. Help me be the one I truly am. Amen

For further thought

What is your image of God? Do you need more than one image to feel how God embraces you completely, body and soul?

June

The Bible's divine body imagery – 2 Tears

Friday 3 June
Our loving bond with God

Read Isaiah 49:13–18

Can a woman forget her nursing-child, or show no compassion for the child of her womb? Even these may forget, yet I will not forget you.

(verse 15)

Isn't it amazing those times when we feel like we bond or connect with someone? There might be those whom we've known for a long time that we share a special bond with. But we can also feel connection with someone we hardly know. Sometimes it's hard to explain why, and other times we can feel how we share a bond because of similar experiences, thoughts or interests. When a loving connection is there, I think we also have more of a will to understand that person.

God wants a loving bond with every one of us, and I think that is why we need many images of God. No image is ever full enough. But maybe even more important, I think it is different for each of us what image awakens the loving bond between ourselves and God. To some the image of God as a father speaks about a steadfast love. To someone else the image of God as mother does the same. I think they both fit on the throne in Isaiah's vision. Many images of God can coexist within us, so we can have many ways to find the loving link between ourselves and God.

When we feel like we bond or connect with someone, it is almost as if we feel like we are sharing something holy, and I think we are. It is like we experience a little bit of God's eternal love; the love that wants to understand, and will never forget us. God is there; in a mother's love for her child, and in many other relationships

† God of life, thank you for that nothing can separate us from your love. Help us trust your love, each new day. Amen

For further thought
Experiencing a loving bond can feel holy. How do we treat what is holy to us? Could that say something about God's love for you?

Saturday 4 June
In God's hand

Read Psalm 145:8–21

You open your hand, satisfying the desire of every living thing. The Lord is just in all his ways, and kind in all his doings. The Lord is near to all who call on him, to all who call on him in truth.

(verses 16–18)

A hand can protect and give comfort. A hand can create and direct. There is a sculpture made by the Swedish artist Carl Milles called, 'The hand of God', and I think it gives a beautiful image of what it can be to be in God's hand. The sculpture is a big hand lifted up, toward the sky. In the palm of the hand, a man is standing on his two feet, and it looks like he is finding his balance in the hand while he is also, at the same time, stretching himself to see maybe the world, his surroundings, what the future holds. That is one way to be in God's hand: to stand up, meet life and the future, while finding balance and strength in the palm of God's hand.

God is near, to all of us. Sometimes we might sense it as a protective or comforting hand when we somehow feel that we are not alone. We might pray that God's loving hand will be there to direct us into a path that is right for us. We might every now and then see traces of God's creative hand when we discover grace in the nature around us. But we can also remind ourselves how the source for strength and balance can be in God's hand.

The sculpture of a big hand lifted up. I like to think of it as a hand opened up to bless us. God is near, and we can stand up in God's hand, open to God's blessings when we meet the world and our future.

† God of life, be near with your loving hand. When we worry about what the future might hold, let us know that your hand is a source of strength to trust. Amen

For further thought

Does it matter from where we get our strength and balance? Is there a difference if God is our source of strength, or something else?

Being church

1 On the way

Notes by **Katie Miller**

Katie is an Ordained Pioneer Minister in the Church of England working in East London on the Becontree Estate, once considered the largest social housing estate in Europe. She has previously worked in communities of social housing in Speke, Liverpool and in Norwich. Prior to ordination, she worked both as a climate researcher, lecturing in environmental science, and as a theatre director, poet and playwright. She is married to Bill and they have three adult children. Katie has used the NRSVA for these notes.

Sunday 5 June (Pentecost)
Waiting

Read Acts 2:1–13

Amazed and astonished, they asked, 'Are not all these who are speaking Galileans? And how is it that we hear, each of us, in our own native language?'

(verses 7–8)

Living in East London, we are blessed with a very multi-cultural congregation. East London has always been a gateway for those newly settling in the United Kingdom. We rejoice in our particular congregation in members from many African and Eastern European nations. This adds depth and texture to our worship and, I would contend, gives us the best 'bring and share' lunches, as delicacies from all over the world are eaten alongside the biscuits and cheese sandwiches.

As we explore our theme of 'Being church' – and more specifically this week, being 'On the way', it is important to remember that the disciples were asked to wait for the Holy Spirit. Waiting is not always easy. We want to act, but waiting reminds us of our dependence on God. We cannot set out on the way without the Holy Spirit. And when the Spirit comes, as we see in this passage, each hears the good news in their own language. The uniqueness of each nation is celebrated. We are not first asked to become uniform, but God speaks to us in ways we will understand. We need to be on the way together, embracing and celebrating each other.

† Lord help us to wait to be filled with you and, as we go forward, may we go forward together to rejoice in the uniqueness of each of our brothers and sisters.

Monday 6 June
Twelve apostles again

Read Acts 1:12–24

Then they prayed and said, 'Lord, you know everyone's heart. Show us which one of these two you have chosen to take the place in this ministry and apostleship from which Judas turned aside to go to his own place.'

(verses 24–25)

Just on the edges of our parish, we have the West Ham United men's football team training ground. I often see a crowd of fans waiting at the gate for autographs as I sail past on the top of the number 5 red double decker bus. (I have never quite cured myself of the habit of wanting to sit on the top deck at the front of the bus – it gives such a great view.) The team is doing pretty well as I write this, in the top half of the Premier League. I don't pretend to be a football pundit, but I know that playing with ten men rather than eleven is not a good thing!

Being 'On the way' is about being a team. It about praying about each person and where they fit in the ministry. It's about going together. We need one another. We need each person in the role to which God has called them. We do that by each taking our role. The disciples here were a player down. Judas is described in these verses as turning aside to go to his own place. There is a great sadness in those words. The role he should have taken was important and he needed to be prayerfully replaced. We are on the way together. Everyone is needed including us.

† Thank you that you have called us each to a purpose in your kingdom. May we not turn aside to our own way but move forward together.

For further thought
Do I see myself as part of the team, a person who is needed?

Tuesday 7 June
New members

Read Acts 2:29–42

So those who welcomed his message were baptised, and that day about three thousand persons were added. They devoted themselves to the apostles' teaching and fellowship, to the breaking of bread and the prayers.

(verses 41–42)

As I write this, we are over six months into the restrictions brought about by coronavirus. Like many others, we have had to reassess what it means to be church, to be on the way when we cannot meet in person – or can only meet in person in restricted ways. Looking at the four things mentioned in this passage, I have to say that each one has been a challenge in its own way. It has been a steep learning curve of camera angles, sound, uploading, learning new skills. The apostle's teaching has been recorded, live streamed; sermons and interactive online Bible studies uploaded; Bible notes put through people's doors. We went months without breaking bread together and now it is amid hand sanitiser, masks and socially distanced pews. We list prayers on our webpages and social media, and try to be there for each other down the phone. Not always easy in a community where not everyone has internet access.

Yet God is faithful and adds to our number. Each new member changes us and each new member should change us, bringing new perspectives, new experiences. Some new members have only found us because we have been thrown out of the comfort of our Sunday services in the building. They have found us online and in the new places we find ourselves.

† Lord help us to see who you are adding to us and, as we welcome them, know that they will change us.

For further thought

Have I seen who God is adding to our number? Where do I need to be for them to hear?

Wednesday 8 June
Getting organised

Read Acts 6:1–7

Therefore, friends, select from among yourselves seven men of good standing, full of the Spirit and of wisdom, whom we may appoint to this task.

(verse 3)

It's not always possible to predict the needs that will arise. Over lockdown, we found ourselves partnering with the local authority to deliver food and medicines to those in our community who had no one else to shop for them. My main memory of those first few months will be standing in endless lines at supermarkets, three or four different lists in hand. The people on the tills became familiar with our faces. Every chemist shop in a mile radius of the church started to recognise us. It wasn't a task we set out to do, it wasn't in our outreach plan, it was a need to which we responded.

The early church found that there was a need they were not meeting. The Hellenist widows were being neglected, so the church commissioned members to undertake this task. It can be so easy to overlook prayer in the practical tasks. Here was a very practical task yet the church set high qualifications for those who were to undertake it. They needed 'to be of good standing, full of the Spirit and wisdom'. Then they prayed and laid hands on those who were chosen. Part of getting organised on the way is being flexible to new needs, seeing these practical tasks as important, setting high standards and in all things committing those who serve to prayer.

† Lord, help us to see the needs around us and to respond prayerfully and practically.

For further thought

What practical needs are in my community? Who is being called to this task? How can we commission them to go?

June

Being church – 1 On the way

Thursday 9 June
All welcome

Read Acts 11:1–18

If then God gave them the same gift that he gave us when we believed in the Lord Jesus Christ, who was I that I could hinder God?

(verse 17)

'Is it all right if I come to your church?' The same young woman would ask me the same question once a year. Every year I would tell her, of course, she didn't have to ask, she could come any time. Then she would turn up with her son, just about once a year, but she would come. I don't know what exactly made her feel she had to ask permission. I can guess. She may not have felt that she met the picture of a regular churchgoer. But what is that? Personally I was delighted the year her young son turned up in full fancy dress.

Peter was well schooled in what was profane, what was unacceptable. It took a vision, his being told three times and perhaps most importantly his witnessing the Holy Spirit at work in others, for him to change his mind, to see differently. 'If then God gave them the same gift that he gave us when we believed in the Lord Jesus Christ, who was I that I could hinder God?' is his conclusion. As church on the way, we need to be open to seeing the Holy Spirit in all people, especially those who have not always been welcomed. Who in our community is feeling the need to ask if they are welcome?

† Lord help us to see where your Holy Spirit is working. Open our eyes and change our hearts and minds to see you in new places.

For further thought

Who do I assume is not as welcome? How can I make sure they are welcomed?

The church gets established

Read Acts 11:19–26

When he came and saw the grace of God, he rejoiced, and he exhorted them all to remain faithful to the Lord with steadfast devotion.

(verse 23)

'The church down the road is doing a fantastic job.' It's sometimes hard to hear that. Or worse, perhaps, as a colleague of mine was recently told by a key member of her congregation, 'I have decided to go to that other church where more is happening.' My colleague had the grace to bless the person in their new venture. A leader in a church near us said to me only this week, 'We have so many people in our church who are equipped and ready to serve, we don't know what to do with them all.' I managed a smile.

Things are beginning to happen among the scattered church in our reading today. People are doing things differently and God is blessing them. The church in Antioch is growing and the gospel is fruitful among Hellenists not just Jews, so Barnabas is sent to check things out. It is to his great credit that 'when he came and saw the grace of God, he rejoiced'. Barnabas was, as the passage records, a good man. Being church on the way is always about seeing the bigger picture. It is always about rejoicing at the church growing, wherever that is, even if our own fellowship is struggling, even if the other church does things differently. Not only that, it is about committing our resources to the wider church, not just our small corner. Paul gives a year of teaching to this new fellowship, giving his gifts and talents to their growth.

† Lord help us to rejoice with those who rejoice and to give away our gifts and resources to others.

For further thought

Am I rejoicing when the church is growing in other places? What resources am I giving away to other fellowships to build them up?

June

Being church – 1 On the way

Saturday 11 June
The end of the beginning

Read Acts 28:23–30

He lived there for two whole years at his own expense and welcomed all who came to him, proclaiming the kingdom of God and teaching about the Lord Jesus Christ with all boldness and without hindrance.

(verses 30–31)

There is water pouring through the roof of our church: not a new problem, I know. As I write the rain is lashing down and I know I will have to run over to church and check the large bins we have under the key leaks. This way the bins can be emptied before they overflow and ruin the wooden flooring. The water is also destroying the plaster. We are working on repairs but it's a long haul and sometimes takes up far too much of our time. As I said, not an unusual problem in more economically challenged communities. But this is not what our church is about. We do not invite you to admire the plaster – or indeed sigh at its demise – we are about proclaiming the good news of salvation.

Paul's message has not changed; he knows his calling to preach the good news. He does not lose focus. Here we find Paul at the end of his ministry still doing the thing God told him to do, and apparently tirelessly: 'From morning until evening he explained the matter to them, testifying to the kingdom of God and trying to convince them about Jesus both from the law of Moses and from the prophets' (verse 23). Although not all were convinced, he continues. There are many distractions in the Christian life, the roof will leak, not all will be convinced. We are called to be faithful to that which God has asked us to do and to continue in that faithfulness.

† Lord help us to see what is important, to hold firm to all that you have called us to do.

For further thought

What has God called me to do? Is that the thing taking my time and energy? Am I still on the path I set out on?

Being church

2 The Church – and the churches

Notes by **John Proctor**

 John is a minister of the United Reformed Church. Now retired, he has served in a Glasgow parish, a Cambridge college and the URC's central office in London. John has written commentaries on Matthew (BRF, 2001) and the Corinthian letters (WJK, 2015), and several Grove booklets on New Testament themes. He is married to Elaine and they live near Cambridge. John has used the NRSV for these notes.

Sunday 12 June
The Church is people

Read Romans 16:1–16

Greet Prisca and Aquila, who work with me in Christ Jesus, and who risked their necks for my life … Greet Rufus, chosen in the Lord; and greet his mother – a mother to me also.

(parts of verses 3–4 and 13)

Paul had never visited this church. But many roads led to Rome, and the early Christians were very mobile. Paul knew many of the members from contact and companionship elsewhere, and here he greets twenty-six of them by name. Names are people, each with a story, background, relationships and character. Paul's brief greetings are lenses on a world of varied experience, shared faith and practical love.

Christian discipleship was not an easy option. We read of stress and effort, of risk to liberty and life, of imprisonment, and several times of hard work.

Christians valued one another deeply. They were family, 'sisters and brothers' in Christ. One lady had been 'a mother' in the church, not only in her own household but beyond it too. Paul calls his readers 'saints'. They were God's holy people, with privileges and responsibilities.

One responsibility was to value and honour one another. The command to 'greet' would remind them to do this. This church in Rome was quite a diffuse company, spread across a network of house fellowships. Paul's greetings urge them to keep in touch, to notice, respect and support one another, just as he names, remembers and encourages so many of them.

† Remember Christians you have known who are now worshipping and working elsewhere. Pray for some of them. Think about making contact with one or two.

Monday 13 June
Inter-church aid

Read 2 Corinthians 8:16–24

We are sending the brother who is famous among all the churches for his proclaiming of the good news; and not only that, but he has also been appointed by the churches to travel with us while we are administering this generous undertaking for the glory of the Lord.

(part of verses 18–19)

Paul's financial collection was a major project, involving many of the churches that he had helped to start. He asked these fellowships, made up largely of Gentile Christians, to gather money for the church in Jerusalem. Both of his letters to Corinth mention this plan (1 Corinthians 16:1–4; 2 Corinthians 8 and 9).

In part, this gift would be a straightforward piece of Christian sharing. The Jerusalem church was going through a time of hardship. They needed help – and fellow believers in other places had the means to give this. Yet the gesture was important for other reasons too.

It was a mark of gratitude. The Christian good news had come out of Israel, bringing promise and blessing into the Gentile world in the name of the Messiah Jesus. So now, for Gentile Christians to give to their Jewish sisters and brothers would be a way of saying thank you.

It was also a sign of the church's unity, of a love that brought Jew and Gentile together in Jesus. Here was a company of people overcoming ancient divisions of race, language and culture, and giving one another some very practical help.

Paul wanted to be responsible. Money must be handled with care, if people are to give confidently. So our reading today talks about the three people Paul sent to Corinth to gather the gifts. Titus knew the Corinthian church and they knew him; his companions were trusted and backed by other churches. These people can be relied on, says Paul, to deal honestly and to make sure the gifts fulfil their purpose.

† Generous God, help me to give gladly, carefully and confidently, to places of need, to the work of your kingdom, to the support of the church. For Jesus' sake. Amen

For further thought

Remember people who have given to you over the years – time, care and material gifts. Thank God for the difference they made to your life.

Tuesday 14 June
No distinction

Read Galatians 3:23–29

In Christ Jesus you are all children of God through faith. As many of you as were baptised into Christ have clothed yourselves with Christ. There is no longer Jew or Greek … slave or free … male and female; for all of you are one in Christ Jesus.

(parts of verses 26–28)

Our reflection yesterday mentioned the unity of the early Christian church. This new movement brought Jew and Gentile together in ways that overcame long-standing barriers of culture and custom. Galatians explains what makes this unity possible. Times have changed. The coming of Christ has launched a new era.

For centuries, says Paul, the Jewish law had both negative and positive effects. It constrained the chosen people; Paul's language in verse 23 is quite bleak. Yet the law also nurtured habits of learning and conduct. That's the positive meaning of the word translated 'disciplinarian' (verses 24–25) – in other versions 'tutor, schoolmaster, guardian' – shaping a young person's life until years of freedom arrive.

'But now' (verse 25), in 'the fullness of time' (4:4), the coming of Christ has brought new freedom. Faith in Christ is open to all, Jew and Gentile alike. This faith is a great leveller. It marks people out as children of Abraham, not as a matter of genes and biology, but because they carry his spiritual DNA. Abraham was the prototype believer, and those who believe in Jesus belong to his heritage, as members of the family of faith.

Christian baptism is a mark of equality too. The ancient covenant rite of circumcision privileged Jews over Gentiles, and men over women. Whereas baptism mirrors faith, by making no such distinction. At the baptistry, there is no rank in race, or grading by gender, or status from social class, slaves too may claim the freedom that is in Christ. Christians are one body, one fellowship, one people – in the name and the company of Jesus.

† Can you recall Christians with whom you have known deep friendship, whose background is very different from your own? Thank God for those people and pray for them today.

For further thought

'All one in Christ Jesus.' Is this view of the Christian church realistic and relevant now?

Wednesday 15 June
Suffering and glory

Read Ephesians 3:1–13

This is the reason that I Paul am a prisoner for Christ Jesus for the sake of you Gentiles … so that through the church the wisdom of God in its rich variety might now be made known to the rulers and authorities in the heavenly places.

(verses 1 and 10)

You may have noticed that this week's readings come from seven letters, sent to seven different churches. This is a complete set of Paul's church contacts, as we have them in scripture; his other letters were to individuals. Yet among the seven, Ephesians stands a little apart. Some people think it was a kind of circular – to Christian communities in and around Ephesus. Certainly it has a wide viewpoint, looking at the church as a whole, rather than at issues and individuals in one local congregation. Paul describes his ministry in a variety of ways.

He was a confidant of God (verse 3). He knew the plan. Good news was going out across the world. God was bringing Jew and Gentile together, showing that no worldly barrier could stem the flow of grace. The church is a visible sign of the power and goodness of God. Earth and heaven, sit up and take notice (verse 10).

Paul was a servant and a saint (verses 7–8), a representative of Christ and one of God's holy people. He had not deserved any favour from God, but 'grace had been given' (verses 2 and 7–8). He counted his work as an honour and makes light of the suffering to which it has led.

For he was writing from captivity (verse 1). We do not know where. Paul was locked up a number of times. Serving Christ had been costly. But he tells his friends not to be anxious (verse 13). God's purpose is moving forward. Paul's pains are helping the people he loves to discover the glory of Christ.

† Remember a place where Christian witness is costly today. Pray for people there who are keen to share the gospel. Ask God to give them wise words and faithful lives.

For further thought
Where do you see grace overcoming worldly barriers today?

Thursday 16 June
Welcoming church workers

Read Philippians 2:19–30

I hope in the Lord Jesus to send Timothy to you soon … who will be genuinely concerned for your welfare … I think it necessary to send to you Epaphroditus – my brother and co-worker and fellow soldier, your messenger and minister to my need.

(parts of verses 19–20 and 25)

Paul was a team player. Keeping contact with a wide network of churches was not a task to manage alone. His letters often mention co-workers, people whom he liked, valued and relied on. Here are two of them – one a colleague of long standing, and another who offered support at a difficult time.

Timothy was younger than Paul, and Paul refers to him as a son (verse 22). That surely implies affection; it may also cast Timothy as an apprentice, absorbing Paul's skills as they worked together. He had first joined Paul in his hometown of Lystra, and probably helped him to plant a church in Philippi (Acts 16:1–11). Later he made two more visits to the area (Acts 19:22; 20:3–6), so the Christians in Philippi would have known him well. Now Paul speaks of sending him again, when 'I see how it will go with me' (verse 23). A decision was expected about Paul's custody, and Timothy would wait for this before leaving him.

Epaphroditus would travel first, surely carrying this letter. He was a Christian from Philippi, and the church there had sent him to support Paul in prison. (It was often possible for friends on the outside to bring a prisoner gifts and supplies.) Yet now, although Paul is still not free, he feels the time has come for Epaphroditus to go home. Paul commends him gratefully, for his commitment and the care he has given on the Philippians' behalf. Across great distances, the early Christians took trouble to keep in touch, to maintain friendship and to give one another material help.

† Pray for Christians in jail: for those around the world who have been imprisoned for their faith; and for others, perhaps locally to you, who have come to faith while they are in prison.

For further thought

'Brother or sister, co-worker, fellow-soldier, messenger, minister to need' – which of these roles do you fulfil for other people?

June

Being church – 2 The Church – and the churches

Friday 17 June
Sharing news

> **Read Colossians 4:10–18**
>
> *Aristarchus my fellow prisoner greets you, as does Mark the cousin of Barnabas … Jesus who is called Justus greets you. These are the only ones of the circumcision among my co-workers … Epaphras, who is one of you, a servant of Christ Jesus, greets you … Luke, the beloved physician, and Demas greet you.*
>
> (parts of verses 10–14)

Paul ends this letter with greetings from six companions, as well as his own handwritten farewell. Three of the six are Jewish by birth and background, and three are Gentile. We meet several of them elsewhere in the New Testament.

Aristarchus came from Thessalonica in northern Greece. He was alongside Paul in the thick of a riot in Ephesus, they travelled with money for Jerusalem, and sailed under armed guard to Rome (Acts 19:29; 20:4; 27:2). Clearly Paul trusted him, and he knew about the cost of Christian witness.

Mark had stumbled in his early attempts at mission, and Paul was reluctant to work with him again (Acts 15:37–38). The mention of him here suggests a reconciliation. Failure and quarrel had not had the last word. Church tradition, of course, links him to one of the four gospels.

Colossians shows Demas and Paul on good terms. But later Demas left him, lonely and disappointed. On that latter occasion Luke was the only friend to remain with Paul (2 Timothy 4:10–11). If this is the Luke of the Gospel, and the author too of Acts, it is interesting that Acts switches several times from 'they' to 'we'. Luke apparently travelled a long way with Paul, in miles and in friendship.

From this company of real, complex, ordinary, Christian people, came greetings to Colossae. To Nympha, who hosted a church in her home. To Archippus, who had an important task to fulfil. And on to Laodicea, a few miles away, with greetings to the church there too.

† Lord Jesus Christ, thank you for the people whose lives interlock with mine. Please help us to build good relationships, even when things go wrong.

For further thought

'Stand mature and fully assured in everything that God wills' (verse 12): would you find it helpful, or intimidating, to make that your aim as a Christian?

Saturday 18 June
Bringers of good news

Read 1 Thessalonians 3:1–10

In fact, when we were with you, we told you beforehand that we were to suffer persecution; so it turned out, as you know … But Timothy has just now come to us from you, and has brought us the good news of your faith and love.

(verses 4 and 6b)

The church in Thessalonica was born in conflict. Its members were brand new Christians. But as the gospel made an impact in the town, and people took an interest, a strong reaction had arisen. There were angry scenes, threats and violence, and legal action against the church's leaders. Paul and his companions, whose preaching had launched the church, had to leave town very hastily.

As he travelled on, Paul surely wondered if his friends in Thessalonica could weather this storm. There was little he could do for the moment. But his mind was full of questions, anxieties and prayers. Had they lost heart? Had their faith collapsed? Could any help be offered? So as the weeks went by, Paul decided to send Timothy back to Thessalonica. As a quieter personality, he would not attract much attention in the town. He could mix and mingle with the local Christians, learn their news, lift their spirits, and listen to their doubts and fears.

Timothy's mission fulfilled its aims. He brought good news back, of a church holding steady and sure – of solid faith, grateful memories and warm greetings. Paul's heart rejoiced. His prayers were bright with thanks and joy. He had cared deeply, and suddenly anxious care was transformed into glad relief.

We have read this week about some of the networks of contact and friendship that linked the earliest churches. In today's verses we glimpse the intense personal love and care that gave these networks their strength.

† Do you know anyone who carries a deep sense of disappointment, who fears that good work has come to nothing? Ask God to lift that person today and remind them of the Spirit's power.

For further thought

Should we expect to see intense personal love and care in our churches today? If so, what can you do to nurture this?

June

Being church – 2 The Church – and the churches

169

Readings from Ezekiel

1 Vision of glory

Notes by **Nathan Eddy**

Nathan is a father, friend, minister in the United Reformed Church, poet, Hebrew language nut and an ever-hopeful home gardener. He recently completed a PhD in Psalms and now works in Jewish-Christian relations as Interim Director of the Council of Christians and Jews, the oldest interfaith charity in the UK. Nathan lives with his family, including a Schnauzer puppy named Arthur, in London. Nathan was editor *of Fresh From The Word* from 2014 until 2021. Nathan has used the NRSVA for these notes.

Sunday 19 June
Vision of God

Read Ezekiel 1:1–14

In the thirtieth year, in the fourth month, on the fifth day of the month, as I was among the exiles by the river Chebar, the heavens were opened, and I saw visions of God.

(verse 1)

What does God look like?

On a summer's day, by a canal in a strange land, a north wind blew a glowing cloud toward the priest Ezekiel. Four glowing creatures were visible, with four faces and four wings. Their wings touched; perhaps they were arranged in a square. A spark of fire flashed in their midst.

The opening chapters of Ezekiel are his 'call' narrative: that moment, as with Isaiah in the temple in Isaiah 6, when God appears, commissions and sends out. The verses also describe how Ezekiel was sent into exile around 597 BCE – ten years before the destruction of Jerusalem and final exile of its people.

The comparison with Isaiah's temple vision is significant. Ezekiel is a priest (verse 3), and his language is temple language. Fire, lightning, thunder and dark cloud: these are elements familiar from Psalms which undoubtedly reflect temple worship. Ezekiel invites us into the conceptual world of the temple – at times, a challenge for Christians who may be more accustomed to prophetic criticism of the temple.

To read Ezekiel is to experience God with all our senses, as we do in worship. For this reason, Ezekiel of all the prophets presents perhaps the greatest challenge to readers today. What do you see? What do you hear? Where will God send you?

† God of the prophets, open our eyes, unblock our ears and grant us your vision; raise up your prophets among us.

Monday 20 June
A sound of tumult

> **Read Ezekiel 1:15–28**
>
> *When they moved, I heard the sound of their wings like the sound of mighty waters, like the thunder of the Almighty, a sound of tumult like the sound of an army … And there came a voice from above the dome over their heads.*
>
> (parts of verses 24–25)

What does the word of God sound like?

Yesterday, we looked and *saw* with the prophet; today we *listen* and fall in worship.

As Ezekiel's description continues, he sees a high wheel next to each creature that moves with them. And above the creatures is an ice-like expanse: a dome spread over their heads and wings. As the vision comes closer still, Ezekiel hears their wings: a sound like a thundering waterfall or the thundering voice of God. His eye drawn upward, he sees a sapphire throne fixed to the dome and a fiery figure sitting in the throne, set in radiance 'like the bow in a cloud on a rainy day' (verse 28). As the psalmist says, 'in your light we see light' (Psalm 36:9).

A friend of mine recently posted a picture of Derwent Dam in the north of England on Facebook. In the image, a huge volume of white water cascades down the massive stone face. Almost as an aside, my friend noted that the sound of a waterfall reminds him of the voice of God.

In the stories of the Sinai revelation, the sound of God is so terrifying that the people beg the prophet to stand in for them, lest they die; and the people promise to listen to the prophet who is able to stand before the Holy One (Deuteronomy 5:26–27). In some Jewish traditions, the people hear only thunder at Sinai, but Moses discerns the words of God in the tumult and records them for the people.

Realising he is in the presence of God, Ezekiel falls to the ground (verse 28). The only response to the thunder of God's voice, truly, is silence; silence and worship.

† God of thunder, help us hear your word afresh this day, discern its meaning and live it out.

For further thought

In Hebrew, the word for 'noise' or 'sound' is also used for 'voice' and 'thunder'; God's voice in the Hebrew Bible is an awesome, terrifying sound.

June

Readings from Ezekiel – 1 Vision of glory

Tuesday 21 June
Spirit of life

Read Ezekiel 2:1–3:3

He said to me, O mortal, stand up on your feet, and I will speak with you. And when he spoke to me, a spirit entered into me and set me on feet.

(verses 1–2b)

This short chapter is full of contrasts: God's words and Ezekiel's stunned silence; God's commands for Ezekiel to speak and Ezekiel's silence; Ezekiel's obedience and the warning of Israel's intransigence.

Yet one feature is not a contrast, but a beguiling overlap. In the verses quoted above, a 'spirit' enters Ezekiel and helps him stand. This spirit, the Hebrew word *ruach*, is above all the awesome, empowering wind or 'spirit' of God which bore the storm cloud in Ezekiel 1:4. In the familiar story of the valley of dry bones later in the book, the wind or breath of God comes from the four winds and revives the bones (37:9–10). Similarly, here the divine spirit lifts Ezekiel up, animating him and giving him courage. Paradoxically, the spirit of God is what makes God God, but also what makes Ezekiel Ezekiel.

We see in this process that the awesome beauty of God in Ezekiel's visions is also moral through and through. God has a very practical, down to earth and challenging task for Ezekiel: to call Israel back to God. It is God who gives the spirit of life; yet Israel must decide to heed God's words, and so live. Life is not just a gift to be passively received, but a decision to be made; a way to walk.

The final note is hopeful. In the first of many symbolic actions, Ezekiel not only hears God's word, but *eats* it. We've reflected on the appearance of God, and the sound of God's word, and here we have the *taste* of God's word; and it is as sweet as honey.

† Empowering God, lift us up on our feet, show us the way, and give us the courage to walk it.

For further thought

In Psalm 19, God's law is described as 'sweeter than honey' (19:10); perhaps the reference evokes the meditative practice of reading of scripture aloud.

Wednesday 22 June
Divine house arrest

Read Ezekiel 3:12–27

Go, shut yourself inside your house … I will make your tongue cling to the roof of your mouth, so that you shall be speechless and unable to reprove them, for they are a rebellious house.

(parts of verses 24 and 26)

A new chapter, a new vision: yet this vision results in Ezekiel 'going in bitterness in the heat of my spirit' (verse 14). Why is Ezekiel's spirit bitter? Is it a reflection of God's anger towards Israel, or Ezekiel's anger at his thankless task? For the great Jewish theologian, Abraham Joshua Heschel, Ezekiel here embodies the suffering of God as God seeks his people. For Heschel, the prophet is not just a robot-like conduit for the word of God, but a friend and partner of God who suffers with God in order to reconcile God and Israel. 'The prophet is not a mouthpiece, but a person,' Heschel writes; 'not an instrument, but a partner, an associate of God' (*The Prophets*, Vol 1. New York: Harper, 1969, p. 25). Like Jeremiah, Ezekiel feels God's word burning in his very bones (Jeremiah 20:9).

It is perhaps for this reason that God strips Ezekiel of speech itself in the verses quoted above. As the people reject the prophet, so God withdraws the prophet from their midst. God's healing powers in the prophet are not available to the people, as long as they will not listen. Ezekiel remains under a kind of divine house arrest in the readings to come.

Chinese artist, Ai Weiwei, portrayed what he called his own house arrest in an exhibit I saw in London in 2015: ceramic scenes of the artist under home surveillance by uniformed guards, who watch his every move. Like an artist, Ezekiel will make his own house arrest a stage to symbolise a message of judgement to his people.

† God of the housebound, give grace to those in need; give courage to those in danger; give life to those who seek you; and orient us to your voice.

For further thought

What artists or writers come to mind as prophets of our own age? How does their life relate to their art?

Thursday 23 June
Lost for words

> **Read Ezekiel 4:1–17**
>
> *Lie on your left side, and place the punishment of the house of Israel upon it; you shall bear their punishment for the number of the days that you lie there.*
>
> (verse 4)

Under divine house arrest, Ezekiel is commanded to undertake striking symbolic actions. Ezekiel must lay on his side for months, during which time he must eat siege rations. He must portray Jerusalem on a brick, and, as if playing God, lay up siege works against it. In the next chapter, he will even be commanded to shave his head and beard in a kind of ritual humiliation. Throughout, Ezekiel 'bears the punishment' of his people (verse 4), serving as a kind of a scapegoat, the animal in Leviticus 16:20–22 which bears the guilt of the people and makes atonement for their sin. The intent seems to be to show the people the events of destruction which were surely coming, and to goad them into action to prevent it.

These symbolic actions make for hard reading. Whatever the people's sin, is it right that God wreaks such destruction and death? Recently, scholars have suggested we read these passages as 'trauma literature'. Ancient Israel was a traumatised people, deported from their homes and sent into a foreign land. Ezekiel himself, struck speechless, confined to his home, bears the marks of what today we might today call post-traumatic stress disorder. Ezekiel and all of his fellow exiles were struggling to come to terms with what had befallen them.

In this light, perhaps Ezekiel's actions can be seen as a way to healing and wholeness. God had not abandoned his people. God's punishment was harsh, but God was still the God of Israel, still loved his people, and still sought their restoration.

† Wherever we have not heeded your prophets, God, forgive us. Help us turn and listen, and live.

For further thought

In a recent film, the climate change activist, Greta Thunberg, reflects powerfully on her own loss of speech as a young child in reaction to the climate crisis. How are her actions today prophetic?

Divine destruction

Read Ezekiel 10:1–8, 15–22

Go within the wheel-work underneath the cherubim; fill your hands with burning coals from among the cherubim, and scatter them over the city.

(part of verse 2)

In chapters 8 and 9, Ezekiel has witnessed the acts of idolatry in the temple; and here we see the consequences. Although the language in chapter 10 is strikingly similar to the beatific vision of God's glory in chapter 1, the result is horrifying: the gradual withdrawal of the divine presence from the temple, and the destruction of Jerusalem. In the verse above, a priest-like figure tends coals in a worship setting, but not for the good the city. Instead, these worship elements are turned against the city, burning it.

In the ancient world, God's presence and urban well-being were connected. If a god was present in the temple, his home, it was deemed to be secure. A city was inviolable unless the god chose to leave. In the reading for today, Ezekiel is providing a kind of theological interpretation, or behind-the-scenes glimpse, of the destruction of Jerusalem at the hands of the Babylonians in 587 BCE. The cherubim rise up, the glory of the Lord enthroned above them, and depart from Ezekiel's sight (verse 19).

For all its beauty, the vision is harsh. Yet chapters 37 and 40 depict their reversal.

'My dwelling place shall be with them; and I will be their God, and they shall be my people,' God promises Ezekiel at the end of chapter 37. 'Then the nations shall know that I the Lord sanctify Israel, when my sanctuary is among them for evermore' (37:27–28).

† In the words of Psalm 122:6–7: 'Pray for the peace of Jerusalem. "May they prosper who love you. Peace be within your walls, and security within your towers."'

For further thought

God's holiness does not mean that God cannot abide sin; God's holiness is precisely that God will forgive. But God's forgiveness must be sought and lived out.

June

Readings from Ezekiel – 1 Vision of glory

Saturday 25 June
Divine re-creation

Read Ezekiel 11:14–25

I will give them one heart, and put a new spirit within them; I will remove the heart of stone from their flesh and give them a heart of flesh, so that they may follow my statutes and keep my ordinances and obey them. Then they shall be my people, and I will be their God.

(verses 19–20)

We end this week back where we began: in Chaldea, Babylon, among the exiles. The cherubs, having borne the divine majesty as far as the East Gate in the vision of Jerusalem in 10:19, now depart the city altogether, settling on the mountain 'east of the city' (verse 23) – the Mount of Olives. Ezekiel's visions have jumped in space and time: in chapter 1, in the 'present' in Babylon after the destruction of Jerusalem, the divine majesty has appeared to him arriving seemingly from heaven, where God has been exiled from the city he loves. In subsequent visions, Ezekiel was transported *back* in time to Jerusalem, where the awful events leading up to God's exile are explained. At the end of the reading today, we are back in the 'present', in Babylon.

We have traversed a horrible terrain of divine punishment and absence. To modern ears, the message is harsh; yet there are analogies to the way we might understand catastrophes today. Climate change, for example, can be understood both as a tragedy to be lamented, and as a calamity that we have brought on ourselves.

But Ezekiel does not leave us in despair. He promises that God will not only be present to the exiles (verse 16); God will also return them to the land of Israel. And God won't just return the people, but create them afresh; God will empower them to hear and obey freely and joyfully.

Ezekiel does not let us off the hook, but he gives us hope. God tips the balance, and is at work within and among us, for the sake of restoration. Will we listen, and follow?

† God of restoration, work in me that I might hear and have the strength to change my life and follow. Help me be an instrument of your reconciliation. Amen

For further thought

In Ancient Israel, one did one's thinking with the heart; there is no word for 'mind'. A new heart promises entirely new cognitive and emotional powers.

Readings from Ezekiel

2 Restored to life

Notes by **Noel Irwin**

Noel is a Belfast boy and a Methodist minister. In 2000 he moved to Sheffield: firstly working for the Church of England as a community outreach worker, then as Superintendent of the Methodist Mission in the city centre. After working as Director of the Urban Theology Unit in Sheffield, he is now Tutor in Public Theology at Northern College Manchester and trains Church Related Community Workers for the United Reformed Church there. In his spare time, he enjoys running in the hills and Brazilian jiu-jitsu. Noel has used the NRSVA for his notes.

Sunday 26 June
Taking responsibility

Read Ezekiel 18:1–17

What do you mean by repeating this proverb concerning the land of Israel, 'The parents have eaten sour grapes, and the children's teeth are set on edge'?

(verse 2)

I have quoted the proverb in this verse, perhaps, more in the last five years or so, than any other verse in the Bible. When my son complained loudly, after the Brexit referendum in 2016, that he would no longer be able to study in Europe in the future, this was wheeled out. Reflecting on my struggle to deal with my sectarianism, this was quoted. Even watching a feature on the increasing rates of obesity among young people, this got an airing. Over the years, pastoral situations I have had to deal with: domestic abuse, alcoholism, actual poverty and poverty of aspiration, have sometimes, sadly, been passed from one generation to the next.

It's interesting that Ezekiel and Jeremiah both complain that people are using this proverb, not as an explanation, but as an excuse, as individuals and as a community in refusing to take any responsibility. The loving kindness of God means, while our actions resonate through generations, each generation has a fresh start. We are neither trapped nor judged, under God we have the capability to break free by embracing the ways of God (verses 5–9 and 14–18) which alone bring true freedom.

† Pray for those who feel trapped because of their past, that they may know the freedom, love and mercy of God.

Readings from Ezekiel – 2 Restored to life

Because your heart is proud

Read Ezekiel 28:1–19

Because your heart is proud and you have said, 'I am a god; I sit in the seat of the gods, in the heart of the seas', yet you are but a mortal, and no god, though you compare your mind with the mind of a god.

(part of verse 2)

Our reading today is split between proclamation (verses 1–10) and lamentation (verses 11–19) against and over the king of Tyre. This passage has played a role in Christian tradition by its use in creating the story of the 'fall' of Lucifer and thus the origin of the idea of Satan. However, I tell my students that while we may not always take the Bible literally, we must take it seriously. In this context, that includes understanding the imagery the prophet uses, the culture in which those were meaningful and the key issue they were seeking to address. In that light, we see a clear focus on the hubris (excessive pride without reference to God) of Tyre's king.

There is a sense that the 'primary' sin in the Hebrew scriptures is hubris and we see connections with the story of Eden in verses 11–19, particularly in verses 13 and 16. Though, unlike the story of Eden there is no appearance of a tempter, rather the cause of the sin is primarily pride (verse 17).

This incredible picture of the proud prince of Tyre may seem to be long ago and far away, but it's not so difficult to make connections with our world, where we have political leaders who claim they never have to seek any forgiveness from God and who claim to be perfect in every way. In the time of Ezekiel and today, power corrupts, and absolute power corrupts absolutely, while the remedy is given by the psalmist (Psalm 111:10a) 'The fear of the Lord is the beginning of wisdom'.

† Pray for wisdom for political and church leaders; locally, nationally and internationally.

For further thought

Think about what taking scripture 'seriously' means.

Tuesday 28 June
Greatness will fall

Read Ezekiel 31:1–14

Mortal, say to Pharaoh king of Egypt and to his hordes: Whom are you like in your greatness? Consider Assyria, a cedar of Lebanon, with fair branches and forest shade, and of great height, its top among the clouds.

(verses 2–3)

Here we have the fifth oracle against Egypt in Ezekiel, with the aim once again to stress to the people of Judah that there will be no deliverance for them from Egypt. From verses 1–9 we have a poetic allegory which compares Egypt to the greatest tree known to the people of the Ancient Near East, the cedar of Lebanon. Then in verses 10–14 there is what is characterised as both indictment and judgement of Egypt.

God compares the supposed greatness of Egypt to that of Assyria (verses 2–9), but in verse 10 onwards even mighty Assyria is brought down to the grave because of its pride and hubris, echoing the sins of the prince of Tyre which we looked at yesterday. The way the passage works is to move from the greater to the lesser: if God judged the great Assyria, then how much more will Egypt face judgement and destruction.

We know the saying 'Pride comes before a fall', a version of Proverbs 16:18 which has come into our everyday speech. This is true for Tyre, Assyria and Egypt and all the other great nations and empires which have fallen over the centuries. One of the intriguing things of this passage is the outlining how smaller nations benefit from a great one and how they are affected by its fall (verses 6 and 12). As we live in such an interconnected world, we need to be careful about celebrating the difficulties of any other nation, because we may find that our neighbouring country has eaten sour grapes and our teeth are set on edge!

† Pray for those countries around the world who are suffering difficulties and problems – whether it is conflict, natural disaster or whatever. Give thanks to God for the variety of nations and peoples in our world.

For further thought

Reflect on our connectedness and dependency on other countries. Pick a country and explore our links with one another in greater depth.

June

Readings from Ezekiel – 2 Restored to life

Wednesday 29 June
I will seek my sheep

Read Ezekiel 34:1–16

You have not strengthened the weak, you have not healed the sick, you have not bound up the injured, you have not brought back the strayed, you have not sought the lost, but with force and harshness you have ruled them.

(verse 4)

The image of a shepherd as a ruler was a commonplace one in the Ancient Near East and was particularly important for Israel and Judah as David, the shepherd, was the greatest of all their kings. What we have here is an eviscerating indictment of the leaders of Israel: their rule is cruel, they starve their people, and they are not concerned at all for the common good of those who depend upon them. God will have to step in and do the job which they had been appointed to do.

While you will read this in June, I am writing just before Christ the King Sunday in November when some of our verses today are one of the readings. Christ the King became a named Sunday in the church year as a way to counter some of the claims of various European dictators in the twentieth century. The message of the Sunday is very simple and clear: the real ruler is Christ, not those who strut, pose and boast. The dictators have gone, replaced by 'populist' leaders who sometimes claim to defend Christian values to gain appeal. But the passage doesn't require religious pronouncements, it requires loving action in line with God's priorities. 'To do righteousness and justice is more acceptable to the Lord than sacrifice' (Proverbs 21:3).

† Today use Ezekiel 34:4 as a basis for your prayers for others.

For further thought

What do you think about the idea of Christ the King Sunday as a response to dictators? Any new Sundays you would initiate?

Thursday 30 June
Valley of dry bones

Read Ezekiel 37:1–14

Then he said to me, 'Mortal, these bones are the whole house of Israel. They say, "Our bones are dried up, and our hope is lost; we are cut off completely."'

(verse 11)

This is a really striking passage and probably the best-known section of Ezekiel. This is one of four mystical experiences which are all introduced in the same way, with the Spirit of God transporting Ezekiel from one place to another (3:22; 8:1; 37:1; 40:1). Here Ezekiel arrives in a valley where bodies have been left unburied and their bones are bleached by the sun. We tend to picture this scene as the site of a great battle, but we are not actually told that. The prophet obeys the order of God to prophesy to the dry bones (verse 7), the bones start to come together, then Ezekiel is commanded to prophesy to the breath or wind (same Hebrew word) to bring life resulting a huge living community.

Often this passage is seen as being about bodily resurrection, but if we are faithful to the text and the explanation of Ezekiel himself about the vision (verses 11–14), we see that it is about the resurrection of a community and a nation in this world, not of individuals after death. With that in mind the images which come to me, as I read this text, are of the many communities I've visited over the past few years, where shops and businesses are boarded up and a community has been exiled to another place. Can the dry bones of our left behind communities live? There's a 'perhaps' at the end of verse 3, 'O Lord God, you know.' There's also a hope that where God's Spirit is active there can be restoration.

† Lord breathe on our communities which seem dead, dry and hopeless and help them stand up, live again and thrive through you. Amen

For further thought

Where in your community has seemed as dead as the dry bones? Have you experienced the breath/wind/Spirit of God bringing life again to unlikely places?

Restoration

> **Read Ezekiel 39:25–29; 43:1–5**
>
> *I will never again hide my face from them, when I pour out my spirit upon the house of Israel, says the Lord God.*
>
> (verse 29)

Chapters 38 and 39 of Ezekiel have provided fruitful ground for many over the centuries who have seen them has some sort of coded messages about the 'final days'. There is nothing in these chapters which has any phraseology to suggest 'last days' or 'final days'. What there is, in visionary language, is a sense that, even when the odds seem impossible against the people of God, despite everything God will triumph against the forces of evil, they will be able to rest in their land and never will they be afraid again (verse 26). Our selection of verses from chapter 39 are actually a succinct summary of the message of chapters 34–39. They are about restoration, forgiveness and what is key in Ezekiel – the promise of a new, fresh relationship with God.

Then in chapter 43 the final sign of restoration is the return of the glory of the Lord to the new temple. Earlier, Ezekiel had seen the glory of God leaving the east gate in Jerusalem and moving east (chapters 8–11). As he sees it return from the east, he is totally in awe and falls on his face (verses 2 and 3), from which position, the Spirit lifts him up again and places him in the inner court, where, in subsequent verses God speaks to him. The idolatry of the people caused the destruction of the temple, here we see confirmation that there is a future for a restored people, with whom God will dwell forever.

† Are we brave or faithful enough to pray for a vision of the glory of the Lord?

For further thought

What restoration do you, your church and your community desperately need? What are the first steps you need to step to be restored?

Fresh water

Read Ezekiel 47:1–12

Their fruit will be for food, and their leaves for healing.

(part of verse 12)

From chapter 40 onwards, Ezekiel is on a tour of the new temple. He even has a tour guide (40:3), though they don't have an umbrella or sign, but a linen cord and a measuring reed! This, in chapter 47, is the climax of the tour as going outside to the east gate, water is exiting the gate where only the glory of God has passed. Then they go for a walk, the small stream from the temple grows and swells, bringing life with the growing of many trees (verse 7). Ezekiel can't see any further and so the guide gives him a wonderful picture of new and abundant life, with the Dead Sea becoming the Life Sea – using vocabulary lifted from the account of creation in Genesis 1. Beside this river the trees will provide fruit each month, their leaves give healing and all because the source of the water is the temple and sanctuary of God. What a beautiful and amazing picture with very strong connections with Revelation 21–22.

I love the sense here of how God is connected with superabundance, generosity, healing, flowing, bubbling, creating, re-creating, fruitfulness, moving, life giving, changing. This is so different from the 'unmoved mover' of Greek philosophy which has dominated Christian pictures of God over the centuries and is so totally different from the biblical witness of a God who is active, involved, caring, loving and passionate. There is much to think about here from this passage as we, human beings, do the opposite of this passage with our planet, destroying God's creation and re-creation.

† Using some of the words about God in the reflection above, focus your prayers today on God as creator and re-creator.

For further thought

Think about your picture of God in the light of this passage.

The stranger next door

1 Stranger danger

Notes by **Louise Jones**

Louise lives and works in Winson Green, Birmingham, in an embedded, community-based organisation (Newbigin House) which aims to create a sense of family, purpose and social cohesion in a community that is often overlooked, forgotten and misunderstood. Louise is in her early twenties and has a passion for empowering, resourcing and loving those that have slipped through the cracks of our systems to help people see their immense value and worth in Jesus. Louise has used the NIVUK for these notes.

Sunday 3 July
Unexpected wisdom from the stranger

Read Judges 13:2–20

Then the woman went to her husband and told him, 'A man of God came to me. He looked like an angel of God, very awesome. I didn't ask him where he came from, and he didn't tell me his name. But he said to me, "You will become pregnant."'

(part of verses 6–7)

We live in a world where we are taught from a young age not only not to trust strangers, but to ignore them. When I was studying at university and ordered a taxi, I would quietly dread the awkward conversation with the driver. They would ask what degree I was studying and when I said English Literature the driver would invariably enjoy telling me that an arts degree was a waste of time and then give me advice about future career prospects. I was never offended by the drivers' opinions because I simply didn't care about them. The drivers were strangers to me and I had been taught that strangers are, at best, irrelevant. Moving into Winson Green, however, and beginning my work as a community worker in a multi-cultural area where new refugee families would arrive most weeks meant that unless I overcame my apathy for the stranger, I would quickly become very isolated. Manoah and his wife listened to the stranger and his outlandish statement that they will get pregnant. We shouldn't assume that strangers can't speak wisdom into our lives, and this week I will explore the ways strangers have demonstrated that in my context.

† Lord, help us to be open in our interactions with strangers today, and to the possibility that you might be speaking to us through them.

184

Because you were strangers

> **Read Deuteronomy 10:12–22**
>
> *He defends the cause of the fatherless and the widow, and loves the foreigner residing among you, giving them food and clothing. And you are to love those who are foreigners, for you yourselves were foreigners in Egypt.*
>
> (verses 18–19)

In this passage Moses puts forward the ground-breaking idea that people who have experienced the isolation and fear of being a stranger are the best people to welcome new strangers. It astounds me how often people with no experience of homelessness, alcoholism or debt can fall into the trap of giving patronising advice to those going through these situations. Moses suggests that maybe the old foreigners, who have gone through the same difficulties as the new foreigners have something better to offer. Their lived experience means that their advice isn't patronising and has a higher chance of being helpful as the person knows the reality of the situation.

A few years ago, our charity supported Steve, an ex-convict, to set up a project in the local prison distributing holdall bags to prisoners being released. His idea was birthed from his own humiliating experience of being given a clear, plastic bag to put his belongings in when he was released from prison. He hated the shame of having to walk down the street with a bag branded with the prison's name on the side so everyone knew where he had just come from. Only someone who had lived through this experience could have come up with this simple way to give prisoners dignity and a fresh start from the beginning of their release. Fuelled by his own humiliating experience, Steve set out to 'defend' and 'love' future prisoners being released.

† Father, help us recognise the amazing gifts of those around us and show us where we can include those that have overcome certain struggles to be a part of the solution for other people.

For further thought

Did you know the Dutch prison rates have halved since 2004 when they decided to prioritise maintaining the dignity of prisoners and their reintegration into society over the punitive approach of jails in the UK?

Tuesday 5 July
The risk of getting to know strangers

Read Psalm 94:1–11

How long will the wicked be jubilant? They slay the widow and the foreigner; they murder the fatherless. They say, 'The Lord does not see; the God of Jacob takes no notice.'

(parts of verses 3 and 6–7)

Having been a part of the Winson Green community for almost five years, I have recently learned the risk of letting a stranger into your life. Sophie, a local mum, has become a good friend in the last couple of years despite her initial distrust of me as a shiny newcomer to the community. Recently, we got the devasting news that she has untreatable cancer with only months to live. This week I've acutely felt David's cry, 'the Lord does not see' as I've grappled with the unjustness of losing my friend Sophie and with the pain it will cause her three children. Watching Sophie's mother overcome with tears at church made me angry that we live in a world where a young mum can get sick and die. I was also selfishly angry that God had let me get close to Sophie, a woman who was once a stranger to me.

The risk of choosing to love our neighbours is that it's all the more painful if something happens to them. It's easy to feel crippled like David does by the pain in our world, but this week I have learned the power of a community lamenting together. Instead of Sophie's family having to grieve alone, she has a whole community grieving with her. Sophie would have cancer whether I knew her or not, so what a privilege it is to stand with Sophie's family during this time. In an unjust world it is up to us, God's hands and feet, to take notice of the people in pain and to stand with them.

† Lord, thank you that we are never alone in our pain and suffering. We ask that you'd help us to model your heart of love in the midst of pain to those suffering around us.

For further thought

I have found practical acts, such as driving people to hospital appointments, a really easy way to show love in the midst of overwhelming situations.

The tragedy of the idol of safety and security

Read Hosea 8:1–10

With their silver and gold they make idols for themselves to their own destruction … 'They sow the wind and reap the whirlwind.'

(parts of verses 4 and 7)

One of the tragedies of the Western world is the idol that has been made out of safety and security. For example, we are fed the lie that by reducing immigration and increasing border control we are somehow protecting ourselves from danger. But the tragedy is that the exact opposite occurs. Immigration is portrayed in our media as a scary whirlwind that we must try and control, but it is this idol of safety and security that is the dangerous whirlwind. The wind that is being sown in us is that we should distrust people who are different from us. But this passage says that this wind only reaps a whirlwind, in this case a whirlwind of fear, hate and isolation. Tragically these are all the opposite of God's heart for love and inclusion without exception.

One way that we have tried to reduce the fear of difference in Winson Green is through a project called 'Flavours of Winson Green' where women who have relocated from different countries teach a group of paying customers how to cook a dish from their culture. We have found that by creating a space where people see that their difference is valued and celebrated, our community has only been enriched by the stranger. In the kingdom of God there is always room for difference.

† Father, help me not to be scared by people that do things differently from me, instead show me how to be radically inclusive of everyone, indiscriminately.

For further thought

'Every brother or sister in need, when abandoned by the society in which I live, becomes an existential stranger, even though born in the same country', Pope Francis.

Thursday 7 July
The result of isolation and individualism

Read Lamentations 5:1–15

We have become fatherless, our mothers are widows. We must buy the water we drink; our wood can be had only at a price.

(verses 3–4)

The opposite of a healthy community is unhealthy individualism. These verses are taken from a longer inward-looking lament about individuals who have strayed far from God's idea of healthy community and love for one another. They feel sharply the pain of isolation as they struggle to pay for drink and resources with no community to help lighten the burden. The tragedy of the passage is that they still don't realise that the answer to their pain is to look outward for help – instead, they blame strangers for their current distress.

I have found that by living in community and accepting that I cannot do things in my own strength, I have gained a family. I live in a community house with eight other people of all ages and stages of life. I live with a couple in their 50s with a teenage son, a newly married couple in their 30s, an elderly lady, a father of three adult kids, and an 18-year-old staying for a six-month internship. Instead of experiencing distress in losing family members, like the writer of this lament, I find that I have gained a beautiful hybrid family. The benefit of living in multigenerational community is that I have gained a grandma who teaches me to make Yorkshire puddings, a sister to watch trashy movies with, and an in-house mechanic who fixes up my car for free! If we strive to do everything on our own and live in isolation then we miss out on the beauty of strangers who become our family.

† In a world that is built on the power of individualism, help us to see the strength and beauty of relying on and loving one another.

For further thought

Fun fact! One in six families in America is currently living in multigenerational households and studies are showing significant benefits to these families' mental health.

Friday 8 July

Demonstrating God's counter-cultural heart for the stranger

Read Psalm 146

The Lord sets prisoners free, the Lord gives sight to the blind, the Lord lifts up those who are bowed down, the Lord loves the righteous. The Lord watches over the foreigner and sustains the fatherless and the widow.

(part of verses 7–9)

It is easy to read this passage and simply reflect on how amazing it is that God repeatedly strives to free the oppressed. As an English Literature graduate I pay attention to word choices, and it's hard to read the impressive list of verbs in this passage without coming to the conclusion that we worship a God who isn't lazy! David writes that the Lord, 'sets … free', 'gives sight', 'lifts up', 'loves', 'watches over' and 'sustains' those being oppressed. Our God is a God of action, he feels compassion for those being overlooked, and does something about it. However, I don't think we're supposed to read this psalm passively. If we want to become more like God by loving those around us as God does, then that means the impressive list of verbs in this psalm applies to us too! We have a part to play in setting people free, sustaining and loving the stranger.

Sharon, a lady at the heart of the community in Winson Green, is a perfect example of someone that does this despite experiencing many hardships herself. Sharon was friends with a homeless gentleman and after feeling overwhelmed by his situation, she took him into her already crowded home to support him in his alcoholism and ensure he was eating. It would have been easy for Sharon to have pitied him but decide the problem was too big. But instead, she has actively shown God's love for the lost and downtrodden through her quiet act of radical kindness by disrupting her world and taking in a stranger.

† God, give us the courage to be radically loving and kind to those around us. Guide us in seeing what actions we can take to help those being oppressed.

For further thought

In 2019, a report carried out by the organisation Shelter revealed that 1 in 66 people in Birmingham (UK) were homeless, and this is increasing every day.

Saturday 9 July
Loving one another as brothers as sisters

Read Hebrews 13:1–6

Keep on loving one another as brothers and sisters. Do not forget to show hospitality to strangers, for by so doing some people have shown hospitality to angels without knowing it.

(verses 1–2)

During the coronavirus pandemic, our charity got ten times busier during lockdown as we had to think of creative solutions to support the most vulnerable members of the community. I was home alone one day as the doorbell rang. The dishevelled man at the front door had an unkempt beard and old trousers which were falling down. If I'm honest, I felt afraid of this man who aggressively announced he'd been released from prison and wanted food. Our general policy is not to give food out randomly as it creates unhealthy dependency – instead, we invite people to our community meals where we try to create a sense of family/belonging as we share food together.

However, as I stood in front of this stranger who scared me, I felt God whisper, 'treat this man like my son'. So instead of sending him away with a flyer for our community meal I snuck into the kitchen to put together a haphazard food parcel and a hot drink for him to take with him. In that moment I was reminded that we should treat everyone we speak to and interact with as if they are Jesus. We are all made in the image of God and carry God's DNA and therefore we should treat each other with the respect, kindness, time and energy that we would like to be treated with. It's easy to show hospitality to people who are like us but as Christians we are called more importantly to show love to the strangers who are different from us.

† Instead of seeing strangers and neighbours as scary and dangerous, teach us, God, to see them as part of your beautiful, diverse family and show us how to love one another with kindness and dignity.

For further thought

How have this week's readings changed your view of strangers? Is there anything you're going to do differently when interacting with people who are different from you?

The stranger next door

2 A culture of care

Notes by **Dafne Plou**

Dafne is a retired social communicator and a women's rights activist who participates in the women's movement in her country. She's a member of the Methodist Church in Argentina. In her local church, in the suburbs of Buenos Aires, she works in the area of 'Community building and fellowship in liturgy'. She has a big family and loves spending time with her ten grandchildren. Dafne has used the NIVUK for these readings.

Sunday 10 July
Brother's keeper?

Read Genesis 4:1–16

Then the Lord saqid to Cain, 'Where is your brother Abel?' 'I don't know,' he replied. 'Am I my brother's keeper?'

(verse 9)

In 2020, in the midst of the Covid-19 pandemic, I remember reading an article in one of the main newspapers in Argentina where the journalist asserted that 'each home would become a bunker'. And in a way it happened. He also said that the 'bunker-home' would mean much more than what 'home' had meant so far and that this new understanding would change its definition for a long time. This assertion made me think deeply, did I want my home to become a 'bunker'? Of course, I wanted it to be a safe place in a troublesome environment. But a 'bunker', where we stay in fear, distrust, thinking only selfishly of ourselves and closing doors to outsiders?

'Where is your brother? Where is your sister?', asks the Lord even during lockdowns. And we are called to get moving. In our suburban congregation we got organised in a creative quick-response network and our mobile phones became our best allies – not only to respond to any need but also to pray for each other. And we also got to the streets to protest against confusing health policies that increased discrimination and corruption, while wearing our face masks, of course! No bunkers, but open doors and commitment!

† Jesus, challenge us to affirm our commitment to justice and care for each other even in lockdowns and virus crises. Don't let us become icy bunkers. Amen

Monday 11 July
Commandments to live by

Read Exodus 20:12–17

So that you may live long in the land the Lord your God is giving you.

(part of verse 12)

In a very concise style, the commandments sound like harsh orders, compulsory mandates that people must obey in fear. The reading tells us that the people of Israel who were witnessing this crucial moment were trembling frightfully and at a distance, looking how Moses approached 'the thick darkness where God was' (verse 21). A scary setting! Did God plan to control his people with a rigid hand and threats?

Much has been said about the Old Testament law that condemns and the redeeming grace we find in Jesus' gospel. But is there not also love and redemption in God's actions to free the people of Israel from slavery in Egypt? Exodus 20 starts by saying 'I am the Lord your God, who brought you out of Egypt, out of the land of slavery' (verse 2). It speaks of a Father's abundant love and care who saves his sons and daughters from oppression and also wants them to live long in their own land, in peace and justice.

The commandments we are asked to live by do not imply a menace nor a veiled bondage, but a call to build new just and peaceful relations among each other and societies where we feel free to obey our Redeemer, the Holy One, the Lord our God. He teaches us what is best for us, he directs us in the way we should go and promises that if only we pay attention to his commands, our peace would be like a river, and our well-being like the waves of the sea (Isaiah 48:17–18).

† Help us abide by your mandates, God, in just and peaceful relations with our fellow men and women. Let us feel free to obey! In your love. Amen

For further thought

Read or listen to the news today and consider the many ways we defy just and peaceful relations in our world today. What if we followed God's commands? Any ideas?

Tuesday 12 July
Golden rule

Read Leviticus 19:8–18

When you reap the harvest of your land, do not reap to the very edges of your field or gather the gleanings of your harvest. Do not go over your vineyard a second time or pick up the grapes that have fallen. Leave them for the poor and the foreigner.

(part of verses 9–10)

In the 1990s, last century, a new movement grew and got stronger. It questioned how development and economic growth were taking place, for the benefit of a few and to the detriment of many. There was an Earth Summit in 1992 and Christian churches and the ecumenical movement contributed with a new challenging programme on 'Justice, Peace and Creation'. There was a need to discuss in depth the existing economic model that over-exploited natural resources and people, poisoned waters and polluted the atmosphere, and to work toward sustainable development, considering our earth's environmental carrying capacity.

Accumulation, intensive growth and profit are not necessarily compatible with life. In this reading, God is telling us that economic growth filling the barns or pockets of a few should not be the central organising principle of society nor of human relations. Instead, considering how to end with inequalities and taking care of the needs and difficulties common people face daily should be top aims.

In the documents produced by the ecumenical movement during the Earth Summit, we can read debates where delegates affirm that if it is a sin to kill or to steal, then it is also a sin to destroy earth's carrying capacity. All people should be able to enjoy access to natural resources, food, drinking water and clean air. To achieve this, God calls us to build new relationships between people, earth and economic activities. He also wants us to preach hope and commitment to the world so that justice cannot be perverted nor life endangered.

† Guide us with your Holy Spirit to share with others our hope of life on this earth, the home you gave us to look after and enjoy with loving care. Amen

For further thought

How is your local community responding to environmental challenges? Any projects or programmes you could join to learn more, share your interests, contribute to the common good?

Wednesday 13 July
Forgiving neighbours

Read Proverbs 24:27–34

Do not testify against your neighbour without cause – would you use your lips to mislead? Do not say, 'I'll do to them as they have done to me; I'll pay them back for what they did.'

(verses 28–29)

After some fights in the street market between members of different migrant communities there was a need to put an end to controversies and stop violence from escalating. Why were the Bolivian gardeners charged more for their stalls than the rest? Should the Senegalese vendors be allowed to sell those goods of dubious origin? What about mixing in one place crucifixes, images of the Virgin Mary, mandalas and Indigenous symbols? Isn't that profane? How come the Paraguayans put up their national flags in their stands? They live in Argentina after all!

Working for peace in cosmopolitan neighbourhoods is not an easy task, as many of us know. Sometimes one finds that distrust, suspicion and lack of confidence of one another because of race or different ethnic, cultural or religious backgrounds create an atmosphere that endangers social harmony and puts rules of coexistence at stake. Our own church communities suffer from these divisions and it is hard to open opportunities for dialogue and understanding. How do we stop the hunger for paying back for offences, discrimination and mistreatment?

One congregation in a popular area in town decided to celebrate National Day inviting all the different ethnic communities and nationalities in the neighbourhood to share their national dish, music and dances in the church's backyard after an open, ecumenical service. The invitation was accepted with some scepticism at first, but enthusiasm soon grew. Just seeing different national flags on the altar that day created a whole new atmosphere that enabled joint actions to promote understanding and amity for the years to come.

† Jesus, inspire us with your spirit of love and understanding to overcome the barriers that stop us from being true sisters and brothers, in trust and respect for each other. Amen

For further thought

Any migrants or foreigners in your community? How much do you know about their culture? Just search on the internet and work to find ways for inclusion.

Thursday 14 July
Who may abide?

Read Psalm 15

Who may live on your holy mountain? The one whose way of life is blameless, who does what is righteous, who speaks the truth from their hearts.

(verses 1b–2)

n troubled societies, where unrest has become the norm, working for justice and inclusion is a mandate Christians shouldn't avoid. It entails listening to the calls and protests of those who cannot bear any more the structures and actions created by societies that consider them perfectly legal and just but result in the oppression of many.

When I was a young university student, a military dictatorship ruled with an iron hand in my country. 'Law and order' was their motto under national security policies. Some of the chief commanders believed themselves very righteous and attended mass every morning, while the number of human rights violations grew shockingly. The political and social situation was devastating, but we were not left alone. An important number of Christians from different denominations, politicians, activists, human rights defenders and people of good will came together – in spite of fear and threats – to struggle for human dignity, freedom and democracy. For us, the young ones, it was inspiring to see our church leaders demanding justice and speaking truth from their hearts inspired by the Holy Spirit.

Today there are still many situations in which a lot has to be done in order to do away with legal but oppressive structures. Just think of how hard it is to access to justice for victims of gender violence, or to uphold 'Black Lives Matter' high in places where racism, though hidden, is still well alive. For sure, God calls each of us to be someone 'who keeps an oath even when it hurts, and does not change their mind' if justice is our goal (verse 4b).

† God, let us be inspired by the lives of those who have left aside their own safety and conveniences to drive their work for societies where justice, dignity and equality for every person prevail. Amen

For further thought

Think of examples of righteousness today. Is it limited to being 'politically correct'? Any way to go beyond that?

Friday 15 July
Fulfilling the law

Read Matthew 22:34–40

'Love the Lord your God with all your heart and with all your soul and with all your mind.' This is the first and greatest commandment. And the second is like it: 'Love your neighbour as yourself.'

(verses 37–39)

In the movie, *Parasite*, by Korean filmmaker, Bong Joon-ho, disregard of existing inequalities, discrimination in personal relations, and neglect in the implementation of public policies that serve everyone on equal terms end in disaster, violence and death. The film received the 2019 *Palm D'or* in the Cannes Film Festival and four Academy Awards that same year, including Best Picture and Best Director. *Parasite* tells us bluntly that individualism and selfishness appear to lead our societies' main decisions and in today's context of high uncertainty and unpredictability these behaviours can only take us to a dreadful failure.

In an environment where many think they only have to be accountable to themselves, it is difficult to call people to care for others, to pay attention to the unequal conditions and needs in our societies, to find solutions which question wrong decisions that affect the natural world, and to start work for indisputable change. As Christians, are we ready to make visible our love of God with heart and soul and reflect it in love and commitment to our neighbours and our common home?

Brazilian theologian, Leonardo Boff, has for a long time reflected on the state of the relation between human beings and the world they inhabit. He believes that this situation of post-pandemic is calling us to make a drastic change of paradigm. This would entail coming closer to the Mount of Beatitudes, loving life, demystifying violence, and caring and having mercy upon all living beings. 'Blessed are those whose strength is in you, whose hearts are set on pilgrimage.' (Psalm 84:5).

† God, come and be with us, we need your presence, your teachings and the guidance of your Holy Spirit to be in solidarity with those that need you and make visible your love and justice. Amen

For further thought

Look for images, songs or movies that could be helpful to understand the need of faithful witness of Jesus in our world today.

Saturday 16 July
Members of one another

Read Ephesians 4:25–32

Therefore each of you must put off falsehood and speak truthfully to your neighbour, for we are all members of one body.

(verse 25)

The fire began in the hill area just before Spring Day. It had been a very dry winter and winds were now blowing harshly. The fire soon grew stronger and invaded cultivated fields and pastures, destroying crops and cattle, and threatening farms and villages. There were desperate efforts to stop the fire from spreading to other areas and dozens of volunteers – men and women of all ages – worked together with the firefighters to put an end to damage. But a big row also started between farmers and authorities, till the farmers admitted reluctantly that the fire was a traditional way of getting rid of weeds and clearing the ground before springtime – but that it had got out of hand.

'Fake news', speculation and all sort of stories and lies had circulated on social networks and local media during the fires. And though the truth was hard to take, at least recognition of mistakes and wrong decisions helped to clear up responsibilities and start the process of healing open wounds and working out economical loses.

Surprisingly, villagers and farmers discovered that many had never truly met each other. Suddenly, fighting the fires had given them the opportunity to show their mutual care and concern for each other and the love and dedication they shared for their land and animals. Without planning it, they had entered into each other's lives and there were chances for getting rid of bitterness and anger, consider forgiveness and build lasting trust.

† When destruction and anger seem to dominate our lives and behaviours, give us your peace, Jesus, so that we may recognise our wrong doings and be ready to open our hands and hearts to our neighbours. Amen

For further thought

Share in your church group experiences where people you hadn't noticed became important in their care of others.

Living hopefully with pain and disability

1 Living with pain

Notes by **Jessica Hewitt**

Jessica is a wife and stay-at-home mother from Bedfordshire who has experienced many different forms of pain and trauma, including back injuries and eating disorders. In recovery for alcohol addiction and chronic and acute mental health issues, Jessica trained in counselling and in turn helps other sufferers to find their own recovery paths. Pregnancy and motherhood have offered many opportunities for self-reflection and she is working towards helping more people with her writing and experience. Jessica has used the NIVUK for these readings.

Sunday 17 July
Power in weakness

Read 2 Corinthians 12:1–10

Three times I pleaded with the Lord to take it away from me. But he said to me, 'My grace is sufficient for you, for my power is made perfect in weakness.'

(verses 8–9a)

'Weakness' has always been a word with negative connotations. A weakness could be a chink in armour, a broken link in a chain, or a personal failing. Society likes to hide weaknesses, or cover them up in some way, but what if we saw them as opportunities for growth?

Paul is preoccupied with thoughts of appearing conceited, taking away the spotlight from Christ and bringing it upon himself. He has talked of others' visions and revelations while actively avoiding boasting about his own closeness with the Lord, or bigging himself up. It appears Christ has helped him stay humble, too, by giving him a 'thorn in [his] flesh'. Whether this was a physical or spiritual thorn, we don't know. Through this 'weakness', though, God also gave him sufficient grace and power to continue his preaching, because God makes all things bearable. This weakness allowed him to grow spiritually, to become close to God and to bear all the hardships that living in Christ brought him. We can see our own weaknesses daily, yet we might not often use them to find power in Christ.

† God, grant me the grace to find your power in my own weaknesses, and see them not as a failing, but an opening.

Monday 18 July
Transformed through trauma

Read Genesis 32:24–31

Then the man said, 'Let me go, for it is daybreak.' But Jacob replied, 'I will not let you go unless you bless me.'

(verse 26)

Jacob has quite an experience here. He wrestles with an angel all night and is then physically disabled by him, yet he will still not relent unless the angel blesses him. He is still injured, marred by the encounter, but he has persevered and prevailed through what I can only imagine is extreme pain, all to receive God's grace. He is a changed man after this night, he is given a new name and a new purpose. He has seen the face of God. His limp is a token of this change, this blessing and renewal of character.

My disabilities have surely transformed me, my injuries and scars speaking of trying times – even if they were not directly bestowed by an angel! I recognise the transformation that my trauma allowed, and sometimes exacted upon me. God's grace has helped me to use this trauma as a tool, and I carry my scars as reminders of those experiences. It can be easy to dwell on the memories and only focus on the pain, but those memories serve a much higher purpose when we can see how those moments led us to change ourselves, and choose better things. When I see someone with a disability, I see someone who has overcome. Our traumas can be our transformations, and our scars can be symbols of change, just like Jacob's limp was a symbol of God's blessing and Jacob's indomitable faith.

† Pray for yourself or someone else: Lord, I pray that you would help me see my traumas as a testament to my strength and my personal story, and help me to continue to find strength in them.

For further thought

Jacob could have easily considered himself a victim after that night. What do you think stopped him?

Tuesday 19 July
Advocating through God

Read Exodus 4:10–17

You shall speak to him and put the words in his mouth; I will help both of you speak and will teach you both what to do.

(verse 15)

The first thing that leapt out at me upon reading this passage this time was how the way we see Moses act here is not how I viewed Moses from Bible stories when I was younger. Those stories of Moses leading the Israelites out of Egypt and across the Red Sea and receiving the ten commandments from God showed him as a strong, able leader and a chosen follower. Yet, in this passage, we see him in weakness and fear. In the midst of this anxiety, God gives him an alternative, his brother Aaron. Aaron becomes his advocate.

I strongly believe in the positive power of advocating not only for yourself, but for others. I have felt shame in the past for not being able to speak on behalf of myself, and yet here is God providing an earthly advocate for such a man as Moses. Of course, Moses wasn't yet the man he would become, but perhaps that's even more important – having an advocate helped him on that journey.

I can see how having people act as an advocate for me when I was at my most vulnerable led to me getting the help that was so critical at the time. My mother has been, and always will be, my most willing advocate, and she was definitely motivated by God. I have certainly been blessed by her willingness to stand up for me, and I am now strong enough to stand up for myself and ask for the help I need.

Sometimes, all it takes is the knowledge that someone else has your back. Sometimes, all it takes is standing up for someone else to see what help you need yourself.

† Loving Lord, I pray that I can see and take opportunities to advocate for those in need, or ask for someone to advocate for me when I can't for myself.

For further thought

Is there anyone in your life who might be in need of a godly advocate?

Wednesday 20 July
Unburdened by the king

Read 2 Samuel 9

'Don't be afraid,' David said to him, 'for I will surely show you kindness for the sake of your father Jonathan. I will restore to you all the land that belonged to your grandfather Saul, and you will always eat at my table.'

(verse 7)

This is a difficult passage to digest, and not just because of the names! There's a whole load of history behind the significance of the interaction, and a lot of family drama. We know King David as a wise and just ruler, but his interconnectedness with King Saul's descendants is worthy of a soap opera! Even with all of the bad blood between them, though, here David is opening his doors and laying a place at his kingly table for the last descendant of the man who tried to kill him, purely on the merit of his relationship with Jonathan. Perhaps the only reason Mephibosheth has been lost and discarded by society is the fact that both his feet are lame. In a culture where your ability to physically fight or work was key, it's easy to see how Mephibosheth could have been cast aside.

I too have been lost in the gutter, figuratively and literally. I was ashamed of where I had fallen to when I came from such a good, loving family. The last thing I could comprehend was God wanting me at his table, being blessed when I had fallen so far. Yet, here is David, a king, asking a broken man whose family has been scattered and slain, to come and sit at his table. Even when he has nothing to offer, David recognises what the right thing to do is, and God's graciousness flows through him in this act of kindness. As God worked through David, he too offers us seats at his kingly table when we have nothing to offer him.

† Thank you, Lord, for preparing a place for me even when I feel I have nothing to offer.

For further thought
Is there room 'at your table' for someone who could use an act of kindness?

Thursday 21 July
Hope in unrelenting pain

Read Job 6:8–13

What strength do I have, that I should still hope? What prospects, that I should be patient?

(verse 11)

What a cry for help. Exhausted, broken, overwhelmed by pain... This man can't take any more. Can you imagine being in such pain, physically or mentally, that you just wish for death? That you ask the creator himself to grant it? Have you ever experienced this yourself, or known someone who has?

It's a dark place indeed. It can feel dramatic and chaotic, or it can be quiet and tranquil. For me, there was a resonance in such moments. A taking stock. An acknowledgement of all life is and has been so far. A stillness where I could feel the suspense of a decision. I would swim in my mind between the consequences of my actions, what I might feel, who I might affect. The dichotomy of hopefulness and hopelessness hanging in the air.

Job is certain of the comfort that death will bring. Even in these darkest moments, he is hopeful of being by God's side and free of pain. His echoing question, 'Do I have any power to help myself, now that success has been driven from me?' is so salient. My recovery and helping others on their recoveries has taught me that God has given us all the power to help ourselves. I have learned that there is nothing you can't recover from, although what that recovery looks like is different for everyone. God wants and empowers us to help ourselves, and finding hope is the first step in doing so successfully. The beautiful thing is: God is hope. He is our hope when we can't find any for ourselves.

† God of hope, I pray for all the people who are struggling to find a light at the end of the tunnel, that they find their way to a new day.

For further thought

When you've struggled and come through, what was it that gave you hope to continue?

Friday 22 July
Trust the process

Read Psalm 22:1–15

To you they cried out and were saved; in you they trusted and were not put to shame.

(verse 5)

There is a deeply emotional cycle of hope and despair at play here. The psalmist feels totally abandoned by God, yet he knows his faith in him is in the right place. He acknowledges that others have been spared when they cried out for help, yet he still despairs that he hasn't been rescued already. Knowing that he will be rescued doesn't stop him from expressing his distress and anguish in the moment. But even though he talks as if he is at death's door, he truly believes he will be delivered.

If I could go back and tell myself in my deepest desperations that I was on the right path, I doubt I would have truly believed it. I didn't know if I was ever going to recover parts of myself that I could feel slipping away. There is a phrase that gets thrown around in therapy: 'trust the process'. It's an infuriating one, because the process often looks hard, futile and downright hopeless, but here I am years later reflecting on just how accurate it can be. The process of recovery is so important because of the lessons it teaches. Ironically, they aren't lessons you can read. The mistakes we make, the difficult times we face and the way we face them all prepare us for the next steps in our lives. The psalmist here understands this, but it doesn't stop him from letting God know how tough he's finding his current situation or that he feels abandoned. You can trust in God, and still talk about how hard that can be.

† Lord, let me find the strength to trust in you even when all seems lost.

For further thought
Can you think of any times where you couldn't see the benefit of the process at the beginning, but recognised it afterwards?

Saturday 23 July
Benefits that outweigh the risks

Read Galatians 4:12–20

Where, then, is your blessing of me now? I can testify that, if you could have done so, you would have torn out your eyes and given them to me. Have I now become your enemy by telling you the truth?

(verses 15–16)

Paul's letter to the Galatians is eye-openingly honest. He talks about 'trialling' them with his 'illness', the diagnosis of which is heavily debated. Regardless of what his affliction was, however, the power of Christ worked through him and they welcomed him with open arms. Can you imagine feeling such acceptance from a group of people entirely counter to your own culture, especially if you were suffering from a challenging illness?

I feel as though there is a lot of self-stigma around mental health in particular, in that we might hold ourselves back from making connections with others because of how we fear they may perceive us. We can miss opportunities to spread God's love when we shut ourselves off. Paul questions if he has now become an enemy of the Galatians because he told them the truth. This is a question that plagues many people, and I definitely worry about disaffecting many to whom I tell my truth. That applies to both my faith and my personal journey. Paul is a shining example of someone who felt the fear and did it anyway. He helped start the Christian churches in Asia Minor and risked losing his favour with them when he told them honestly how they needed to get back on the right path. His devotion to God and the benefits of refocusing the Galatian churches was much more important than the prospect of falling out with them. Although there is a risk to honesty, the benefits far outweigh that risk.

† Lord, help us all to speak honestly about our truths, and to know that we are accepted regardless of our flaws or afflictions.

For further thought

Can you think of a time when you decided not to be honest because you thought it would risk too much? What happened? If you would have done it differently, how would you do it now?

Living hopefully with pain and disability

2 Sustained by hope

Notes by **Liz Carter**

 Liz is an author and poet, writing about finding God's treasure in the midst of pain and brokenness, living with long-term illness. She lives in Shropshire with her husband Tim, a church leader, and their two children. Her first book, *Catching Contentment* (IVP, 2018), explores how we can find peace when life doesn't work out as we would hope, and her second book, *Treasure in Dark Places* (Capstone House, 2020), is a collection of poetry and short re-imaginings of encounters with Jesus. Liz has used the NIVUK for these readings.

Sunday 24 July
Supported by angels

Read Mark 1:12–13

At once the Spirit sent him out into the wilderness, and he was in the wilderness for forty days, being tempted by Satan. He was with the wild animals, and angels attended him.

(verses 12–13)

Sometimes we experience the great heights, only to be plunged into the depths – and the contrast is stark. Jesus had just been connected to his Father in a tangible and visual experience of the Holy Spirit, only to be wrenched from the glory and into the desert. For many of us, that wilderness is a familiar place. Maybe some of us feel as if we never escape it, as if we never get to break out of its bonds and come back to safety and freedom. The wilderness looks like different things for different people; for me it is the long-term lung disease I live with, leaving me often in pain and sickness.

Yet words of hope permeate this short passage. Although Jesus was tempted, although he must have been faint with hunger and thirst, he was also attended by angels. Three words which are thrilling in their alluring invitation to us to be drawn into a story where we are not left alone, and we are not abandoned to the desert – even when we are dwelling there for a time, God is attending us. God is by our side, watching for our needs and catching us when we fall.

† Father, thank you that you attend us in our wilderness and never abandon us. May we know the consolation of your Spirit in our brokenness.

Monday 25 July
Jesus' wounds

Read John 20:19–20

Jesus came and stood among them and said, 'Peace be with you!' After he said this, he showed them his hands and side. The disciples were overjoyed when they saw the Lord.

(part of verses 19–20)

They'd been through a myriad of emotions over the past few days. They'd been torn apart and left bereft, wondering what this had all been about. And then the elation as they saw him there, in the room with them:

> *The night was towering and forlorn in its gloom*
> *the day of hopelessness a crushing ravage*
> *but now dawn streaks the sky with scarlet gold*
> *and hope blazes through the heavens*
> *as the day explodes to glorious life*
> *and joy comes in the morning.*

(from 'Sunday Two' in *Treasure in Dark Places*, Capstone House, 2020)

Joy had come to their morning, but it was more than joy. The first words Jesus spoke were of peace, as if to remind his friends that they could access the depths of God even in their shock. In showing them his wounds, Jesus spoke truth over them; the truth of who he was, the truth of the pain he had gone through for them, and the scars that remained. And that's when the joy came, an explosion of exhilaration, of relief and excitement all crowding together in their incredulous minds.

We can know this peace, too, when we are fearful and anxious, when life isn't going as we'd hoped. We can know that Jesus went through so much agony the scars still show; scars that whisper his love through history and through our weary hearts. And we can grasp hold of the inexpressible joy that is only found in the fathomless love of God, joy that sparks us with hope for the path ahead.

† Dear Jesus, wounded for us, may we know the incomprehensible peace you breathe over us, even in our own hurting. May we take hold of living hope and plunge into streams of joy inexpressible.

For further thought

Take courage when you live with your scars, because Jesus went there too. How will you take hold of Jesus' words of peace today?

Tuesday 26 July
Creation groans

Read Romans 8:18–25

We know that the whole creation has been groaning as in the pains of childbirth right up to the present time. Not only so, but we ourselves, who have the firstfruits of the Spirit, groan inwardly as we wait eagerly for our adoption to sonship, the redemption of our bodies.

(verses 22–23)

Waiting can be painful. We wait through our lives for many things, whether for buses or Christmas or illness to be over or grief to ease, and the waiting time can be a grief in itself, especially when there is no end in sight. We so often feel that it's only when the waiting comes to an end that we will find peace and contentment. We've forgotten how to wait, in a world that values immediacy, as people who cannot wait longer than a couple of seconds for a webpage to load.

Yet here Paul portrays the upside-down nature of God's kingdom, as he writes of the profound mystery of the groaning of creation and how our groans are gathered up within this as we wait, with the creation, for liberation. The wait can be heavy with despair, but also can be imbued with a sense of eagerness, of yearning for how things will, one day, be made perfect. We groan along with creation because we know, deep down, that we are made for more, that our bodies will be whole, that our tears will be dried up and that there will be no more grief. And as we wait, hope can trickle through when we turn toward Christ, when we realise that it is *inside* the waiting we find him waiting with us.

> *We join in the groaning of all creation,*
> *Dive into echoes of exultation,*
> *Ache for the song of restoration,*
> *And wait with fragments of tear-washed hope.*

(from 'Friday' in *Treasure in Dark Places*, Capstone House, 2020)

† Father, when we live under the groaning of waiting, may we know your everlasting arms encircling our past, present and future, and the glorious hope to which we are called sustaining us within our wait.

For further thought
Reflect on how creation groaning to be made whole points to the great hope you can take hold of in your painful present.

Wednesday 27 July
Enduring suffering

Read 2 Corinthians 1:3–11

We were under great pressure, far beyond our ability to endure, so that we despaired of life itself. Indeed, we felt we had received the sentence of death. But this happened that we might not rely on ourselves but on God.

(part of verses 8–9)

Amy Carmichael was a twentieth-century missionary who suffered a fall which led to crippling pain, confining her to her sickbed. It seemed too much to bear, after a life of great passion and action among orphans in India, and most of us would probably have found it beyond endurance. But Amy writes of how she discovered a spiritual secret about finding peace in God despite her pain. She discovered that it was in looking to God and relying on God for all her needs where she found rest for her soul, even when her body was hurting. Instead of living in discontent, she chose to live flooded with hope as she continued to dig into the treasures of Christ that she found even in darkness.

Paul, too, was in great difficulty that seemed beyond endurance, and he, too, chose to trust in God, reminding his readers that his own suffering helped bring them comfort in their own anguish, as they found resonance in his struggle. Paul realised that God showers riches on those who trust through the storm, even when the storm threatens to overwhelm, and chose to prioritise praise to God over his own worry and anger.

It is striking that Paul highlights the importance of honesty in the sharing of struggles (verse 8), knowing that his modelling of honesty would help those reading his letter when they need to share their own pain, but reminding them, ultimately, that God is their deliverer. We, too, can find great comfort in sharing of our difficulties with others, and in an encouragement to look to hope.

† Lord, when we are battered by life and our struggle seems beyond endurance, remind us of your hope that brings freedom, and teach us the secret of contentment as we trust you through our storms.

For further thought

Read some writings of Amy Carmichael, reflecting on her tenacious courage in the most trying of times. Hear the whisper of hope through her words.

Thursday 28 July
Crushed but not defeated

Read 2 Corinthians 4:7–10

But we have this treasure in jars of clay to show that this all-surpassing power is from God and not from us. We are hard pressed on every side, but not crushed; perplexed, but not in despair; persecuted, but not abandoned; struck down, but not destroyed.

(verses 7–9)

When watching *The Great Pottery Throwdown* (a television show about a group of potters creating pieces from clay) earlier this year, I was struck anew how fragile the pots were and how easily shattered they were during and after the process of crafting, firing and decorating. In early church times, people reading this letter would have been familiar with 'jars of clay' in many different forms, and especially familiar with their fragility as well as their beauty and utility. Paul using this metaphor brings a powerful description of our own frailty and the contrasting power of the treasure we are carrying – the truth of the gospel.

The hope that Paul breathes through these words has sustained many Christians over centuries, because it is hope mixed with raw honesty. He does not sugar-coat the experience of the Christian life or advise us that all will be well when we have faith, as if God is a great vending-machine ready to give us our every wish. Instead, he tells it how it is. We will be overwhelmed, under pressure, persecuted and perplexed. For me, it's a great relief to see scripture admitting the reality of what so many of us face in our lives as Christians living in a broken world. But it's the way Paul balances each phrase with his 'but nots' that so consoles me when things are hard.

We are fallible creatures, living with imperfection, and yet God has trusted us with the greatest treasure of all, and that treasure sustains and upholds us, sparks joy within us and keeps us from falling.

† Lord, when we are perplexed, fill us with confidence in you. When we are crushed, console us with peace beyond understanding. When we are in despair, remind us of the treasure found in darkest corners.

For further thought

Find space today to reflect on Paul's 'but nots'. Ask God to whisper his breaths of hope through the truth of these words of scripture.

Friday 29 July
Jesus' self-emptying

Read Philippians 2:2–11

Who, being in very nature God, did not consider equality with God something to be used to his own advantage; rather, he made himself nothing by taking the very nature of a servant, being made in human likeness … humbled himself by becoming obedient to death – even death on a cross!

(part of verses 6–8)

My husband is a church minister, and when my children were small they would sometimes wander up and stand by his side while he was preaching, lifting their arms to be picked up. As his children they loved his presence and had confidence in their rights to be cuddled wherever they were, even if Daddy was wearing his scary robes.

Jesus gave up his rights to his Father's presence, emptying himself of his royal status. I cannot even imagine the pain of this emptying out of himself, and I am in awe at his humility, not counting himself of a higher status than others, and thus not eligible for suffering. Instead, he left glory and got into our mess, willing to take on our sin, out of his Father's presence, unable to wander over and ask for a hug.

And it's because of his obedience and humility that we can be set free from the bondage of sin and the burden of our own struggles, because he is God with us, because he has been raised and exalted to the highest place. Because of his emptying of himself, which cost him everything, we can run right up to the Father and say, 'Up, Daddy!' And we will be lifted in everlasting arms, held close and comforted.

When we look to follow Jesus' example of humility and self-denial, we dig into the resources to wait through our own suffering with hope and anticipation for what will one day become reality, when every knee will bow and every tongue confess that Jesus Christ is Lord.

† Jesus, we are amazed at your great love for us. We are stunned by your emptying of yourself so that we can be free. We bow to you and confess that you are Lord.

For further thought

How can you follow Jesus' example of humility and emptying himself in your life today?

Fresh From The Word 2023

Thinking ahead, now is the right time to order *Fresh From The Word 2023*.

Order now:

- direct from IBRA
- from your local IBRA rep
- from the Lion Hudson website: www.lionhudson.com
- in Christian bookshops
- from online retailers such as Amazon, Eden and others

To order direct from IBRA

- website: **shop.christianeducation.org.uk**
- email: **ibra.sales@christianeducation.org.uk**
- call: **0121 458 3313**
- post: **using the order form at the back of this book**

Fresh From The Word is available for Kindle, and in ePub and PDF format from online retailers such as Amazon and Eden.

How are you finding this year?

Let us know how you are finding this year's daily Bible reading notes. If you are on Facebook or Twitter, we would love to hear your thoughts, as little or as often as you like! You never know, it may also encourage others to investigate The Word and form a deeper connection with our fellow readers.

 www.facebook.com/freshfromtheword

 www.twitter.com/IBRAbibleread

Would you consider leaving your own legacy to help spread the Good News?

IBRA and *Fresh From The Word* are only possible through you, the readers, and your donations. At this moment, when the world is changing rapidly, we need your help. A gift in your will to IBRA's International Fund will help continue its Bible reading legacy of 140 years. Every penny of your donation goes directly towards enabling hundreds of thousands of people around the world to access the living Word of God.

> *For while bodily training is of some value, godliness is of value in every way, as it holds promise for the present life and also for the life to come.*
>
> **1 Timothy 4:8 (ESV)**

It was the vision of Charles Waters to empower people in Britain and overseas to benefit from the Word of God through the experiences and insights of biblical scholars from around the world. The goal was to strengthen and encourage people in their homes and situations, wherever they were. His legacy lives on today, in you, as a reader, and in the IBRA team, across the globe.

Our work at IBRA is supported by sales of our books, and since 1882 we continue to ensure that 100% of donations to the IBRA International Fund go to benefit our local and international readers. We are blessed every year by those who leave a legacy in their will – ensuring that their hopes are carried on and fulfilled by IBRA, when they have risen into eternal life with our Lord. To continue this important work, would you consider leaving a legacy in your will?

To find out more please contact our Finance Manager on 0121 458 3313, email ibra@christianeducation.org.uk or write to International Bible Reading Association, 5–6 Imperial Court, 12 Sovereign Road, Birmingham, B30 3FH.

- To read more about the history of IBRA go to the inside back page.
- To find out more about the work of the IBRA International Fund go to page 369.

Saturday 30 July
An end to war wounds

Read Micah 4:1–4

They will beat their swords into ploughshares and their spears into pruning hooks. Nation will not take up sword against nation, nor will they train for war anymore. Everyone will sit under their own vine … and no one will make them afraid, for the Lord Almighty has spoken.

(parts of verses 3–4)

My lungs are riddled with scars, caused over years by degenerative disease and countless infections. In our lives, our scars keep showing even when we are healed, just as Jesus' did after his resurrection. We have wounds that go deep, wounds others have afflicted upon us and wounds we have afflicted upon ourselves, as well as wounds from life's struggles and burdens. It sometimes feels as though there is no end in sight to the wars we wage and the pain that we bear.

Micah was a prophet with a heart for the marginalised and oppressed (4:6), and for God's justice and mercy (6:8). In this passage he shares God's priorities of a kingdom of peace, where war will be no more, and his call to repentance for those who have trampled others. We can draw courage from the cry for restoration at the very centre of the gospel. We can dig deep into the treasure God showers us with while we are waiting for that restoration and while the wars still rage on, while being consoled with the knowledge that there will be an end to our war wounds, there will be a cease to our dread, for God has spoken.

Imagine a world of peace, where justice reigns and perfect love has cast out all fear. We see glimpses of this kingdom here in the painful now, and the anticipation of it and yearning for it carries us forward, ever pressing on and persevering in the love of God, as hope sustains us and guides us on our way.

† Lord, thank you that you speak perfect love into our lives, casting out fear. Thank you for your heart of justice, restoration and peace. May we reflect your kingdom principles in all that we do.

For further thought

Read Micah 6:8, reflecting on the person God calls you to be. How can you bring his justice and mercy into a hurting world?

Setting sail

1 Make yourself an ark

Notes by **John Birch**

Based in South Wales, John is a Methodist Local Preacher, he writes prayers and Bible studies for faithandworship.com, and is amazed at where these are being used and how God has blessed lives through them. Some prayers have been adapted for use within choral and more contemporary worship settings. John has several published books and in his spare time sings folk songs and, with his wife Margaret, has an allotment, walks and explores the country in a campervan called Lola. John has used the NIVUK for these notes.

Sunday 31 July
The seas are formed

Read Genesis 1:6–9

And God said, 'Let there be a vault between the waters to separate water from water.' So God made the vault and separated the water under the vault from the water above it. And it was so.

(verses 6–7)

Standing at the old harbour in town, it is easy to imagine ships of all sizes sailing down the estuary toward their destination. Apparently, in 1480, a ship loaded with 10,000 slates from English quarries sailed into town: repairs for the local castle gatehouse. That must have been quite a sight!

The sea is a part of our lives. We are not sailors, but we walk the coast and beaches and watch for migrating birds. Looking out to where sea touches sky, it is easy to understand the writer's picture of an immense dome with water both above and below, separated from the earth on which we stand. We know about water in Wales!

Those sailors of old would have been familiar with the dangers awaiting them as they neared land, and local beaches have their share of ancient wrecks. But that dome-like sky, from which the stars and moon shine on a good night, would have guided them to port and safety. The dome speaks to me of God's goodness and provision reaching around and above us all, embracing this world in his love, and though the journey may not always be smooth, God will bring us safely to our destination.

† Pray for all who spend their working lives on what can often be dangerous seas.

Monday 1 August
First, make your boat ...

Read Genesis 6:13–18

But I will establish my covenant with you, and you will enter the ark – you and your sons and your wife and your sons' wives with you.

(verse 18)

Water is essential for life; it is a gentle stream or refreshing shower, but it can also be a monsoon or tsunami, like that which swept across Japan in 2011 with waves up to 39 metres high, killing thousands and laying waste an enormous expanse of the country. Nearer to where we live, torrential rainfall causes riverbanks to burst and water to pour through homes and businesses. It disrupts lives for months, leaving victims to pick up the pieces and get on with life as best they can.

Noah's ark was substantial, the size of one and a half football fields, but without a rudder, so the destination of those on board was totally in the hands of God. Noah had detailed plans to follow, and God trusted him to succeed. But this was no ordinary flood. This was more than the disruption some of us have experienced through storm damage. It was more than picking up the pieces afterwards and getting on with life. This was a new beginning, not humanity resuming the lifestyle of the past that had so broken God's heart. This was life starting afresh with the faithful Noah and family.

And isn't that a picture of what happens when we give our lives to Christ? God does not ask us to build an ark, but he provides the means, through repentance and faith, to leave the past behind, make a fresh start and find new life. And as with Noah, God leads us safely there.

† Pray for those for whom floods are a regular occurrence, that God might give them both the strength and help they need to recover and start anew.

For further thought

If water is so essential for life, is there anything you can do as an individual or family to reduce the amount that is wasted?

Setting sail – 1 Make yourself an ark

August

A valuable fleet

> **Read 2 Chronicles 9:20–22**
> *The king had a fleet of trading ships manned by Hiram's servants. Once every three years it returned, carrying gold, silver and ivory, and apes and baboons.*
>
> (verse 21)

I read the Old Testament and I am thinking 'ancient civilisation' and all that those words conjure up in my mind. Yet here is King Solomon, reigning in the late Bronze Age (970–931 BC) and responsible for Jerusalem's glorious first Temple – a king who controlled maritime trade routes out of Edom, Arabia, India, Africa and Judea, making huge sums of money through taxation, conscripted labour, tributes and gifts from foreign countries, and using a system of land and sea trading backed up by his powerful navy.

Solomon's ships brought back from their voyages not only precious goods but exotic animals, possibly to amuse his many wives and concubines, or as a zoo to educate his people, we do not know. The same source tells us that 'The king made silver and gold as common in Jerusalem as stones' (2 Chronicles 1:15). The story of this maritime trading empire would not be out of place in a history of Elizabethan times in the UK.

How does this news snippet about Solomon speak to us? Well, maybe we should reassess any preconceived ideas we might have about ancient civilisations. They were turbulent days, but so are ours today. The king's friends got key jobs, dealers made their fortunes, workers were exploited, trade deals and back-handers were common, all backed by his army and navy. Perhaps we need to ask ourselves how God sees the world now, some three thousand years later, and whether he is happy with the progress we have made.

† Pray for leaders in the business world, that they might deal fairly with their employees and those who supply their goods.

For further thought
Have you ever given thought to the source of the food you eat and the clothes you wear, and might that inform your future choices?

Wednesday 3 August
Ships of war

Read Daniel 11:40–45

At the time of the end the king of the South will engage him in battle, and the king of the North will storm out against him with chariots and cavalry and a great fleet of ships. He will invade many countries and sweep through them like a flood.

(verse 40)

In their many forms boats bring pleasure and thrills, they rescue victims of flooding, aid movement of refugees, harvest the sea's resources, carry goods and people around the world, and are part of a nation's military might. Here, we read of a great fleet of ships and an army sweeping through countries like a flood. Suddenly all those strategic alliances between nations, such as those struck by Solomon in yesterday's reading, seem very fragile.

However, this is Daniel and there is more here than just a massive power struggle between two powerful kingdoms in the north and south. This was a prophetic warning of what was to come, including the invasion of the 'Beautiful Land' of Israel, a massacre of Jerusalem's population and an altar to Zeus set up in the Temple. But beyond the immediacy of a 'near future' many commentators see a picture of what could be the final scenes of history, a war waged by the antichrist (the king of the North) and his enemies, where he will meet his sudden end on the holy mountain, Jerusalem's temple mount.

I am familiar with Bible prophecies that have their fulfilment in the birth of Christ, but this reminds me that there is so much within the words of the Old Testament if we are prepared to let it speak to our hearts and minds.

Prophecy points to the future, but also the world in which it comes from. However, it is unlikely that the last battle of this world will involve chariots!

† Pray for those sailing in treacherous waters as they flee from conflict and seek refuge in foreign lands.

For further thought
Wars have been a part of history since the earliest days of humans on this planet – why might that be and are they inevitable?

Thursday 4 August
Slave transport

> **Read Deuteronomy 28:64–68**
>
> *The Lord will send you back in ships to Egypt on a journey I said you should never make again. There you will offer yourselves for sale to your enemies as male and female slaves, but no one will buy you.*
>
> (verse 68)

I like to think I keep my promises, but occasionally an apology is necessary because I forgot something I signed up to, so I know I'm far from perfect. Keeping promises is important because trust is the issue. Relationships can break down without trust, as we know only too well in the political sphere.

At the centre of the Old Testament is an agreement, a 'covenant', between God and his people, and trust is at the heart of it. 'If you will be a holy people and follow me, then a blessing will follow!'

But this is not a one-sided agreement. For Israel, having a land to call their own was the blessing they sought from God. At the start of this chapter, Moses and the elders do their best to persuade the people to take God's word seriously. There is a blessing to follow if they say 'Yes!' to their side of the agreement, but the consequences of not doing so are bleak. They will find themselves shipped off as worthless slaves into Egypt, the very place from which God had brought them out of slavery. Is that really what they want?

Now, this might seem like God adopting a rather crude reward and punishment approach, but even Jesus gave people stark choices in his teaching – we sometimes need reminding that not taking seriously the promises we make, particularly to God but also with each other, can have serious consequences.

† Pray for honesty and trust among those who lead both locally and nationally within the country.

For further thought

God's people struggled to remain a 'holy people'. Can you empathise with their dilemma based upon your own experience?

Friday 5 August
A ship for a baby

Read Exodus 2:1–10

Then Pharaoh's daughter went down to the Nile to bathe, and her attendants were walking along the river-bank. She saw the basket among the reeds and sent her female slave to get it. She opened it and saw the baby. He was crying, and she felt sorry for him. 'This is one of the Hebrew babies,' she said.

(verses 5–6)

The Egyptian pharaoh, worried that the Hebrews among them were getting too numerous, ordered the drowning of all baby boys in the Nile. So, one desperate mother hatches a plan to hide her baby son. It seems a strange one, setting a baby adrift on a river, but this was not a case of totally abandoning the child. Sailing in this papyrus ark which, like Noah's, had a waterproof coating of tar and pitch, Moses had his sister Miriam keeping watch as Pharaoh's daughter appeared to partake of the Nile's health-giving waters. At which point Miriam, and God, step in.

From a point of vulnerability, Moses rises to be the one who leads God's people out of Egypt, the very country where he grows up, adopted into the royal family. It is a story that has echoes in that of Joseph (of the legendary colourful coat), taken from the pit where his brothers abandon him and into Egypt, where he becomes a powerful official in the land.

God uses people like Moses, Joseph, you, and me to do his work in the everyday business of life. We may not see the bigger picture, but God can work out his purpose through the ups, downs and coincidences that have put us where we are. It may lead us to positions of power or service, and both are equally valuable. We need to ask God how best we can serve him in the here and now.

† Pray for all those who are caring for newly born babies, particularly in areas of the world where resources such as clean water are scarce.

For further thought

Have you ever wondered what God might want you to do? Why not try asking now?!

At journey's end

> **Read Genesis 8:13–22**
>
> *Then God said to Noah, 'Come out of the ark, you and your wife and your sons and their wives. Bring out every kind of living creature that is with you – the birds, the animals, and all the creatures that move along the ground – so they can multiply on the earth and be fruitful and increase in number on it.'*
>
> (verses 15–17)

On Monday we left Noah building an ark, and now he is back on dry land after his voyage, in a different place and with a new start, his reward for a faithful life and obedience to God's direction. And with this new start comes a promise, the restoration of God's creation – seedtime and harvest, night and day. Whether you understand this story as history or myth, it still speaks to us.

I am reminded of the Mayflower, which in 1620 took 102 Puritans across the Atlantic to a 'Promised Land', arriving just before a harsh winter which would have been disastrous but for the help of the indigenous people among whom they established their colony. New starts can sometimes be difficult, but God provides.

Noah's first act was to set up an altar and worship his saviour. Moses did the same after the Exodus, and God's response in each case was a promise of blessing.

As a family we have made several new starts over the years, as jobs and circumstances dictated, and each one came with challenges as we moved away from friends, family, colleagues, schools and churches where we felt 'at home'. But God has been with us and used us wherever we dropped anchor.

Now, after almost 30 years in one place, I wonder if our physical journeying with God is over (the spiritual one never ends), but pray that should the call come that we, like Noah, will be faithful and allow God to take us safely where he needs us.

† Pray for those who have tough decisions to make today, that they might find the help and advice that they need.

For further thought

How easy has it been in your journey of faith to hear and respond to God's call, and are you still listening?

Setting sail

2 All hands on deck

Notes by **Ian Fosten**

Ian has ministered within the United Reformed Church in Norfolk, Suffolk and on Holy Island (Lindisfarne). He is director of a community theatre in Lowestoft where he lives with his wife and two youngest children. He runs open-mic poetry readings and has a particular interest in landscape and spiritualty. Ian has used the NIVUK for these notes.

Sunday 7 August
A sailor's faith

Read Psalm 107:23–30

Then they cried out to the Lord in their trouble, and he brought them out of their distress.

(verse 28)

As we maintain a nautical theme this week, I read today's psalm and respond, 'Yep, I've been there!'

Forty years ago, I sailed a little boat out onto a lake near my home. The launching point was sheltered, but out in open water both wind and waves increased to way beyond the capability of this inexperienced sailor, or his tiny craft. I lowered sail and tried to row back – but the wind was too strong. I prayed.

Unlike the sailors in the psalm (and Jesus friends on a stormy lake), God's instant response to my split-second prayer for help came not in the miraculous calming of wind and waves, but as three clear statements: 'You got yourself into this! I am most definitely with you. I will help you work out the solution.' With plenty of 'fear and trembling', I raised the sail once more. Over the next hour, I inched back towards the slipway, learning how to use the wind safely, avoid capsize and not be swamped by the waves.

Forty years on, my heart still races as I recall this incident, though my soul delights in the lesson learned that day – and repeated so often since.

† Lord of wind and waves, fears and inexperience, build within me a faith that is humble, robust and a blessing to everyone I meet. Amen

Monday 8 August
Passengers at sea

Read Acts 27:1–11

Much time had been lost, and sailing had already become dangerous …
But the centurion, instead of listening to what Paul said, followed the
advice of the pilot and the owner of the ship.

(parts of verses 9 and 11)

In today's reading, Paul's story is an eyewitness account of a ship struggling against dangerously adverse wind and weather. This eyewitness is commonly thought to be Luke himself. As the drama unfolds, there is real tension in the dilemma posed by conflicting opinions – should they press on through winter storms, or wait until the safety of springtime? We feel, also, real dread in the decision reached by the centurion, eager to fulfil his duty, and the pilot and owner, eager to complete a voyage without the cost of over-wintering. Given such strong imperatives, maybe we can sympathise with their unwillingness to listen to the caution of the prisoner, Paul.

If you had been in their shoes, would you have heeded Paul's warning?

I am often struck by how harshly and unrealistically society judges people who are expected to make faultless decisions, without the benefit of being able to predict the future. Doctors, social workers, parents, even politicians, will either be taken for granted if events prove them right, or pilloried if their decisions are undermined by unforeseen events.

As Christians, even with access to prayer and the guidance of the Holy Spirit, I don't think that we often, if ever, have detailed foreknowledge of how the future will pan out. What we can do is pray for wisdom and clear sightedness in the difficult decisions we face. We should pray too, with understanding, empathy and love, and without any excessive readiness to judge, for people we know who have to make hard decisions which affect the lives of others.

† Today, dear Lord, may I be slow to judge the difficult decisions that people in authority have to make, and seek, instead, to understand their motives and their needs. And nurture in me, too, the gifts of empathy and fairness. Amen

For further thought

Watching, listening to or reading the news today, notice whether or not people who make tough decisions are treated with understanding and fairness.

Tuesday 9 August
A busy traveller

Read Acts 18:18–22

When they asked him to spend more time with them, [Paul] declined. But as he left, he promised, 'I will come back if it is God's will.' Then he set sail from Ephesus.

(verses 20–21)

Reading of Paul's travels leaves me feeling breathless – in just these few verses he takes in Corinth, Syria, Cenchreae, Ephesus, Caesarea, Jerusalem and, finally, Antioch. 'How did he fit it all in?', I wonder. How did he maintain that frenetic pace, yet still provide a meaningful ministry? The Jews in the synagogue in Ephesus hoped he might slow down sufficiently to spend a little more time with them, but the best that Paul could offer was a, 'maybe, if things work out that way'.

I'm left thinking that Paul, because of a powerful sense of urgency at this stage of his work, took on a 'travel light and pack in as much as possible' approach to his calling. In that he was phenomenally effective. But I don't believe that such intense busyness is the only, nor necessarily the best, Christian lifestyle model to adopt – neither did Paul at less hurried times in his ministry.

So, alongside my admiration for globetrotting Paul, I'm hearing an even stronger voice reminding me of the importance of giving other people proper and sufficient time. For me, that might mean listening patiently to the child as he tells a long-winded story. It means making the phone call to the person who I know from past experience is never brief, rather than merely sending them a quick text. And, maybe, that means spending unhurried time listening to God, rather than rattling off my spoken prayers in haste before plunging into the clamouring needs of the day.

† Lord of my busyness, and also of my rest, help me to see time as a gift and not as something to be chased. Amen

For further thought
Spend ten minutes with God in prayer: no words, no agenda, just a time of quietness.

Wednesday 10 August
All hands on deck

Read Acts 27:27–44

*Just before dawn Paul urged them all to eat. 'For the last fourteen days,'
he said, 'you have been in constant suspense and have gone without
food ... I urge you to take some food. You need it to survive. Not one of
you will lose a single hair from his head.'*

(parts of verses 33–34)

As a difficult situation edges towards potential disaster, Paul, who
had predicted this outcome, chooses not to sulk or keep aloof
and mutter, 'I told you so!' Instead, he offers some cool-headed,
practical wisdom and encourages his fellow travellers to prepare
themselves for the possibility of the ship being wrecked, by having
something to eat. In what appears to be a deliberate echo of the
Lord's Supper, Paul took some bread, gave thanks and broke it, and
then they all ate – I guess that was a visual reminder that even in
the midst of the storm, God the provider was present.

While many us of might crave a life characterised by peace and
harmony (I certainly do!), I've lived long enough to realise that
globally, locally or personally, unexpected change, fallings-out
and disruption are inevitable components of everyday living.
Mindful of this, I find Paul's behaviour on the boat encouraging
and inspirational. Our Christian calling is not to keep out of the
way of disruption, even less are we called to offer 'told you so'
judgements from the sidelines. Our calling is to be the ones who
offer sustenance in the midst of panic, and to be oases of peace
for the benefit of people who are caught up in the storm. We can
do this not because we are super women or men, but because
we have learned to tightly hold the hand of the one whom Jesus
taught us to think of as the very best kind of parent – God, in
whose hand all things are safely and eternally held.

† When I'm caught up in storms, help me, dear Lord, to find sufficient peace, wisdom
and presence of mind that I may be useful and not a burden. Amen

For further thought

How hard is it not to sneak some satisfaction in being proved right,
or to say to those who doubted you, 'I told you so!'?

Thursday 11 August
Merchant shipping

Read Isaiah 23:1–3

Wail, you ships of Tarshish! For Tyre is destroyed and left without house or harbour … Be silent, you people of the island and you merchants of Sidon, whom the seafarers have enriched.

(parts of verses 1–2)

For much of the twentieth century, the town where I live was relatively prosperous. In addition to a thriving fishing industry there were large employers of skilled labour, from ship building to electronics. By the year 2000, most of those industries had either dwindled to a faint shadow of their former glory or gone completely. Consequently, comments posted on websites which feature the town as it used to be frequently yearn for 'the good old days', while declaring the present and future as being without value or hope. Older people, who in their youth remember the town bustling with activity shake their heads and wonder, 'How has it all come to this?'

Isaiah's prophecy is to people experiencing the crest of prosperity and warns that material success is a transient thing, especially when it has become an end in itself and the basis of the community's self-worth. Behind the prophecy lie implied questions: when commerce dwindles, your prosperity dries up and your ships lie idle and rotting, what have you got left? What would define your community then?

When Paul wrote to Christians living in the prosperous city of Corinth (1 Corinthians 13), he addressed these questions and declared that neither wealth, status nor fame are sufficiently durable to give a community lasting value. That can only be found in relationships built upon self-giving love, and people can only rise above their tendency towards self-centredness and competitiveness when they draw upon the God we know in Jesus – the source of that self-giving love.

† Gracious God, may your love working in and through me add true and durable value to the lives of all among whom I live. Amen

For further thought

What attitudes and actions might characterise a lifestyle that makes generosity to others its priority?

Setting sail – 2 All hands on deck

August

Friday 12 August
Breakfast on the beach

Read John 21:1–13

Jesus said to them, 'Come and have breakfast.' None of the disciples dared ask him, 'Who are you?' They knew it was the Lord. Jesus came, took the bread and gave it to them, and did the same with the fish.

(verses 12–13)

Among the many poems written by the English clergyman poet, George Herbert, is a sonnet entitled, 'Prayer'. The poem consists of a wonderful scatter of images, none of which alone explains prayer, but which, when gathered together, build up an understanding of prayer. Among these marvellously varied images, my favourite is, 'heaven in ordinary', and throughout my adult life I have found real delight in those experiences when God seemed more real than ever in ordinary events, actions and people.

In today's reading, I glimpse a true 'heaven in ordinary' moment when, having just experienced a remarkable catch of fish, Jesus presents his disciples with a simple, hospitable invitation: 'Come and have breakfast.'

This invitation is all the more remarkable because it is offered in the context of Jesus having very recently been executed by the Romans – so his being there at all is spectacularly extraordinary. Yet, before the questions and hard-to-get-your-head-around explanations, comes the practical, familiar invitation to share food, restore strength, and enjoy each other's company, just like they had done in recent times.

The simple yet hugely enabling gift of hospitality is something that most of us can exercise. It need not involve elaborate catering, in fact it is probably best if it does not, but may be something as ordinary as offering a cup of tea, or just making space for someone to sit down and share your company for a while.

† Loving God, you welcome me, you nourish me, you let me rest. Build up in me this gift of hospitality that I shall be a place where friend and stranger find welcome, refreshment and peace. Amen

For further thought

What ordinary opportunities for welcome and refreshment do you enjoy? What simple hospitality can you offer to other people today?

Saturday 13 August
Who needs a boat?

Read John 6:16–24

They saw Jesus approaching the boat, walking on the water; and they were frighted. But he said them, 'It is I; don't be afraid.' Then they were willing to take him into the boat, and immediately the boat reached the shore where they were heading.

(part of verses 19–21)

As I read today's passage, my mind and imagination went straight to the miraculous element in the story – Jesus walks on the water to his disciples in their boat. But even as that familiar image was forming, it was nudged to one side by an unexpected memory. I remembered how my mother once asked me to take her for a sail on a local river. The breeze was light, and we made slow progress. We were heading for a lunch stop a mile or so downstream; my father, who had chosen to walk along the riverbank, reached our destination well ahead of us. On arrival, I'm pretty certain he chuckled and said, 'What took you so long?'

Through the lens of that family memory I wondered if, compared to rowing a heavy boat in the dark, through big waves and against the wind, it was simply quicker for Jesus to walk and so arrive there first? It was not so surprising that they saw Jesus and reached the shore simultaneously if, in the darkness and noise of the wind, the shore was much closer than they had supposed?

I do not doubt that it is within the power of God to work miracles, but might this miraculous story also be teaching us about travelling differently than by our normal means? How often do we persevere with customary ways of doing or thinking because, well that's what we always do – isn't it? Perhaps Jesus, in this story, says to us, 'Today, why not leave your heavy old boat behind, and take a walk instead?'

† Lord, forgive me if I hang on to unsatisfactory ways of doing or being because I am afraid of change or of trying something new. Instead, wake me up to how your Spirit is leading me, that I may travel light and in your company. Amen

For further thought

Who needs a boat, when you can walk? Is that a helpful question for reviewing and refreshing aspects of life where you are feeling a bit stuck or overburdened?

Readings from Ecclesiastes

1 Vanity of vanities

Notes by **Rev Mandy Briggs**

Mandy is a Methodist minister who lives in Bristol. She is the Education Officer at the New Room (John Wesley's Chapel), the oldest Methodist building in the world. Twitter: @NewRoomBristol @mandbristol. Mandy has used the NRSV for these notes.

Sunday 14 August
Vanity of vanities

> **Read Ecclesiastes 1:1–15**
>
> *I saw all the deeds that are done under the sun; and see, all is vanity and a chasing after wind.*
>
> (verse 14)

Welcome to the book of Ecclesiastes!

You may already be familiar with the beautiful passage in chapter 3 which tells us that there is 'a time for everything', but have you ever taken time to read the whole book?

The author, named here as the Teacher, is thought to have probably been King Solomon. The tone of the book is fascinating – there is a lot of wisdom, philosophy and reflection, but also a real sense of world-weariness and a search for authenticity and meaning.

One of the words that frequently crops up is 'vanity', so it may be helpful to consider what this means. Vanity is defined as having inflated pride in oneself or one's appearance, or describing something that is vain, empty or valueless. In a world where vanity plays itself out constantly through enhanced and altered photos and videos on social media, it is sometimes a challenge to consider what is real, true and authentic.

The author of Ecclesiastes has lived life, sometimes to excess, but has not found peace or satisfaction. Instead he is grappling with a question: what really matters? When all around seems hollow, where is value to be found? Where is meaning? Where is God?

† God of authenticity, speak to us this week and help us consider what really matters as we study this intriguing book.

Chasing the wind

Read Ecclesiastes 1:16 – 2:11

*And I applied my mind to know wisdom and to know madness and folly.
I perceived that this also is but a chasing after wind.*

(verse 17)

In the nineties action film, *Twister*, teams of 'storm chaser' scientists compete against each other to track and measure violent tornadoes which regularly sweep across Oklahoma. They engage in a race against time and the elements to deploy new technology which will analyse the 'twisters' and provide information that will hopefully save people's lives in the future.

In this section of Ecclesiastes, 'chasing the wind' is not so much about tracking tornadoes but more about following something that is ultimately unsatisfying. The writer has so far lived a life of pleasure and excess. He considers himself wise and lists his accomplishments, achievements and indulgences. In the eyes of the world, this man would be considered a huge success. If he lived now, articles would be written and TV shows made. But as he looks back he cannot see value in all that he has done and he does not feel happy or fulfilled.

It has been suggested that an alternative name for this part of the book could be 'Solomon's Confession'. There is a real sense of dissatisfaction and yearning.

The passage leaves me wondering what things we chase after now as individuals and in society in general. What fulfils us, and what leaves us with a sense that we are 'chasing the wind'? It is easy to cram our lives full of things the world may consider successful and yet feel completely empty. But it doesn't have to stay that way.

† A prayer of St Augustine in modern language: You have made us for yourself, O God, and our hearts are restless until they can find rest in you.

For further thought

Consider what life has been like over the last couple of years and how your values have changed/not changed because of those experiences.

Tuesday 16 August
Simple pleasures

Read Ecclesiastes 2:12–26

There is nothing better for mortals than to eat and drink, and find enjoyment in their toil. This also, I saw, is from the hand of God; for apart from him who can eat or who can have enjoyment?

(verses 24–25)

The TV show *Succession* is a popular American series which explores a family fighting for control of a global empire. Knowing that the head of Waystar Royco, Logan Roy, is ageing, his children and extended family pitch themselves into a battle to take over at the top. It's dark and dysfunctional and has also proved to be extremely popular, winning a clutch of TV awards.

The writer of Ecclesiastes might be sympathetic to Logan Roy's situation. If indeed this is King Solomon writing then succession will have always been at the back of his mind – who will come after me and how will they rule? What will they do after all my hard work? He has to concede that he has no idea and no control, which is extremely frustrating and adds to his mood of cynicism. However, in this gloom there is a shift in his tone. He suggests that we might as well try to enjoy life – eating, drinking and working – because it all comes from God.

I'd like to suggest that today we might understand this thought in terms of the phrase 'simple pleasures'. The writer has already dismissed a life of excess as the way to happiness and fulfilment. Maybe the activities of each day – completing a task, enjoying a meal – are enough. We are encouraged to see them not as unimportant or mundane, but opportunities to give thanks for the provision and goodness of God. They may even bring wisdom and joy.

† God, when things feel complicated, help me to notice and appreciate the simple pleasures that are gifts from you.

For further thought

At the end of today, make a list of all the things you have appreciated about the day. Nothing is too small!

Wednesday 17 August
For everything there is a season

Read Ecclesiastes 3:1–8

For everything there is a season, and a time for every matter under heaven.

(verse 1)

Today's reading is the most famous and well-known passage in Ecclesiastes by a long way. It's poetic and well loved – it is often shared at funerals and thanksgivings and other times where reflective words are required. It has been suggested that this is one of the most beautiful passages in the Bible, words which are deeply profound but also extremely simple to understand.

There is a time for everything.

The writer of Ecclesiastes may generally be wondering 'why bother' all through the rest of the book but the fact remains that, despite all the questioning and world weariness in his writing, Ecclesiastes 3:1–8 does contain a hopeful note. By asserting that 'there is a time for everything', I hear the assurance that things will not always be as they are now. They will change. Just as there is a time to weep, so there is a time to laugh. Just as there is a time to mourn, so there is also a time to dance.

Life is not static. It moves and changes and we move and change with it. This passage reminds us that God is present in all of our experiences and in the cycles of the earth. In all that we hope for and in all that we strive to understand, in all that we struggle with and all that we celebrate, God weaves everything together. No experience is lesser than the other; all are recognised, heard and acknowledged.

These words speak of hope, of love, of real life and of the assurance that no matter how we feel, God is present.

† Loving God, help us to recognise your presence in all of the times and seasons of our lives. If we are celebrating, dance with us. If we are sorrowful, comfort us.

For further thought

Spend some time reading today's passage again. Can you write your own version?

Thursday 18 August
God's gift

Read Ecclesiastes 3:9–22

For the fate of humans and the fate of animals is the same; as one dies, so dies the other. They all have the same breath, and humans have no advantage over the animals; for all is vanity.

(verse 19)

Have you ever been to a pet service?

Churches in the UK often hold annual services where animals and birds are brought to church by their owners for a blessing (a good example can be seen in the TV series *Vicar of Dibley* in the episode called 'Animals'). Apart from Palm Sunday, it may be the only time in the year where you can see a Pekinese in a pew and an Alsatian walking down the aisle! The aim of pet services is to thank God for all living creatures and to celebrate creation in all its winged or four-legged glory.

In today's passage from Ecclesiastes, however, the writer is thinking about death. Today's musing is that humans have no advantage over animals, because all die in the end and are turned to dust anyway. He won't be drawn on whether or not 'the human spirit goes upwards and the spirit of animals goes downwards to the earth'. The best he can suggest is for everyone to enjoy their work, no matter what they have been given to do.

In our age of work-related stress and deadlines, we are taught that busy is good, stress is necessary, and we are judged by what we do, not how we are.

Contemplating the beauty of the natural world and God's creatures may enable us to gain more perspective on this. We are loved whoever we are and whatever our work may be.

† Give thanks for all those who work to protect animals, including vets, rescue organisations and conservation projects.

For further thought
Read Matthew 6:25–34.

Friday 19 August
The tears of the oppressed

> **Read Ecclesiastes 4:1–16**
>
> *Again I saw all the oppressions that are practised under the sun. Look, the tears of the oppressed – with no one to comfort them! On the side of their oppressors there was power – with no one to comfort them.*
>
> (verse 1)

Today the writer briefly turns his attention to the use of power.

He writes compassionately about 'the tears of the oppressed' and recognises the injustices perpetuated by those using power inappropriately and cruelly to create unfair systems. He doesn't dwell on this topic but the phrase he touches on is important. These words provoke compassion and are also a call to action. The call is to share help and comfort with those immediately in need, but also recognise and challenge the root causes of suffering and need. Take food banks for example. Many churches and individuals give generous donations of food and time.

But we are also called to radically challenge the societal systems which lead to people needing to use them in the first place. Or as Archbishop Desmond Tutu says in a quote widely attributed to him: 'There comes a point where we need to stop just pulling people out of the river. We need to go upstream and find out why they're falling in.'

These are hard questions and can't be answered satisfactorily in a short reflection. So, I am encouraged that the writer goes on to praise the value of friendship and standing together. We do not have to face this complicated world alone. But we do need to exercise warmth and compassion and be brave enough to challenge the systems which are built on oppression and suffering.

† God of the oppressed, bring your comfort to those in need. Lead us as a global community into new and hopeful places of freedom and justice.

For further thought

A group of older world leaders called 'The Elders' work together for peace and human rights. Find out more at theelders.org

Saturday 20 August
Guard your steps

Read Ecclesiastes 5:1–17

With many dreams come vanities and a multitude of words; but fear God.

(verse 7)

I wonder what your thoughts have been about the book of Ecclesiastes this week? For me, the attitude and approach of the writer is intriguing. In some ways his cry of 'everything is meaningless!' may help us to keep the trivialities of life in perspective. But there are also moments when I long for him to shake off the cynicism and be a bit more positive – come on, say something encouraging and uplifting!

At heart I believe the writer of this book is urging us to hold a mirror up to life. I think he wants us to consider what matters most and what is authentic. He wants us to consider what is worth striving for and what can be laid down. His reflections on the world may have caused us to reflect – but his advice as we move on is to consider our words and our actions and to use them wisely. He encourages us to follow through on our promises, keeping an awareness of our covenant relationship with God, looking in a clear-eyed way at the world and working with humility and contentment at the tasks we are given.

As we prepare to hear from a different contributor from tomorrow, I'd like to encourage you to consider how far we have already travelled through the book. What verses have particularly spoken to you so far? What have you found comforting – and what has been challenging? What have you found out about Ecclesiastes that you have never realised before – and how does it speak today?

† God of wisdom, thank you that the words of this book, written so long ago, can still speak to us today.

For further thought

How many services have you been to which feature Ecclesiastes? Do some online research to see what reflections and sermons you can find which comment on this book.

Readings from Ecclesiastes

2 Wisdom is better than might

Notes by **Catherine Williams**

Catherine is an Anglican priest who works as a freelance spiritual director, retreat conductor and writer. She is also involved with vocational discernment and ministerial development within the Church of England. Living in the English town of Tewkesbury, Catherine is married to Paul, also a priest, and they have two adult children. In her spare time, Catherine enjoys reading, singing, theatre, cinema, and poetry. She keeps chickens and is passionate about butterfly conservation. Catherine has used the NRSVA for these notes.

Sunday 21 August
Being human

Read Ecclesiastes 6:1–12

For who knows what is good for mortals?

(part of verse 12)

This week we are exploring the second half of the book of Ecclesiastes. A figure called the Teacher shares with us his perception of being human. Life and death feature heavily in his assessment. He is a realist and, at times, quite despairing of humanity. In today's passage, he sets the scene for us by suggesting that wealth, long life and a large and prosperous family are worthless if we are not able to find joy in each day. He is quick to point out that many things in life are empty, and evil often has the upper hand. While we are used to finding positive messages in scripture, it's helpful to have biblical material that enables us to relate to our darker and more depressing experiences of life. Our journey through life may have many ups and downs, and we don't always have answers for why difficulties and injustices come our way. Being able to air some of these situations, and acknowledge the challenges of being human and living in community with others, can help us reassess our relationship with God and our ongoing need for the awareness of God's presence in our lives.

† Lord Jesus, walk with me as I explore the human condition this week. May I be open to all that you wish to teach me.

Monday 22 August
Life and death

Read Ecclesiastes 7:1–14

The heart of the wise is in the house of mourning.

(part of verse 4)

If you have ever suffered a significant bereavement you will know that being confronted by the death of someone you love makes you consider deeply your own mortality. Our lives come sharply into focus when we recognise the truth that we will die at some point, and our earthly life will cease. During my ministry, I've conducted many funerals, and it's a privilege to sit in the home of the deceased and pastor the mourners. The work is intense but also deeply authentic. When bereaved, we can no longer sustain the masks we often wear in public and the emotions and sentiments that emerge are raw and from the heart. Our passage today suggests that wisdom is to be found more readily in this setting than in celebration and partying, which is often a surface response to life.

Days of adversity, suggests the Teacher in Ecclesiastes, are times to ponder. It's good to be joyful when life is going well, but God is Lord of both good times and bad, and to be found in both as we aim to live life in all its fulness. 'Blessed are those who mourn', taught Jesus in the Sermon on the Mount (Matthew 5:4), indicating that we recognise more strongly our reliance on God when times are tough. Wisdom comes from serious grappling with life's challenges, from not holding onto a nostalgic longing for the past, but by looking forward to the new work that God is doing and embracing it.

† O God, you are the Lord of heaven and earth. Help me to trust you through all the ups and downs of my life. May I live wisely and well in your light.

For further thought

Which events in your life have enabled you to grow in wisdom? In what ways might you share that wisdom with others?

Tuesday 23 August
Wise faces

Read Ecclesiastes 8:1–15

Wisdom makes one's face shine, and the hardness of one's countenance is changed.

(part of verse 1)

Think of someone you know who is considered wise. What do they look like? How do you know they are wise? The Teacher in Ecclesiastes suggests that wisdom can be discerned in people's faces. The wise, he says, have faces which shine, and which are softened by wisdom. A face which shines is indicative of God's presence – think for example of Moses coming down from Mount Sinai after meeting with God, or Stephen whose face is like that of an angel as he gives his testimony prior to martyrdom. The light and grace of the Holy Spirit – the counsellor – can radiate from the faces of those who are close to God.

The Teacher further suggests that the wise act prudently toward those in authority, knowing that there are times and ways for difficulties to be overcome, and injustices to be resolved. The wise resist certainty and humbly reserve judgement on others since the future is in God's hands and no one, however wise, can predict it. Taking hold of the good gifts that God has given us, finding satisfaction in our work, and taking simple pleasure in eating and drinking is sufficient to bring joy into each day, and build the resilience necessary to cope with the unfairness that society so often promotes. The wise wait patiently, in hope, aware that God is a just judge and will act.

† Lord, help me to believe that you will act where injustice and prejudice prevail. Enable me to be part of your righteous action.

For further thought

What simple things bring you pleasure? Start noting down the joy you find in each day and give thanks for it.

Wednesday 24 August
Seize the day!

Read Ecclesiastes 9:1–16

Whoever is joined with all the living has hope, for a living dog is better than a dead lion.

(verse 4)

The Teacher in Ecclesiastes continues to observe injustice all around him and concludes that only one thing is certain: everyone will eventually die. He surmises that morality and good deeds count for little since the same outcome happens to all, irrespective of behaviour. Though the wise and righteous are in the hand of God, even they do not know how God will act toward them. Everything seems futile and full of vanity, and even the person who saves a city through wisdom rather than might is neither rewarded nor remembered.

In the light of this, the Teacher concludes, we should all seize the day, because it's better to be a living dog, counting for little, than the dead king of the beasts. We are urged to live life to the full, enjoying all that is good, fostering loving relations with each other, dressing as if for a festival, and working to the best of our ability. Here is where positivity is located and God's approval found. As Christians, we know that Jesus came so that all might enjoy fulness of life. Living deeply in the moment and finding fulfilment and joy in every day is the antidote to the random ups and downs of life's fortunes. Post-resurrection we need not look at life in such a despairing way as the writer of Ecclesiastes. We know that nothing can separate us from God's love shown in Jesus Christ, and we need not fear death, for eternal life with God is assured.

† Lord God, help me to live deeply in each moment and to seek you with my whole heart.

For further thought

What patterns of thinking or behaviour do you need to change in order to live each day more fully?

Thursday 25 August
Wisdom and folly

Read Ecclesiastes 10:1–15

If the iron is blunt, and one does not whet the edge, then more strength must be exerted; but wisdom helps one to succeed.

(verse 10)

Recently we bought a new set of kitchen knives. We've been married for over 30 years and were still using the set we were given as a wedding present. I decided it was time to replace them. Using the new set for the first time I nearly sliced through my thumb – they were so sharp! It occurred to me we'd been using a blunt set of knives for years, but hadn't noticed. No wonder it took so long to prepare certain foods. The new set of knives came with a knife sharpener, and now I know that I should keep whetting the blades so that they stay sharp and do their job well.

In today's reading, the Teacher gives a series of proverbs that illustrate the difference between wisdom and folly. The wise succeed because they use their minds, think ahead and are prepared for what may come. The Teacher suggests the wise incline toward what is right, and their words are pleasing to others. The foolish on the other hand face in a different direction and are more likely to wander off. They speak without thinking, chattering on and on without saying much; digging a pit which they fall into themselves. They lack direction, not knowing even the simplest route. To be both human and made in the image of God is to be a mixture of foolishness and wisdom. Acknowledging our need for God enables us to reach out in the right direction and not go astray.

† O Lord, when I act foolishly, help me remember that I'm made in your image. Fill me with the wisdom and grace of your Holy Spirit.

For further thought

Look through the proverbs in this passage carefully. Which ones speak to you, and why? What might God be saying to you or your community?

Friday 26 August
Highlights and shadows

Read Ecclesiastes 11:1–10

In the morning sow your seed, and at evening do not let your hands be idle; for you do not know which will prosper, this or that, or whether both alike will be good.

(verse 6)

The Teacher continues to be a realist. He encourages his readers to be diligent and hard-working, enjoying the good things in life at the same time as recognising that not everything that happens to us will be positive, for we do not have ultimate control over life's events. We cannot tell what will work out and what won't, and if we keep waiting for fine weather we will never begin. We are exhorted to keep going, trusting that everything is God's work. This 'not knowing' can be liberating as we let go of the need to turn events to our advantage, or control outcomes. Rather, suggests the Teacher, it is better to give freely and joyfully – our time, our gifts and our wealth – so that others may flourish.

'Do not worry about your life' says Jesus in Matthew 6. God knows what we need and will provide for us. In turn, we are to trust that God is working for good in all things and that though we cannot always recognise his hand, the plan is often much bigger and more complex and subtle than we can possibly imagine. The Teacher encourages us to follow our heart and desires, banishing anxiety and rejoicing in life while we can, because it is so fleeting. Whether old or young we are to rejoice through each day, taking the good and the bad, the highlights and the shadows, in our stride.

† Lord God, help me to give thanks every day. Teach me how to truly rejoice.

For further thought
If you are able, donate to charity today or give of your time or gifts in a way that will help others.

Living in the light of death

Read Ecclesiastes 12:1–14

Remember your creator in the days of your youth.

(part of verse 1)

In the final chapter of Ecclesiastes, the Teacher returns to the importance of our awareness of death. Using a series of poetic images, he illustrates for us what the final stages of life may be like. The elements, a decaying house, the natural world, the end of commerce and finally a funeral procession all spark our imagination. There are many ways that our life may come to an end and for each of us, it will be different. Finally, we will become as dust on the earth and our breath will return to God who breathed life into us. There is no mention of eternal life, no answers to life's big questions, and no resolution to the situation we find ourselves in. Rather we are encouraged to confront our mortality in our youth, look to God our creator, keep his commandments and live our lives aware that God sees and knows every detail. It's a wake-up call to embrace the present and look for God always and everywhere.

As Christians, we can embellish this picture with the assurance that through the life, death and resurrection of Jesus death is not the end, and doesn't have the final word. Death is a natural part of life, a process to be gone through in order to enter fully into eternal life with God. The message of Ecclesiastes to live life to the full, finding joy in simple pleasures; taking the rough with the smooth remains a good maxim for daily living, as does the entreaty to be in awe of God throughout our life.

† Lord Jesus, thank you that through your death and resurrection the promise of eternal life is offered to all.

For further thought

What do you most want people to remember about you after you've died?

The rhythm of life

Notes by **Carla A. Grosch-Miller**

 Carla is a practical theologian and poet living in Northumberland. Her books include *Psalms Redux: Poems and Prayers* (Canterbury Press, 2014) and *Lifelines: Wrestling the Word, Gathering up Grace* (Canterbury Press, 2020). She teaches and writes about congregational trauma and practical theology. She is an avid year-round North Sea 'skins' swimmer (without a wetsuit) and long-distance walker, and is deeply grateful for the love of family (husband, children and grandchildren) and friends and for the beauty of creation. Carla has used the NRSVA for these notes.

Sunday 28 August
Birth and the struggle to be

Read Genesis 25:19–28

The children struggled together within her; and she said, 'If it is to be this way, why do I live?' So she went to inquire of the Lord.

(verse 22)

The beginning of life is romanticised. Even for those who have pushed a human through their birth canal, the dewy new life that emerges is so breath-stoppingly love-flooding that the pain and struggle is quickly forgotten. But the truth is that birth itself is a life-and-death struggle. In this time of vastly reduced infant and maternal death rates for many of us, we forget that.

Not only is birth a struggle, but becoming who we are is a struggle. 'Why do I live?' haunts; it is the curse (and blessing) of consciousness. We are made to search for meaning and purpose. And like Rebekah, we turn to the Creator for answers. Our faith traditions are long rambling discourses in response to that question and to the question 'How then shall I live?'

This story is the genesis of Jacob, who will gain the name 'Israel' on the banks of the Jabbok after wrestling all night. The name means 'those who struggle and strive with/for God'. So the journey began for Jacob, and so it continues for all of us.

† Creator of all life, meet us in our struggling and our striving, and make us who we can be for you. Amen

Monday 29 August
Childhood and life restored

Read 1 Kings 17:17–24

Then he stretched himself upon the child three times, and cried out to the Lord, 'O Lord my God, let this child's life come into him again.'

(verse 21)

The death of a child is a parent's worst nightmare. There is no ending so final, no pain so unbearable.

Then there are the lesser deaths that children endure: the traumas of war, poverty, abuse, neglect. Research shows that what most enables children (or adults) to endure, survive and potentially thrive after damaging life events is the presence of one warm, caring person. Resonant care – the kind that enables a child to experience the love that affirms their being – saves and heals. Elijah's physical covering of the widow's son and his impassioned cry is a metaphor for that kind of care. It is the kind of care that hallows earth and searches heaven, the kind of care that gives life.

There is a child deep within each of us. Perhaps that child was neglected or abused. Perhaps that child became accustomed to being ignored or used. Perhaps that child was caught up in larger events or forces beyond the control of caring parents. Still, she longs to be heard and comforted. Still there is a spark of life harboured within her heart under heavy layers of grief. Still there is the possibility that the warm and resonant care of another person will bring her back to life. For we are made for love and by love we are restored.

Jesus speaks in the Gospels of the necessity of being like a child if we are to enter the kingdom of God. Hand in hand with those who care, our child-like spark and wonder can be restored. And we will walk together into the love that knows no end.

† Good and gracious God, only you know the pain that children bear. And only you can enable us to love that pain into possibility. Make it so. Amen

For further thought
Is it time to tell a trusted other of your childhood pain? Is it time to listen to someone else's pain?

The rhythm of life

August

Tuesday 30 August
Committed love

Read Genesis 24:50–67

Then Isaac brought her into his mother Sarah's tent. He took Rebekah, and she became his wife; and he loved her. So Isaac was comforted after his mother's death.

(verse 67)

Marriage customs and practices change over time. Isaac and Rebekah's marriage was arranged; she was purchased by his father's servant and brought home. In Hebrew Bible times, when a fertile woman had to survive five live births to keep the clan's population stable, women were sexual and domestic property and men had the right to bed any woman who did not belong to another man. Polygamy and concubinage were more than acceptable. Upping the birth rate was the primary driver of sexual ethics. By the time Jesus was born, the understanding of marriage had begun to change and the Roman practice of monogamy became accepted among the Jewish people. Jesus lifted women's status when he declared that men no longer had the unilateral right to divorce (Matthew 19). Slowly over time the full personhood of women has become more accepted. And now, as the human population doubled between 1960 and 2000 and the strains on the ecosystem are everywhere evident, the concern has become overpopulation. Sexual ethics are no longer driven by a need for maximal procreation.

While marriage practices and customs change, one thing does not: the human need for loving companionship. Committed relationships that are mutually respectful allow each person to grow fully into who God desires us to be. We are comforted in the ancient sense of the word – strengthened – by our mates. Marriage, committed relationships and strong friendships provide a crucible that enables our maturity and responsibility not only to each other but to God and to the wider world. Thanks be to God for the gift of love

† O Love that never lets us go, enable me to be faithful, honest and kind in my love for others. Amen

For further thought
How today will I show my gratitude to those whose love sustains me and enables me to grow into who I am meant to be?

Pro-creativity

> **Read 1 Samuel 2:18–21**
>
> *His mother used to make for him a little robe and take it to him each year, when she went up with her husband to offer the yearly sacrifice.*
>
> (verse 19)

You may remember Hannah's anguished cry for a child (which the priest Eli at first attributed to drunkenness) and her promise to give the child to God in 1 Samuel 1. She fulfilled the promise. When the longed-for child was weaned, Hannah and Elkanah delivered him to the priest.

Stories like this are counter-cultural in the highly individualistic West. Not only are promises lightly made and not always kept, but the thought of giving a deeply loved and longed-for first child to a religious institution grates against the understanding that life is about personal wish fulfilment. Still, though, our souls hunger for the clarity of vision and commitment that looks beyond our paltry lives to a greater reality, a greater good.

The desire to bear children can come from this hunger. It is by nature forward-looking, hard-wired for the survival of the species. But it may also be a profound expression of hope, of the possibility of contributing to the divine-human project for the flourishing of life. In a not inconsiderable sense, we bear children as a gift to the future. And when we cannot, the pain can be deep.

Do all creative endeavours arise from the same longing? I think so. And now that the earth is overly full of the human family and choking and changing as a result, is it time to direct our creativity toward a greater good that may not involve procreation?

† Holy One, grant us clarity of vision and commitment to direct our creativity. Receive our creations as gifts of love and use them for the flourishing of all life. Amen

For further thought

What am I creating with my life? For whom? For what?

The rhythm of life

August

The dignity of work and justice

> **Read Genesis 3:17–19**
>
> *By the sweat of your face you shall eat bread until you return to the ground, for out of it you were taken.*
>
> (verse 19a)

Many of the stories in the first chapter of Genesis are aetiological – they were told to explain the rhythm of life. We can imagine the clan seated on the ground around a fire at night, a young person asking: 'Why do we have to work so hard?' Sadly, Eve is blamed (Adam couldn't say 'No'?), but the curse of toil is explained.

This story also reflects the move from a nomadic to an agrarian society. Human beings have always had to work in order to eat. First, we hunted and gathered. Then we began to cultivate crops and do home cottage work. Cities arose as places for people to trade goods. With the Industrial Revolution in the West, work moved into large-scale buildings and the population of cities exploded. More recently information technology has changed the shape and experience of work in the developed world. And most recently the global Covid-19 pandemic impacted if, how and where we work.

There is a dignity to work. By working we feed ourselves. By working we contribute to the well-being of the community. By working, if we are fortunate, we discover and develop skills and gifts.

But working can also be exploitative. No matter how societies are organised, the well-resourced few benefit the most from work done by low-paid women, men and children. The gap between the richest and the poorest within and between nations continues to grow, a phenomenon widely criticised by the biblical prophets. We all have to work, but why must so few benefit so much while so many live in poverty?

† God, grant me the dignity of work and the integrity to speak and act for justice. Amen

For further thought

What is the gap between the rich and the poor in your country? What is the church saying or doing about it?

Making the most of it

Read Proverbs 31:10–31

Give her a share in the fruit of her hands, and let her works praise her in the city gates.

(verse 31)

In my first year of seminary, I read the Bible through from cover to cover as an adult. It was early on, at Exodus 20:17 ('you shall not covet your neighbour's wife') when a niggling feeling turned into an insight: the Bible was written by men and for men! Well, goodness me, what a thought! I grew up in a church with a high and a literalist view of scripture. I still have a deep love of scripture but I now read with a broader perspective.

This morning's passage is about an elite family. The man takes his public place with the elders. The woman has servant girls and wears fine clothes. Although her sphere is limited to the home (she is the good housewife), it is painted as expanding beyond making clothes and food to farming and trading. She is saintly in patience, kind and wise – a paragon of virtue. She is praised by her husband.

Not all of us are privileged or wealthy. Not all of us have partners who appreciate our toil. What is here in this passage for every woman? For every person?

Perhaps it is something about making the most of wherever we find ourselves. I once heard it said: 'It's not the cards you are dealt with, but how you play them.' There is the possibility of grace in every circumstance. Sometimes it is a grace just to survive the day. Sometimes grace overflows and we are able to share it out. Always we can seek to rise above our limitations to grasp the broader horizon.

† Gracious God, give me a grateful heart and the wisdom to find the grace and possibility in each day. Amen

For further thought

What is your view of scripture? How do you make sense of passages that don't reflect your real-life experience?

The rhythm of life

September

Saturday 3 September
Death

Read Genesis 23:1–20

Abraham rose up from beside his dead, and said to the Hittites, 'I am a stranger and an alien residing among you; give me property among you for a burying-place'.

(part of verses 3–4)

The hallowing of death is a hallowing of life. Evidence of human burial practices are our earliest clues to the existence of religion. In the face of death we are electrifyingly aware of the preciousness of the gift of life and the need for an understanding and a language that is large enough to encapsulate its mystery.

I accompanied my mother from her diagnosis of metastatic cancer until her death. All of life was in those weeks: love, searing pain, conflict, new possibility. I never felt more alive. The simplest moments were profound and graced. I emerged from that time as if from a cocoon, with new skin and gossamer wings.

The week I wrote these reflections, I turned sixty-five. David and I were spending a week in a cottage on the North Sea coast in northern England, not too far from where we live. The time was a respite from the gruelling reality of pandemic anxiety and too much work. I am wrestling with aging. David is a bit older, with an underlying health condition; the Covid pandemic brings extra risk of death. I contemplate death gingerly: mine, his, that of other loved ones. It deepens my appreciation for life. I gird my loins, summon my love and courage, grasp today fiercely and gently.

I give thanks for the whole of the journey: the rhythm of days, the solace of night, the warmth and call of love, the joys and the challenges and the wonder of life, and finally for the return Home at the end. Thanks be to God for it all.

† Source and End of all of life, may I come to the end of my days with a song of praise on my lips. Amen

For further thought
'You who painfully separate the fibres of my being so as to penetrate to the very marrow of my substance and draw me to Yourself.' (Teilhard de Chardin on aging, illness and death)

The rhythm of life

September

248

The Gospel of Luke (4)

1 Faith and opposition

Notes by **Rt Rev Dr Peter Langerman**

Peter is a pastor in a Presbyterian Church in Durbanville, Cape Town, and he is the Moderator of the General Assembly of the Uniting Presbyterian Church in Southern Africa. He is married to Sally and they have four daughters. Peter is passionate about the dynamic rule and reign of God. He believes that God invites all to be part of God's transformative mission through love, and that the most potent and powerful agent for the transformation of local communities is the local church living out faithfulness to God. Peter has used the NIVUK for these notes.

Sunday 4 September
A strong challenge

Read Luke 12:1–21

I tell you, whoever publicly acknowledges me before others, the Son of Man will also acknowledge before the angels of God. But whoever disowns me before others will be disowned before the angels of God.

(verses 8–9)

In these post-modern, post-Christendom, post-Covid days, church leaders are grappling with the challenge of trying to get people interested in the matters of faith again. Confronted by the 'I'm spiritual not religious' mantra of the modern person, the church does all it can to try to make the gospel more appealing and attractive to twenty-first-century people.

In our attempts to woo reluctant persons back to church, we can only marvel at Jesus' attitude, which appears to be the total opposite. He seems to make it very difficult for people to follow him, and even those who want to do so are warned off. In this passage he takes on the Jewish religious leaders; warns people of the dangers of God's judgement; assures them that when persecuted they will be supported; and tells a cautionary tale of a farmer who, in our estimation, acted wisely and prudently.

Not a method calculated to attract a crowd or pander to the felt needs of his would-be followers, Jesus makes it very clear what is in store for those who hear the call to follow him and be a disciple. What about you, how will you respond?

† Dear God, help me to be willing to follow you, no matter the cost.

Monday 5 September
Flower children and bird watchers

> **Read Luke 12:22–40**
>
> *Then Jesus said to his disciples: 'Therefore I tell you, do not worry about your life, what you will eat; or about your body, what you will wear. For life is more than food, and the body more than clothes.'*
>
> (verses 22–23)

We live in a world where people are more anxious than ever. The strains of modern life, the uncertainties created by the Covid pandemic, the fears that come from an obscure future, and the pain of everyday life all combine to make us a people that worry.

In Jesus' day, the people that followed him were, mostly, peasant farmers and humble tradespeople who earned just enough each day to live that day. The level of anxiety under which they must have lived must have been unbearable. So, when Jesus tells them not to worry, they must have drawn closer, but his advice seems unworkable.

Jesus tells them that the key to being free from worry and anxiety is to observe the flowers and to watch the birds. I can imagine some may have switched off at this point, deciding Jesus was just out of touch with reality. Jesus then reveals a profound truth: their heart will be where their treasure is. In other words, what you love you invest in and what you value reveals what you love. If we treasure, value, and invest in the things that are important to God, then God will have our heart – our entire life – and God will care for us as God cares for the birds and flowers.

Where is your treasure, where is your heart? Are you anxious about the present or the future? Jesus assures you today that it is God's pleasure to look after you and ensure that you flourish if you will trust him enough to care for you.

† Dear God, please free me from anxiety, worry and fear as I place my heart, and my treasure, in your hands.

For further thought

Be on the look-out today for others who might be worried, anxious or stressed and let them know you care.

Tuesday 6 September
Not peace but division

Read Luke 12:41–59

I have come to bring fire on the earth, and how I wish it were already kindled! But I have a baptism to undergo, and what constraint I am under until it is completed! Do you think I came to bring peace on earth? No, I tell you, but division.

(verses 49–51)

Sometimes, in our desire to 'market' Jesus to a world that doesn't know much about him, we present him as a caricature. He is gentle Jesus, meek and mild, peaceable, always benign, serene, docile, and placid. What we fail to consider, is that, if Jesus was like this, what was it about him that caused such offence and was so threatening? Meek and mild, gentle souls are hardly considered a threat to the powerful and strong, yet Jesus was clearly seen as a threat to the religious and political authorities. He was such a dangerous threat that they conspired to have him executed.

Jesus here lays down a marker for his disciples in every age. Following Jesus will not always be the popular choice, and it may lead to conflict, even within your own family. The disciple has to be constantly alert and ready – complacency is a deadly enemy. From those to whom much has been given, much will be expected and failure to share is not an option.

It is interesting in these passages how frequently Jesus stresses the need for generosity and kindness and warns his disciples of the dangers of hoarding and selfishness. In our dog-eat-dog world where we are encouraged to get ahead and accumulate resources, Jesus' advice seems oddly out of place. Yet we all know examples of people who got what they desired only to be desperately unhappy and people who are content, even though they have very little.

To be content with what we have is to live counter-culturally in this day and age.

† Dear God, help me to be content with what you have given me and to be generous in giving of myself to and for others.

For further thought

Look for opportunities today to share something – time, energy, kindness, compassion – with someone else.

Wednesday 7 September
Repentance

Read Luke 13:1–17

But unless you repent, you too will all perish.

(part of verse 5)

I have a love-hate relationship with GPS devices. I find them very helpful in finding my way to places I have never been before, but sometimes they take me by routes that I would rather not take. Often I think I know better than the GPS, and there have been times when I have second-guessed the GPS, gone the wrong way, and had to make a U-turn.

Repentance is not a popular word today. It sounds judgemental and preachy. It's a word that we seldom use outside of a religious context. Yet the Greek word for 'repentance' means to change direction, to make a U-turn. When you are going in the wrong direction, the worst thing you can do is continue going in that direction, and the best thing you can do is turn around and head in the correct direction.

That is the point Jesus is making in this passage. Unless we turn around, we are headed into danger. One of the most severe wrong turns the people had taken in Jesus' day was around the Sabbath laws. There were specific rules about what did and did not constitute work on the Sabbath. Healing was considered work and was prohibited, but Jesus heals a woman and challenges their rules.

Jesus wanted them, and us, to understand that God longs to set people free. Doing the will of God, being obedient to God and following God is precisely what we should be doing every day of the week. For them repentance meant understanding this. What does it mean for you?

† Dear God, help me to turn from things that I know to be wrong in my life and follow you.

For further thought

If you have something that is keeping you bound, what can you do to be freed?

Thursday 8 September
Of mustard seeds and yeast

Read Luke 13:18–35

Then Jesus asked, 'What is the kingdom of God like? What shall I compare it to? It is like a mustard seed … It is like yeast'.

(parts of verses 18, 19 and 21a)

When I read this passage, two thoughts come to mind. The first is of my mother-in-law's home where she had, on a shelf, a tiny mustard seed encased in plastic with this verse attached. The other is that one of our daughters loves to bake bread and she is very good at it. It is a treat at a family meal to have the smell and taste of a freshly baked loaf of home-made bread on the dinner table.

Jesus here uses two familiar images to convey the truth of the kingdom, the rule and reign, of God, to his followers. The mustard seed is tiny, but it grows into a huge shrub. You only need a small amount of yeast for a rather large batch of dough, since the yeast permeates and spreads itself through the dough causing the bread to rise and fill out.

Similarly, the rule and reign of God might begin in small and insignificant ways, but those small beginnings can have a giant impact. In our inter-connected world, we sometimes refer to this as the 'butterfly effect': a small change in an inter-connected complex system might have wide-ranging and far-reaching effects.

We so often think that our small acts of kindness, our generosity and compassion do not change the world, but we do not know what impact our ordinary, seemingly insignificant acts might have on the world. This passage culminates with Jesus weeping over Jerusalem because they missed their opportunity to do something significant and change the world. Let's not miss ours.

† Dear God, help me to see that even small acts of kindness, generosity and compassion can yield great fruit for your kingdom.

For further thought

Think about someone close to you who needs a kind word or an encouraging act and reach out to them today.

The Gospel of Luke (4) – 1 Faith and opposition

September

Friday 9 September
Family meals and dinner parties

Read Luke 14:1–14

For all those who exalt themselves will be humbled, and those who humble themselves will be exalted.

(verse 11)

I am not sure what family meals such as at Christmas etc are like in your home, but they can sometimes be chaotic affairs. Despite the meticulous planning and the attention to detail, it seems that things can just conspire together to go wrong. The meal gets burnt, family members end up fighting over trivial issues, no one wants to help with the clean-up, and, at the end of the day, we are absolutely exhausted, and we vow 'never again'. Maybe we think this passage give us an excuse to justify cancelling these family get-togethers.

On the other hand, it's my pleasure both to host and to attend dinner parties. Sometimes these dinner parties are with close friends. Sometimes they are with people I don't know all that well in order to get to know them a little better. Most often we invite people to a dinner party with the expectation, which often happens, that they will invite us in return.

In this passage Jesus is not saying we should not have Christmas dinner with our family members, but he is highlighting the dangers of doing things for others in order to get something in return. In God's economy, we should never operate on the basis of a *quid pro quo,* but we should be kind and generous to those who could never repay us. To do so is to do for others what God does for us. God welcomes us in and lavishes good things upon us, things which we did not earn or deserve because it is in God's nature to be generous.

† Dear God, thank you for your generosity in my life. (Take a moment to list the ways in which God has blessed you.)

For further thought

How can you demonstrate kindness and generosity today to someone without expecting anything in return?

Saturday 10 September
Grace is free, but it's not cheap

Read Luke 14:15–35

Then the master told his servant, 'Go out to the roads and country lanes and compel them to come in, so that my house will be full. I tell you, not one of those who were invited will get a taste of my banquet.'

(verses 23–24)

Because God freely bestows grace upon us, and because grace is something we can never earn nor deserve, there is a tendency to think that grace is cheap in that it doesn't cost us anything. What this week's readings should have made plain to us is that, while Jesus invites us to follow him on the path of discipleship, those who do so must be prepared to count the cost.

Dietrich Bonhoeffer (1906–1945), the German theologian, popularised the concept of cheap grace, by which he meant grace which we receive without calling forth from us any radical change in our lifestyle, thinking or behaviour. While we grapple in each age to determine which behaviours are permissible and which are prohibited for Christians, we miss Jesus' main point. Those who accept the gracious invitation to follow Jesus have got to be prepared to put it all on the line, to give up everything, to surrender every other claim. Without that willingness, it is all just a sham. Jesus was not averse to telling people who wanted to follow him that they had to give up something in order to do so. The Gospels are littered with examples of people for whom this was too high a price.

How will we respond to the grace which Christ offers to us freely? Will we say, 'Yes, please' and leave unchanged, or will we receive that free gift and give God all our brokenness, sin, sorrow, regret and failure in return? For when we do so, God is able to take all that and transform it into something beautiful and precious.

† Dear God, I thank you for your grace and I give you all of myself in return.

For further thought

If there is something that you are holding on to that is affecting your relationships, ask God to help you give it up.

The Gospel of Luke (4) – 1 Faith and opposition

September

The Gospel of Luke (4)

2 Teaching in parables

Notes by **Bruce Jenneker**

Bruce is a retired South African Anglican priest living in Cape Town. During 35 years of ministry, worship, liturgy and Christian Formation have been his primary occupation. He served as Canon Precentor at both Washington National Cathedral, St George's Cathedral, Cape Town, as Precentor at Trinity Church Copley Square, Boston, and as Director of Liturgy at Trinity Church Wall Street in New York City. He has been a frequent speaker at conferences and retreats. Bruce has used the NRSV for these notes.

Sunday 11 September
Words of life

Read Luke 15:1–10

The Pharisees and the scribes were grumbling and saying, 'This fellow welcomes sinners and eats with them.' … [Jesus replied], 'there will be more joy in heaven over one sinner who repents than over ninety-nine righteous people who need no repentance.'

(parts of verses 2 and 7)

Galilee's tradition of cultural diversity and political autonomy made for a resentful acceptance of Roman domination. Rural and agricultural, it was caught between the power of Rome and Jewish religious authority. Heavily taxed by Rome and constrained by Jewish law, it was a crucible for social, political and religious unrest.

Like those of Martin Luther King Jr, Nelson Mandela and Desmond Tutu, the words of Jesus touched people where they lived, addressed their troubling questions, and offered a vision of hope and freedom. From the very beginning, the religious and the political authorities were profoundly critical of his words which challenged the status quo and advocated a dignity and liberty the authorities were determined to constrain.

Jesus was prophetic: his words confronted the present with a vision of a redeemed future; his actions were symbolic of that redemption breaking into the present.

In this parable of recklessly going after what is lost, Jesus overturns conventional wisdom to usher in this radical new way of thinking. The individual is worth every risk and sacrifice. No one is forgotten, left behind or excluded. This is not merely right or just, it is the source of goodness and joy.

† God, your embrace includes everyone: empower us with your love to seek those cast out and finding them, to rejoice with you.

Words for a living hope

The Gospel of Luke (4) – 2 Teaching in parables

Read Luke 15:11–32

But we had to celebrate and rejoice, because this brother of yours was dead and has come to life, he was lost and has been found.

(verse 32)

Preachers have found in this well-known parable a story about a prodigal son, a story about a reckless father, a story about a selfish elder brother. Ultimately, this is a parable of a finding father's forgiveness and the restoration of the dignity of his son who was lost and is found.

This is the last in Luke's series of three 'lost and found' parables. The coin was lost. The woman began and completed the search. The sheep was lost. The shepherd started and achieved the rescue. The son left his father. It was the father who kept diligently watching for his son's return, and when his son was still far away, began making the preparations for an extravagant welcoming celebration. It was the shepherd, the woman, the father who made the relationship whole again.

Jesus highlights the reckless permissiveness of the father; he not only allows his son the freedom to depart, but finances the adventure and celebrates his return. The finding father gives lavishly from his abundance, unreservedly. It is the amazing grace of his – and significantly our – Father that Jesus proclaims: our Father who gives the life of his Son to save everyone from all that separates us from God's love and restores them to loving intimacy with God.

That is who our God is and what our God does in the amazing grace of our salvation – it is handsomely shared so that everyone is returned to God's embrace: no one is forgotten, no one is excluded, and no one is left behind.

† God of every time and place: let your love reach us and make us whole, then empower us for your work of redeeming all things.

For further thought

Spend some time reflecting on the ways our Father has forgiven and restored you. In what ways were you lost?

Tuesday 13 September
Words of a convicting truth

Read Luke 16:1–18

No slave can serve two masters; for a slave will either hate the one and love the other, or be devoted to the one and despise the other. You cannot serve God and wealth.

(verse 13)

This sounds like a clip from today's news. A manager has misappropriated his employer's assets and is about to be fired. Because he doesn't want to be reduced to manual labour or be forced to beg, he shrewdly decreases the debts of those indebted to his employer, hoping to gain the erstwhile debtors' support to secure a livelihood after he loses his job. Surprisingly, the employer commends the dishonest manager for his shrewdness.

Luke places this parable between those of the prodigal son and the rich man and Lazarus. Both concern wealth and its use in the order of things, and in both cases that order is reversed. The parables of Jesus in Luke are all concerned with the reversal of the temporal order so as to redeem it and restore it to the divine order. And that is precisely what the dishonest manager does here: what was at risk or lost, is saved or found.

Status, wealth and power are indices by which the world measures merit and well-being. In Luke, Jesus proclaims that worth, dignity and security are not guaranteed by any of these. Rather, they are 'false saviours' that mislead us. In the parables of Jesus, the values of the world are turned upside down and inside out.

Where do we find our security? The choice is always ours – to choose so 'that among the swift and varied changes of the world, our hearts may surely there be fixed where true joys are to be found.' (*Book of Common Prayer* 1979, Collect for the Fifth Sunday of Easter, p. 219).

† God of goodness and truth: inform our minds and guide our desires, that we will choose only what leads to fullness of life with you.

For further thought

What are the 'false saviours' that have misled us? Are our hearts still fixed on some of these?

Wednesday 14 September
Words to open closed minds

Read Luke 16:19–31

Abraham replied, 'They have Moses and the prophets; they should listen to them ... If they do not listen to Moses and the prophets, neither will they be convinced even if someone rises from the dead.'

(verses 29 and 31)

There are more references to wealth, money and possessions in Luke than in the other gospels. Luke's Jesus proclaims that trusting in wealth poses the danger that we will offer to it the allegiance that properly belongs to God: 'Where your treasure is, there your heart will be also' (Luke 12:34).

In this parable Jesus proclaims two challenging gospel messages: that giving wealth the ultimate priority in one's life is foolhardy, and that faith requires trusting belief. The rich man's wealth insulated and blinded him, robbing him of a truly good life. Not accepting and believing the teachings of Moses and the prophets, prevented him from knowing the true meaning of life.

Following Jesus demands that we make urgent and critical choices. What will define our way of life? Will we put our trust in wealth, money and power? What will inform our patterns of living? Will we shape our lives by self-serving, materialistic and consumerist values?

Luke's Jesus proclaims that the only security is the unconditional, unmerited, unreserved grace and love of God offered full and free; and the only trustworthy word is the hallowed word of God incarnated in the Only-begotten, Jesus Christ.

It is interesting to note that it was this parable that challenged Albert Schweitzer to leave his comfortable life in Europe to go to Africa as a medical missionary. (S. MacLean Gilmour and George A. Buttrick, *The Interpreter's Bible*, vol. 8, Abingdon, 1952, p. 289).

† God of time and eternity: reveal to us the true meaning of life, that always choosing righteousness, we will be brave witnesses of Christ.

For further thought

Allow this passage to challenge us afresh: 'what will define our way of life?'

The Gospel of Luke (4) – 2 Teaching in parables

September

Thursday 15 September
Words that unlock and reveal

Read Luke 17:1–19

One of them, when he saw that he was healed, turned back, praising God with a loud voice. He prostrated himself at Jesus' feet and thanked him. And he was a Samaritan.

(verses 15–16)

This is a collection of sayings: warning about failing, exhortation to forgive, pronouncement about faith, reminder of the duty of slaves, and the parable of the ten lepers. The vocation to faithfulness links these sayings.

'Increase our faith', the disciples plead (verse 5), these demands are too daunting. All that is needed is a fragment of faith, Jesus replies.

Luke locates the story 'between Samaria and Galilee'. It is a predictable event for the time. Also predictably, once healed, Jesus commands them to do as the law commands. On their way, one 'saw that he was healed, turned back' and praising God, came to thank Jesus. Samaria and Galilee share borders; there is no region between them. Luke is saying that the great work of the gospel occurs in the 'spaces in-between', those 'thin', unexpected places often hidden in plain sight, where the ordinary and extraordinary meet. Be alert to recognise God's action in them.

Luke's Gospel invites a recognition of Jesus, calls for a response, a turning around, a reversal. The tenth leper sees, understands and turns around, going back to thank Jesus – his gratitude overriding his obedience to the law. Seeing and recognising God's action in ordinary and extraordinary contexts is a requirement of faith. Acknowledging one's need and asking for help is a necessary step on the pilgrimage of salvation. Turning one's life upside down, conversion and gratitude are its hallmarks.

The basic requirement is faith, a committed and unwavering trust – received as a gift and nurtured as a vocation, with gratitude; surprisingly demonstrated by the stranger, the object of prejudice, a Samaritan.

† Saving God, you are anywhere and everywhere: supply our needs, relieve our distress, make us whole, that we will live to your praise and glory.

For further thought

Are there things from God that we haven't seen? The unnoticed gift, the surprising healing, the encouraging word? Let's look again and give thanks.

Words of life's ultimate challenge

Read Luke 17:20–37

Those who try to make their life secure will lose it, but those who lose their life will keep it. I tell you, on that night there will be two in one bed; one will be taken and the other left.

(verses 33–34)

For Judaism, dramatic, supernatural signs would announce the advent of the Messiah. Jesus overturns this belief, saying to the Pharisees, 'The kingdom of God is among you.' Jesus warns the disciples that God's reign – its present reality and final consummation – is hidden. Some will recognise it, others will not. In the 'in-between time', confusion, suffering and rejection require patient forbearance and steadfast faith – when everything is falling apart.

I am writing this on 10 October 2020 which is Day 197 of lockdown in South Africa during the global Covid-19 pandemic. 'It is a gloomy moment in history. Not in the lifetime of most people has there been so much grave and deep apprehension; never has the future seemed so incalculable. The economic situation is in chaos. The political cauldron seethes with uncertainty. It is a solemn moment. Of our troubles no one can see the end.' This analysis appeared in *Harper's Magazine*, 10 October 1857, 163 years ago. We have been here before.

We are vulnerable, our trusted securities are bankrupt, despair and despondency grip us. Our confidence in the 'reign of God' is threatened. But God's reign is always nothing less than God's unwavering, constant solidarity with us, no matter what, or where, or when.

There is an 'anchor' that holds 'in the storms of life' (words from the hymn written by Priscilla J. Owens in 1882). Not a magic panacea but the enduring solidarity of God.

† God, our Rock and Salvation: let your sustaining presence strengthen our faith, and renew our hope, that we will trust the security of your grace.

For further thought

What signs of the kingdom are we looking for? The miraculous overthrow of our problems, or grace in the midst of them?

Saturday 17 September
Words of life

Read Luke 18:1–17

I tell you, this man went down to his home justified rather than the other; for all who exalt themselves will be humbled, but all who humble themselves will be exalted … whoever does not receive the kingdom of God as a little child will never enter it.

(parts of verses 14 and 17)

Luke's parables are always about God: windows through which we can glimpse who God is and who we are called to be in relation to God. They invite us to recognise God's action, understand it, be converted by it, and by it come to redemptive self-knowledge and wholeness.

Although the characters in the first parable are an unjust judge and a persistent widow, it reveals that God is supremely good, compassionate and eager to bless. God is present to us, attentive and ready to engage us.

The widow comes seeking justice. In the world of the New Testament, widows were of no account. Women had no access to the courts, only men did. Widows were poor, voiceless and powerless, on the margins of society, without any assurance of justice. Jesus announces that God is the source and guarantee of justice, especially to the vulnerable and the outcast – a truth that speaks powerfully to our world beset with systemic racism and oppression that are often tolerated and condoned by those in power.

In the second parable there is a significant shift from unrighteousness to self-righteousness, from the lack of virtue of the unjust judge to the complacency and hypocrisy of the Pharisee. God knows the secrets of our hearts, and eagerly waits to embrace us – as we are – in order to redeem us.

Demonstrating and summing up his gospel, Jesus calls the children to him and blesses them: it is simple faith and childlike trust that are the desired responses of those who hear Christ's message, offering themselves and all they are to God.

† Loving God, you know and accept us: redeem, renew and restore us, that by your grace we can become what you made us to be.

For further thought

Have we over-complicated the message of Jesus? Come again today, as little children to your loving Father.

Brother, sister, let me serve you

1 What does God require?

Notes by **Shirlyn** Toppin

Shirlyn is a presbyter in the Methodist Church. She believes passionately in the preaching of the word of God, without compromise or fear, and exercising a pastoral ministry of grace. She enjoys various forms of leisure and relaxation and her favourite pastime is shopping. Shirlyn has used the NRSVA for these notes.

Sunday 18 September
The pattern (1)

Read Mark 10:41–45

But it is not so among you; but whoever wishes to become great among you must be your servant, and whoever wishes to be first among you must be slave of all.

(verses 43–44)

At first glance, Jesus appeared to rebuke James and John for desiring a great position in the kingdom. Closer inspection of Jesus' response shows that it's not directed only at the two, but also at the other ten disciples and every believer. It is doubtful we are surprised by any of this – either by the brothers' request or the anger of the other disciples (an emotion maybe rightly justified). Is it possible the other disciples were angry because the brothers dared to ask *first*, not because of their forthrightness?

Society's concept of greatness and leadership would applaud this as ambitious and career-oriented, clearly opposite to how the kingdom of God operates, where greatness is measured in service and not entitlement. Jesus dispelled this notion of attaining prominence by saying, 'It is not so among you', meaning those who should not be governed by human (earthly), but by kingdom principles.

This is pertinent and valuable advice for all who are actively engaged in a serving ministry with an inclination to seek recognition and reward, rather than fulfilling the call of Jesus to share his life and values. Are you willing to serve without acclaim and expectation? Join me on a journey of rediscovering that genuine service must imitate Jesus' teaching and ministry.

† Heavenly Father, Jesus came 'not to be served, but to serve' (verse 45). Help us to follow his way of life and serve without expectations. Amen

The pattern (2)

Read Psalm 23

You prepare a table for me in the presence of my enemies.

(part of verse 5)

Have you ever wondered why David mentioned the Lord's 'prepared' table as comforting reassurance, amid the fear in Psalm 23? Gratitude comes to mind, but much more than being appreciative of the Lord's generous act of kindness and grace. David portrayed the Lord as a gracious host who takes the initiative to offer service – captured in one word, hospitality.

Hospitality goes beyond the mere provision of a meal as it includes a protective responsibility – the guest of the Lord is assured of safety, despite being surrounded by foes. Hospitality also highlights the invitation to fellowship with the Lord as an honoured guest, dining at his table – an experience familiar to many people when invited to share a meal in someone's home, with thoughtful consideration given to dietary and possibly religious requirements, ensuring that the guest feels honoured.

Jesus' hospitality to his disciples at the Last Supper shows him serving bread and wine, not for satiation only, but as a future pattern to act as an example of his servanthood. We too are invited as honoured guests in the celebration of Holy Communion, not only as participants of the ritual, but in remembrance of our purpose summed up in the dismissal prayer after communion in the Methodist Worship Book (1999), p. 159, 'May we who have received this sacrament be strengthened in your service.' Hospitality as an act of service is an inextricable part of discipleship, which should not be hindered by differences or cultural barriers.

† Lord, help me to remember when we engage in service to others, I am serving you. Amen

For further thought

Sharing of a meal is hospitable service. How willingly are you prepared to be the gracious host instead of the honoured guest?

Loving receiving

> **Read Matthew 26:6–13**
>
> *But Jesus, aware of this, said to them, 'Why do you trouble the woman? She has performed good service for me.'*
>
> (verse 10)

The dynamics of service has changed in today's reading and Jesus is on the receiving end. The dinner host is Simon, but the person honouring the guest is a woman, name unknown in Matthew's account, but named as Mary in John's Gospel. She was extravagantly generous in her material gift and actions, which garnered praise from Jesus but judgemental criticism from the disciples. It shows that the value placed on material possession is the same today as it was then, and who is deemed worthy of receiving has not changed. Many charitable organisations may agree with the disciples and, like the disciples, they would have also missed its significance. It was not the costliness of the gift that counted, but the service rendered. Unknowingly, her action was symbolic – but knowingly, it was an emotional and physical display of serving in kindness. Her actions should teach us that: service is sacrificial (verse 7), service is willing participation (verse 10), service would not be recognised (verse 8) and service would be condemned (verse 9).

The woman's unabashed service contradicted the expected behaviour of the day. She didn't care about the repercussions, knowing her conduct would generate criticism about inappropriateness and immorality. The propelling force for loving service made her forfeit material possession, her expected role as a woman and her status. In today's context, self-consciousness and the perspective of others may determine whether we are prepared to serve sacrificially – sometimes acceptance is the thing we value most. But, we cannot allow gender, opinion, or prominence to restrict how and to whom we offer service.

† Loving God, help me not to withhold all that I am and have in service to you and others for the glory of your kingdom. Amen

For further thought

What will you willingly sacrifice in an act of loving service for Jesus?

September

True fasting

Brother, sister, let me serve you – 1 What does God require?

September

Read Isaiah 58:5–12

Is it not to share your bread with the hungry, and bring the homeless poor into your house; when you see the naked, to cover them, and not to hide yourself from your own kin?

(verse 7)

People of faith throughout the ages have participated in the act of self-denial of food to promote a deeper sense of spiritual awareness in their lives. Other religions also fast as part of their practice and belief. Yet the concept of fasting has changed over the years and the restriction of food intake has extended to include fasting from technology, certain patterns of behaviour and dietary regulations. The reading from Isaiah has challenged us to accept that fasting is not just an inward spiritual exercise, but an outward act manifested in serving and service. Isaiah's audience believed that the personal discipline of sacrificing food was devoted worship to God, and though their intentions may have been genuine, they overlooked its significance. Their worshipping practice was severely condemned. Instead of ministering service to others, it became self-serving and hollow, with false humility and blindness to injustices.

I believe that Isaiah's denouncement of the ritualistic spiritual discipline needs to be revisited by the church and individuals, especially during the season of Lent. The personal aspect of fasting must clearly fulfil Jesus' command to 'love your neighbour as yourself' (Mark 12:31). Natural disasters, wars and situations such as the Covid-19 pandemic are opportunities for us to respond with loving service to one another. The challenge is not simply expressing individual acts of kindness, but sustained acts of service.

Social justice issues must be given greater priority than rituals for inner change, and focus given to acts of service that bring liberation, independence, and self-worth.

† Merciful Father, may the abstinence of food not make me abstain from offering love, justice and liberation to others. Amen

For further thought

True fasting from food and possession is not self-serving but benefitting to all God's people.

Thursday 22 September
Kindness given

Read 2 Kings 4:8–17

Let us make a small roof chamber with walls, and put there for him a bed, a table, a chair, and a lamp, so that he can stay there whenever he comes to us.

(verse 10)

'Do not neglect to show hospitality to strangers, for by doing that some have entertained angels without knowing it' (Hebrews 13:2). A most appropriate and pertinent Bible verse to support the two-fold account of hospitality in today's text. The kind service rendered was done in expectation of a miracle, yet the miracle was the result of a selfless act.

We can agree that the Shunammite woman's initial kindness in verse 8 was more than charitable, but she goes further and extends her hospitality by erecting an overnight room on the flat roof of her house. Her supposedly 'open door'-ness though a makeshift room did not overshadow her hosting initiative, a costly investment of money and time. What was the compelling factor for her kindness? Was it that she suspected that Elisha was a holy man of God – and she wanted a miracle, maybe? I would like to believe that the nature of her kindness was indicative of her character, and not tied to her wealth or expectation. Her invitation to a meal was not because of a perceived status but kindness done in service – she willingly served rather than expecting service to be done to her because of her affluent position.

Some may argue that the 'open house'-like concept should be encouraged, and shown especially to those of the migrant communities. Equally, some may see this as unwise, and instrumental in creating unnecessary chaos and pain.

† Father, it's easy to ignore the call to extend kindness to those we perceived as strangers. Help me to show compassion and care. Amen

For further thought

Is it risky to have a stranger stay overnight in your home? How would you feel if you were that stranger?

Brother, sister, let me serve you – 1 What does God require?

September

Kindness returned

> **Read 2 Kings 4:18–37**
>
> *She came and fell at his feet, bowing to the ground; then she took her son and left.*
>
> (verse 37)

The saying that 'kindness costs nothing but means everything' connects with today's story of kindness returned. It illustrates that expressing kindness should never be about getting something back, despite the fact that there are often unexpected benefits.

There is a Cadbury's chocolate advert on TV about a man returning lost items found in his garden to his neighbour's garden. One day he finds a bar of chocolate and before he can return the uninvited object (not thrown over accidentally), a young boy pops his head over the fence and tells him he does not have to throw that one back. The action of the child captures the concept of kindness returned, more so, unexpectedly. The Shunammite woman's kindness was returned in two forms: first, a child, and second, the child's new life from death. It's unlikely that Elisha believed that the wealthy woman would need his service, which reminds us that service is not always materialistic, but can be emotional, physical and spiritual.

Additionally, service is personal. Elisha's staff was ineffective in Gehazi's hands, whereas Moses performed miracles with his staff (Exodus 4:1–4). More so, service is demanding. The woman's persistence for Elisha to respond personally to her plea was successful. His repeated actions of praying and lying on the boy before God restored life-giving breath in the boy's body seems simple – but it could have been spiritually exhausting for Elisha.

Ironically, kindness done without expecting kindness to be returned often breaks open the way for such kindness. This should always be the mark of Christian service.

† Lord Jesus, thank you that we do not have to repay the debt you paid for our salvation. Amen

For further thought

Consider a situation that would benefit from your selfless kindness.

Saturday 24 September
What must I do?

Read Luke 18:18–30

There is still one thing lacking. Sell all that you own and distribute the money to the poor, and you will have treasure in heaven; then come, follow me.

(part of verse 22)

The commandments were kept, but a sense of unfulfillment remained. The ruler's quest for spiritual guidance so that he could attain eternal life was shattered by Jesus' response. His presuppositions needed to be realigned with 'one thing lacking' – which was a practical and personal sacrifice. These apparently small, but uncompromising, changes expected by Jesus seemed severe. To give up worldly comfort for eternal reward was too radical, demanding and troubling for the ruler, for the disciples and possibly for us. It was not simply a matter of selling the possessions and taking the money on a new itinerant ministry. No, the proceeds from the sale would be given to the poor, the ones who were least likely to reciprocate such generosity.

Mistakenly, the ruler understood serving to be religiosity, but Jesus dismantled his beliefs and proposed a new path that would be financially debilitating and emotionally demanding - monetary blessings to the poor, and his life to Jesus. This level of serving highlights the costliness of discipleship, where the truth is undiluted, and the expectation is 'all or nothing'. The criteria for a serving ministry include letting go of things that prevent us offering wholehearted surrender and commitment.

Feelings of incompleteness were the catalyst for his search, and the clear directives given by Jesus – though sobering – were essential for him to grasp the true significance of what God requires. As difficult as it might be, putting the less fortunate first remains the heart of ministry, 'Truly I tell you, just as you did it to one to one of the least of these who are members of my family, you did it unto me' (Matthew 25:40).

† Heavenly Father, help me to surrender all I am and all I have for your service and glory. Amen

For further thought

How do you feel about totally entrusting everything to God? Is exercising wholehearted faith something of the past?

Brother, sister, let me serve you – 1 What does God require?

September

269

Brother, sister, let me serve you

2 Love one another

Notes by **Catrin Harland-Davies**

Catrin is the Director of the Centre for Continuing Ministerial Development at the Queen's Foundation in Birmingham, where she works with those preparing for, or newly embarked on, ordained ministry, and ministers who want to develop their learning and professional expertise. She is a New Testament scholar, with a particular interest in the life and leadership of the early church. She enjoys walking, doing cryptic crosswords and learning languages, and is particularly fond of a good political rant. Catrin has used the NRSVA for these notes.

Sunday 25 September
Maintaining constant love for one another

Read 1 Peter 4:8–11

Above all, maintain constant love for one another, for love covers a multitude of sins. Be hospitable to one another without complaining. Like good stewards of the manifold grace of God, serve one another with whatever gift each of you has received.

(verses 8–10)

'Your children are not yours – they are just lent to you for a while...' This sugar-coated sentiment came to my attention as a meme on social media. Twee it may be, but there is truth there: that children are entrusted to our care. But really, I noticed it because it followed this: 'Be nice to your children – they'll choose your nursing home!' Again, a truth hidden, this time behind humour: that vulnerability shifts, and human relationships are usually interdependent.

The first epistle of Peter is written to congregations in Asia Minor, to encourage them in difficult times. These few verses focus on their shared life together, calling them to love and serve one another. The readers are reminded that they are not owners of their gifts, but stewards. Their gifts – material or spiritual – are given to them by God, to use for God's good purposes.

And more than that, they are stewards of one another. Each of them is a beloved child of God, and God has entrusted his children to one another's care, service and love. How might it transform our relationships, if we thought of our fellow Christians as entrusted to our care – and ourselves entrusted to theirs?

† God of love, help us to love one another constantly, not as a burdensome duty, but as a sacred charge.

Monday 26 September
What's in a name?

Read Acts 4:32–37

Now the whole group of those who believed were of one heart and soul, and no one claimed private ownership of any possessions, but everything they owned was held in common.

(verse 32)

Names can tell us something about a person – maybe what their parents hoped for them, or something about their heritage or origins. Names that people have chosen for themselves tell us something about what they hope for, or how they see themselves or would like to be seen. But a nickname – a name given to you by others – tells us about how a person is seen by others. It may be complimentary or insulting; perhaps it relates to their appearance, habits, preferences or personality.

Joseph, the landowning Cypriot Levite, had a nickname. It was a positive one, and it clearly stuck, as he is known by it throughout the remainder of the book of Acts. He is called Barnabas, one who is the very embodiment of encouragement.

It is interesting, in this ideal or idealised picture of the earliest days of the church, in which all apparently share, that Barnabas is singled out. Perhaps it is because, of all this Jerusalem community, he is the one known across the expanding church, or perhaps because he is known to Luke, the probable writer of Acts.

It may be for both these reasons, but maybe it is also because his gift embodies something of his personality. He is an encourager. We may think of encouragement as about words and emotional support. Giving is often generous, but can be self-centred. But when the two come together – when words of encouragement and support are backed up by actions that make it real, and when generosity is offered to build up the recipient and deepen their discipleship – how powerful the act becomes. The son of encouragement indeed!

† God of love, help us to love one another constantly, not as a burdensome duty, but as a sacred charge.

For further thought

What gifts has God given you, to build others up? They may be material gifts, talents, or aspects of your being – or perhaps all three!

Stop trying to like and start trying to love

Read Acts 9:10–19

So Ananias went and entered the house. He laid his hands on Saul and said, 'Brother Saul, the Lord Jesus, who appeared to you on your way here, has sent me so that you may regain your sight and be filled with the Holy Spirit.'

(verse 17)

There are a couple of tropes of Christians found in fiction, film, and popular imagination – some more likeable than others. One of the kindest tends to be of someone who is benignly holy, and who likes everyone. This image always stirs up a deep insecurity in me. I aspire to be holy, too, but there are people whom I dislike. I know that life is messy, and I am more complex than a caricature on a screen, and yet, I often feel that it ought to be true; that I should like everybody.

I don't know with what emotions Ananias went to visit Saul, on Straight Street, Damascus, but surely there would be more than a little trepidation. In his place, my deepest instinct would not be friendly. Did he expect to like Saul? I doubt it. Did he like him when he met him? The story doesn't say, but it does say is that he calls him 'Brother'.

Brothers – and sisters, for that matter – don't always like each other much. There are arguments, jealousies and fallings out. But that can belie a deep and profound mutual love. Siblings who squabble may still be there for one another when it matters.

'Brother Saul', says Ananias, to his enemy. And in that simple phrase we encounter a profound truth – the commandment is not to 'like one another', because liking is a matter of personality and instinct, and may be beyond our control. We are called instead to 'love one another', and love is a choice, and an attitude of heart.

† Think of the people in your life, whom you struggle to like – or perhaps profoundly dislike. Admit that honestly before God, and then pray for yourself, that you might still love them.

For further thought

How well do you balance an acceptance that you won't like some people, with a commitment to love them all the same?

The Tabithas in our midst

Read Acts 9:36–42

All the widows stood beside him, weeping and showing tunics and other clothing that Dorcas had made while she was with them.

(verse 39b)

We know very little about Tabitha – only that she was charitable, and a seamstress. But in my imagination, I know her well …

She's in your local church, serving on every committee. She's not as quick on her feet as she used to be, and these days coming out in the evenings is a bit of an effort, but she's still there, loyally, for every service, every church fête, every meeting. When there was no one to be Church Secretary, she volunteered. She's on the flower rota, washes the communion linen, plays the organ.

She's behind the coffee urn after the service, and always supplies chocolate biscuits. She'll sit with you for half an hour, because she notices that you're looking a little down, and she can be depended upon to visit when you're in hospital. And the children love it when it's her turn to lead the Junior Church!

She takes a coffee and sandwich out to the man sleeping rough in the church porch, and invites him into the warm. She remembers everyone's birthdays; she knows that Mrs Smith needs help finding the hymns, and Mr Jones needs a hand getting to the communion rail.

She's not often thanked, but she doesn't mind. We probably take her for granted a bit. Until she's gone. Then we realise what she means to us – to our community. Which of us then wouldn't send for Peter, the rock, and beg for his help? Who wouldn't want a second chance to appreciate the Tabithas, whose quiet acts of charity and kindness become, unnoticed, the rock of our church…?

† Compassionate God, we give thanks for those whose dedication and charity are the often unacknowledged strength of our community, and whose service and commitment stand as a witness to your love, and an example to us.

For further thought

Who in your church, or in the wider community, have you forgotten to thank? How will you show your appreciation for all they have done?

Brother, sister, let me serve you – 2 Love one another

September

Thursday 29 September
Unusual kindness on the seashore

> **Read Acts 28:1–2**
>
> *The natives showed us unusual kindness. Since it had begun to rain and was cold, they kindled a fire and welcomed all of us round it.*
>
> (verse 2)

Beleaguered, tired, captive, hungry, endangered, cold and wet, and now vulnerable and at the mercy of strangers, who shared neither his culture nor his faith … You can see why a hospitable welcome came as such a relief to Paul, that he described it as 'unusual kindness'.

What might unusual kindness look like in our society today? On the beaches of a Mediterranean island, refugees coming ashore might find volunteers ready to welcome them, feed and clothe them, help to reconnect them with their loved ones, and translate or advocate for them in their contact with authorities. Those, like Paul, whose boats are lost at sea are too often less fortunate, and strangers may honour them and prepare them for burial, knowing no name but wanting to restore their human dignity.

Perhaps unusual kindness might be found not merely in the one who welcomes, but also in the one who arrives among strangers. Perhaps the act of unusual kindness might be accepting vulnerability, arriving, powerless, in the midst of a community, showing gentle compassion and grace, challenging structures and systems of unequal power, subverting our expectations. Perhaps it might be to sit with the outcast, with those at the bottom of society's pecking order, or at the top – to take time to engage in conversation with Pharisees or Samaritan women, tax collectors, scribes, Roman centurions or those with conditions that make them 'unclean'.

And if Jesus modelled for us an extraordinary act of unusual kindness, perhaps 'unusual' kindness should, for us, become usual, habitual, a part of everyday discipleship.

† God of kindness, kindle in us a spirit of kindness. Make it a habit in us to reach out a hand of friendship to all in need.

For further thought

What opportunities are there in your community for those newly arrived not only to be shown, but to show, kindness? Does this matter?

Friday 30 September
More blessed to receive than to give?

Read 2 Corinthians 9:1–15

Each of you must give as you have made up your mind, not reluctantly or under compulsion, for God loves a cheerful giver. And God is able to provide you with every blessing in abundance, so that by always having enough of everything, you may share abundantly in every good work.

(verses 7–8)

'It is more blessed to give than to receive.' According to Paul (Acts 20:35), these are the words of Jesus. This may be why they seem important to him, and why he commits a significant amount of energy to persuading the Corinthian church of their truth.

The history of giving in the church is rich but complex – in particular, European Christians sending money, missionaries, books and much more to newer or less wealthy churches, sometimes with little regard for how useful the offerings might be. I'm sure that many of those gifts have blessed the receivers, and I'm certain that they have usually blessed the givers. But this has also created unhealthy power dynamics, and we might be forgiven for suspecting that the blessing of the giver (and I write as one of the givers) has often been the point.

Paul's collection is for the Jerusalem church, from wealthier, but arguably 'junior' communities. I wonder how easy it might be for the parent church – the seat of apostolic authority, in those early days – to accept help from the daughters. We don't know how it was received, but we might hope that it was with all the graciousness that might be needed in that situation!

The Western church is learning to receive. As mission partners arrive from the places it has previously evangelised – ambassadors from growing churches, to help those in decline – we must remember again that all communities have riches to offer, and all need humility to receive. Giving is costly, receiving is hard, but both are needed if all are to be truly blessed.

† Generous God, as Christ received water for his refreshment, hospitality for his enjoyment, and companionship for his comfort, give us the humility to receive. As Christ gave himself, give us the generosity to give. Amen

For further thought

What do you need to receive from others? What gifts do you find it easy to accept? Are there others that you find harder? Why?

The peace of Christ

Read Colossians 3:12–17

And let the peace of Christ rule in your hearts, to which indeed you were called in the one body. And be thankful. Let the word of Christ dwell in you richly; teach and admonish one another in all wisdom.

(part of verses 15–16)

This is a beautiful image of what a community, characterised by mutual love, can be. Following a list of the kind of behaviour *not* to engage in and a call to be renewed and united, it's striking and compelling. Through an attitude of compassion, kindness, humility, meekness and patience, the church can become a place of forgiveness. Then above all, it should be a place of love. And finally, it is to be a place of peace – the peace of Christ.

Peace characterises many appearances of the risen Christ; he stands among the disciples and declares, 'Peace be with you' (John 20:21). Peace sounds lovely, calm, easy. But the reality is that it can be hard, especially the peace found in a community of forgiveness. We can build peace by forgiving and forgetting minor offences – not dwelling on the abruptness of a brother or sister who may just be having a bad day, for example. But we cannot build peace by tolerating injustice, and we cannot demand forgiveness of the victim of bullying or abuse – and it cannot come at the expense of justice!

The kind of peace spoken of here – the peace of Christ – comes through the hard work of acceptance, challenge, grace, justice-seeking, humility and love. Christ's peace is not merely the absence of conflict, and can even build a safe environment for robust disagreement. Rather, it builds a community where all know that they are in need of grace, and where all long for, pray for, work for and rejoice in transformation.

Peace be with all of us.

† Pray for peace, for courage to work for peace, for passion to maintain a just peace. Pray for those who have no peace. Pray for the grace to forgive and the humility to be forgiven.

For further thought

Forgiveness and justice are both worthy aims, and both essential in building a community of peace. Does pursuing one undermine the pursuit of the other?

Brother, sister, let me serve you – 2 Love one another

October

Readings from 1 Kings

1 United kingdom

Notes by **Ellie Hart**

Ellie is a Bible teacher, blogger, artist and the author of *Postcards of Hope* (BRF, 2018). She is passionate about reading the Bible in community, about understanding it well and allowing it to change our hearts and lives. She is especially enthusiastic about helping people to read and reflect on OT poetry and narrative. After 10 years in overseas missions she now lives in Derby, England, with her husband Andrew, three children and a loveable but disobedient brown dog. Ellie has used the NRSVA for these notes.

Sunday 2 October
Adonijah sets himself up as king

Read 1 Kings 1:1–18

Now Adonijah, son of Haggith exalted himself, saying, 'I will be king'; he prepared for himself chariots and horsemen, and fifty men to run before him.

(verse 5)

The kingdom of the twelve tribes of Israel, finally united under David, is at a perilous moment of transition. The now elderly king is weak and not even a beautiful young woman is able to stir him. As David's weakness becomes known, we see Adonijah, fourth son of David and the next in line, decide that this is his moment to take power.

It's very telling that the writer tells us that Adonijah 'exalts himself'. Handsome, strong and overindulged by his father, Adonijah might well have been the kind of king the people wanted and I've no doubt that he thought he would make a rather marvellous king. So he gathers together horses and chariots and arranges his own 'coronation'.

But David had understood what Adonijah did not: 'you deliver a humble people, but the haughty eyes you bring down' (Psalm 18:27).

Adonijah thought he could exalt himself and take power with horses, chariots, men and powerful friends, while David knew that his glory and power was his only 'on loan' from God. Those who steal it for themselves, especially at the expense of others, won't get to live in God's blessing.

† Lord, I declare that all glory and power belong to you. When I am tempted to exalt myself or grab at power, show me a better way. Amen

Readings from 1 Kings – 1 United kingdom

October

Monday 3 October
Solomon becomes king

Read 1 Kings 1:28–48

So the priest Zadok, the prophet Nathan, and Benaiah son of Jehoiada, and the Cherethites and the Pelethites, went down and had Solomon ride on King David's mule.

(part of verse 38)

My friend Audrey lives on a beautiful peaceful farm in Derbyshire, not far from where I live. I love going to visit her, but the only way to get there is to drive down the winding lane that crosses a deep steep-sided valley. It's dark with trees and on wet days can be flooded at the base. It scares me a little, but you have to go down in order to go up.

Going down before you can go up seems to be a pattern in the lives of people in the Bible. Joseph is enslaved and then imprisoned before becoming the Pharaoh's right-hand man; David flees for his life before becoming king; and Christ himself lays down his life in utter humility before the Father exalts him to the highest place of all.

So where Adonijah gathers horses and chariots to gain power, king-to-be Solomon rides to Gihon to meet Nathan the prophet on a mule owned by his father. The succession happens in the end, not with a show of strength or demonstration of power but with an anointing by a man of God. Only then, with an authority given, not taken by force, can Solomon step up to David's throne and take his place as king.

As we follow God and step up into the roles that he has appointed for us, we need in our hearts to be following this pattern, as we did in baptism, to go down before we go up.

† Lord, help me to let go of my need for recognition and glory and choose to walk the path of humility before you, trusting that at the right time, you will raise me up.

For further thought

How can you lean into the idea that to be 'seen' by God is more important than being noticed or honoured by people?

Solomon asks for wisdom

> **Read 1 Kings 3:3–15**
>
> *'Give your servant therefore an understanding mind to govern your people, able to discern between good and evil; for who can govern this your great people?' It pleased the Lord that Solomon had asked this.*
>
> (verses 9–10)

I often stumble when people ask what gift I would like for, say, Christmas or a birthday. I just don't know what to ask for. I can't even imagine how I would respond if I heard God ask me the question that he asks Solomon in this passage. 'Ask what I should give you.' I wonder if Solomon asked for a bit of time to think about it!

You can understand how young Solomon would be feeling the weight of governing Israel, now, just as God had promised to Abraham, 'so numerous they cannot be counted' (verse 8 and Genesis 13:16). And though he perhaps hasn't shown a great deal of godly wisdom so far in his dealings with David's old enemies, his choice of wife and allies, Solomon hits a sudden high with his request for the wisdom to govern the people well. Other men might have asked for power or riches, long life or the sudden disappearance of his enemies. But King Solomon asks for wisdom. And in return for this bubble of humility, this insight into his own weakness, he is given it in overflowing abundance.

Wonderfully, James reminds us that God is still outrageously generous with wisdom to all those who ask: 'If any of you is lacking in wisdom, ask God, who gives to all generously and ungrudgingly, and it will be given to you' (James 1:5). Rather than operating only out of our experience and common sense, we also have the opportunity to ask for godly insight into the challenges we face. What will you do with this invitation to ask for wisdom?

† Lord, in the face of our suffering, bewildered world, give us both your wisdom and the opportunity to use it. May those in authority also act in godly wisdom so that your blessing ripples out.

For further thought

Solomon's wisdom becomes a blessing for Israel, and also for the whole of the known world. How can you use godly wisdom to bless others?

Readings from 1 Kings – 1 United kingdom

October

279

Wednesday 5 October
A wise ruling

> **Read 1 Kings 3:16–28**
>
> *The king said, 'Divide the living boy in two; then give half to one and half to the other'. But the woman whose son was alive said to the king – because compassion for her son burned within her – 'Please my Lord, give her the living boy; certainly do not kill him!'*
>
> (verses 25–26a)

Have you ever had to sit an exam knowing that everyone would see the results? This is Solomon's big moment to prove himself – the turning point for him in the eyes of his people, the great demonstration of his godly wisdom. And yet I've struggled with it over the years. After all, who are these women, and what's the point of including this story above all the other times where Solomon resolved disputes or gave judgements, if not to demonstrate the superlative wisdom for which he became famous.

Two prostitutes, of no social standing – one grieving, one desperate – and a heartbreakingly unsolvable question. If all Solomon does with his wisdom is trick a woman into revealing her indifference to the child, to manipulate these vulnerable women, then that feels pretty unsatisfactory to me.

Perhaps though, through this judgement, Solomon actually demonstrates a deep and powerful truth: that in the heart of a parent, the need for justice is trumped by compassion for their child. The wronged woman would rather let go of her right to justice than see her child suffer. Far from being a weakness, I wonder if this is a window into the heart of God. That although he is a God of justice, he is also a God of compassion, and that when his people cry out to him, compassion wins. Again and again in scripture we see this played out when in spite of Israel's sin, idolatry and rebellion, the God of justice still responds out of the compassion of a parent – listening and loving; forgiving and restoring.

† Lord, as we lean into your deep, burning compassion for us, may we become people that act out of compassion and love rather than a need for our own justice.

For further thought

Solomon makes time for these desperate, broken, marginalised women and gives the gift of listening to their story. Could you do this in your life?

Solomon builds the temple

Read 1 Kings 6:1–14

So Solomon built the house, and finished it.

(verse 14)

After years of exile in Egypt and then wandering in the desert, and then the terrible cycles of rebellion and return to God in Judges, God's people are finally settled in the land that was promised. And King Solomon is allowed the honour of building a place on earth where God's presence can dwell.

I'm a starter. I just love starting new projects, especially art or craft ones. From getting the idea, daydreaming about what's possible and how it could be done, to collecting materials and sketching out possibilities. That's all full of life for me. Finishing things…? Now that's a different story! More often than not I lose enthusiasm part of the way through knitting a jumper or crocheting a blanket and they lie unfinished and gathering dust.

Solomon on the other hand, both starts and finishes the temple, God's house. The building itself is far from showy, simply designed to replicate the spaces inside the tabernacle, with not even a beam from the outer structure disrupting the integrity of its walls. Solomon follows the plans God gave his father and creates a building which is so much more than it looks from the outside.

Amazingly, it's built in complete silence, with every stone quarried and shaped at a distance. This place where God is going to dwell is a place of absolute peace from the very beginning. It's clear that in some way it matters not only what you build for God, but also how you build it.

† Lord, as we build the things you call us to build in your name, may we have the perseverance, strength and courage to complete them and to be a temple of your peace and presence on earth.

For further thought

Solomon's plans called for simplicity on the outside, beauty on the inside and integrity all the way through. How can you reflect that?

Readings from 1 Kings – 1 United kingdom

October

The ark arrives and the cloud settles

The glory of the Lord filled the house of the Lord.

(verse 11b)

Have you ever climbed a mountain, or even a really big hill? All along the way you are looking ahead to the peak, focusing on how to get there, judging how far you still have to go. You keep going because of the promise of that high point yet to come, where you'll be able to rest, perhaps enjoy your lunch, and revel in the beautiful view.

The arrival of the ark in the temple is a pinnacle moment in the history of the people of God. Since the days of Abraham, they have been looking forward to, longing for and climbing towards this point. All the promises of God that they have been holding onto – the promise of a land they could call home; of a people too numerous to count; of a Davidic king on the throne; of peace on every border and honour among the nations – have all finally become a reality. And now the temple is finished and God's very presence comes to fill it.

Cherubims' wings still cover the entrance to the holy of holies, just as they did to the garden of Eden, but God himself is present with his people. The cloud settles down and finally the people who have followed the cloud are able to settle too, with God at the very centre of their city, and their lives.

† Lord, thank you that you have always been committed to being present with your people whether wandering or settled, and that even in their rebellion you faithfully brought them to a place of rest.

For further thought

The ark was brought into the centre of Jerusalem with great celebration. How can you bring God's presence into the very centre of your life today?

Saturday 8 October
The Lord's response to Solomon

Read 1 Kings 9:1–9

If you will walk before me, as David your father walked, with integrity of heart and uprightness, doing according to all that I have commanded you … then I will establish your royal throne over Israel for ever, as I promised your father David.

(parts of verses 4–5)

In a moment of clarity in chapter 8, Solomon realises that God's glory couldn't possibly be contained in this temple he has built and that his position is perhaps more precarious than he had thought. It would be so easy to walk away from this spacious, blessed place and back down into the struggles of the valley. You only have to forget who it was who brought you here.

Wisely and passionately he leans into God's compassion and cries out to him in prayer asking forgiveness and mercy for the sins which he knows his people will commit in the future. And God responds with this beautiful promise and a sharp warning: I will bless you, but don't take that blessing for granted. If you forsake me and worship other gods, I will cut you off from this land and from this house.

This is one of many 'If … then … but …' promises that God makes in the Old Testament. There is no free pass for God's people. If they neglect the law and chase after lifeless 'gods' then all the blessing – all the fulfilment of promises made to Abraham, David and Solomon – will be taken away.

God's blessing comes at the cost of loyalty and obedience to him. He is abundantly gracious, compassionate, slow to anger and abounding in loyal-love for his people, but he keeps this promise too. And as you read on into 1 and 2 Kings you'll see Solomon, the later kings and the people descend into dreadful unfaithfulness to God and eventually the people are carried off into exile, the temple destroyed.

† Lord, help us to not take you, your presence with us or the blessing you bring us for granted. When we are tempted to run after empty 'gods' would you gently restore us to your side. Amen

For further thought
Consider what false 'gods' you might be tempted to put your trust in. How can you choose each day to lean into God instead?

Readings from 1 Kings – 1 United kingdom

October

Readings from 1 Kings

2 Divided kingdom

Notes by **Deseta Davis**

Deseta is assistant pastor of a Pentecostal church in Birmingham. Her main vocation is as a prison chaplain helping to bring hope to those who are incarcerated. She obtained an MA in Theological Studies and previously worked as a tutor in Black Theology, bringing the study of theology to a range of people who had not considered such study. Deseta is married to Charles, and they have two grown-up children and a granddaughter. Deseta has used the NIVUK for these notes.

Sunday 9 October
United we stand

Read 1 Kings 12:1–24

He followed the advice of the young men and said, 'My father made your yoke heavy; I will make it even heavier. My father scourged you with whips; I will scourge you with scorpions.'

(verse 14)

In a recent training session, the discussion turned to the issue of churches not working together, even in the same neighbourhood. The result is that the same tasks are repeated over and again in each church causing an outward show of disunity. It was deemed that God's love would be much more visible if churches were willing to put aside their differences and work together for the greater good of the community and of the gospel.

The turn of events we explore this week shows the outcome of divisions and rifts. The people come, ready to pledge loyalty to Rehoboam and ask him to reduce the hard labour and taxes of his father king Solomon. Rehoboam, not learning from his father's mistakes, ignores the sound advice of the older sages and follows the advice of his peers.

What begins is the period known as the divided monarchy and what remains are two weakened, far less powerful and less important states that spend much of their time arguing and fighting with each other.

Churches today could take the example of this narrative and work together, creating a great synergy where much more would be achieved knowing that 'divided, we fall'!

† United God, may we as a church be one as you are one in the Trinity: Father, Son and Holy Spirit.

Monday 10 October
I've got the power

Read 1 Kings 12:25–33

*Jeroboam thought to himself, 'The kingdom is now likely to revert …
If these people go up to offer sacrifices at the temple of the Lord in
Jerusalem, they will again give their allegiance to their lord, Rehoboam
king of Judah. They will kill me and return to King Rehoboam'*

(parts of verses 26–27)

The Snap! song about power is a song that all humans would wish to sing at some time or another in their lives, as power is something that we all crave to some extent. There are many definitions and examples of what power is and what it can do, but it tends to have the notion of influence (whether good or bad).

Today, we see how power negatively affects Jeroboam. He accepts and believes the prophecy made to him by the prophet Ahijah (11:31–39) that he would be king and would have a great enduring dynasty if he followed the statutes and walk in the ways of God. Yet he soon forgets the promises of God and becomes afraid that the people would desert him and go back to king Rehoboam in Jerusalem. He had a great fear that religious unity would form political unity. He became so desperate to keep the power he had gained that he took matters into his own hands and started to imitate the worship to Jehovah God and build shrines and erect golden calves.

Power was much more important to him than the promises of God, so much so that he was willing to disobey God and get rid of anyone else who got in the way. He was a prime example of power corrupting and absolute power corrupting absolutely.

Rehoboam's actions caused a deeper division between the two kingdoms. His policies signified a political and religious break with Judah not only in geography but in worship and fellowship, never to be united again.

† Almighty, all powerful God, help us not to take matters into our own hands but to trust you to deliver what you have promised, knowing you have the ultimate power.

For further thought

What does power mean to you? How do you deal with power?

Readings from 1 Kings – 2 Divided kingdom

October

Tuesday 11 October
Forgive your enemies

Read 1 Kings 13:1–10

Then the king said to the man of God, 'Intercede with the Lord your God and pray for me that my hand may be restored.' So the man of God interceded with the Lord, and the king's hand was restored and became as it was before.

(verse 6)

Having established himself in the northern kingdom, King Jeroboam is making an offering on his manmade altar at Bethel. A nameless stranger turns up and shouts a warning that another king would sacrifice the bones of Israel's priests on the altar. This made King Jeroboam very angry due to the fact that burning human bones on an altar would desecrate it and thus prove that Jeroboam's kingdom was not of God. Determined to attack this man of God, Jeroboam stretches out his hand, which becomes paralysed.

After the king begs for healing, the man of God does not reject him or turn his back on him, he intercedes for the rebellious king. He forgives the fact that the king was ready to arrest him and asks God for healing.

When we see the hand of God move in our difficult situations, due to the acts of unbelievers, what is our response? Do we pray for their healing or do we act in our own desires and shun them? It is very easy to become proud and arrogant but God still healed king Jeroboam, even in his sin. The man of God did not judge him even though he was in the wrong. We are also not to judge but learn to forgive, love our enemies and pray for those who persecute us. I have prayed many times in arrogance, with a sense of pride, but this narrative is telling me to pray good and not bad for people, even though they may be in the wrong.

† Forgiving God, we ask that you forgive our sins as we forgive those who sin against us. Help our prayers to be ones of love and forgiveness rather than pride and arrogance.

For further thought

Is there anyone in your life that you need to forgive? Try praying loving prayers and ask God to help you to forgive.

Leading with integrity, following with insight!

Read 1 Kings 13:11–34

The old prophet answered, 'I too am a prophet, as you are. And an angel said to me by the word of the Lord: "Bring him back with you to your house so that he may eat bread and drink water."' (But he was lying to him.)

(verse 18)

This is a very sad end to a young man who stands up against the odds and speaks truth to power. He suffers the consequence of deceit from one who claims to be a prophet, yet this old prophet does not seem to have any consequences for his deception.

The fact that this old prophet spoke lies to the man of God may be a sign of the depth to which those in the northern kingdom had fallen, taking the prophets of Jehovah with it. Rather than prophesying and speaking truth to King Jeroboam, this old prophet stooped to the level of lying to the man of God.

As we have seen throughout the week, this is another example of how the failings of leaders often have catastrophic effects on their followers. The old prophet states that he has been sent by God, but the man of God is too quick to believe rather than going back to check with God. As leaders, we have a real obligation to lead with integrity. We may not go out to deceive intentionally, as this prophet did, but we need to remember that what we do and say will impact upon those who follow us.

This story also puts responsibility on those of us who follow. We need to research what we are told. We cannot take everything at face value, wherever it comes from. We all have to live with the consequences of our beliefs and actions. As my mother told me on numerous occasions, 'not everyone has your best interests at heart'!

† Gracious God, teach us to have a discerning spirit and to hear what you have to say about any given situation and not follow blindly.

For further thought

As a leader, how do you lead with integrity? As a follower, how do you check your facts and research what you have heard?

Readings from 1 Kings – 2 Divided kingdom

October

Evil

Readings from 1 Kings – 2 Divided kingdom

October

> **Read 1 Kings 14:1–18**
>
> *You have done more evil than all who lived before you. You have made for yourself other gods, idols made of metal; you have aroused my anger and turned your back on me.*
>
> (verse 9)

'Am I evil, Miss? It was only an accident. Am I evil?' This question was asked as I sat giving pastoral care to someone who had been charged with a crime. This made me wonder what it meant to be evil. The term raises many questions such as whether evil is a part of nature or nurture, and whether children can be evil, as in some cases very young children have been classed as such. Then there is the issue of who dictates what is evil.

There are people in society who, being notorious for the crimes that they have committed, are categorised as evil. In the worst cases, their names are used interchangeably with the word evil – for example, I have heard people call others 'Jezebel', meaning they are evil.

Throughout the Bible, the name of Jeroboam has become synonymous with sin and evil. There are no fewer than twenty-one times in the Bible where he is charged with having caused Israel to sin. Yet others, such as the wicked King Ahab, turned from sin and was forgiven by God (1 Kings 21:27–29).

Many people have discussed the term and the issue of evil, some believing there is no hope for someone who is evil. However, this does not take away from the fact that no one is beyond redemption. As much as we do wrong, God is willing to forgive if we turn to him. Romans 5:20–21 tells us that 'sin didn't, and doesn't, have a chance in competition with the aggressive forgiveness we call *grace*' (MSG).

† Gracious God, thank you for your aggressive forgiveness which we call grace and help us to remember that where sin abounds, grace abounds much more.

For further thought
Reflect on what it means to be evil and whether anyone is beyond redemption.

Friday 14 October
Jehovah Jireh

Read 1 Kings 17:1–16

*'I am … [making] a meal for myself and my son, that we may eat it –
and die.' Elijah said to her … 'first make a small loaf of bread for me
from what you have and bring it to me, and then make something for
yourself and your son.'*

(parts of verses 12–13)

I have been told many stories by our elders from the Caribbean
who, having nothing for their next meal, would fill a pot with water
and put it on the fire and pray for God to provide food. Invariably
their prayers were answered and someone would come with food.
Today it may seem ridiculous to some people – but for others it is
still a reality. Trusting in God to provide!

The poor widow in today's story did not expect to live beyond the
last meal she was preparing. Elijah tested her faith and asked her to
first make him some bread *before* cooking for herself and her son.
I wonder how many of us would do such a thing today?

Yet I note that the poorest people seem to be the kindest people.
When I have gone abroad on mission, the people would share with
their neighbours whatever we had bought for them, stating that
their neighbours were in need as well. It was also their pleasure to
share the little they had with us missioners, who had much more
than they did. They could be offended if we refused. They believed
strongly that God would provide for them as they shared with
others.

Jehovah Jireh, the God who provides, provided food for Elijah
from both the dirty scavenger raven and then from the very poverty-
stricken widow. Those who are starving today may wonder about
the God who provides, but I tend to find them to be the ones with
real faith in Jehovah the Provider.

† God our Provider, may those of us with more than enough put our hands and
resources to help those who do not have enough. Help us not to be selfish but to
be loving and giving.

For further thought

Reflect on what you can do to help those in need today.

Saturday 15 October
The God who answers... he is God

Read 1 Kings 18:20–39

'Then you call on the name of your god, and I will call on the name of the Lord. The god who answers by fire – he is God.' Then all the people said 'What you say is good.'

(verse 24)

God on Mute (Kingsway, 2007) is a book by Pete Greig, the founder of a prayer movement, who prayed intensely when his wife had a brain tumour. He speaks about the torment, the doubt and the fear when God is silent. He also tells of his struggles with his faith and the outcome.

We all have times when it seems our prayers go unanswered and God is silent! In our desperation, he is quiet and seemingly has no answers.

In today's text, we see Elijah challenging the people, asking them to prove the real God. The one who answers ... he is God, Elijah says. The worshippers of Baal pray, shout, cry and even slash themselves with swords and spears until their blood flowed. Sometimes we may feel to do all these things, yet God is still silent. It can become a real test of our faith and at times we have to make a tough decision, do we follow a god that seems not hear us in our direst need, do we keep the faith?

Elijah made ready the altar and prayed one deep, meaningful prayer – and God answered by fire.

In the times when God is silent, it is good to remember the times when he has answered us, when he has provided for our need. We may never know or understand why he is silent, but how we react to his silence is important. He may not answer when and how we think he should today, but tomorrow he may answer with fire!

† Loving God, it is difficult to pray when you seem silent. Help us to trust you during these times rather than lose faith.

For further thought

In the reading, people self-harmed, trying to get the attention of some deity. Today, many do so because of underlying mental health issues. How can you help them?

Nation shall speak unto nation

1 A vision of peace

Notes by **Liz Clutterbuck**

Liz is a priest in the Church of England and leads an inner-city congregation in North London. She combines parish ministry with research, specialising in exploring how church impact and church growth can be better measured, so that we can understand more about which missional initiatives work best and where. Liz is passionate about social media, film, baking, and travel – and loves it when she manages to combine as many of her passions as possible! Notes based on the NRSVA.

Sunday 16 October
Vision of peace

Read Isaiah 2:1–5

He shall judge between the nations, and shall arbitrate for many peoples; they shall beat their swords into ploughshares, and their spears into pruning hooks; nation shall not lift up sword against nation, neither shall they learn war any more.

(verse 4)

A century ago our world was recovering from the impact of the First World War and the 1918 influenza pandemic. Barely two decades into the new century, much had changed: some empires had fallen, new nations founded, millions of lives had been lost, and technology was beginning to enable people to communicate with each other.

During the war, radio communication developed significantly, enabling warnings of gas-attacks to be sent ahead to troops. By 1922, the value of radio for the civilian population had also become evident and, as a result, 'swords were beaten into ploughshares' – out of combat, the British Broadcasting Corporation (BBC) was founded, a century ago this week.

By 1927, the BBC held the motto: 'Nation shall speak unto nation', with a mission 'to inform, educate and entertain'. The founding of the BBC and its development in the 1920s and 1930s was a vision for peace between nations, in keeping with the words from Isaiah. Sadly, of course, that peace still seems far away. Nevertheless, in celebration of those high ideals, we will use aspects of the BBC to explore this week's theme.

† How does the media enable you to pray for places beyond your own community? What relationships do you have with other nations?

291

New heavens and new earth

Read Isaiah 65:17–25

But be glad and rejoice for ever in what I am creating; for I am about to create Jerusalem as a joy, and its people as a delight. I will rejoice in Jerusalem, and delight in my people; no more shall the sound of weeping be heard in it, or the cry of distress.

(verses 18–19)

The prophet Isaiah speaks of the Lord's glorious new creation, a new Jerusalem. We know this prophecy is being fulfilled in the kingdom of God brought forth by Jesus' resurrection and ascension. A kingdom where God's people are delighted in, and where weeping is no more and where 'wolf and lamb shall feed together' (verse 25). It is a bright vision, full of joy and hope.

Sir John Reith – the BBC's founder – was full of similar optimism when he created this new institution. It was his vision that it should entertain as well as inform and educate, making the BBC more than just news. I wonder what he would think of the BBC's output a century later? Multiple TV channels, digital radio stations, podcasts and international services.

Of course, the BBC is not the new Jerusalem! For many, the BBC is where they receive reliable news about world events – whether in Britain or via BBC World. And, owing to the state of our world, that news often includes or induces weeping. One of my earliest memories of the BBC is hearing Kate Adie reporting from Tiananmen Square in 1989, dodging bullets as she described what was happening. Fortunately, joyful news is also part of the BBC's remit. The coronation of Queen Elizabeth II in 1952 was an event that proved the worth of its television broadcasting, as millions globally watched what BBC cameras filmed.

The BBC, on the one hand, reminds us of how different God's kingdom is to what we have on earth, while also giving us a taste of the joy that will be experienced there.

† God of the new creation, keep our eyes fixed upon the promise of your new Jerusalem as we continue to pray for the world in which we live.

For further thought

Where are the signs of hope and joy in the news today? Where can you see God at work in our world?

Peace in trusting the Lord

Read Isaiah 26:1–12

Those of steadfast mind you keep in peace – in peace because they trust in you. Trust in the Lord for ever, for in the Lord God you have an everlasting rock.

(verses 3–4)

The congregation I serve is blessed with a number of members who are in their 80s and 90s and who have been worshipping in our church for decades. Many came to London from the Caribbean and grew up with a strong emphasis upon learning scripture by heart. Regularly, in our morning prayer meetings, I will begin the readings of the day and see them joining in without needing to look at the Bible in front of them. Whenever I express my envy of their gift, they tell me of the comfort that the psalms bring them. When they awake worried in the middle of the night, they can quickly draw upon reassuring verses from the psalms or from verses like these in Isaiah, and find peace.

Every human needs peace and, in our world of many faiths and none, people do so in different ways. Those of you outside of Britain may be surprised to hear that the BBC gives space for a moment of peace during what is often the most frenetic time of the day – the early morning, when life and news is at its busiest. The two most popular BBC radio stations, Radio 4 (news and other spoken word programming) and Radio 2 (a music station) include a 'Thought for the Day' and 'Pause for Thought' first thing in the morning. Religious leaders and thinkers provide a couple of minutes of reflection that is a moment of peace in the midst of whatever the events of the day are. Frequently, listeners who consider themselves non-religious will speak of the great impact that these short meditations have upon their lives.

† Spirit of peace, fall afresh upon me this day. May I trust in the peace that only you provide.

For further thought

Do you make enough space for times of peace in your daily life? Is there a new or different spiritual practice that you could try that might lead you into God's peace?

Wednesday 19 October
Wars cease

Read Psalm 46

He makes wars cease to the end of the earth; he breaks the bow, and shatters the spear; he burns the shields with fire. 'Be still, and know that I am God!'

(verses 9–10a)

If you own a smart phone, do you have it set up to receive news alerts? I'm never sure if this is a helpful or unhelpful feature, but the BBC – along with many other news outlets – offers it. Sometimes it feels as though it only ever tells me about the terrible things happening in the world – acts of violence, natural disasters, deaths of well-known figures, or the latest number of infectious disease cases. There are mornings when I wake up, reach for my phone to check the time and, in the process, discover a shocking piece of news.

Sometimes the endless barrage of news – of bad news – can become overwhelming. We just want it to stop! In these moments, it's helpful to remember the words of the psalmist: 'Be still, and know that I am God!'

Our God stills stormy waters, he brings peace where there is war, and justice where injustice reigns. In the stillness, we can hear the voice of God more clearly and know his purpose for us and the world.

Something I found helpful in my prayer life is to make the time to be still. To tune out the noise of the world and sit in silence, knowing God's presence with me. It's a time when my phone is off and the alerts of world news cannot interfere. Being still and knowing God.

† Creator God, we pray that you would bring peace to your world. We bring before you all places where there is violence today and pray for your intervention.

For further thought

Do you find yourself addicted to the news? Can you give yourself space from the endless alerts and instead be still and know God?

Thursday 20 October
Just judges

> **Read Deuteronomy 16:18–20**
>
> *You must not distort justice; you must not show partiality; and you must not accept bribes, for a bribe blinds the eyes of the wise and subverts the cause of those who are in the right. Justice, and only justice, you shall pursue.*
>
> (verses 19–20a)

When people from outside the UK first encounter the BBC, they are often surprised by the fact that it does not show adverts and is strictly impartial. As the state's broadcaster, being unbiased (especially regarding politics) is important. The British are used to this, it has been a feature of the BBC since its charter was awarded in 1927, but it means that we find news stations with a clear bias from other nations quite a strange concept.

Of course, the problem is that being unbiased is near-impossible. Virtually every day, the BBC receives complaints about bias. No human is without bias – our culture, upbringing, faith and all sorts of other factors shape how we see and describe our world. Before training for ordination, I was a historian and the very first lesson in reading historical sources is 'What is the bias of the writer?'

Only God is without bias. That is what Israel is being taught by the Lord in this passage. They have reached the promised land and this is how God is calling them to govern themselves. They are called to pursue justice, godly justice, so that their community will flourish in the land God has given them.

But humans are not God. We succumb to the temptation of judging by our own standards, instead of God's. We are inherently biased and struggle to overcome that. How different would our world be if we were to pursue only godly justice?

† God of justice, open our eyes to our deeply held bias, and the injustices we perpetuate in the world. Help your church to pursue your justice instead.

For further thought

News sources (TV, newspapers, websites) usually have some form of political bias. Could you take in news from a source you wouldn't usually read, in order to gain a fuller picture of how different people think?

Friday 21 October
'Peace' when there is none

Read Jeremiah 6:9–15

To whom shall I speak and give warning, that they may hear? See, their ears are closed, they cannot listen. The word of the Lord is to them an object of scorn; they take no pleasure in it.

(verse 10)

Many of the readers of *Fresh From The Word* will live in communities where the Christian faith is not a widely held belief. In the words of the prophet Jeremiah, 'their ears are closed' to God's word.

One of the elements of the BBC that can surprise people from outside the UK is its commitment to religious broadcasting. Earlier this week, I mentioned the brief reflections offered during morning radio shows, but there is more. Right from the outset, Christian content was broadcast on the BBC. In 1922, Revd John Mayo – a vicar in Whitechapel in East London – gave the first radio sermon, in which he expressed his amazement that this technology could be used to preach to so many people.

Songs of Praise, broadcast on BBC TV every Sunday since 1961, is consistently one of the highest viewed programmes, with a million people tuning in weekly. During the Covid-19 pandemic, the BBC played an important role in broadcasting a weekly national service by the Church of England, enabling people to worship in their homes while church buildings were closed.

Many in Britain pour scorn upon those who are Christian. Yet, in spite of opposition, the BBC continues to be a place from which the word of God is broadcast. It provides comfort and sustenance for those already within the church, and the possibility of new ears opening, hearing and believing.

† Loving God, we lift to you those who scorn our faith in you. Open their ears, their minds and their hearts to your word so that they may come to love you as we do.

For further thought

How could you share God's word in a new way in your local community?

Saturday 22 October
God of peace and our practice

Read Philippians 4:8–9

Keep on doing the things that you have learned and received and heard and seen in me, and the God of peace will be with you.

(verse 9)

The last century has been witness to significant changes in the media and its influence in our world. One hundred years ago, newspapers were the primary conduit of information – often taking days to report on events from around the world. Now, many of us live in societies where news seems to arrive instantaneously. Social networks like Twitter and Facebook enable anyone to report on what they are witnessing to a global audience, and for it to be seen immediately.

Society has learned much about media in this time, including the fact that it is a powerful tool – both for good and for bad. The BBC is generally seen as a force for good, but it cannot afford to be complacent. We've seen in recent years, the effects of political parties controlling media and information. In some places, preventing access to media has been a way of suppressing minorities or opposition.

In the words of these verses from Philippians, we need to remember 'whatever is true, whatever is honourable, whatever is just, whatever is pure, whatever is pleasing, whatever is commendable …' (verse 8). We need to seek the truth amidst the 'fake news' of our day. We need to work together to see the gospel truth heard and understood in our increasingly secular world.

Through the change and tumult of the last century, God has remained our constant. Our calling is to keep on doing the things that we have learned, received and heard in Jesus and the apostles, and to work to bring about God's peace on earth.

† Constant God, remind us again of your truth. We pray for those places and people where untruth reigns and light struggles to shine in the darkness. Lord, bring your peace.

For further thought

Do you fact-check the news that you read or watch? Could you develop a discipline (or encourage others to) of checking before you share a story online?

Nation shall speak unto nation

2 Speaking truth to power

Notes by **Noel Irwin**

For Noel's biography, see p. 177. Noel has used the NRSVA for his notes.

Sunday 23 October
Appointed over nations

Read Jeremiah 1:4–10

Then I said, 'Ah, Lord God! Truly I do not know how to speak, for I am only a boy.'

(verse 6)

Our reading comprises the first half of what we know of as the 'call narrative' of the prophet Jeremiah. One of the things which has stuck with me from when we looked at 'prophecy' when I was a student, was the professor telling us prophecy in the bible was 'forth telling' not 'fore telling'. It is not about predicting the future, it is about understanding the realities of the present well enough to see how the future will look if things do not change.

Prophets were not always listened to in the time of Jeremiah, but they were certainly taken seriously. So, what would this sort of prophet look like in our time and context? I don't see how they would be a pastor or a minister if they are to be 'appointed over nations and kingdoms' (verse 10), as they would not have that sort of audience. I write this on the birthday of the young British footballer, Marcus Rashford, who having a devout Christian mother and having suffered poverty himself, is using his voice and platform for children who are going hungry in our wealthy nation. He is perhaps a prophet for our time, the God of Jeremiah has surely put words in his mouth today.

† Pray for those who are addressing the issue of food poverty and for justice that children will not go hungry.

298

Confronting God

Read Psalm 82

God has taken his place in the divine council; in the midst of the gods he holds judgement.

(verse 1)

This reading might come as a shock for those who picture God as a King who rules by himself, with no need or desire of input from other counsellors – whereas the picture in Psalm 82, the 'divine council', is much more like a British prime minister presiding over their team of senior ministers. Here we have God plus lesser spiritual beings, who are not afraid to disagree! The psalmist rebukes them, not for disagreeing, but because they don't share God's heart: 'How long will you judge unjustly and show partiality to the wicked?' (verse 2). Then in verses 3 and 4, he gives a plea for justice for all those who are particularly vulnerable, finishing in verse 8 by asking God to sort it out and be a God standing on the side of the poor and the oppressed. Bold stuff from the psalmist!

I love how this psalm holds together ambiguity and certainty. In terms of ambiguity, in our world of social media we are quick to judge ourselves as good and our opponents as evil. There is nuance and uncertainty in the account of the heavenly council, which we would do well to take note of. There is also certainty, as someone I knew in Northern Ireland said cryptically, 'Not all cats are grey in the dark night of politics'. What they meant was that, at times, there are issues which are 'good' or 'evil'; all is not ambiguous/grey. They were speaking about violence in Northern Ireland and apartheid in South Africa. Perhaps today it would be the scourge of racism and the destruction of the climate?

† Pray through a contemporary 'hot' topic – trying to hold together both ambiguity and certainty in your prayers.

For further thought

What issues are you certain and uncertain about? Why do you think the way you do in terms of scripture, tradition, reason and experience?

Nation shall speak unto nation – 2 Speaking truth to power

October

They abhor the truthteller

> **Read Amos 5:1–10**
>
> *They hate the one who reproves in the gate, and they abhor the one who speaks the truth.*
>
> (verse 10)

Yesterday we saw how there can be ambiguity and argument on political matters, even in heaven! A tool of discernment in trying to understand what is wrong and evil, which Amos provides for us throughout his book, is that the way the poor are treated signals the health of a society and how it stands in relation to the judgement of God.

For those who are unhappy with the way the poor are treated, who stand with God, there is often pressure to simply be quiet and not speak out against injustice. In Israel, judgement was given at the city gates – those who try to judge impartially face hatred and judges are bribed to rule in favour of the rich and against the poor (verses 10 and 12).

Growing up in Northern Ireland, there was a saying relating to 'The Troubles': 'Whatever you say, say nothing'. This was an encouragement not to upset anyone, not to rock any apple carts, not to speak about what was dividing us as communities. So we were simply nice and polite to one another in the churches, as the violence and the killing continued unabated. Speaking out and critiquing injustice and wrong in society was at the heart of the prophets of the Hebrew Bible. As contemporary Christians and followers of Jesus this must be one of our core ministries as well, not just to provide foodbanks (wonderful as that is) but to ask why they are necessary as, just in the time of Amos, the rich continue to get richer and poor poorer.

† Give thanks for all who speak out against injustice, and ask for the grace to listen when the 'truthteller' is speaking to us and our community.

For further thought

Think about what being a 'truthteller' means today in church, community, society and world.

Against false prophets

> **Read Micah 3:5–8**
>
> *Thus says the Lord concerning the prophets who lead my people astray, who cry 'Peace' when they have something to eat, but declare war against those who put nothing into their mouths.*
>
> (verse 5)

Micah was unusual because he prophesied to both the northern kingdom of Israel and the southern kingdom of Judah. In this chapter, he is pointing out that there are prophets who, if they are fed well enough, will prophecy good things like 'peace' – whereas, if they're not paid, they will prophecy 'war' and 'conflict'. One commentator, rightly, tied this in with the 'cash for questions' scandal in the British Parliament in the 1990s – pointing out that politicians should ask questions because they are important, not just because they have been paid to ask them by vested interests. In the same way, prophets should honestly speak the words given to them by God and not because they were being paid.

Latin American Liberation Theology speaks eloquently of 'the preferential option for the poor' – in other words, preference being given to the needs and well-being of the poor and powerless, which should be the default position of the Christian church. Yet in our text and in much contemporary church and political life, we see 'the preferential option for the rich', which has been the dominant voice and practice over the centuries.

The prophet Micah does not just speak out against these prophets for hire, but he also says they will be punished. Those who have led the people of God astray will no longer hear from the Lord. In verse 7, we see the consequences of their actions – they will face disgrace and shame. Then Micah, in verse 8, speaks of the validation of his own message against the injustice of the rulers. He listens to the voice of God and so he is filled with power, justice and might and above everything, with the Spirit of the Lord.

† Pray for all you know are called to speak the word of the Lord. Pray for courage when it becomes clear to them God's message will be neither easy nor comfortable.

For further thought

In our times there are cries of 'fake news' from various quarters. As a Christian how do you tell 'fake' from 'real'?

Nation shall speak unto nation – 2 Speaking truth to power

October

Does the Lord not see it?

Read Lamentations 3:25–36

*When human rights are perverted in the presence of the Most High,
when one's case is subverted – does the Lord not see it?*

(verses 35–36)

The context of the book of Lamentation is Jerusalem being destroyed by Babylon in 587 BCE, with the great and the good of the population being hauled off into exile. The author of the book is anonymous (though the Greek translation says it is Jeremiah), they are among those who have been left behind, they are mourning and asking huge questions such as, 'Why this has happened?'

You'll be pleased to know chapter 3 is the most hopeful chapter (albeit with a very cautious sense of hope) in the book! On both sides, there are chapters of lament at its deepest. When I read Lamentations, my brain seems automatically to switches to pictures of bombed and destroyed cities, near and far, both in terms of time and distance.

Very often, when the powerful of the world commit injustice, they rely on their misdeeds being done in secret. Perhaps one of the blessings of the age we live in, where so many people have camera phones and access to the internet, is that it is perhaps more difficult to hide abuses of human rights than it used to be. Of course, I recognise that the above can also be a curse as well as a blessing – technology does not have a built-in moral compass! The message and hope of Lamentations is this: 'God sees', 'God knows', 'God cares'. In this I am reminded of the words of Jesus in Luke 12:2, 'Nothing is covered up that will not be uncovered, and nothing secret that will not become known.'

† Pray for victims of torture and unjust imprisonment around the world.

For further thought

Pray in a focused way using resources from organisations like 'Action by Christians Against Torture' and 'Amnesty International'.

Not to please mortals

> **Read 1 Thessalonians 2:1–8**
>
> *For our appeal does not spring from deceit or impure motives or trickery, but just as we have been approved by God to be entrusted with the message of the gospel, even so we speak, not to please mortals, but to please God who tests our hearts.*
>
> (verses 3–4)

One of the things we have seen in many countries in the recent past has been a breakdown of trust in politicians and institutions (including the church), allied to a breakdown of civility in discourse between those with opposing political/moral/social views. Truth is seen as the exclusive purview of my group, this is of course exacerbated by the 'echo chamber' effect of social media, where our own biases are constantly confirmed by people who are just like us.

What Paul in Thessalonians throws into our contemporary malaise is not an echo chamber confirming bias and refusing any contrary opinion, but a focus on a truth which is constantly open to being tested by God. Remember in Paul's time the heart was considered to be the part of the body which functioned as the seat of reason and rationality, not about feelings and emotions. Also at a time of huge distrust in this Christian community, Paul brings trust not just in terms of the Christian message, but an entrusting of themselves to the Thessalonians (verse 8). This entrusting involves a tenderness reflected in verses 7 and 8. I particularly love the nursing mother image of verse 7. The character of the messenger and message are one.

The decision the Thessalonians have to make is whether they will accept what is being offered to them or be cynical, seeking ulterior motives in Paul and his fellow missionaries. Truth, trust and tenderness – though we are in very different times from Paul – are still the keys to the renewal of the church and also of society.

† Loving God, we pray that we will be open to truth, trust and tenderness in church and community. May we rise above any tendency to cynicism and see the best in others as you see in us. Amen

For further thought

How can we engage with systems and governments to seek systemic change without becoming embroiled or aligned with politics?

Nation shall speak unto nation – 2 Speaking truth to power

October

Armour of God

Read Ephesians 6:10–20

For our struggle is not against enemies of blood and flesh, but against the rulers, against the authorities, against the cosmic powers of this present darkness, against the spiritual forces of evil in the heavenly places.

(verse 12)

Here the author of Ephesians sums up the argument of his book, in a passage which is one of the best known in the whole of the New Testament: the opposition we receive from a fallen world is not an excuse to stop serving, the fallen world is the reason for our service. The battle is ultimately spiritual, but that does not mean we should abrogate our human response to it.

As an example, in verse 12, the spiritual realities are connected to political realities. The word 'against' is used five times with a movement from earth (rulers, authorities) to heaven (cosmic powers, spiritual forces). The causes of injustice, war, poverty, environmental destruction and the like are connected to realities which are spiritual and earthly. Reversing those causes is not just about opposition to and struggle against any particular 'blood and flesh' ruler or party, nor is it just about engaging in spiritual warfare. No matter how effective we are in changing human systems, if the spiritual dynamics are not addressed, those changes will quickly degenerate into legalistic systems that become perverted, just as the Law did in Israel. Similarly, if we are successful in tearing down spiritual strongholds but do nothing with the human systems they empowered, the injustice and oppression they served remains virulent. Ephesians calls us to tackle both.

This makes sense to me as I look at my own struggle against sectarianism and watch those who find the message of 'Black Lives Matter' so difficult to engage with. Everything is connected!

† Pray for all victims of injustice, specifically those in your community and area. Pray for insight to see connections and structures which need to be engaged with, as opposed to simply blaming individuals.

For further thought

Engage with material on 'Institutional Racism' and then re-read Ephesians 6:10–20.

Readings from 1 Corinthians

1 Walking as one

Notes by **Joshua Taylor**

Joshua is the Vicar of St John's Anglican Church in Timaru, New Zealand. He's married to Jo, with three daughters (Phoebe, Esther, and Eve), and together they've been exploring what it means to be a family on mission. Joshua completed his master's thesis on consumerism and its impact on how we do church. In his spare time, he loves to spend his days off being mocked by fish while holding a fishing rod, or playing in his pottery studio. Joshua has used the NRSV for these readings.

Sunday 30 October
Called to be Saints

Read 1 Corinthians 1:1–19

To the church of God that is in Corinth, to those who are sanctified in Christ Jesus, called to be saints, together with all those who in every place call on the name of our Lord Jesus Christ, both their Lord and ours.

(verse 2)

Have you ever experienced nostalgia? The idea that 'back in my day things were better'. Some of my favourite nostalgic memories are of watching Saturday morning cartoons with my brother, trout fishing with Dad, or frosty mornings on a rugby pitch.

I think we often have nostalgic views of what the early church was like. We say things like, 'If only we could get back to the 'early church'. But 1 Corinthians tells us what some of it was really like: quarrelling, jealousy, envy, ignorance, bad theology, deception, arrogance, people sleeping with their stepmother (seriously, read chapter 5!), suing one another, visiting prostitutes, husbands and wives leaving one another, idol worship, greed, and generally failing to love one another.

This is no perfect church. These are people like you and me in the process of ongoing transformation to become more Christ-like by the power of God's Spirit. In the opening words of 1 Corinthians, Paul calls the people of the church 'saints'. It seems that Paul knows who they are in Christ and who they can become if only they will embrace it.

† Lord, may we by your Spirit become all you have created us to be, in Jesus name, Amen

Monday 31 October
We preach Christ Crucified

Read 1 Corinthians 1:20–31

For Jews demand signs and Greeks desire wisdom, but we proclaim Christ crucified, a stumbling block to Jews and foolishness to Gentiles, but to those who are the called, both Jews and Greeks, Christ the power of God and the wisdom of God.

(verses 22–24)

The cross was a brutal form of capital punishment that the Roman's inflicted on criminals and political enemies. The lowly of society who committed crimes against the empire were the people nailed to the cross, not saviours or kings. To many Romans, the fact that Christians worshipped this crucified God would be a joke.

Corinth was a place of great opportunity. It hosted tourists for the Isthmian games, second only to the Olympics. Corinth was booming economically and beckoned entrepreneurs. It was a deeply competitive and ambitious place. For people who love winning, competition and strength, the gospel news of a crucified Messiah was shocking.

The cross has always been divisive in the sense that it turns over conventional wisdom. In the misery and suffering of the cross, Jesus accomplished a victory over the powers of death and evil. The church has wrestled with what this means. In its early days, the church suffered persecution at the hands of the Roman Empire, but from the fourth century on, the relationship changed and in many places the church rose to power. A complex relationship between religion and politics was formed. Many terrible things were done in the name of Christianity and we live in the wake of these events. As Christians, we must examine our relationship to power and our relationship to the values of the world at large. Are our lives defined by Jesus, and by his death and resurrection, or are we using another measuring stick? Do we add religion on as a gloss over our lives – lives that are determined primarily by other priorities?

† Lord Jesus, may we gaze at your uplifted love on the cross in awe and worship. May our thinking be shaped by this act of self-giving love, that our lives may reflect your love in the world. Amen

For further thought

What is your reaction to the crucifixion of Jesus? What feelings does it evoke? What thoughts or questions does it raise for you?

Tuesday 1 November (All Saints' Day)
Wisdom from the Spirit

Read 1 Corinthians 2:1–16

My speech and my proclamation were not with plausible words of wisdom, but with a demonstration of the Spirit and of power, so that your faith might rest not on human wisdom but on the power of God.

(verses 4–5)

The church at Corinth, to whom Paul was writing, was influenced strongly by Graeco-Roman thinking which was shaped by philosophers such as Plato and religious traditions which emphasised wisdom and spiritual knowledge. It appears that one of the main problems that was evident in the church at Corinth was that some people were claiming to have superior wisdom and insight, and insisting that they were more spiritual than others. This caused arguments and divisions in the church.

Paul argues that true wisdom isn't what the Corinthians might think. It isn't found through human insight and knowledge. Rather Paul argues that true wisdom is found in the revelation of God through Jesus' life, death and resurrection. This wisdom is given and received, not earned or conjured up. Practically speaking, this makes all the difference in the world. Many of the divisions within the Corinthian community were between those who proclaimed themselves to be 'wise' versus those who were perceived to have less 'spiritual knowledge'. To talk about wisdom as received by God, through the power of the Holy Spirit, places the emphasis on God's action and gives no room for anyone to boast about being super-spiritual.

For us today this is an important point. Where we might be tempted to be puffed up with pride for our theological knowledge, our prayer life or whatever spiritual badge we might think we have earned, Paul grounds us with the reminder that all the wisdom that counts is given by God through the gift of Jesus Christ.

† Lord, may we boast in Christ alone. When we are tempted to count ourselves wise, give us humility and keep our eyes on you. Amen

For further thought

What do you boast in? Are there areas in your life where pride has taken root, or you count yourself above others?

Wednesday 2 November
Laying foundations

Read 1 Corinthians 3:1–23

According to the grace of God given to me, like a skilled master builder I laid a foundation, and someone else is building on it. Each builder must choose with care how to build on it. For no one can lay any foundation other than the one that has been laid; that foundation is Jesus Christ.

(verses 10–11)

I have recently taken up pottery as a new hobby. I've very quickly fallen in love with the whole process from start to finish: working up the clay, throwing it, trimming it, firing and glazing it. What I've noticed is that if I don't get things right at the beginning, it never quite works out. I can't throw a pot with clay I haven't spent time 'working' on the bench and I can't glaze over a wobbly pot that hasn't been centred. The first steps really matter. The foundations are important.

In today's reading, we see that Paul also knows just how important foundations are. When crafting or building anything, the foundations are the first and most important piece. Paul says that like a master builder, he has laid a foundation, and that foundation is none other than Jesus. It seems that the Corinthians were tempted to lay other foundations – such as their favourite teachers, like Apollos. However, Paul makes it very clear that it is folly to build on anything other than Jesus. The problem of building on wobbly foundations is not uniquely Corinthian. Throughout the centuries, the church has been tempted to build on elements other than Jesus Christ. However, through renewal, the church has been brought back consistently to the foundation of the gospel. This foundation is the steady ground on which we share common life together. Paul calls for a unity in faith, and that is always built by placing Jesus at the centre.

† Lord Jesus, may you be the foundation of our faith and our life together, that we may be one. Amen

For further thought

In our churches and ministries is Jesus the foundation? What other foundations are we tempted to build upon?

Thursday 3 November
Servants of Christ

Read 1 Corinthians 4:1–21

Think of us in this way, as servants of Christ and stewards of God's mysteries. Moreover, it is required of stewards that they be found trustworthy. But with me it is a very small thing that I should be judged by you or by any human court. I do not even judge myself.

(verses 1–3)

We live in a celebrity culture. Magazines, blogs, Instagram accounts and television shows present us with people to follow. The red carpet is an object of fascination in the twenty-first century, but the culture of celebrity is nothing new. People have always engaged in versions of this kind of behaviour. We've been exploring Corinthians and have seen how Paul has found himself in the middle of a popularity contest that he never signed up for. The Corinthians have been judging their leaders by human standards. They are impressed with human wisdom, strength and beauty.

Yet here in chapter 4, Paul outlines what matters: it is God's commendation that counts. As an apostle, Paul has been called by God to be a servant of the church and he makes it clear that this isn't always glamorous. It couldn't be further from the acclamation and glitz of the red carpet of Hollywood. Paul gives a list of his experience as an apostle: weakness, hunger and thirst, a poor reputation, homeless, weariness, persecution, and more.

Yet amid all this, Paul sees God at work in his ministry. He follows a crucified Messiah – one who gave his very life for the sake of the world. In the pattern of Jesus, Paul gives his life too as a servant for Christ's sake. Paul imitates Jesus and then urges the Corinthians to imitate him. Paul knows that what counts the most is not what other people think of him but what Jesus has done for him and what Jesus is doing through him.

† Heavenly Father, Paul didn't live an easy or comfortable life, yet he lived one that imitated your Son, Jesus. Help us to imitate Paul's example in a life of servant-hearted living, for Christ's sake. Amen

For further thought

Who do we look to for affirmation? Does our sense of identity and worth come from the opinion of others or is it grounded in the love of God?

Readings from 1 Corinthians – 1 Walking as one

November

Clear out the old yeast

Read 1 Corinthians 5:1–12

Your boasting is not a good thing. Do you not know that a little yeast leavens the whole batch of dough? Clean out the old yeast so that you may be a new batch, as you really are unleavened.

(verses 5:6–7a)

When I was a teenager I remember bringing a friend to a Christian camp. This friend wasn't from church and so I was a little worried that the experience might be rather weird. I remember cringing as our music team performed a 'Christian version' of the theme tune from the 1990s sitcom, *Friends*. I could see the look of amusement on his face and felt embarrassed. From then on, I felt that the church shouldn't be weird. I thought that Christians should be just like everyone else. Yet over the years, I have changed my mind.

In 1 Corinthians 5, Paul reminds the church at Corinth that they are to be distinctive. Paul references a report of sexual immorality in the church. It's hard to believe now, but once upon a time, Christian ideas about sex were considered revolutionary. In Roman society, several sexual activities outside of marriage were broadly accepted – such as sex with prostitutes, courtesans and slaves. In fact, there was a double standard when it came to sex. Wives were expected to honour their husbands by remaining faithful, yet men were allowed a lot of freedom to have sex with others as long as they weren't someone's wife or a freeborn virgin. Paul's sexual ethic, in line with the teachings of Jesus, was transformational in that it benefited women and children and contributed to social cohesion and flourishing in the community. Paul is concerned for the Corinthians and makes it clear that they are called to be different and to bear witness to the fulness of life available in Jesus Christ.

† Lord, help us to be different in the best kind of way, that people may see our lives and experience your love and goodness. Amen

For further thought

What do you think about Christians being 'different'? Is there a time that being different has been difficult for you?

Saturday 5 November
Unite with the Lord

Read 1 Corinthians 6:1–20

When any of you has a grievance against another, do you dare to take it to court before the unrighteous, instead of taking it before the saints?

(verse 1)

In today's passage, we see another example of division in the Corinthian church. There was a court case going on between two of the believers in the Corinthian church. One member of the church (let's call him Jimmy) had defrauded another member of the church (let's call him Bob). So, Bob took Jimmy before the civil magistrates to sort the matter out publicly. Seems fair enough right? Jimmy took Bob's money, so Bob takes Jimmy to court. But Paul says no! Paul is outraged at the way they have approached the conflict they're facing, but why? Doesn't it seem fair that Jimmy should be punished for his crime against Bob?

We must be careful not to use this passage to justify letting crimes go unpunished or letting people be treated unjustly in the name of Christianity. God is a just and good God. This isn't suggesting the church should sweep problems under the rug. Instead, this passage is a call for the church to grow up. It is a call to recognise not only our rights, but also our responsibilities. Paul consistently encourages the church at Corinth to 'be who they are', to become the people God has made them through Jesus Christ. Unity in the church is an important witness to the world and so Paul calls to take this seriously. This week's readings have been all about 'breaking down divisions'. In our politically divided and fractured world, Christians are called to be an example of unity. It doesn't mean we all agree with one another but rather that we seek reconciliation and restoration.

† Lord Jesus, in a fractured and broken world, help us to be a people united in our commitment to reconciliation and love. In Jesus' name we pray. Amen

For further thought

Are you friends with people who disagree with your politics or beliefs? Or do all your friends think like you?

Readings from 1 Corinthians

2 Spiritual guidance

Catherine Sarjeant in conversation with **David Painting**

Catherine and David co-write a 'Thinking Allowed' blog in which they think aloud with each other, while others listen in! This week's readings have been created in conversations. You can find out more about Catherine in the bio and notes she has written next week; David's bio in on p. 65. Catherine and David have used the NRSV for these notes.

Sunday 6 November
Rules or relationship?

Read 1 Corinthians 7:1–9

Do not deprive one another except perhaps by agreement for a set time, to devote yourselves to prayer, and then come together again, so that Satan may not tempt you because of your lack of self-control.

(verse 5)

There seems to be a tendency in humankind that whenever we percei there to be a problem about something, we try and solve it by makin rules! Here's an example: the Corinthians were worried about the sexu immorality all around them and wanted to create rules, even with marriage, to solve the problem.

There are two ways to make something that seems unsafe, safe. Yo can surround it with rules – do's and don'ts, policing the rules wi fear of punishment – or you can choose how to behave based on yo knowledge of God's love. This was the challenge in Eden – we we created to understand right from wrong through relationship with Go but instead chose independence. And in the absence of that relatior knowledge, we relied on rules to guide us. The problem is that inste of protecting, rules, however well intentioned, can quickly becor shackles. Think about Legion, he was chained up to protect himself a others, but in the end, the chains themselves caused harm. In truth, was only when he met Jesus, only in relationship, did he became free

Perhaps we face the same danger as in the days of the Scribes a Pharisees, focusing on rules rather than relationship. Like them, we c become hyper-anxious about getting things wrong to the point where becomes exhausting and paralysing. 'Are you tired? Worn out? Burn out on religion? Come to me... I won't lay anything heavy or ill-fitti on you. Keep company with me and you'll learn to live freely and light (part of Matthew 11:28–30, MSG)

† Father, help me live in relationship with you.

Monday 7 November
Freedom and responsibility

Read 1 Corinthians 8:1–13

But take care that this liberty of yours does not somehow become a stumbling block to the weak.

(verse 9)

Yesterday we saw how the Corinthians sought to control sin by shackling it with rules. At the other extreme, today we see them abusing their freedom and thereby causing others to stumble! It's not unlike the debate in 2020 about freedoms. Whether we should limit our freedom to meet together for worship, to walk the streets when we wanted, to choose what to wear or what not to wear. It's not a new issue, it generated as much heat for the Corinthians as it did for us.

Paul sets out the principle in Philippians where he encourages us to have the same mind that is ours in Christ Jesus, who though in very nature God, did not count equality with God something to be grasped, but emptied himself.

In short, for the sake of those more vulnerable than you, there is something greater than your freedom at stake. True, you have the liberty to eat meat offered to idols (or whatever freedom you might be being asked to curtail). For you it may make no material difference, bring you no harm. But for a younger believer or a believer from a different background, your freedom might be their downfall.

† Father, help me protect the vulnerable around me. Guide me in what to give up or do so I am not a burden to them knowing you.

Thinking Allowed

If our mission is to make Jesus visible, we must be like him, individually and collectively. If the world sees us as a people who stand on our rights, insisting on exercising our freedoms – even when it potentially puts others in danger – are we really representing the one who gave up everything?

Readings from 1 Corinthians – 2 Spiritual guidance

November

Tuesday 8 November
Servant of Christ

Read 1 Corinthians 9:1–23

For though I am free with respect to all, I have made myself a slave to all, so that I might win more of them.

(verse 19)

So, Paul has shown us that choosing how to live isn't about rules, and it isn't about our freedoms, it's about Jesus. It's about our relationship with him and the relationship we long for others to have with him. Paul doesn't just teach this, he lives it out. Never allowing his rights to get in the way of drawing himself and others closer to God.

This is so different from the way the world works. God always steps down to where we are, in order to lift us up to where he is. Whereas the world often raises itself up at the expense of pushing others down – from systems that protect those who have, at the expense of those who have not, to leaders lording it over their people, drawing power to themselves for their own benefit rather than that of those they serve.

And it works both ways round, not only do leaders sometimes exalt themselves, but we sometimes encourage that culture, raising up leaders who fit into a particular mould. Rather like the Israelites when they chose Saul, choosing a man who looked like they thought a king should look; strong, vociferous, sure of himself!

But true leadership is more like a shepherd than a Saul. Like the shepherds we met in Romania, who lived with the sheep, knew them, smelled like them. Who gave up the right to warmth and safety in order to keep the sheep safe. Who led, not as a badge of status but as a means of being first in the place of danger.

† Father, thank you that you stepped down to be with us. Help me to step down to be alongside others.

Thinking Allowed:

If you are a leader, what ways can you use to step down to be with those you lead? If you are being led, how can you avoid putting pressure on your leaders to be that which they are not?

Wednesday 9 November
Gift or giver?

Read 1 Corinthians 10:1–24

So if you think you are standing, watch out that you do not fall. No testing has overtaken you that is not common to everyone. God is faithful, and he will not let you be tested beyond your strength, but with the testing he will also provide the way out so that you may be able to endure it.

(verses 12–13)

God gives good gifts, but so often the gift becomes the goal. The people followed Jesus hoping to see a sign, not because they wanted to be with him, or changed by him. Similarly, the passage points out that the Israelites revelled in God's gift of food and water, rather than in the one who had given. Focusing on the gifts, being motivated by them, rather than acknowledging and loving the giver is idolatry.

All the good gifts from God are intended to point past themselves to God. In the gift of communion, bread and wine point to a God who so loved us that he held nothing back. We enjoy the good gifts for what they are, but we also see beyond them to the generous, loving God who gave them. If we don't, that which was designed to bring life will end up bringing death. As with the Corinthians, if we focus on the gifts of food and drink, gluttony is fuelled bringing a death to our health as individuals and a greed that leads to inequality corporately. Focusing on the gift rather than the giver is sin and sin always lead to something dying.

On the other hand, moving our focus from the gift provides a way of escape from temptation and allows us to enjoy the gift safely. Loving the giver becomes about relationship rather than rules or things.

† Lord, thank you for the gifts you give. May they lift you, not me, up.

Thinking Allowed

It's great when we receive good gifts from God, let's make sure we give him thanks. But how do we make sure we keep worshipping the giver, rather than allowing the gift to become central?

Readings from 1 Corinthians – 2 Spiritual guidance

November

When scripture is hard!

Read 1 Corinthians 11:1–16

Judge for yourselves: is it proper for a woman to pray to God with her head unveiled? Does not nature itself teach you that if a man wears long hair, it is degrading to him?

(verses 13–14)

Angels, hair, beauty, authority, headship – just some of the controversial issues in today's reading! Rather than trying to provide a definitive answer to the problems of the passage, let's ask the question, 'How do we approach scriptures that are difficult to understand?'

During the various lockdowns, jigsaw puzzles became more popular – a picture formed from many small, interlocking pieces that have to be assembled. When you take a piece, you have just a small part of the whole and you have to try and identify where it fits. If the overall picture is a seascape and the piece you have is blue, it can be hard to know whether it is a piece of sky or sea! The key to completing a jigsaw puzzle correctly is to know what the big picture is supposed to look like – and then fit the edge pieces together to provide a framework for everything else. The picture on the box is crucial!

Now, compare that with the Bible – with each verse being a piece of jigsaw puzzle. How do we know where any individual piece fits? For example, a piece taken from Psalm 14 says, 'There is no God' which taken on its own might lead us to a very strange picture! The piece next to it gives the context: 'The fool says in his heart … there is no God'!

The key to understanding scripture is the same as to understanding a jigsaw puzzle – we need to know the picture that the whole is supposed to show, we need a framework into which all the pieces fit.

If Jesus is the full revelation of God, then he is the picture on the box, the framework that any verse or passage must fit into. If the verse doesn't sound or look like Jesus, if it doesn't point to him, then we must be looking at the 'piece' in the wrong way, or trying to fit it in the wrong place.

† Father, help me not to feel like I have to understand things when I don't. Jesus, may I always see you as the big picture, the full revelation of God.

Thinking Allowed

So, what of our reading, what is it teaching about the roles of men and women? The context, as ever, must be Jesus. Whatever the passage means, it has to fit that context.

Friday 11 November
Meeting together

Read 1 Corinthians 11:17–34

When you come together, it is not really to eat the Lord's supper. For when the time comes to eat, each of you goes ahead with your own supper, and one goes hungry and another becomes drunk.

(verses 20–21)

Why do we come together? Probably for all sorts of reasons, some good, some perhaps, not always so good! It's great to meet up with friends, wonderful to enjoy the music, great to be inspired by the message. But sometimes these can displace the main reason: to be with and to be like, Jesus.

Paul describes a church in which this has become an extreme! In key ways, God has been pushed to the margins as they focus on satisfying their own desires. Greed, divisiveness, and drunkenness are what this church is at risk of being known for – which is very bad news indeed because the church is the body of Christ, the visible representation of Jesus to the world. So, when people see us being church, they are seeing our presentation of Jesus. If they see us ignoring the poor, we declare that Jesus doesn't care about them either. If they see some in the church lording it over others, it declares that Jesus does the same.

This misrepresentation is a form of blasphemy – it is a declaration about God which is untrue. And that's why Paul says communion is so important. More than anything, it graphically reminds us of who God is and what he is really like. It holds up a mirror to our own behaviour and calls us back to what is central. Communion is always about coming together, where we are all the same before God, all receiving grace from the same Lord.

When we are like that, when leaders step down to serve, when the poor are fed, when the oppressed are freed, the real Jesus is made visible.

† Father, thank you for the beautiful gift that sharing communion is. Help me be aware my privileges, so I come to the table with and not above others.

Thinking Allowed

Why do we go to church, what attitude do we go with? Who do we as church represent – Jesus or someone else?

Gifts of the Spirit

Read 1 Corinthians 12:1–11

Now there are varieties of gifts, but the same Spirit.

(verse 4)

Paul reminded the people that they should always look beyond gifts to the giver, a great foundation to talk about the gifts of the Spirit – they can be so dramatic, so visible that we might otherwise get distracted by the gifts, and mistake them for godliness. Outward things are much easier to identify than inner qualities, but if we stop at those, we don't really know the person at all. This is all too common – we see someone with extraordinary gifts and, on that basis, call them to roles where their character is found wanting. A person might look strong, but actually have a weak character.

We need to remember that the Spirit who gives gifts also produces fruit. We must not be so impressed by one that we ignore the other. God, who has attributes of power, majesty, wisdom and reach exercises them through his love, mercy and grace.

Jesus exercised the gifts as signs that the kingdom was breaking in, not as a means of impressing people: he healed because he hates the effects of sin, he raised the dead because of his compassion on the grieving, he fed the crowds because they were hungry, he spoke words of knowledge to point people to freedom. In short, the outward signs were motivated by his inward character, the gifts of the Spirit expressed through the fruit of the Spirit (Galatians 5).

† Thank you, Jesus, that you know me. Grow in me a character that reflects you to carry and use the gifts you give.

Thinking Allowed

The Bible says that we look at outward appearances, but God sees the heart (1 Samuel 16:7). Are we more impressed by the gifts than the fruit? How can we develop both?

Readings from 1 Corinthians

3 The higher way of love

Notes by **Catherine Sarjeant**

Catherine describes herself as living in a messy place. A messy place where she is being treated for PTSD and still has the effects of trauma playing out. She lives in this messy place with Jesus – a place where she is weak and he is strong. She co-leads a small house church, helping others meet Jesus in their messy places too, learning together that he walks with us to bring order to the chaos. Catherine has used the NRSVA and NLT for these notes.

Sunday 13 November
One body

> **Read 1 Corinthians 12:12–31**
>
> *On the contrary, the members of the body that seem to be weaker are indispensable, and those members of the body that we think less honourable we clothe with greater honour, and our less respectable members are treated with greater respect.*
>
> (verses 22–23, NRSVA)

Some things happened when I was younger that caused trauma. As often happens in these circumstances, in order to survive emotionally and physically, parts of me separated themselves from each other. I lived in fragments, each part distant and uncommunicative with the others, each ready to react to new situations with their different defence mechanisms. Each day was a battle to override and hide parts so that I could function. Living in a body with many parts that is fighting itself (sometimes literally) is exhausting!

I've spent the last few years learning how to value each of the parts, recognising that they carry precious and beautiful things that make me who I am. Learning to have compassion for myself and grace for all parts has helped me become more able to work as a whole.

And the same is true for the church as a body. How exhausting for different parts to be squabbling, some hidden or suppressed, others taking over positions of power. Paul points out that the body is not really a body without the parts working together as a whole with a common purpose. It is a lesser version of what is possible. The body functions not as 'I', but as 'we'. One body many parts. All working together. A wonderful, hopeful picture for trauma survivors – and for the church!

† Father, thank you that every part is precious in your body. Show me how to work together as a part of that body.

The greatest is love

Read 1 Corinthians 13:1–13

And if I have prophetic powers, and understand all mysteries and all knowledge, and if I have all faith, so as to remove mountains, but do not have love, I am nothing. If I give away all my possessions, and if I hand over my body so that I may boast, but do not have love, I gain nothing.

(verses 2–3, NRSVA)

Some of my trauma was rooted in abuse of power – by people in positions of authority. As a result, my relationship with God, the ultimate authority figure, began by me understanding him to be scary, imposing his will, constantly trying to catch me out and picking up every little fault.

Over the years, people have tried to bring healing to me by 'breaking this, casting out that, taking authority over the other'. But, as with my experience, the nature of abuse is often to do with power, with control, with imposed demands. Hearing people praying with a similar tone, however well intentioned, is more likely to trigger trauma than bring healing.

The passage tells us that 'love does not insist on its own way', it does not demand, does not control. Healing began when I met people who exhibited more of this: instead of standing over, they stood alongside. People who patiently waited for me to articulate things – sometimes waiting for weeks. People who showed kindness in the midst of my brokenness. People not judging the words that I spoke out of that place of hurt. People who were generous with their time and relationships. People who defended me, saw the injustice and gave space for the pain and anger to be heard. A love that didn't impose or try to fix me, that didn't attempt to be my saviour, but pointed me gently to God.

There's a place for deliverance, there's a place for all the gifts. There's always a place for love.

† Father, thank you for making your love known in Jesus. Help me to love like you love me.

For further thought

Fear has often been used as a tool in evangelism. If perfect love casts out fear, consider, does God have a better way?

Tuesday 15 November
Prophecy and tongues

Read 1 Corinthians 14:1–25

Dear brothers and sisters, if I should come to you speaking in an unknown language, how would that help you? But if I bring you a revelation or some special knowledge or prophecy or teaching, that will be helpful.

(verse 6, NLT)

The first time I walked into church as an adult, there was a man, walking down the aisle, ranting at the preacher. The congregation was alarmed and fearful and responded by praying in tongues. It all felt very scary to me, people seemingly out of control – reinforcing my negative view of God! Nobody explained what was going on – my first encounter with gifts of the Spirit was not ideal!

Years later, I understood that speaking in tongues wasn't about God taking control or forcing me to say words, but rather a gift allowing my spirit to cry out to God. I learned that tongues transcend the limitations of human language, allowing me to express worship or pain that would otherwise remain trapped.

I was chatting one day to a friend who was open, but probably not yet in a relationship with God, and we somehow got onto the subject of 'tongues'. She was intrigued, asking what it was about and what it sounded like. So, I spoke in tongues so that she could hear. It spoke deeply to her spirit, she sensed in those words, something of God, giving an opportunity for me to share more of his love. Her first experience of the gifts, a little more comfortable than mine!

Whether we are speaking in tongues or bringing a prophecy or word, if we don't deliver it reflecting God's love, we are not communicating God.

† Father, thank you for the gifts you give. Test my motives in using those gifts.

For further thought

Consider whether this might be the case: tongues helps us heal personally while prophecy (sometimes given as a 'tongue') helps us heal collectively.

Readings from 1 Corinthians – 3 The higher way of love

November

Making space

> ### Read 1 Corinthians 14:26–40
>
> *Well, my brothers and sisters, let's summarize. When you meet together, one will sing, another will teach, another will tell some special revelation God has given, one will speak in tongues, and another will interpret what is said. But everything that is done must strengthen all of you.*
>
> (verse 26, NLT)

As people learn how to hear God and respond, it can be messy! It was like that in the early church – people who had never been included before (women and Gentiles, for example) had no idea what was appropriate and those who had been involved before had very fixed ideas about how it should be done! Chaotic, noisy, people shouting out across the room and asking what was going on, everyone talking at the same time, some too timid to speak, others dominating proceedings.

We found ourselves accidentally planting a church (long story!) that often felt like this. Some folk had a traditional church background, others had none. Many had been hurt by their previous experience of church, some of us had complicated mental health issues. We've learned to look for God in the mess, to see the glimpses in our own lives and those we seek to serve, to hold on to and encourage that which is of God while trying not to be distracted by the rest! It's wonderful and joyous, real and amazing – as well as painful …

The point Paul is making feels similar. His aim is not to squash or suppress, but to provide a safe place for all to bring what they have, however ill-formed! It isn't about creating a rigid or legalistic structure – when he says two or three, he doesn't mean that the fourth person should be reprimanded! It isn't about leaders creating order for their convenience, to serve their vision or to make it easier or slicker. It's about giving space – honouring all the parts – no one part dominating, so that the body can be body, not just a leg or an arm!

A church without the gifts of the Spirit is less than it could be; a church without love is dead.

† Father, thank you for the Holy Spirit. Shine a light on places I am using gifts to build my kingdom not yours. Show me how and when to use the gifts you give to build your church.

For further thought

How can we make space for everyone to contribute, whatever their background, however messy they might make things?

We are an Easter people and hallelujah is our song

Read 1 Corinthians 15:1–22

And if there is no resurrection of the dead, then Christ has not been raised. And if Christ has not been raised, then your faith is useless and you are still guilty of your sins.

(verse 16–17, NLT)

I started my healing journey from a pretty hopeless place – I didn't know God, even though I'd been in church for years. I still thought of him as scary and frightening, so the thought of being raised to spend eternity with him didn't feel like good news!

At the same time, I doubted that I would be raised, because of that sense of God being perfect and me being very imperfect. A double whammy to relationship, leaving me with either needing to be perfect in order to relate to God, or to cower and hide from him. I'd absorbed this view of God through the words and actions of those in authority who purported to represent Jesus.

The resurrection from where I was sitting didn't look like good news, but this passage talks about the resurrection being *the* good news! When the resurrection is divorced from the character of Jesus, approaching or living with God can sound scary, but when we understand it in the light of who he is, it becomes life-transforming.

Far from being impersonal or scary, the resurrection appearances are lovingly tailored to the needs and situation of each person that he meets: Mary desperately needs to know that Jesus hasn't abandoned her, so he waits till she is alone to meet and reassure her. Peter needs space to process his betrayal, so Jesus arranges a breakfast meeting away from the crowd. Paul wasn't even part of the original group, so Jesus meets him on the road to Damascus.

Recognising this restored hope and transformed my view of God. Suddenly, Jesus being raised became good news – someone to meet gladly, even in a place of imperfection.

† Thank you for the good news of resurrection and all it means. Thank you that you want to meet with me right where I am.

For further thought

Why is the resurrection good news for you?

Readings from 1 Corinthians – 3 The higher way of love

November

Friday 18 November
A new body

Read 1 Corinthians 15:35–57

Our bodies are buried in brokenness, but they will be raised in glory.
They are buried in weakness, but they will be raised in strength.

(verse 43, NLT)

One of the early outworkings of the PTSD was a 'flop' response. It meant that at times, irrespective of where I was, when the PTSD triggered, my body would collapse. Awkward! Of course, as an adult, it was the last thing I wanted, but fragmented parts reacted to what they perceived as danger in the only way they knew how.

For others, issues of body image, physical illness, ageing or disability affect our perception. And added to all these, Paul brings the sense of our bodies being weak with regards to temptation and the damage sin can do.

For all sorts of reasons, we can end up being disappointed with our bodies.

But whatever the cause of our disappointment, the good news is that there is something new coming, the completion of a renewal process begun here! A new body as originally envisaged – one that is capable of holding all parts as a whole – full healing, complete restoration, all that the fall introduced, cleansed, set aside and made new.

Jesus' resurrected body had scars – they were part of the new perfection, not glossed over but beautified. This knowledge slowly transformed my disappointment and anger at my body to one of kindness and acceptance. And that in itself has brought a measure of healing – while I still creak from years of hockey, I no longer collapse as much!

If you're struggling right now, be encouraged by the hope that is to come and don't be afraid to find professional help where it's needed now.

† Lord, help me be honest about how I feel about my body, help me to cast off any shame and to be kind to me as you are kind.

For further thought

How can knowing this impact our perception?

Go large

Read 1 Corinthians 16:1–24

Keep alert, stand firm in your faith, be courageous, be strong. Let all that you do be done in love.

(verse 13–14, NRSVA)

Here's what had happened. Someone with a tested gift of prophecy (Agabus in Acts 11) had received a word from God that there was going to be a famine in Jerusalem. Paul (and others) had written to other churches, asking them to support the Jerusalem church. The letters were received before the famine happened; they were responding to a need that hadn't happened yet! Meanwhile, the church in Jerusalem had to swallow their pride and receive help from churches they had planted, churches that they potentially saw as younger, less wise, less important.

I love this picture of big church, the body that is comprised not just of individuals, but of many local churches, acting together in faith. The church. That's the church we are called to build, against which not even the powers of hell can prevail!

Are we seeing this bigger body of Christ as the church? If we give to others, it is easy to wonder if will we have enough for our own needs. If we send our people to serve, will we be able to run our own programmes? If we cooperate with other groups, will our uniqueness become blurred? The problem is the thought that it is 'our'… whereas Jesus said: 'I will build *my* church.' It isn't 'ours' at all, it is *his*. We can only participate in building his church by being like him – sacrificial, faithful and loving.

Paul encouraged the Corinthians to have a bigger view of the body; they gave freely of their people and resources and the church was built.

† Father, open my eyes to the bigness of your church.

For further thought

How can we be part of that bigger body while yet being committed to our local expression?

Readings from 1 Corinthians – 3 The higher way of love

November

A colourful Bible

Notes by **Gail Adcock**

Gail is Family Ministry Development Officer with the Methodist Church, working as part of the Children, Youth and Family Team, equipping and resourcing those working with families across the UK. She has a primary education background and was family pastor at Stopsley Baptist Church for 10 years. Her book *The Essential Guide to Family Ministry* was published in 2020 (BRF). She lives in Hitchin with husband, Matt – along with their young adult sons, they are all supporters of Tottenham Hotspur FC. Gail has used the NRSVA for these notes.

Sunday 20 November
A colourful covenant

Read Genesis 9:8–17

When the bow is in the clouds, I will see it and remember the everlasting covenant between God and every living creature of all flesh that is on the earth.

(verse 16)

Rainbows have become a symbol of so many things in contemporary life: displayed in windows as a symbol of hope during the pandemic. A heart-shaped rainbow badge I wear as a welcome of diversity and affirmation. On rainy days the sight of a rainbow as clouds clear and sunlight breaks through.

Here's a vibrant reminder of God's covenant, a definitive promise to never again destroy what's been created. With God's full commitment to keeping it without condition for all generations.

The spectrum of colours speaks of the vast array of God's creation, peoples dispersed across the globe but all uniquely made and equally loved by God. And of the colourful multitudes – many species of creature we share this planet with.

All existing in an ecosystem of God's love and care that's covered by a radiant rainbow.

Yet it's a covenant made between God and us, so what is our part? We can't match God's gesture but we can commit to being people of hope in the places we move and walk in. To extend that same generous love to those who find themselves disconnected or on the margins of society. To everyone regardless, just as God does.

† Every time we glimpse a rainbow, remind us we are your hopeful people, God, and help us to be alert to those who feel marginalised.

Monday 21 November
A green plant

Read Genesis 1:29–31

'And to every beast of the earth, and to every bird of the air, and to everything that creeps on the earth, everything that has the breath of life, I have given every green plant for food.' ... *God saw everything that he had made, and indeed, it was very good.*

(verses 30–31)

'Eat your greens!' I wonder how many of us heard that phrase when we were children? For most of my childhood, the only vegetable I ate was peas. Thankfully I've graduated to a wider, more colourful diet now! In these verses we encounter how God's generosity knows no bounds: every green plant has been given for our food and nourishment. The bounty of creation offered to keep us fit and well as God supplies food that he knows will sustain our whole being.

And if God knows what we require in such basic terms to fuel our bodies, how much more might he understand our wider needs? For human connection or meaningful work endeavour? For rest and relaxation? If we paused to consider these things, and how God can provide for us, we might reach the conclusion that it's of no interest or concern to God. There are far more pressing demands on his time and priorities surely higher up his list. Yet God's care extends to our entire being, beyond simply what we put in our mouths at mealtimes. As our creator and sustainer, God longs to see us thrive: spiritually, physically, mentally and emotionally. There is no part of our being that he is uninterested in.

Finding ways to explore the full dimension of our humanity is of infinite interest to God. He continues to speak the same message of goodness across all he has created including us: 'it was very good.'

† God, thank you for the bounty of food I can enjoy. Help me to be more aware, in the fullness of who I am, made in your image, of what else I need from you.

For further thought

Give some thought to where in your own life might God want to provide for you beyond your physical needs.

A colourful Bible

November

A blue robe

Read Exodus 28:31–35

On its lower hem you shall make pomegranates of blue, purple, and crimson yarns, all round the lower hem, with bells of gold between them all round.

(verse 33)

These are fascinating, elaborate instructions that we read here, detailing the garments to be made for priests: 'sacred vestments' full of vivid hues of colour and intricate embellishments that adorn this blue robe. It comes to life before our eyes, in all its glory, a little like the wonderful creations of those taking part in the TV programme, *The Great British Sewing Bee*.

In that programme, contestants begin with simple bolts of fabric and then cut, sew and fashion a stunning array of garments for people of different ages and for a variety of purposes. What would they make of this 'pattern' offered in these verses I wonder? There's an exceptional function for this robe, one that's made for glory and beauty, to be worn in the presence of God. One that's meticulously made, with a hem adorned with 'bells of gold' that ring, announcing the priest's arrival in the holy place. It's definitely not something that could be worn with a hope of remaining invisible or unseen by God.

Sometimes we may wish to not draw attention to ourselves; we live and move through our days keeping a low profile. Not always wanting others or God to be fully aware of us. And yet this invitation extends to us as well, to draw near to God as he holds this beautiful robe ready for us to wear. 'Put it on', he urges, 'try it on for size' and be with me awhile. Would we feel worthy of such a splendid robe? Possibly not, but God's invite remains to join him in the holy place.

† Lord God, grant me the boldness to come into your presence, thankful in the knowledge that you have clothed me in your rich grace and mercy.

For further thought

When might there be times I am reluctant to come into the presence of God and why might this be?

A red cord

> **Read Joshua 2:1, 15–21**
>
> *'But if you tell this business of ours, then we shall be released from this oath that you made us swear to you.' She said, 'According to your words, so be it.' She sent them away and they departed. Then she tied the crimson cord in the window.*
>
> (verses 20–21)

There are so many echoes in this account that centres around Rahab and the crimson cord. Echoes of other times and events in scripture: the passing over of households with crimson blood on the doorframes, the crimson blood of Christ shed for us in his death. Echoes backwards and forwards of God's encounters with his people and ongoing desire to be light and life for and with them. The crimson cord is a thread that we can follow through to our current day as we share in the bread and wine, commemorating Christ's death in communion. It's a thread that connects us to all God's people through history, that draws our attention to the continuation of God's story that unfolds among us today.

Returning to Rahab and the spies in this intimate scene of secrecy as they plot their escape. The crimson cord is a powerful symbol of promises made. Promises to protect and preserve life as long as both parties remain true to their word. Echoes here too of God's rainbow covenant being a sign of ongoing commitment to all peoples. In this instance, however, our attention is drawn to how that it isn't one-sided and the fact that there is a crucial part for us to play in response to this covenant. The crimson cord connects us and God always, through into eternity. A symbol of trust and hope as we follow in the footsteps of faithful believers who came before us.

† Thank you, God, that I am connected by this crimson cord to your bigger story for humankind. Guide my steps as I seek to walk with you day by day.

For further thought

What does my response to this covenant with God look like and how might I express my commitment to it or not?

A colourful Bible

November

A seller of purple

Read Acts 16:11–15

A certain woman named Lydia, a worshipper of God, was listening to us; she was from the city of Thyatira and a dealer in purple cloth. The Lord opened her heart to listen eagerly to what was said by Paul.

(verse 14)

These encounters with female figures in scripture are deeply moving for me as a woman of faith. Here is Lydia, a woman of status, a businesswoman who has established for herself a degree of independence due to her enterprising work. Established as a figure in her local community, no doubt, a trader of purple cloth, we encounter her here as she meets with other women. It's an empowered gathering as they engage in discussion with Paul, listening to what is said, reflecting and considering it all in light of the lives they lead. I'd have enjoyed being there alongside them as their conversations unfolded; creating these kinds of spaces continue to be important for us today as we wrestle with questions of life and faith.

Yet for all her accomplishments, Lydia has recognised a gap in her life, something missing that her wealth and status don't fill. Her response: to be baptised and extend hospitality. Both joining and welcoming the new community she and her household are part of. We can express our belonging as part of the body of Christ in different ways, being inclusive of others has a place at the centre of faith. As Lydia welcomes these relative strangers, she reflects our shared calling demonstrated throughout Jesus' ministry. To seek to be those who are alert to creating community that benefits all its participants, whether of new or mature faith and everything in between.

† Lord, help me to be alert to how I can be inclusive of others, noticing those who may feel they don't belong, and being a welcoming presence as I walk in faith.

For further thought

In what ways have you experienced a sense of belonging to your faith community? How could you help others experience the same?

Friday 25 November
Radiant and ruddy

Read Song of Solomon 5:9–16

My beloved is all radiant and ruddy, distinguished among ten thousand. His head is the finest gold; his locks are wavy, black as a raven. His eyes are like doves beside springs of water, bathed in milk, fitly set.

(verses 10–12)

In 2019, Matt, my husband, and I celebrated our silver wedding anniversary. As we looked back at our wedding photos, seeing the youngsters we were (less grey and wrinkled!), we couldn't quite believe it! Surely by now we'd have got to grips with married life and have it down to a fine art …? But it continues to be a voyage of discovery, learning new things about each other, loving and adapting together as life unfolds.

Here in Song of Solomon, the beloved conjures up a sensuous poetic image of the one they love. Comparing their features with beauty found in nature: doves, streams, jewels, spice, lilies, myrrh, ivory, cedar trees and gold. It's a rich, luxurious picture, celebrating all that is exquisite about the object of their affection. A glorious sight that conveys the power of emotion felt: a deep, true love.

This description reminds me how love is a gift to us, freely given, and how important intimate relationships are to us as human beings. If we love generously, wisely and well, our relationships are able to thrive. If our love is meagre, tight-fisted and self-centred, our relationships can be like pot-bound plants that stifle growth.

There's the suggestion here too of the strong bond of love between God and us, his people – of how God gazes on us with delight and gladness, the sight of us bringing him great joy! Do we often consider that's how God sees us? Might this be transformative in our relationship with him and others if we truly grasped how deeply God first loved us?

† Remind us, God, how precious love is – not something to exhaust, abuse or discard. Help us learn the language of loving generously.

For further thought

Consider the ways you treasure the love shown to you by others. How are you able to express your love and return it?

A colourful Bible

November

Saturday 26 November
Gold sash and white hair

Read Revelation 1:12–20

I saw one like the Son of Man, clothed with a long robe and with a golden sash across his chest. His head and his hair were white as white wool, white as snow; his eyes were like a flame of fire, his feet were like burnished bronze.

(part of verses 13–15)

Some years ago, when our children were young, we visited a night-time light exhibition as a family. It was in the forest and, being out after dark, exploring the woods, seeing the trees and exhibits lit up in colourful, bright ways prompted so much awe and wonder – in them and us! They were overjoyed as they followed each twist of the path and turned each corner, discovering new sights. I can still see their astonished faces now.

These verses prompt a similar response in me as I read them: the sheer magnificence of setting eyes on the Son of Man resplendent, glittering and shining. The brightness of his presence emphasised by the mentions of the golden sash, flame of fire, white wool and burnished bronze. He glows! It's almost overwhelming and too much to behold.

It is only the sound of his voice that grounds the moment, as he speaks compelling words of truth. Words that shine a radiant beam of the essence of our faith: 'I am the first and the last, and the living one. I was dead, and see, I am alive for ever and ever' (verses 17–18). What was darkness is now eternal light, what was dead and buried is risen to new life, what was hopeless is now full of promise. These words fan the flames of belief. And all of this demands a response as to whether I choose to believe, taking steps into the mystery of faith, even though my questions are still many.

† Radiant and glorious Lord, let your light illuminate my life and being. Let me still be captivated in your presence as you speak words of everlasting truth over me.

For further thought

When are the times and where are the places I experience the bright presence of God? How important are these to me?

The beauty of holiness: tabernacle and temple

1 The wilderness tabernacle

Notes by **Andy Heald**

Andy is a professional communications, marketing and fundraising consultant, and has led fruitful young adult and small group ministries. He is an active pilgrim and is exploring a calling to serve a fatherless generation. In 2019, he sold his home in Sussex and, with his wife and three young daughters, he began travelling Europe in a motorhome, exploring God's principles of faith, freedom and family and living a different way. He has used the NIVUK for these notes.

Sunday 27 November (Advent Sunday)
Make a sanctuary

Read Exodus 24:15–25:9

Then let them make a sanctuary for me, and I will dwell among them. Make this tabernacle and all its furnishings exactly like the pattern I will show you.

(verses 8 – 9)

Following Jesus, we sometimes experience personal wildernesses, such as tough situations, unfamiliar places or mental challenges. These are unknown territories, beyond our comfort and safety. God uses them to grow our faith and enable us to become closer to him. To grow through these experiences, we must depend on him and trust him more. But we cannot do this alone.

Thankfully, like the Israelites, we are not alone in our wilderness. God chooses to dwell with us too, dwelling in our hearts through faith (Ephesians 3:17). Learning that God was 'moving in' probably shocked, and even scared, them – but I imagine they were relieved and joyful too! We can identify with these feelings. However harsh our wilderness, whatever trials we face – God is with us and we can find joy.

Even better, in the uncertainty of these situations, God doesn't make us guess what we, the 'temple of his Holy Spirit' (1 Corinthians 6:19) should look like – he's provided the 'instruction manual'. Jesus is 'the pattern'. We can read God's word, listen to his Spirit and, as our hearts are inspired, bring our offering, as they did. Then, as we are built as God's sanctuary, we'll experience his presence and the blessings with it.

† Lord, thank you that you want to dwell in me. Please show me the pattern for your dwelling place that you want me to become.

333

Monday 28 November
The ark

Read Exodus 25:10–22

There, above the cover between the two cherubim that are over the ark of the covenant law, I will meet with you and give you all my commands for the Israelites.

(verse 22)

God promises the Israelites that if they are fully obedient to him, they will be his treasured possession … a holy nation (Exodus 19:5–6). To show them what keeping the covenant would look like, he gives them the Law. What's more, he loves his children so much that he places physical evidence of his promise in the very heart of his dwelling place – the ark of the covenant. Here too, in this most holy place, which is made of the rarest and most valuable materials, is where he will communicate with them.

As we each wander in our wilderness, being built up as God's dwelling place, we must be aware of our own ark. 'I will put my law in their minds and write it on their hearts' (Jeremiah 31:33b). Our heart towards God is as precious as pure gold and we too must keep our hearts holy, as is fitting for his worthiness. As God provided the instructions, resources and skill to the Israelites to build the ark, we too can trust him to do the same for us. After all, he has already given us the 'atonement cover' that we need to meet with him, through Jesus and his death on the cross. With his law in our hearts and the covering for our sins, whatever our external circumstances, we can rest in God's presence everywhere we go.

† God, thank you for your promise that I am your treasured possession and for making a way for me to meet with you. Please help my heart be a holy and beautiful place for you.

For further thought

The Israelites gave their precious gold for the ark. Even in the wilderness, is there anything precious you need to give God to make a place for him?

Tuesday 29 November
The craftspeople

Read Exodus 35:30–36:8

So Bezalel, Oholiab and every skilled person to whom the Lord has given skill and ability to know how to carry out all the work of constructing the sanctuary are to do the work just as the Lord has commanded.

(verse 1)

The work of being built as God's holy dwelling place may (sometimes) feel like a daunting task but we don't have to do it alone – in fact, we can't. Some days – especially when we're in a tough, wilderness place – it's hard to read God's word, or find a few minutes to pray, let alone find joy in trials, feed the poor, heal the sick and live up to God's standards. Thankfully, he's prepared a team, other members of his family – his church – to help. These are our craftspeople.

Our 'tabernacle' is part of a spiritual house, where we are 'living stones' (1 Peter 2:4–6). Like Bezalel and Oholiab, God has placed people around us to build us up as his sanctuary, as he has commanded. Each will have different skills, depending on your need – instead of engravers and designers they will be experts in following Jesus, perhaps in the workplace, marriage, parenting or other part of life.

You can recognise them as the people who love you; they build you up, not knock you down. They are filled with the Spirit of God, wisdom, understanding, knowledge and the ability to teach. What's more, they will have willing hearts to help – perhaps so much that they too may need to be restrained from giving!

Perhaps you have friends like this already? If not, seek them out and remember that you are a craftsman for someone else too! Our journey with Jesus is not solitary, but one where we confess our sins, spur one another on to good works and become the holy priesthood that God promises.

† Father God, thank you for preparing a skilled team to help build me up as your holy dwelling place. Show me those who will help me – and those who I will build up too.

For further thought

Who are (or might be) the Bezalels and Oholiabs in your life? Indeed, who can you be a gospel 'craftsperson' for?

The work is finished

Read Exodus 39:32–43

The Israelites had done all the work just as the Lord had commanded Moses. Moses inspected the work and saw that they had done it just as the Lord had commanded. So Moses blessed them.

(verses 42–43)

How do you feel when you bring something you've made to be approved by someone you respect? Excited? Daunted? Fearful? Even cooking for guests can make me feel a bit nervous. Will it taste good? Will they like it? I wonder how the Israelites felt when they brought the finished tabernacle to Moses to be inspected. Would it meet the standards God set? Would he be pleased with them? It could have been a terrifying experience… what if they'd got even one of the many details wrong…?

As God's dwelling place today, we are a work in progress – not yet the finished article. Therefore, we can sometimes feel nervous when we approach God. But thankfully, because of Jesus' sacrifice we can approach God in faith and with confidence!

This event in the Israelite's wilderness journey invites us to cast our eyes into our future, where we too will be inspected – on judgement day. We mustn't diminish the significance of judgement, but we must remember that it's also a triumphant moment, 'where the righteous will shine like the sun in the kingdom of their Father' (Matthew 13:43). The Israelites built the tabernacle just as the Lord had commanded and so Moses blessed them! By following Jesus faithfully, becoming more like him (the perfect child of God), we can look towards our inspection (judgement day), not with trepidation, but with joy! The blessing we receive then will be more than the temporary dwelling place that God has chosen for us now. He will complete the work in us, and he will dwell with us (Revelation 21:3)!

† Jesus, thank you that because of your grace and sacrifice, one day, your work in me will be finished and I will dwell in your presence for eternity.

For further thought

Ponder the beautiful truth of grace; that, for us, the law is not the path to righteousness – the finished work of Christ is.

The cloud of the Lord

Exodus 40:17–27, 34–38

And the glory of the Lord filled the tabernacle. In all the travels of the Israelites, whenever the cloud lifted from above the tabernacle, they would set out; but if the cloud did not lift, they did not set out – until the day it lifted.

(part of verses 35–37)

Often, we only realise we are in a wilderness when we suddenly don't know where we are. Away from our usual path, without our familiar landmarks, we are lost. This is unsettling at best, petrifying at worst. It can even paralyse us – without any sense of direction, without paths or signs to follow, we have no idea where to go.

I imagine that God's arrival among the Israelites was scary but that it also brought great comfort. His presence was so dangerous that even Moses could not enter the tent, but it was clearly visible, all the time. And he would now show them all the way to go. No longer did they have to wait for Moses to return from a mountaintop meeting.

As a pilgrim, much of my focus is in learning how to follow where Jesus is leading me. I've often thought it would be simpler if he was as visible as a cloud, or a pillar of fire. In reality, he has made it easier than that – he has not only shown us the way, but he is the Way! Through his death and resurrection, unlike the Israelites, we can enter his presence, and pray. Because he lived with us as a man, we have his teachings and his example. What's more, he has sent us his Holy Spirit as our comforter and guide (John 14:15–17)! To follow Jesus, we must live as he did (1 John 2:6). To see where he is leading, we must seek the kingdom, sacrifice our own desires, and obey his commands.

† King Jesus, thank you that I can come into your presence. Help me to recognise you, hear your voice, understand your teachings, learn from your example and follow you when you move.

For further thought

Read the Gospels to see how Jesus taught his disciples. Observe his actions. Can you learn and apply anything to your life?

The beauty of holiness: tabernacle and temple – 1 The wilderness tabernacle

December

Friday 2 December
Carrying the tabernacle

Read Numbers 4:1–15

After Aaron and his sons have finished covering the holy furnishings and all the holy articles, and when the camp is ready to move, only then are the Kohathites to come and do the carrying. But they must not touch the holy things, or they will die.

(part of verse 15)

Carrying God in us is a significant responsibility, it requires the right level of reverence and it has purpose – to show him to others, and show that we are his people. Kohath was Moses, Miriam and Aaron's grandfather, and thus the Kohathites were considered the most important of the Levites. It is likely that because of their elevated status within the tribe of priests appointed by God, they were selected to carry the ark and most important parts of the tabernacle. Yet their responsibility only extended so far and their proximity to God was restricted, they were not even allowed to gaze on or touch these holy things, or they would die.

As God's children, we are made as his image-bearers, yet we fall short of his glory (Romans 3:23). Like the Levites, we too are God's chosen, royal priesthood (1 Peter 2:9) and also to be his dwelling place. Like the Kohathites, we have been entrusted with the care of the most holy things. Like them, we too must remember the specific responsibilities we've been given. We are to carry his holy presence before others, but we are not 'ready to move' without his saving grace. We must first be made holy, cleansed of our sins. Only Jesus, our high priest, deals with our sins, by his merciful sacrifice on the cross.

And he does! His salvation prepares us. We are ready to go and can have confidence to share our faith with others. Therefore, our responsibility is to move, to take up our cross and humbly follow Jesus so that he is seen through us.

† Thank you, Jesus, that you have dealt with my sin, so that I may be in your presence. Lord, help me to humbly carry your image so that others see you in me.

For further thought
Read Genesis 1:27 and Hebrews 1:3. Consider God's image and how he made his children. How does Jesus show us the exact likeness of God?

The ark brought to Jerusalem

Read 2 Samuel 6:12–19

Wearing a linen ephod, David was dancing before the Lord with all his might, while he and all Israel were bringing up the ark of the Lord with shouts and the sound of trumpets.

(verses 14–15)

It's no wonder, really, that David was so joyful that he abandoned himself in praise to God, leaping and dancing (much to the embarrassment of his wife, Michal).

Even though God came to dwell with his people, travelling with them everywhere, bringing them out of the wilderness into the promised land and going into battle with them, the Israelites still managed to turn away from him. For a time, they didn't consult him, and once, the ark was even stolen by the Philistines! Plus, because they had forgotten the strict rules about carrying God's presence, in an earlier attempt to bring the ark to Jerusalem (the Israelites' holy city), God had killed Uzzah, and David became afraid of God, worried that he wouldn't be able to bring the ark to himself (1 Chronicles 13).

There are times in our lives too, when we turn away from God, when we don't consult him and when we choose to walk without him, when we forget his ways and the consequences of our disobedience. Yet, thankfully, nothing can separate us from God's love! However far we may have strayed, we can turn back to him and believe; he will welcome us into his open arms. This is cause for us to leap and dance in celebration with all our might, too!

What's more, this passage points us towards the day that we will be fully restored and reunited with God in the holy city, the new Jerusalem, where we will dwell and praise with God forever. What wonderful thing to look forward to (especially when in a wilderness)!

† God, thank you that nothing can separate your children from your love. Jesus, help me never to forget you but instead, joyfully celebrate who you are and your presence dwelling with me!

For further thought

Read Revelation 21. Whatever season of life you may be in, wilderness or other, let this vision encourage you and give you hope and joy.

The beauty of holiness: tabernacle and temple – 1 The wilderness tabernacle

The beauty of holiness: tabernacle and temple

2 The Jerusalem Temple

Notes by **John Proctor**

For John's biographical details, please see p. 163. John has used the NRSV.

Sunday 4 December
From tent to house

Read 2 Samuel 7:1–17

The Lord will make you a house ... I will raise up your offspring after you, who shall come forth from your body ... He shall build a house for my name, and I will establish the throne of his kingdom for ever.

(parts of verses 11–13)

Many a congregation has felt the need to build, to move on from makeshift premises into a permanent church building. There they can worship more confidently and offer a visible Christian presence in the community. Today's text remembers a similar moment in Israel's story, a thousand years before Christ.

The tent of meeting had been a focus for faith on the Exodus journey. But now time had passed, and the people were firmly settled in the Holy Land. King David wanted to make firmer arrangements for worship too, and spiritual adviser Nathan urged him on.

Yet God's finger was on the pause button. Not yet. David had to be reminded. God had already helped Israel for a long time, without asking for any sort of fixed abode. Such a God cannot be programmed, packaged or pinned down. So now God would take the initiative again, by building a 'house' for David (verse 11) – a dynasty, a royal family, stretching far into the future. Then the next generation of that family – Solomon, as it turned out – would build a 'house' for worship (verse 13), where the people could honour God.

So, David would actually achieve less than he hoped. But God would do much more. For even when we want to fix things, God remains in charge. We must often construct – buildings, plans, ideas, ambitions. Yet even our best work can never contain the purposes of heaven. These stretch ahead of us, paving the future with unexpected grace.

† Remember people who plan and look after church buildings – who budget, design, construct, repair, clean and maintain. We need them, and they deserve our prayers.

Monday 5 December
Touching place

Read 1 Kings 8:5–13

Then the priests brought the ark of the covenant of the Lord to its place … underneath the wings of the cherubim … There was nothing in the ark except the two tablets of stone that Moses had placed there … And … a cloud filled the house of the Lord

(parts of verses 6 and 9–10)

Solomon has become king. After 7 years of building work (6:38), the temple is complete. The promises we read yesterday in 2 Samuel 7 have unfolded into reality. Now is the dedication day. Everything is ready to be offered to God. The focal point will be the ark of the covenant. It will be put into the very heart of the building, the holy of holies.

The ark speaks of history, of a tried and tested relationship. This God has staying power. Israel had carried the ark, and her faith had carried her, through long years of journeying in the desert. The ark tells of God's covenant goodness, guarding and leading the people through changing times.

The ark itself was a box, of precious wood overlaid with gold (Exodus 25:10–16). Inside it, two stone tablets held God's commands, to remind Israel of the demands and duties of her faith. At the centre of worship was law to live by, to shape the efforts and encounters of the days and the years. This God cares about practical matters – about liberty, community, family and honesty.

The carved wooden cherubim were mighty angels. They spread a protecting shadow over the ark (6:23–28, and Exodus 25:17–22), to signal majesty and to frame a space for mercy. Here is a touching place between earth and heaven.

Yet amid all the beauty and splendour, there is no direct image of Israel's God – no icon, portrait, statue or figurine. The cloud is heavy with invisible presence. God is overwhelming, mysterious and intimately close at hand.

† Gracious God, when I worship, please keep me reverent and confident. Help me to remember that you are mighty and mysterious, yet also trustworthy, sure and near. In Jesus' name. Amen

For further thought

What do you most need from worship at the moment – a reminder of God's goodness, direction for faithful living, a sense of God's near presence?

The beauty of holiness: tabernacle and temple – 2 The Jerusalem Temple

December

341

Tuesday 6 December
Name and nature

Read 1 Kings 8:14–30

Have regard to your servant's prayer ... that your eyes may be open night and day towards this house, the place of which you said, 'My name shall be there' ... Hear ... your people Israel when they pray towards this place; O hear in heaven your dwelling place; heed and forgive.

(part of verses 28–30)

Years ago somebody set fire to the telephone junction box in my road. Melted wires, perished connections – and all communication was lost. Over the next few days, a repair crew patiently re-connected everything, until service was restored. We needed the junction box. Many of our contacts and concerns went through it.

The Jerusalem Temple was a kind of junction box, a contact point between earth and heaven, and a focus for many concerns. God's people Israel would pray 'towards this place' (verse 30). And Solomon asks that God keep watch on 'this house' (verse 29), to tune in to the people's prayers. The Temple was a witness. It testified that God was interested and involved in the nation's life. It spoke too of the character and nature of God.

The Temple was not exactly God's residence. But it was a 'house' for the name of the Lord. That had been the promise (2 Samuel 7:13), and Solomon's prayer recalls it many times over (verses 16–20 and 29). By honouring God's name, the Temple told of God's nature too. For the Lord had been revealed on Mount Sinai, not as name only but as a living and loving presence: 'The Lord, the Lord, a God merciful and gracious, slow to anger, and abounding in steadfast love and faithfulness' (Exodus 34:6). That is what God's name meant in Israel. The Temple was there to hold the name high, to remind Israel of the character and concerns of her covenant Lord. Those who prayed 'towards this place' could be confident in the God who heard them.

† Hallowed be thy name. God of the ages, may your nature and goodness be known and honoured, in my life, through your church and around your world. In the name of Jesus. Amen

For further thought

'Name speaks of nature.' What do the people around you hear in the name 'Christian', and what can you do to influence that message?

How lovely is thy dwelling place

Read Psalm 84

Happy are those who live in your house, ever singing your praise. Happy are those whose strength is in you, in whose heart are the highways to Zion ... O Lord of hosts, happy is everyone who trusts in you.

(verses 4–5 and 12)

This is a pilgrim psalm, a journey in three stages. It starts far from Jerusalem, in longing and desire (verses 1–4). The psalmist's speech and spirit reach out to the temple. How delightful it would be to settle there, amid the music and worship! Then the second act moves forward, along the pilgrim way (verses 5–8). We hear of highways and scenery and a landscape brought to life. Water wells up from arid ground as the pilgrims pass by. If the poet stretches a point here, the point itself is a good one. Confidence in God makes the very colours of creation seem brighter. The world is a different place when your heart is ready to worship. Finally, the third act speaks of arrival, of lingering in God's presence and resting in joyful trust (verses 9–12).

You can trace these movements through the three words of blessing in the psalm. 'Happy' say many English translations. The first blessing (verse 4) is a word of yearning, of spiritual thirst seeking refreshment. The second (verse 5) is purposeful, forward-looking and energetic. Eventually, we reach secure contentment (verse 12), a deeply satisfying homecoming to God.

The whole psalm shows how much the Temple meant, as a magnet for Israel's love and praise. Yet it also invites the reader to make an inward journey. The three movements – of heartfelt longing, committed approach and confident trust – mark the route. Do not be afraid to travel, is the message. Join the way of faith and commitment. 'Draw near to God, and he will draw near to you' (James 4:8).

† Pray for anyone you know who is feeling distant from God at the moment. Ask that they may find courage and confidence to draw near.

For further thought

What helps you to approach God? Scripture? Prayer? Companions? Solitude? Loud praise? Silence? Or something else?

The beauty of holiness: tabernacle and temple – 2 The Jerusalem Temple

The temple burnt down

> **Read 2 Kings 25:8–21**
>
> *Nebuzaradan, the captain of the bodyguard, a servant of the king of Babylon ... burned the house of the Lord, the king's house, and all the houses of Jerusalem ... broke down the walls around Jerusalem ... carried into exile the rest of the people who were left in the city.*
>
> (parts of verses 8–11)

This is a wretched and awful chapter in the Old Testament story. Jewish people still remember it with tears on Tisha B'Av, the ninth day of the fifth month, around the end of July. The year was 587 BC. Solomon's Temple had stood for almost 400 years, as sign and centre of the people's faith. Yet the kingdom was divided into two through most of that period. Jerusalem was in the southern half, called Judah.

This split surely made Israel and Judah easier prey for aggressive neighbours. Indeed Babylon, the great power of the day, had conquered Judah a decade earlier. Temple treasures and many thousands of people were taken away, leaving the community weak and dispirited (24:10–16). So ten years on, when Judah's king rebelled against his colonial masters (24:20), the contest was never going to be equal.

Babylon's reaction was decisive and brutal. Jerusalem was utterly wrecked and ruined. Burning, destruction, plunder, slaughter and slavery gouged a deep and ugly scar across land and memory. A few people were left to work the ground, but the strength of the community had gone, marched across the desert to serve an alien regime (25:11–12).

Yet God was not so easily taken out of the picture. Faith learned to be resilient and tenacious. Even the exile became a time of spiritual renewal, and it led eventually to return and rebuilding. Hope endured. The temple rose again. And Babylon fell. Empires are temporary. God is permanent.

† War is still pretty merciless. Some communities in our world today have been damaged in terrible ways. Pray for the people involved, and for all who work for peace and offer help.

For further thought

Where have you seen tenacious faith, surviving tragedy and rising to new life? What can you learn from what you have seen?

Friday 9 December
The enemy has destroyed everything

Read Psalm 74:1–11, 22–23

Remember your congregation, which you acquired long ago, which you redeemed to be the tribe of your heritage. Remember Mount Zion, where you came to dwell ... How long, O God, is the foe to scoff? Is the enemy to revile your name for ever? .... Rise up, O God, plead your cause.

(verses 2, 10 and 22a)

This anguished psalm comes from a city devastated and desolate, after the terrible events we read of yesterday. It holds before God the sorrow and shame of the remnant community in Judah – the people that Babylon left behind. Where their lovely Temple once stood, was only emptiness, rubble, jagged edges and charred remains. A matching void in their hearts was littered with the leftovers of faith, the grit and dust of painful memory, and the shattered beauty of inconsolable grief.

Humanly speaking, there was no hope, no horizon with dawn rising beyond. No prophet or seer in Judah 'knows how long' (verse 9) things would be this way. Only God could make a difference. Yet it seemed that God had checked out, turned against the people and abandoned them. So the psalm is a desperate prayer for God to stir.

'Remember' is the plea. Remember your people, O God. Remember your powerful deeds, when you gathered Israel to yourself. Remember your place, where you chose to be worshipped (verse 2). Come and see the wreckage and the ruin (verse 3). Enemies have risen against you (verse 23), it is time for you, God, to 'Rise up' and act (verse 22).

Lament psalms like this (and there are quite a few of them) offer words and a way to speak back to God when life brings us sorrow, hurt and fear. Agony is not sanitised and measured; it is angry and miserable. Yet God can hear this, can share it with us, and can remember grace when all that we remember is grief. The cross of Christ tells us that.

† Pray for anyone you know who is living with loss – of health, of trust, of hope, or of someone they love. Ask that they may be able to share their situation with God.

For further thought

When you feel sorrow and anger, do you find that you can share your heart with God? Does it help to do this?

The beauty of holiness: tabernacle and temple – 2 The Jerusalem Temple

December

Rebuilding

> **Read Haggai 1:1–15**
>
> *And the Lord stirred up the spirit of Zerubbabel son of Shealtiel, governor of Judah, and the spirit of Joshua son of Jehozadak, the high priest, and the spirit of all the remnant of the people; and they came and worked on the house of the Lord.*
>
> (verse 14)

Fifty years after the fall of Jerusalem, a big group of exiles came back from Babylon. They were keen to rebuild the Temple and actually began the job (Ezra 1–3). But it was a false start. When resentful neighbours blocked the work (Ezra 4:4–5), the community lost heart and turned to other concerns.

Enter Haggai. His brief ministry – a few months in 520 BC – made a big impact. He was a motivator. He could stir people. He urged them to tackle God's work, and not invest all their energies in their own well-being. He believed that God would bless a community which takes worship seriously. When life finds a centre in worship, this gives stability and confidence to everything else – whereas, without worship a community is liable to flounder and fragment.

Perhaps people were shaken by his message. They were certainly stirred. They got stuck in, with firm leadership and plenty of willing commitment (verse 14). The building work actually took four more years (compare 1:1 and Ezra 6:15). This was a task to push forward but not to rush. The finished product had to be dignified and durable.

Haggai's work clearly made a difference. When the project was stuck, he got it moving again. When the people lost vision, he gave them a target. When the community needed a focal point, he pointed them to God. And if assurance was needed, he spoke God's 'I am with you'. Which reminds us in Advent of Jesus, God with us in flesh and always (Matthew 1:23; 28:20).

† Lord Jesus Christ, God with us in person, may your presence motivate and guide me in times when I get stuck, on days when I lack vision, through seasons when I need assurance.

For further thought

How do you strike a balance between church involvement and what you do for home, family and self? How often do you review this balance?

The beauty of holiness: tabernacle and temple

3 Jesus and the Temple

Notes by **Delyth Wyn Davies**

Delyth is a Learning and Development Officer for the Methodist Church in Britain based in Wales. She has worked as the National Children's Work Officer for the Presbyterian Church of Wales and as Wales Co-ordinator for BMS World Mission. She has translated over 35 Welsh language Bible story books for children, edited Welsh language Christian song books and is involved in gobaith.cymru, a Welsh language website with downloadable Welsh hymns and worship song lyrics. Delyth has used the NRSVA for these notes.

Sunday 11 December
The Lord will come to his temple

Read Malachi 3:1–4

See, I am sending my messenger to prepare the way before me, and the Lord whom you seek will suddenly come to his temple. The messenger of the covenant in whom you delight – indeed, he is coming, says the Lord of hosts.

(verse 1)

The temple has been an important and significant feature of God's relationship with his people for generations. In the Old Testament, the temple was the symbol of God's presence, a dwelling place among his people and a place set aside for worship. In the New Testament, this concept takes on a new meaning and significance in and through Jesus. This week's theme of 'Jesus and the temple' spans the Old Testament and the New Testament and today's reading from the book of Malachi, like a trailer for a film conveying a sense of excitement and anticipation, sets the scene for the coming of the Messiah and his reign in God's eternal temple.

Central to the passage is God's relationship with his people and his desire to restore, or rather, renew his covenant with them and make his dwelling place among them. By Malachi's time, the temple had been rebuilt for almost a century but the priests and the people had neglected their commitment and worship to God. Malachi's message of the Lord coming to the temple is one of hope and forgiveness in anticipation of the coming of the Messiah bringing restoration to those who receive him.

† As we celebrate the coming of the Messiah, may we welcome you Lord in our lives and be open to your renewal and restoration.

Zechariah's vision

Read Luke 1:5–17

Now at the time of the incense-offering, the whole assembly of the people was praying outside. Then there appeared to him an angel of the Lord, standing at the right side of the altar of incense. When Zechariah saw him, he was terrified; and fear overwhelmed him.

(verses 10–12)

Following a foretaste of the Messiah's coming in Old Testament prophecies, the first episode of the story of Jesus begins with the dramatic telling of Zechariah's visit to the Temple in Jerusalem. In the fulfilling of an ordinary duty as part of his priestly role the extraordinary happens as he unexpectedly receives a vision from God.

At the time of Zechariah, there were around twenty thousand priests divided into groups of about a thousand. When it was the turn of their division to be on duty, lots would be cast to decide who would enter the sanctuary to burn the incense. Going to the Temple was therefore a once in a lifetime privilege. So, for Zechariah, the experience would have been overwhelming, but in addition he meets an angel, hears that he is to become a father at a ripe old age, and is the first to hear that God's promise to send the Messiah is being put into action. Wow!

At the same time, people were praying to God outside. As the smoke from the incense arose they would have been in awe of the mystery surrounding the Temple and would be waiting expectantly for the priest to emerge from the sanctuary to receive a blessing. The burning of the incense was a symbol of their worship to God and led to a cleansing of sins and a new beginning. But as this drama unfolded, little did they realise how significant this visit to the Temple would be in history and how it marked the beginning of a new blessing from God.

† Thank you Lord for those times when you work in unexpected ways, giving us a new insight into the wonder of your presence. May we be ready to be surprised by you and respond faithfully.

For further thought

Zechariah was at the Temple having been chosen by lot – but was it by chance? How does this fit in with your understanding of providence?

Tuesday 13 December
Jesus as a boy

Read Luke 2:41–52

When they did not find him, they returned to Jerusalem to search for him. After three days they found him in the temple, sitting among the teachers, listening to them and asking them questions. And all who heard him were amazed at his understanding and his answers.

(verses 45–47)

Today's passage tells another dramatic story about a visit to the Temple – but this time the focus is the boy Jesus. As this is the only record of Jesus between his early childhood and mature adulthood, the story gives us a glimpse of both his humanity and divinity in his formative years.

In some cultures, we would react with horror to the fact that his parents managed to lose their child on the journey back from the visit to Jerusalem. But they weren't being negligent. It was natural for people to travel together in groups, often with the women and children at the front and the men behind. Jesus, who was considered almost an adult, could have been in either group.

When they find him, he is in the temple school where the rabbis taught. He was actively engaged in a dialogue, receiving respect and admiration. His explanation to his parents indicates the importance of the Temple to Jesus, but more significantly his use of the word 'Father' is the first record of Jesus' acknowledgement of who he was, God's Son – a prophetic statement at the time.

Jesus' young age is highlighted several times in the text. It is a reminder of the contribution that young people bring to God's people. One of the most profound things I have experienced working for a church which puts an emphasis on listening to the voices of young people was when a 10-year-old said that the church should not be afraid. A simple sentence which challenged me in different ways and surely a prophetic statement for today.

† Lord Jesus, as we wonder at the mysteries of your incarnation, we thank you for growing up as one of us. Help us to grow in wisdom and to be a prophetic voice for you.

For further thought

Being part of the faith community was key in Jesus' formation. In what ways can your church become a more welcoming, inclusive and intergenerational community?

The beauty of holiness: tabernacle and temple – 3 Jesus and the Temple

December

The Word tabernacled among us

Read John 1:6–18

And the Word became flesh and lived among us, and we have seen his glory, the glory as of a father's only son, full of grace and truth ... No one has ever seen God. It is God the only Son, who is close to the Father's heart, who has made him known.

(verses 14, 18)

I'm fascinated by words and their meanings. In the Welsh language, the word '*trigo*' to some people means 'to live somewhere', and for others it means 'to die'! It is the first of these meanings, to dwell, which gives focus to today's meditation. This passage from John's Gospel is one of the clearest statements about who Jesus is. Set in the context of the prophecies relating to John the Baptist and Jesus, we are given an exposition of the role of Jesus that is packed with powerful imagery spanning all time.

One striking word is the one used by John to explain that the Word 'lived among us'. The meaning of the Greek word is 'tabernacled', which means encamped. Different words are used in various Bible translations but the word 'tabernacled' draws out distinct motifs which relate to the role of the tabernacle in the Old Testament – the moveable temporary dwelling place of God with his people, as the Jews travelled through the wilderness. It was a simple and ordinary structure compared to the grandeur of the more permanent Temple built by Solomon 500 years later. It was here that the ark of the covenant with the ten commandments was kept. It was a place of worship where sacrifices to atone for sins were made to God. It was where God's presence was made known to the Israelites, as he filled the tabernacle with his glory. In John's account, these motifs are fulfilled in Jesus who, as both God and human, came to live with and die for his people – and God's glory and presence is revealed in him.

† Lord God, we praise you and give you thanks that your glory is revealed to us in your son, Jesus Christ. May we be aware of your indwelling at all times. Glory be to you.

For further thought

Charles Wesley's hymn invites Love Divine to 'fix in us thy humble dwelling'. How can we experience and share the indwelling of Jesus' love?

The temple of his body

Read John 2:13–22

Jesus answered them, 'Destroy this temple, and in three days I will raise it up.' The Jews then said, 'This temple has been under construction for forty-six years, and will you raise it up in three days?' But he was speaking of the temple of his body.

(verses 19–21b)

The Passover was the most important Jewish festival, with every adult male Jew living near Jerusalem visiting the Temple to worship God. Jews living further afield would make an effort to visit at least once. As part of the worship they would offer sacrifices and they were expected to pay Temple taxes to cover costs. What Jesus found in the Temple courts was that high prices and additional charges were incurred by those whose sacrifices were deemed inadequate by inspectors, and pilgrims who had to exchange currencies also faced additional charges. No wonder Jesus was angry! They were blatantly and unjustly exploiting worshippers, probably excluding some, and they were destroying the essence of true worship, of what really pleased God his Father.

Jesus' actions naturally led to different reactions. While his disciples reflected on scripture which speaks of total commitment to worship in the Temple (verse 17 and Psalm 69:9), the Jewish leaders angrily asked Jesus by what authority he had acted. His reply seems somewhat presumptuous and his enemies twisted these words later to challenge him at his own trial. With hindsight, the Gospel writer is able to explain that the temple that Jesus speaks of is his own body (contrasting what the Jews had taken literally to mean a physical building) – along with Jesus' deeper spiritual meaning as to who he really was. The destruction and rebuilding of the Temple is paralleled with Jesus' death and resurrection, when his self-sacrifice would replace the need for sacrificial rituals at the Temple, opening the way to worship God through him.

† Lord Jesus, you are the true temple where we meet God. Help us to worship in spirit and in truth and live our lives by your example so that we bring glory to you.

For further thought

The temple scene was far removed from being a place symbolising God's presence and glory. What can get in our way when worshipping God?

The beauty of holiness: tabernacle and temple – 3 Jesus and the Temple

December

351

Christ as high priest

Read Hebrews 8:1–12

We do have such a high priest, who sat down at the right hand of the throne of the Majesty in heaven, and who serves in the sanctuary, the true tabernacle set up by the Lord, not by a mere human being.

(verses 1b–2, NIV)

It's so easy for us to go about in our daily lives to focus on the earthly, the here and now, and forget that our lives in Christ relate to things which are beyond the present. This passage from the letter to the Hebrews reminds us that our focus on Jesus and the temple, it moves away from the earthly to the heavenly, from the temporary to the eternal as it culminates in the role of Christ as high priest in the heavenly tabernacle in God's new covenant with his people.

Jesus has just been described in Hebrews 7 as the perfect priest, the one who never sinned and did not need to make any sacrifices as other priests, and yet he became the sacrifice to replace all sacrifices. It is this 'such a high priest' who is exalted in glory alongside God in the true sanctuary and the one with whom we can relate.

It has always amused me that Methodist ministers in the UK do not retire but 'sit down' at the end of active service in ministry. It raises the question of whether ministers actually retire or does their ministry continue in a different form. In Judaism, it is said that there were no seats in the temple as priests did not sit while they were serving there. But Jesus is said here to have 'sat down' with God, a clear indication that his sacrifice was once and for all – and yet he continues to serve as mediator of the new covenant who draws us beyond the earthly to experience God's heavenly glory.

† Jesus Christ, our high priest exalted in heaven, we offer our praise and thanksgiving for your sacrifice and for the forgiveness for sins. Help us to know you better and trust in you.

For further thought

The parallels between the old and the new in the passage point to the superior ministry of Jesus as high priest. What does Christ's ministry mean to you?

Confidence to enter the temple

> **Read Hebrews 9:11–14; 10:19–25**
>
> *Therefore, my friends, since we have confidence to enter the sanctuary by the blood of Jesus, by the new and living way that he opened for us through the curtain (that is, through his flesh) … let us approach with a true heart in full assurance of faith.*
>
> (verses 19–20 and 22)

The writer to the Hebrews gives theological insight here into the way that Christ's sacrifice has opened the doors for his followers to approach God in confidence to a relationship with him. First, there is the contrast between the earthly old covenant sanctuary and the heavenly new covenant sanctuary because of Christ's death on the cross. Then there is the invitation to enter into God's presence in the heavenly sanctuary through faith in Christ's sacrifice and forgiveness of sins. One can sense the joy and thankfulness of the writer in encouraging his readers to be sure of their faith in Christ as both their high priest and sacrifice.

As I reflect on these rich theological thoughts which are oozing with conviction, I'm reminded of the richness of the traditional 'plygain' carols sung across Wales at Christmas. Plygain carols are full of scriptural teaching, not only about the Christmas story, but how Christ's coming fits into the bigger picture of God's redemption plan from the Fall to eternal life. They can often include themes such as prophecies, Christ's death and resurrection, salvation, repentance, godly living and reaching out to others. These old Welsh language hymns were written not only for worship but to teach biblical truths and build people up in their faith in the same way as the writer penned his letter to the converted Jews.

We may struggle to understand some pieces of scripture but what this passage does is to incite confidence to enter the eternal temple to worship God through what Christ has done for us.

† He made us mere mortals God's sons and his daughters, eternal dwellers of heaven above; to live in his presence in glorious brilliance, to praise the Redeemer for his love. (Rhys Prichard, 1579–1644, my translation)

For further thought

The passage ends with a call, 'to provoke one another to love and good deeds, and encouraging one another' (verse 25). How important is accountability to you?

The beauty of holiness: tabernacle and temple – 3 Jesus and the Temple

December

The beauty of holiness: tabernacle and temple

4 The Christian community and the temple

Notes by **Tim Yau**

Tim is a Pioneer Missioner working for the Anglican Diocese of Norwich. His role is to establish a mission community in Round House Park, a new housing development in Cringleford. He also is a Diocesan Mission Enabler, encouraging missional practice across the region: 'not trying to get people to go to church, but trying to get the church to go to the people'. He's frequently found immersed in the latest sci-fi cinematic epic, and loves mini-adventures with his family. Tim has used the NIVUK for these notes.

Sunday 18 December
Public presence

Read Acts 2:37–47

Every day they continued to meet together in the temple courts.

(part of verse 46a)

In modern Western secular society, it is difficult to find a contemporary analogy for the ancient Jerusalem Temple. It wasn't just for worship, but it embodied national, cultural and political values. Its monumental presence within Jewish religious identity had the gravity to draw people from across the Roman Empire and with them came money, power and influence.

Today, the UK isn't governed by religion. Although the last vestiges of Christendom are still present, they are often viewed with suspicion, sentimentality or indifference. What often seems to drive British culture is consumerism and individualism: 'I shop therefore I am'. So the closest we get to the temple is the shopping mall: a public space exemplifying compulsion for shopping and choice.

Jesus had strong words to say about temple practice, but he still used the space to preach and teach his message. The apostles continued this model because that's where the pilgrims, priests and the poor converged.

When I lived in a suburb of Peterborough, we didn't have church buildings to meet in but there was a shopping mall that served the city on the edge of our estate, so we met there to tell Jesus' story. Where's your equivalent public space?

† Lord Jesus Christ, give us your eyes to see where the people are, and give us your courage to go and be there with them. Amen

Time of transformation

Read Acts 3:1–10

Now a man who was lame from birth was being carried to the temple gate called Beautiful, where he was put every day to beg from those going into the temple courts.

(verse 2)

She laid face down on a busy thoroughfare between a Hong Kong train station and a shopping centre, while thousands of commuters stepped over her empty tapping bowl. This grovelling emaciated elderly woman was desperate, but nobody saw her.

Beggars are found everywhere, many are homeless, suffering from addiction and mental health issues, and their needs are complex. In the UK, we are advised not to give them money or food as it can fuel a culture of dependency and prevents them getting involved with local social care systems. Street beggars are seen as a nuisance by some, a problem to be fixed, and an indictment of our welfare state.

When regularly faced with the poverty and suffering of the marginalised, it can become just a background feature of our lives. It's not that we've become heartless, cynical or too distracted to care, it's just the culture we live and breathe. Those Hong Kong commuters were no worse than me on an English high street saying, 'Sorry' when asked for some spare change.

In the Gospels, we see intimate encounters between Jesus and suffering people who are desperate for transformation. Jesus didn't see humanity as a problem to be fixed, but as individuals to be loved. So, when Peter and John met the lame beggar on the way to the Temple, they didn't just fulfil their religious obligation by tossing him a few coins, neither did they debate the worthiness of his predicament, but instead they gave him their full attention and brought his need to God.

The marginalised are transformed and brought into the heart of the temple.

† Creator, you made us in your image, help us to bear your likeness. Jesus, show us how to live and who to live for. Spirit, guide us to those who need transformation. Amen

For further thought

'Blessed are you who are poor, for yours is the kingdom of God. Blessed are you who hunger now, for you will be satisfied' (Luke 6:20–21).

Tuesday 20 December
Divine disruption

Read Acts 22:1–11, 17–21

When I returned to Jerusalem and was praying at the temple, I fell into a trance and saw the Lord speaking to me.

(verses 17–18a)

I've never been in a trance or had an ecstatic vision where I've been transported into the heavenly realm and encountered the divine presence of God. It's not that I don't believe in them – there are plenty of examples in the Bible when prophets witness something amazing and try to describe it through their fallible human lens.

The New Testament has two mentions of the word trance: the first is in Acts 10 when Peter is shown a vision which causes him to understand that the gospel was also for non-Jews; the second is here, when Paul recounts how God revealed to him that he is to be sent to the non-Jews too. Both these instances initiated a massive ideological shift for the church, which transformed it from being a Jewish sect into the diverse global entity it is today. The trance is God's disruption tool.

In church history there are many examples of pilgrims, monastics and mystics who've dedicated their time to place, prayer and practice. Like Paul in the temple and Peter on the rooftop, sometimes God breaks in and changes everything.

During 1994, I lived in Chicago with the Jesus People USA. The neighbourhood was riddled with poverty, gangs, drugs and prostitution. One afternoon, feeling overwhelmed by the hopelessness of the place I prayed, 'Who's going to do something about this?'

God answered saying, 'You are!'

In that disruptive moment, I swapped my life-plan for God's kingdom plan and it changed me forever. That's the closest I've got to a trance. Are you willing to be disrupted by God?

† Jesus, we dedicate our life to you, forgive us when we presume to know God's will without listening to the Spirit's guidance. Lead us into all truth and disrupt our plans with holy purpose. Amen

For further thought

What are the places you can make pilgrimage to, the prayers you can pray, and practices you can adopt to seek God's will for your life?

Wednesday 21 December
Prudent partnerships

Read 2 Corinthians 6:14–18
For we are the temple of the living God.

(verse 16b)

Being a priest of the national established Church of England comes with benefits and baggage. My clergy collar allows me access to places and people that others wouldn't have. However, my religious public role sometimes puts people off and is a barrier to belief. Last century, Christian religion was seemingly synonymous with British culture, it was difficult to unpick the two. Today, it is a different story – church is no longer at the privileged centre. Religious practice hasn't disappeared, but diversified and embedded in multiple ways. Christian religion was monolithic, now it is one choice among many beliefs systems.

The British government has attempted to codify this stance in stating British values as: 'democracy, the rule of law, individual liberty, and mutual respect for and tolerance of those with different faiths and beliefs, and for those without faith' (www.gov.uk). This statement recognises that we are not a religiously homogenous nation any more.

In the reading today, Paul does not want the Corinthian church to hide from the world, but neither does he want them to form intimate partnerships with those who are following a way of life antagonistic to God's kingdom way.

The Jerusalem Temple was a holy symbol set apart from the impurity and sin of the world. In contrast, the church is a symbol of a renewed people set apart by the Holy Spirit for God's activity in the world. We're a holy church for holy action, which means we have to be wise about who, how and when we partner with others. Will they walk in the same direction with us for God's kingdom life?

† Lord Jesus Christ, give us your godly wisdom and discernment to live well in this world. Let all our relationships reflect righteousness, light and harmony for the sake of the common good of all. Amen

For further thought

Are there idols in your life? What objects, relationships or ideals that you give worth to are pulling you away from your devotion to God?

The beauty of holiness: tabernacle and temple – 4 The Christian community and the temple

Radical reconciliation

The beauty of holiness: tabernacle and temple – 4 The Christian community and the temple

Read Ephesians 2:11–22

And in him you too are being built together to become a dwelling in which God lives by his Spirit.

(verse 22)

In 2011, the newspaper headline read: 'Fears raised over plans for Cringleford housing' (Norwich Evening News, November 26, 2011). The Round House Park project built new homes in the village, but it was met with concern by local residents: 'It was a lovely village, but we are seeing it ruined by excessive house building.' 'Wildlife and the village community could be damaged.' 'It'll be a nightmare.'

Where do you go with such division? When something is changing radically, it's inevitable to think about what will be lost and to put up barriers against difference. But what if we focused on what we might gain?

The developers created crossing points, through community infrastructure, green spaces and play parks, therefore the place is full of young families. As a church we've offered a warm welcome, filled with generosity and hospitality, offering neighbourliness through kindness and joyful relationships. When I see the land being prepared for building work, I pray for the future residents. I ask God that we would be a village that welcomes the newcomer.

Paul declares Jesus as the 'cornerstone'. At the time, this was the principal stone placed at the corner of a building. It was usually the largest, densest and the most carefully constructed in the foundations – from it, everything else was built. Paul wanted the non-Jews and the Jews to be formed together as a 'holy temple in the Lord' (verse 21), unified by Christ, not separated by their cultural differences.

Jesus lived a life of selflessness, love and peace, tearing down barriers of mistrust and pointing to a new way of living. What are you building your life on?

† Lord Jesus Christ, you reconciled humanity to God. Through your work of peace, we can be reconciled with each other. Give us courage to reject fear, enact peace and be built together anew. Amen

For further thought

Who is divided from your community? How can your church offer hands of peace to them? Is there anyone you need to make peace with?

Symbols of sacrifice

Read Romans 12:1–13

Offer your bodies as a living sacrifice, holy and pleasing to God – this is your true and proper worship.

(verse 1b)

A host of Chinese faces gathered at the graveside of my grandfather. A substantial metal container appeared, and armfuls of paper money and paper effigies of everyday items began to be burned as an offering to him for a prosperous afterlife.

In the traditional Chinese culture of my father, they venerate their ancestors. In practice, this involves the ritual burning of 'joss paper', also known as spirit money. The belief is that the more you burn, the more likely it is that your ancestors will smile on you and give you a trouble-free life. When bad things do happen, it's because you haven't appeased your ancestors enough, so you burn more offerings.

In the Western world, we tend to think of religion in terms of a way of life or a belief system, so the idea of offerings and sacrifices seems strange. However, in other cultures and in the ancient world, it was what worship was about. The Jews maintained a highly detailed written code for offering animal and vegetable sacrifices to God. At the time of Paul writing to the Roman church, the Jerusalem Temple was the focus for all the Jewish religious sacrificial ritual.

This focus on transactional sacrifice was open to abuse. You could play the system and act in any way you wanted, as long as you were seen to offer the appropriate sacrifice to assuage God's judgement. In response, Paul encourages the Roman Christians to offer their whole lives as a 'living sacrifice' not just religious rituals, in the way they lived for God in thought, word and deed every day.

† Lord Jesus Christ, your sacrifice offered on the cross tore the Temple curtain in two and allowed all access to God. May we not squander that freedom, but live lives of gratitude and worship. Amen

For further thought

And what does the Lord require of you? To act justly and to love mercy and to walk humbly with your God (Micah 6:8).

Saturday 24 December
People of priests

Read 1 Peter 2:1–10
You also, like living stones, are being built into a spiritual house to be a holy priesthood.

(verse 5a)

Incense billowed across the congregation, the priest bowed to the altar while two attendants pulled back his liturgical vestments. Puzzled, I asked my theological college principal, 'What's going on?' Blankly he replied, 'I have no idea!'

To the uninitiated, the forms and functions of a priest can appear impenetrable, the ritual and regulations perplexing. I wonder if some of my colleagues play on the bewilderment of outsiders to create an air of spiritual mystique. Today, an Anglican priest is simply an ordained person who preaches, celebrates the sacraments and provides pastoral care. This definition does not cover the whole mission and ministry of the church, so creates space for others.

At Mount Sinai, God spoke to Moses telling him to say to the Israelites: 'Now if you obey me fully and keep my covenant, then out of all nations you will be my treasured possession. Although the whole earth is mine, you will be for me a kingdom of priests and a holy nation' (Exodus 19:5–6).

From Aaron and the Levites came the Jewish priesthood, they fulfilled a variety of temple duties, but ostensibly their role was to mediate between God and his chosen people, the Jews. Jesus transformed that model; he became the great high priest (Hebrews 4:14), the one who mediates between humanity and God.

Peter's letter explains that we don't need the temple with its sacrificial system and priests anymore because, through Jesus, all Christians must be priests to the world, representing all humanity before God – and God before all humanity. We're built together to be the priesthood of all believers.

† Lord Jesus Christ, you are our priestly role model, the symbol of God's kingdom way to live. Give us strength to represent you to the world and grace to represent the world to you. Amen

For further thought

How can your skills, talents and abilities be built into God's spiritual house? Where is God calling you? How can you be a priestly presence?

Christmas with Matthew

Notes by **Kristina Andréasson**

You can read more about Kristina in her bio on p. 149. Kristina has used the NRSVA.

Sunday 25 December (Christmas Day)
God with us, also in the periphery and beyond

Read Matthew 1:18–25

'Look, the virgin shall conceive and bear a son, and they shall name him Emmanuel', which means, 'God with us'. When Joseph awoke from sleep, he did as the angel of the Lord commanded him.

(part of verses 23–24)

Merry Christmas! Wherever you might be, I wish you a blessed Christmas Day. I hope the radiant light from the manger reaches out to you and that the angels' singing touches your heart, *even* if you feel like you are somehow in the periphery of Christmas celebrations and a glittery Christmas morning.

Christmas with Matthew is Christmas with Joseph, and there is something so beautiful and relatable about that. Joseph is there, but he's in the periphery. I try to find Joseph among us. I see him as the rather quiet one at Christmas dinner. I sense his gentle smile from a couch watching excited loved ones open their gifts. I find Joseph by the till at a mall, wrapping someone else's Christmas gift. And I see Joseph exit the tube station. He stops, smiles, as he hears the carol singing, and then continues his way through the happy gathering.

I think many of us can have moments when we relate to Joseph, when we are close to the Christmas joy, but somehow, at the same time, in the periphery. But in the periphery, the angel was close to Joseph, close with the promise: God is with us.

† God of life, be with us all this Christmas Day. Let your loving light reach into the peripheries of Christmas miracles, and beyond. Amen

Monday 26 December
With help of knowledge we search the star

Read Matthew 2:1–6

Wise men from the East came to Jerusalem, asking, 'Where is the child who has been born king of the Jews? For we observed his star at its rising, and have come to pay him homage.'

(part of verses 1–2)

A beautiful Christmas tree is important in the church where I currently serve. The church is just next to a roundabout so, apart from church visitors, everyone who drives past will see the tree. Finding the perfect tree is not as simple as just ordering one. Instead, the site manager, the administrator and I go to a 'Christmas tree place' outside London and search. All of us need to go, because one has Christmas tree experience and knows the right measurements and type of tree, another one knows how to drive and read the map, and one is artistic and knows how to spot a beautiful tree. Together we search and, hopefully, we find The Tree.

The wise men were astrologers, scientists of their time. They used their knowledge, science, to search and follow the star to its destination. By doing so, they tell us how science and knowledge go very well with faith. Faith tells us about hope when knowledge can't. But in our search for hope as bright as a shining star, our knowledge, science of today, should not be pushed aside. We need it as we, strengthened by the stubborn hope that is in faith, search for solutions for our planet, our future, society around us and our own lives. Just like the wise men, we might need to be more than one, as we all carry different gifts and knowledge. Sometimes, help from others is what we need in our searches, whether it is about big global issues, or something small, yet important, as the perfect Christmas tree.

† God of life, as we search in our world and in our lives, bring us together so we can share the knowledge and science that takes us closer to your loving light. Amen

For further thought

When was the last time new knowledge also gave you a new hope? Do you have knowledge that might help to create a new hope?

Tuesday 27 December
It is not too late to find great joy

Read Matthew 2:7–12
When they saw that the star had stopped, they were overwhelmed with joy.

(verse 10)

Have you ever wished upon a star? Maybe we tend to do so more around this time of year than otherwise. I hope that some of your Christmas wishes have come true, and that you've found moments in the past days filled with joy. I love how the wise men were overwhelmed with joy when they finally found the place where the star had stopped. I believe we can also find and come close to that joy in precious Christmas moments, whether it is a moment with loved ones, a Christmas carol that moves us, or a simple candle lit with hope.

But at first, the wise men went to the wrong place. When they finally got it right, they were late. We celebrate their arrival first in January. But still, they were overwhelmed with joy. We might have some wishes, that we still carry in our hearts, whatever our Christmas has been like so far. The wise men's joy is still to come. But the star shines brightly for them – and also for us, for wishes that we still carry within. Whatever wish you have, that hasn't really come true this Christmas, the star still shines and tells us it is not too late to find great joy. And the joy is not fixed to certain days in December. Like the wise men, we might find it later. So keep wishing, keep hoping, keep praying. The star shines for the entire world, and tells us about a God who wishes all of us to find precious moments in life, where we are overwhelmed with joy.

† God of life, you who know every single heart's list of wishes, help us all to find moments of great joy. Amen

For further thought

Does life have to be perfect in order to feel great joy? We may be able to find joy even in times when we wish things were different.

Wednesday 28 December
Where are the angels now?

Read Matthew 2:13–15

An angel of the Lord appeared to Joseph in a dream and said, 'Get up, take the child and his mother, and flee to Egypt, and remain there until I tell you'.

(part of verse 13)

It is only a few days after Christmas, but it is almost as if I can see the back of Joseph and Mary, who once again sits up on the donkey, now with her newborn wrapped in her arms. Fleeing to safety. And as they get further away, it is as if the angels' singing goes silent and the radiant light from the manger loses its power. 'Not yet!', I want to say, 'Come back and stay a bit longer! We need you; we need the hopeful light and the angels' singing.' But they flee to another country, like so many families before and after. I realise how lucky I am, not knowing exile in my own life.

But in London, a large city, so dark and cold this time of year, with so many people moving around, you somehow sense that, close to you, there will be those who could tell you what exile is like… It makes me look for the holy family again. And blurred together with our time, I need to ask this: the angels promised peace on earth – where are they now? The holy family is now out of sight, but we can still see other families in exile, all over the world. Maybe that's how we get the angels to sing again, by trying to see those families, and not only waiting for angel magic but *being* what those families need. The holy family helps us, reminds us, to treat others as we treated them, with comfort and joy. That might make angels sing again.

† God of life, in a world where people still flee in fear, like you once did, help us to be angels for each other. Help us to find ways to spread comfort and joy. Amen

For further thought

Singing about 'peace on earth' can clash with our world with violence and fear. But how would it be if we stopped singing?

Thursday 29 December
Christmas and weeping

Read Matthew 2:16–18

A voice was heard in Ramah, wailing and loud lamentation, Rachel weeping for her children; she refused to be consoled, because they are no more.

(verse 18)

It is a Swedish Christmas tradition to celebrate St Lucy. It is done by a choir dressed in white. Most have candles in their hands, while the one who is Lucy wears the candles in her hair. Apart from the candles, you make sure that it is completely dark, to symbolise the Christmas message about light in the darkness. But there is one more thing. St Lucy always wears a red ribbon around her waist, as it was a sword that killed the saint. The red ribbon speaks about suffering and pain. I focus on the red ribbon and can almost hear what we in Sweden call a 'Ramah-cry'. A 'Ramah-cry', from Rachel's weeping, is the kind of scream that is filled with despair and what seems to be never-ending pain.

A heart can carry joy which shines like the most beautiful Christmas decoration. And a heart can also carry what is captured in Lucy's red ribbon – hurt and pain, darkness of some kind. Sometimes those feelings coexist, also during Christmas. And that is okay. A holy night has the strength to meet a 'Ramah-cry'. From painful despair to the smallest tear that runs down our cheek, we don't have to push it aside or sparkle glitter over it.

A 'Ramah-cry' is cried out for all the weeping that still exists, in our lives and in our world, although it's Christmas. The cry is captured in St Lucy's red ribbon – and there, weeping meets the message about a light that never fades, light that no darkness or pain can conquer, the light of life.

† God of life, thank you for embracing us wholly. Receive what is good, but also our tears this Christmas. Let us sense your eternal light in moments of darkness and pain. Amen

For further thought

Could it be that when we our tears meet the light from the manger, it is easier for true joy to also take place?

Friday 30 December
Nazareth and everyday life

> **Read Matthew 2:19–23**
>
> *He made his home in a town called Nazareth, so that what had been spoken through the prophets might be fulfilled, 'He will be called a Nazorean'.*
>
> (verse 23)

My childhood best friend contacted me. We hadn't spoken in years. But now that we'd spoken, it almost felt like it was only yesterday that we'd last been in contact. It made me think back to when I was a young teenager, and my friend and I spent almost every day together. I didn't think of my most amazing memories from that period of my life, neither did I think of the worst – instead, it made me remember the everyday things, those days that were just normal days to me. I remembered scents, situations, music, tastes and little conversations that were just there as a part of normal everyday life happening. Memories of things that I probably would have considered quite normal and not very exciting back then. Looking back, it now felt more like a part of my life story and therefore important somehow.

I think many of us can look back on growing up and, between the highs and the lows, maybe find smells, music, tastes or situations that were somehow once part of our normal everyday life. Whether we look back on it thinking it was good, bad or somewhere in between, it is a part of our life story. Our lives are not only shaped by the best, but also the hardest moments. Jesus grew up in Nazareth. At that time, it was considered just a normal city, not talked about that much, just a normal place. Our normal everyday life can feel important to us later, but Jesus, the Nazorean, somehow tells us that our everyday life is always important to God.

† God of life, not a single day is unimportant to you. Surround every new day with your love, as you have promised to be with us always, to the end of age. Amen

For further thought

When you look back on normal days, everyday life, can you find God's hand there, God's grace appearing on a totally normal day?

Christmas with Matthew

December

Saturday 31 December
Looking back with Matthew

Read Matthew 1:1–17

And Salmon the father of Boaz by Rahab, and Boaz the father of Obed by Ruth, and Obed the father of Jesse, and Jesse the father of King David. And David was the father of Solomon by the wife of Uriah.

(verses 5–6)

Do you look back on the year that has passed today? Does it matter? I think sometimes it does. We can find things that are important, like small treasures for us to keep as we meet the new year. We might have learned something, discovered something about ourselves. Something might have made us stronger, or given us a realisation of some kind.

Matthew also looks back, by looking at Jesus' genealogy. Does it matter to us? I think it can.

As a woman I can't help but to focus on three ladies being mentioned: Rahab, Ruth and Bathsheba. Rahab has been called the 'prostitute', but she was a brave and clever woman, and is mentioned here as a relative of Jesus. Ruth has her own book in the Bible and is also listed in Jesus' family tree. Bathsheba is often remembered as the seductive woman in the bath – but it was David who took her, and here she is mentioned with her husband, Uriah, as a relative of Jesus. When we look back with Matthew, we find three women, showing us that they are more than they have sometimes been made out to be.

When we look back on the past year, we can sometimes find moments of strength or realisation. Like the people mentioned in Matthew's first chapter, gathered together in Jesus' genealogy, there is a God who needs us all and who believes we are more than we sometimes might think ourselves. Looking back, there might have been moments when we've sensed this. Let us keep that as a part of who we are when we enter the new year.

† God of life, we give thanks for all that has been good in the past year. Show us how you continue to call us with love as we prepare to meet a new year. Amen

For further thought

Can you relate to anyone in Jesus' genealogy? What does it mean to you that he or she is mentioned in Jesus' family tree?

IBRA scheme of readings 2023

Our journey through The Word next year will take us through the following themes:

Getting ready

Biblical library (1): Poetry

The Gospel of Matthew (1)
1. Preparing for ministry
2. Teaching the Kingdom

Healing divisions
1. Divisions in the Old Testament
2. Divisions in the New Testament

The Letter of James

Exploring the Lord's Prayer
1. Pray in this way'
2. Our Father in heaven
3. Your will be done
4. Bread of heaven
5. Deliver us from evil

The Gospel of Matthew (2)
1. Passiontide: the coming of the Kingdom
2. Holy Week: the way of the cross

Celebrations

Judges of Israel
1. Deborah and Gideon
2. Jephthah and Samson

Biblical library (2): History

Places of worship

The Gospel of Matthew (3)
1. Healer and teacher
2. Lord of the Sabbath

God's love in action
1. God's directives
2. Our response

Biblical library (3): Apocalyptic

Who is my family?

Readings in Amos

Gospel of Matthew (4)
1. Parables and controversies
2. Son of Man, Son of God

Faithfulness
1. God's faithfulness to us
2. Our faithfulness to God
3. People of faith

Biblical library (4): Prophecy

He gives his beloved sleep

Readings in 2 Corinthians

Fasting

The Gospel of Matthew (5)
1. He who comes in the name of the Lord
2. Confrontations

Sowing and reaping

Biblical library (5): Narrative

Culture and identity: all one in Christ

Readings in Leviticus

Readings in Esther

Healthy humility
1. Walk humbly with God
2. 'Let the same mind be in you…'

Lighter moments?

Biblical library (6): Law

Hidden heroes and heroines

Ephesians plus
1. No longer strangers
2. A life worthy of your calling
3. Living in the light

Christmas with John

IBRA International Fund

IBRA brings together readers from across the globe, and it is your donations and support that make it possible for our international partners to translate, print, publish and distribute the notes to over a hundred thousand people. Thank you.

Are you able to make a donation today?

How your donations make a difference:

£5 can send an English copy of *Fresh From The Word* to any of our international partners

£10 can print 12 copies of *Fresh From The Word* in India

£25 buys 20 copies of *Fresh From The Word* in Nigeria

£50 would fund 1,000 IBRA reading lists to be sent to a country that does not currently receive IBRA materials

Our partners are based in ten countries, but the benefit flows over borders to at least thirty-two countries all over the world. Partners work tirelessly to organise the translation, printing and distribution of IBRA Bible study notes and lists in many different languages, from Ewe, Yoruba and Twi to Portuguese, Samoan and Telugu!

Did you know that we print and sell 6,000 copies of *Fresh From The Word* here in the UK, but our overseas partners produce another 42,000 copies in English and then translate the book you are reading to produce a further 31,000 copies in various local languages? With the reading list also being translated into French and Spanish, then distributed, IBRA currently reaches over 700,000 Christians globally.

Faithfully following the same principles developed in 1882, we continue to guarantee that your donations to the International Fund will support our international brothers and sisters in Christ.

If you would like to make a donation, please use the envelope inserted in this book to send a cheque to International Bible Reading Association, 5–6 Imperial Court, 12 Sovereign Road, Birmingham, B30 3FH or go online to ibraglobal.org and click the 'Donate' button at the top of the page.

Global community

Our overseas distribution and international partners enable IBRA readings to be enjoyed all over the world from Spain to Samoa, New Zealand to Cameroon. Each day when you read your copy of *Fresh From The Word* you are joining a global community of people who are also reading the same passages. The coronavirus pandemic has impacted on international communications as well as worship gatherings since 2020 but our readings continue to offer support to people worldwide:

Ghana

Our partners in Ghana report:

The short notes and commentaries help leaders in morning services – who are not usually clergy – to conduct the service with ease.

This devotional book has helped many families, and acts as a unifier.

New Zealand

A pastor in Auckland tells us:

It really helped during younger days back home [with] Sunday school and youth groups … I'm now still using it and sharing it with church members.

Kiribati

The direction of one leader's life was changed:

It contributed to my decision to become a Deacon.

India

The Fellowship of Professional Workers in India value the shared experience of following *Fresh From The Word*'s daily readings with a world community:

The uniqueness of the Bible reading is that the entire readership is focusing on a common theme for each day, which is an expression of oneness of the faithful, irrespective of countries and cultures.

United Kingdom

Readers felt sustained by a personal Bible study routine during periods of social restriction ('lockdown') brought about by the pandemic:

[While] the churches are shut it provides a moment of reflection.

It has kept me in touch with the Bible and kept me going at a difficult time.

A global community following God's Word

Readers have kindly shared how IBRA's *Fresh From The Word* reading scheme and notes support their Christian journey:

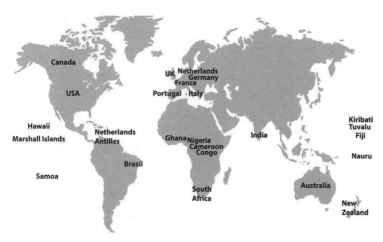

66 *The IBRA readings gave me a firm belief in Jesus which has held me throughout my life.* 99

66 *Without them I do not think that I would read the Bible regularly.* 99

66 *Encouragement to pray.* 99

66 *It has brought me much closer to God and has helped strengthen my faith. It has given me a new outlook to life and people around me.* 99

66 *Enhanced my preaching and Bible study.* 99

66 *I value the IBRA notes for their international and ecumenical perspectives, breaking the bounds of national and theological doctrines and prejudices.* 99

66 *Challenges me to look at things in a new light, inspires me and uplifts me … and the range of writers and subjects that FFTW offers is all part of the inspiration.* 99

66 *Reminds me each morning that God is always by my side.* 99

To find out more visit: **www.ibraglobal.org**

Where do you read your FFTW? Perhaps you have a favourite, unusual or comforting place to enjoy your Bible reading? Email ibra@christianeducation. org.uk to let us and your fellow readers know!

International Bible Reading Association partners and distributors

A worldwide service of Christian Education at work in five continents

HEADQUARTERS
IBRA
5–6 Imperial Court
12 Sovereign Road
Birmingham
B30 3FH
United Kingdom

www.ibraglobal.org

ibra@christianeducation.org.uk

SAMOA
Congregational Christian Church in Samoa
CCCS
PO Box 468
Tamaligi
Apia
Samoa

asst.gsec@cccs.org.ws / lina@cccs.org.ws

Congregational Christian Church in Tokelau
c/o EFKT
Atafu
Tokelau Island

hepuutu@gmail.com

Congregational Christian Church in
American Samoa
P.O. BOX 1537
Pago Pago, AS 96799
American Samoa

gensec@efkasonline.org

FIJI
Methodist Bookstore
11 Stewart street
PO Box 354
Suva
Fiji

mbookstorefiji@yahoo.com

GHANA
Asempa Publishers
Christian Council of Ghana
PO Box GP 919
Accra
Ghana

gm@asempapublishers.com

NIGERIA
IBRA Nigeria
David Hinderer House
Cathedral Church of St David
Kudeti
PMB 5298 Dugbe
Ibadan
Oyo State
Nigeria

SOUTH AFRICA
Faith for Daily Living Foundation
PO Box 3737
Durban 4000
South Africa

ffdl@saol.com

IBRA South Africa
The Rectory
Christchurch
c/o Constantia Main and Parish Roads
Constantia 7806
Western Cape
South Africa

Terry@cchconst.org.za

DEMOCRATIC REPUBLIC OF THE CONGO
Baptist Community of the Congo River
8 Avenue Kalemie
Kinshasa Gombe
B.P. 205 & 397
Kinshasa 1
DR Congo

ecc_cbfc@yahoo.fr

CAMEROON
Redemptive Baptist Church
PO Box 65
Limbe
Fako Division
South West Region
Cameroon

evande777@yahoo.com

INDIA
All India Sunday School Association
House No. 9-131/1, Street No.5
HMT Nagar, Nacharam
Hyderabad
500076
Telangana
India

sundayschoolindia@yahoo.co.in

Fellowship of Professional Workers
Samanvay
Deepthi Chambers, Opp. Nin.
Tarnaka, Vijayapuri
Hyderabad 500 017
Telengana State
India

fellowship2w@gmail.com

Fresh From The Word 2023
Order and donation form

	Quantity	Price	Total
AA200356 *Fresh From The Word 2023*		£10.99	
10% discount if ordering 3 or more copies			
UK P&P			
Up to 2 copies		£3.95	
3–8 copies		£6.95	
9–11 copies		£8.95	
If ordering 12 or more copies please contact us for revised postage.			
Western Europe P&P			
1 copy		£5.95	
If ordering more than 1 copy please contact us for revised postage.			
Rest of the world P&P			
1 copy		£7.95	
If ordering more than 1 copy please contact us for revised postage.			
Donation Yes, I would like to make a donation to IBRA's International Fund to help support our global community of readers.			
£5.00 ☐ £10.00 ☐ £25.00 ☐ £50.00 ☐ Other ☐			
TOTAL FOR BOOKS, P&P AND DONATION			

Title: _____ First name: _____ Last name: _____

Address: _____

_____

Postcode: _____ Tel.: _____

Email: _____

Your order will be dispatched when all books are available. Payments in pounds sterling, please. We do not accept American Express or Maestro International. HOW WE USE INFORMATION ABOUT YOU AND RECIPIENTS OF YOUR INFORMATION: We will use your information in performance of your contract with us and the provision of our services to you including our legitimate interests. For further details please view our full privacy policy and your rights at www.ibraglobal.org/privacy

CARDHOLDER NAME: _____

CARD NUMBER: ☐☐☐☐ ☐☐☐☐ ☐☐☐☐ ☐☐☐☐

START DATE: ☐☐ ☐☐ **EXPIRY DATE:** ☐☐ ☐☐

SECURITY NUMBER (LAST THREE DIGITS ON BACK): ☐☐☐

SIGNATURE: _____

Please fill in your details on the reverse

Ebook and Kindle versions are available from Amazon and other online retailers.

Gift Aid declaration *giftaid it*

☐ If you wish to Gift Aid your donation please tick the box.

I am a UK taxpayer and would like IBRA to reclaim the Gift Aid on my donation, increasing my donation by 25p for every £1. I understand that if I pay less income tax and/or capital gains tax than the amount of Gift Aid claimed on all my donations in that tax year, it is my responsibility to pay the difference.

Signature: _____   Date: _____

Thank you so much for your generous donation; it will make a real difference and change lives around the world.

Please fill in your address and payment details on the reverse of this page and send back to IBRA.

☐ **I have made a donation**

☐ **I have Gift Aided my donation**

☐ **I would like to know more about leaving a legacy to IBRA**

☐ **I would like to become an IBRA rep**

☐ **I enclose a cheque (made payable to IBRA)**

☐ **Please charge my MASTERCARD/VISA**

Card details will be destroyed after payment has been taken.

Please return this form to:

**IBRA
5–6 Imperial Court
12 Sovereign Road
Birmingham
B30 3FH**

You can also order through your local IBRA rep or from:

• website: shop.christianeducation.org.uk
• email: ibra.sales@christianeducation.org.uk
• call: 0121 458 3313

Registered Charity number: 1086990